THE MOST COMMONLY MISSPELLED WORDS ARE WORDS WE USE EVERYDAY.

Millions of people like you despair of ever spelling words like *receive* (recieve?) with confidence, or of ever using words like *principle* (principal?) correctly.

The English language challenges even the best spellers, but by using *The Bantam Instant Spelling Handbook* you can quickly improve your spelling and word-usage skills.

The Bantam Instant Spelling Handbook helps you to avoid embarrassing—and often important—mistakes. You'll find yourself writing more and speaking with new authority and an increased vocabulary. This is the only spelling handbook you will ever need.

THE BANTAM INSTANT SPELLING HANDBOOK

THE BANTAM
INSTANT SPELLING
HANDBOOK

Edited by
Katherine C. Hill-Miller

BANTAM BOOKS

TORONTO • NEW YORK • LONDON • SYDNEY • AUCKLAND

THE BANTAM INSTANT SPELLING HANDBOOK
A Bantam Book / May 1986

A Nautilus Book

ISBN 0-553-23933-3

Published simultaneously in the United States and Canada

PRINTED IN THE UNITED STATES OF AMERICA

O   0 9 8 7 6 5 4 3 2 1

Preface: How to Use This Book

The Bantam Instant Spelling Handbook is an easy-to-use reference that will quickly answer your questions about spelling problems. The book contains over 25,000 words, arranged alphabetically, with an emphasis on those words frequently misspelled, misused, or confused in some other way. The book also indicates correct word division, hyphenation, pronunciation stress and spelling of irregular forms. With its coverage of other kinds of problem words—foreign terms, brand names, place names—this book can be an indispensable guide through the field of spelling traps, a handy desk companion to steer you quickly out of many spelling difficulties.

All words in this book are divided at the correct syllable breaks, according to *Webster's Third International Dictionary*, with syllabication indicated by the symbol (·) (e.g., com·ply). Hyphenated words are indicated with the symbol (-) (e.g., good-bye); separate words are indicated by division with no notation (e.g., ice cream). This system allows you to check the use of hyphens easily; it also allows quick decisions about where best to divide a word while typing.

Many entries contain a wealth of information in addition to syllable division and correct spelling. All homonyms—words that sound exactly alike—and other easily confused words are listed in this way:

ac·cede *v.* (*to consent*; see *exceed*)

In addition to correct syllabication and spelling, this type of entry also lists the word's part of speech if needed, gives a brief definition where necessary and cross-references it to the word with which it is most often confused. This system recognizes that numerous spelling errors are not, technically, *spelling* errors at all: they are simply replacement of one correctly spelled word with another. These are the abbreviations used for various parts of speech and to indicate plurals and gender:

n. = noun
v. = verb
adj. = adjective
adv. = adverb
prep. = preposition

conj. = conjunction
pron. = pronoun
pl. = plural
f. = feminine
m. = masculine
pt. = past tense

If the division of a word varies according to its part of speech, it is indicated in this way: in·va·lid (*n*.) : in·val·id (*adj*.).

Because they tend to be so frequently misspelled, this book contains many common words with -tion, -sion, -able, -ible, -or, -er, and -tive endings. The book also lists words that change when endings are added (e.g., cries, fanciful). For ease of reference, words are generally listed under the root words from which they are formed. Thus, "acceptable," "acceptance," and "accepted" immediately follow the root from which they are derived: "accept."

Since many foreign terms have become part of the currency of daily American expression, we have included common foreign words and presented them in roman type (e.g., habeas corpus). Less common foreign terms—words that are perfectly acceptable, but still working their way into standard English usage—are printed in italics for easy identification (e.g., *hacienda*).

Recognizing that daily business correspondence requires the use of trade names, and that certain trade names have become synonymous with types of goods rather than the specific brands they really are, we have also included the correct spelling of some common trademark names (e.g., Xerox, Band-Aid). The names of states and countries are also included if they are in any way prone to misspelling.

For ease of reference, we have omitted words that are not commonly misspelled. Many single syllable words fall into this category, as do the many plurals formed by simple addition of an "s" (e.g., horse, horses). Furthermore, we have excluded simple past tenses, those words in which an "ed" ending does not change the actual spelling of the root word. Finally, though we include foreign terms, we do not include British spellings of common American words, which are often considered secondary spellings (e.g., colour, grey).

This book was conceived, planned and executed with a single goal in mind: ease and accuracy for you, the reader. We trust it will become a reliable guide through spelling difficulties and a well-thumbed presence on your desk.

—Katherine C. Hill-Miller

A

ab·a·cus
  pl. ab·a·ci *or* ab·a·cus·es
a·baft
ab·a·lo·ne
a·ban·don
a·base
a·bash
a·bate
  a·bate·ment
ab·at·toir
ab·bé
  pl. ab·bés
ab·bess
ab·bey
ab·bot
ab·bre·vi·ate
  ab·bre·vi·at·ing
  ab·bre·vi·a·tion
ab·di·cate
  ab·di·ca·tion
  ab·di·ca·tor
ab·do·men
  ab·dom·i·nal
ab·duct
  ab·duc·tion
  ab·duc·tor
a·bend
ab·er·rant
  ab·er·rance
  ab·er·ra·tion
a·bet
  a·bet·ment
  a·bet·ting
  a·bet·tor
a·bey·ance
a·bey·ant
ab·hor
  ab·horred
  ab·hor·rence
  ab·hor·rent
  ab·hor·ring

a·bide
a·bil·i·ty
  pl. a·bil·i·ties
ab·ject
  ab·jec·tion
  ab·ject·ly
ab·jure
ab·la·tive
a·blaze
a·ble
  a·ble-bod·ied
  a·bly
ab·lu·tion
ab·ne·gate
  ab·ne·ga·tion
  ab·ne·ga·tor
ab·nor·mal
  ab·nor·mal·i·ty
  pl. ab·nor·mal·i·ties
  ab·nor·mal·ly
ab·nor·mi·ty
  pl. ab·nor·mi·ties
a·board
a·bode
a·bol·ish
  a·bol·ish·a·ble
ab·o·li·tion
  ab·o·li·tion·ar·y
  ab·o·li·tion·ist
a·bom·i·na·ble
  a·bom·i·na·bly
a·bom·i·nate
  a·bom·i·na·tion
ab·o·rig·i·ne
  ab·o·rig·i·nal
a·bort
  a·bor·tion
  a·bor·tive
a·bound
a·bout
  a·bout-face
a·bove
  a·bove·board
  a·bove·ground

ab·ra·ca·dab·ra
a·brade
  a·bra·sion
  a·bra·sive
  a·bra·sive·ly
a·breast
a·bridge
  a·bridg·er
  a·bridg·ing
  a·bridg·ment *or* a·bridge·ment
a·broad
ab·ro·gate
  ab·ro·ga·tion
  ab·ro·ga·tor
ab·rupt
ab·scess
ab·scis·sa
  pl. ab·scis·sas *or* ab·scis·sae
ab·scond
  ab·scond·er
ab·sent
  ab·sence
  ab·sen·tee
  ab·sen·tee·ism
  ab·sent·mind·ed
ab·sinthe *or* ab·sinth
ab·so·lute
ab·so·lu·tion
ab·so·lut·ism
ab·solve
  ab·solv·er
ab·sorb
  ab·sorb·a·ble
  ab·sorb·en·cy
  ab·sorb·ent
  ab·sorb·er
  ab·sorb·ing
  ab·sorp·tion
ab·stain
  ab·stain·er
  ab·sten·tion
  ab·sten·tious
  ab·sti·nence
  ab·sti·nent

ab·ste·mi·ous
ab·stract
  ab·strac·tion
  ab·strac·tion·ism
  ab·strac·tive
  ab·stract·ly
  ab·stract·ness
ab·struse
  ab·struse·ness
ab·surd
  ab·surd·i·ty
a·bun·dant
  a·bun·dance
a·buse
  a·bus·ing
  a·bu·sive
  a·bu·sive·ness
a·but
  a·but·ment
  a·but·ted
  a·but·ter
  a·but·ting
a·bys·mal
a·byss
ac·a·deme
ac·a·de·mi·a
ac·a·dem·ic
  ac·a·dem·i·cal·ly
  ac·a·de·mi·cian
a·cad·e·my
  pl. a·cad·e·mies
ac·cede *v.* (*to consent*; see *exceed*)
  ac·ced·ing
ac·cel·er·ate
  ac·cel·er·a·tion
  ac·cel·er·a·tor
ac·cent
  ac·cen·tu·ate
  ac·cen·tu·a·tion
ac·cept *v.* (*to receive*; see *except*)
  ac·cept·a·ble

ac·cept·ance
ac·cept·ed
ac·cess *n.* (*entry*; see *excess*)
  ac·ces·si·bil·i·ty
  ac·ces·si·ble
  ac·ces·si·bly
  ac·ces·sion
ac·ces·so·ry
  pl. ac·ces·so·ries
ac·ci·dent
  ac·ci·dence
  ac·ci·den·tal
  ac·ci·den·tal·ly
ac·claim
  ac·cla·ma·tion
ac·cli·mate
  ac·cli·ma·tize
ac·cliv·i·ty
ac·co·lade
ac·com·mo·date
  ac·com·mo·dat·ing
  ac·com·mo·da·tion
  ac·com·mo·da·tor
ac·com·pa·ny
  ac·com·pa·nied
  ac·com·pa·ni·ment
  ac·com·pa·nist
ac·com·plice
ac·com·plish
  ac·com·plish·a·ble
  ac·com·plished
  ac·com·plish·ment
ac·cord
  ac·cord·ance
  ac·cord·ant
  ac·cord·ing·ly
ac·cor·di·on
ac·cost
ac·count
  ac·count·a·bil·i·ty
  ac·count·a·ble
  ac·coun·tan·cy
  ac·coun·tant
  ac·count·ing

ac·cou·tre·ment *or*
  ac·cou·ter·ment
ac·cred·it
  ac·cred·i·ta·tion
  ac·cred·it·ed
ac·crete
  ac·cre·tion
ac·crue
  ac·cru·al
  ac·cru·ing
ac·cu·mu·late
  ac·cu·mu·la·ble
  ac·cu·mu·lat·ing
  ac·cu·mu·la·tion
  ac·cu·mu·la·tive
  ac·cu·mu·la·tor
ac·cu·rate
  ac·cu·ra·cy
  ac·cu·rate·ly
ac·cursed *or* **ac·curst**
ac·cuse
  ac·cu·sa·tion
  ac·cu·sa·tive
  ac·cu·sa·to·ry
  ac·cus·er
  ac·cus·ing
ac·cus·tom
  ac·cus·tomed
ac·er·bate
  a·cer·bi·ty
ac·e·tate
a·ce·tic (*sour*; see *ascetic*)
ac·e·tone
a·cet·y·lene
a·chieve
  a·chie·va·ble
  a·chieve·ment
  a·chiev·er
  a·chiev·ing
A·chil·les
ach·ro·mat·ic
ac·id
  a·cid·ic
  a·cid·i·fi·ca·tion

a·cid·i·fied
a·cid·i·fy
a·cid·i·ty
a·cid·u·late
a·cid·u·lous
ac·i·do·sis
ac·knowl·edge
  ac·knowl·edge·a·ble
  ac·knowl·edg·ing
  ac·knowl·edg·ment
ac·me
ac·ne
ac·o·lyte
a·corn
a·cous·tic
  a·cous·ti·cal
ac·quaint
  ac·quaint·ance
ac·qui·esce
  ac·qui·es·cence
  ac·qui·es·cent
ac·quire
  ac·quir·a·ble
  ac·quire·ment
  ac·quir·ing
  ac·qui·si·tion
  ac·quis·i·tive
ac·quit
  ac·quit·tal
  ac·quit·ted
  ac·quit·ting
a·cre
  a·cre·age
ac·rid
  a·crid·i·ty
ac·ri·mo·ny
  ac·ri·mo·ni·ous
ac·ro·bat
  ac·ro·bat·ic
ac·ro·nym
a·crop·o·lis
ac·ro·pho·bi·a
a·cross
a·cros·tic

a·cryl·ic
act·ing
ac·tion
  ac·tion·a·ble
ac·tive
  ac·ti·vate
  ac·ti·va·tion
  ac·tive·ly
  ac·tiv·ism
  ac·tiv·i·ty
  pl. ac·tiv·i·ties
ac·tor
ac·tress
ac·tu·al
  ac·tu·al·i·ty
  pl. ac·tu·al·i·ties
  ac·tu·al·ize
  ac·tu·al·ly
ac·tu·ar·y
  pl. ac·tu·ar·ies
  ac·tu·ar·i·al
ac·tu·ate
  ac·tu·a·tor
a·cu·i·ty
  pl. a·cu·i·ties
a·cu·men
a·cu·punc·ture
a·cute
  a·cute·ly
  a·cute·ness
ad *n.* (*advertisement*; see *add*)
ad·age
a·da·gio
ad·a·mant
a·dapt
  a·dapt·a·bil·i·ty
  a·dapt·a·ble
  ad·ap·ta·tion
  a·dapt·er
add *v.* (*join*; see *ad*)
ad·den·dum
  pl. ad·den·da
ad·der *n.* (*snake*)
add·er *n.* (*one who adds*)

ad·dict
  ad·dict·ed
  ad·dic·tion
  ad·dict·ive
ad·di·tion *n.* (*something*
  added; see *edition*)
  ad·di·tion·al
ad·di·tive
ad·dle
ad·dress
  ad·dress·ee
  ad·dress·ing
ad·duce
  ad·duc·er
  ad·duc·ing
ad·e·noid
  ad·e·noi·dal
a·dept
ad·e·quate
  ad·e·qua·cy
  ad·e·quate·ly
ad·here
  ad·her·ence
  ad·her·ent
  ad·her·ing
  ad·he·sion
  ad·he·sive
ad hoc
a·dieu
  pl. a·dieus *or* a·dieux
ad·i·pose
  ad·i·pos·i·ty
Ad·i·ron·dack
ad·ja·cent
  ad·ja·cen·cy
ad·jec·tive
  ad·jec·ti·val *adj.*
  ad·jec·ti·val·ly *adv.*
  ad·jec·tive·ly *adv.*
ad·join
ad·journ
  ad·journ·ment
ad·judge
  ad·judg·ing

ad·ju·di·cate
  ad·ju·di·cat·ing
  ad·ju·di·ca·tion
  ad·ju·di·ca·tive
  ad·ju·di·ca·tor
ad·junct
ad·jure
  ad·ju·ra·tion
  ad·jur·ing
ad·just
  ad·just·a·ble
  ad·just·ment
ad·ju·tant
ad lib *n.*, *adv.*
ad-lib *adj.*, *v.*
  ad-libbed
ad·min·is·ter
  ad·min·is·trate
  ad·min·is·tra·tion
  ad·min·is·tra·tive
  ad·min·is·tra·tor
ad·mi·ral
  ad·mi·ral·ty
ad·mire
  ad·mi·ra·ble
  ad·mi·ra·tion
  ad·mir·er
  ad·mir·ing
ad·mis·si·ble
  ad·mis·si·bil·i·ty
ad·mis·sion
ad·mit
  ad·mit·tance
  ad·mit·ted
  ad·mit·ting
ad·mix
  ad·mix·ture
ad·mon·ish
  ad·mo·ni·tion
  ad·mon·i·to·ry
ad nau·se·am
a·do
a·do·be

ad·o·les·cence
  ad·o·les·cent
a·dopt
  a·dopt·a·ble
  a·dop·tion
  a·dop·tive
a·dor·a·ble
ad·o·ra·tion
a·dor·ing
a·dorn
  a·dorn·ment
ad·re·nal
A·dren·a·lin (*trademark*)
a·dren·a·line
A·dri·at·ic
a·drift
a·droit
ad·sorb
  ad·sorb·ent
  ad·sorp·tion
ad·u·late
  ad·u·la·tion
  ad·u·la·to·ry
a·dult
a·dul·ter·ate
  a·dul·ter·ant
  a·dul·ter·a·tion
  a·dul·ter·a·tor
a·dul·ter·y
  a·dul·ter·er
  a·dul·ter·ess *n.*
  a·dul·ter·ous *adj.*
ad·um·brate
  ad·um·bra·tion
ad va·lo·rem
ad·vance
  ad·vance·ment
  ad·vanc·ing
ad·van·tage
  ad·van·ta·geous
ad·vent
  ad·ven·ti·tious
ad·ven·ture
  ad·ven·tur·er

ad·ven·ture·some
ad·ven·tur·ess
ad·ven·tur·ous
ad·verb
  ad·verb·i·al
ad·ver·sar·y
  pl. ad·ver·sar·ies
ad·verse *adj.* (*in opposition*;
  see *averse*)
  ad·verse·ly
  ad·ver·si·ty
  pl. ad·ver·si·ties
ad·vert
ad·ver·tise
  ad·ver·tise·ment
  ad·ver·tis·er
ad·vice *n.* (*opinion given*; see
  advise)
ad·vise *v.* (*to inform*; see
  advice)
  ad·vis·a·bil·i·ty
  ad·vis·a·ble
  ad·vise·ment
  ad·vis·er *or* ad·vi·sor
  ad·vis·ing
  ad·vis·o·ry
ad·vo·cate
  ad·vo·ca·cy
  ad·vo·ca·tor
Ae·ge·an
ae·gis
  pl. ae·gis·es
ae·on *or* **e·on**
aer·ate
  aer·a·tion
  aer·a·tor
aer·i·al *adj, n.* (*relating to
  air; antenna*)
  aer·i·al·ist
  aer·o·bat·ic
  aer·o·dy·nam·ics
  aer·o·nau·tic
  aer·o·nau·ti·cal
aer·i·al *n.* (*antenna*)

aer·o·sol
aer·o·space
Aes·chy·lus
Ae·sop
aes·thete *or* es·thete *n.*
aes·thet·ic *or* es·thet·ic *adj.*
  (*of beauty*; *see* ascetic *and*
  esthetic)
  aes·thet·i·cal·ly *or*
  es·thet·i·cal·ly
aes·thet·i·cism *or*
  es·thet·i·cism *n.* (*see*
  ascetism)
af·fa·ble
  af·fa·bil·i·ty
af·fair *n.* (*a concern*; *see*
  affaire)
af·faire *n.* (*liaison*; *scandal*;
  see affair)
af·fect *v.* (*to influence*; *see*
  effect)
  af·fec·ta·tion
  af·fect·ed
af·fec·tion
  af·fec·tion·ate
af·fi·ance
af·fi·ant
af·fi·da·vit
af·fil·i·ate
  af·fil·i·a·tion
af·fin·i·ty
  pl. af·fin·i·ties
af·firm
  af·firm·a·ble
  af·fir·ma·tion
  af·fir·ma·tive
  af·firm·a·to·ry
af·fix
af·flict
  af·flic·tion
af·flu·ent
  af·flu·ence
af·ford
af·fray

af·fright
af·front
af·ghan
Af·ghan·i·stan
a·field
a·fire
a·float
a·foot
a·fore·men·tioned
a·fore·said
a·fore·thought
a·fraid
a·fresh
Af·ri·ca
  Af·ri·can
Af·ro-A·mer·i·can
af·ter
  af·ter·burn·er
  af·ter·ef·fect
  af·ter·glow
  af·ter·life
  af·ter·math
  af·ter·noon
  af·ter·taste
  af·ter·thought
  af·ter·ward *adv.* (*a later*
  time)
  af·ter·word *n.* (*epilogue*)
a·gain
a·gainst
a·gape *adj.* (*open*)
a·ga·pe *n.* (*love*)
  pl. a·ga·pae
ag·ate
ag·ate·ware
a·ga·ve
age·less
a·gen·cy
  pl. a·gen·cies
a·gen·da
a·gent
age·old
ag·glom·er·ate
  ag·glom·er·a·tion

ag·glu·ti·nate
  ag·glu·ti·na·tive
ag·gran·dize
  ag·gran·dize·ment
ag·gra·vate
  ag·gra·vat·ing
  ag·gra·va·tion
ag·gre·gate
  ag·gre·gat·ing
  ag·gre·ga·tion
ag·gres·sion
  ag·gres·sive
  ag·gres·sor
ag·grieve
  ag·grieved
a·ghast
ag·ile
  ag·ile·ly
  a·gil·i·ty
ag·ing
ag·i·tate
  ag·i·tat·ing
  ag·i·ta·tion
  ag·i·ta·tor
a·glow
ag·nos·tic
  ag·nos·ti·cism
a·gog
ag·o·nize
  ag·o·niz·ing
ag·o·ny
  pl. ag·o·nies
ag·o·ra·pho·bi·a
a·grar·i·an
a·gree
  a·gree·a·bil·i·ty
  a·gree·a·ble
  a·greed
  a·gree·ing
  a·gree·ment
ag·ri·cul·ture
  ag·ri·cul·tur·al
  ag·ri·cul·tur·ist

a·gron·o·my
  a·gron·o·mist
a·ground
a·gue
a·head
a·hoy
aid *v.* (*to help;* see *aide*)
aide *n.* (*an assistant;* see *aid*)
aide-de-camp
ail *v.* (*to be sick;* see *ale*)
  ail·ment
ai·le·ron
air *n., v.* (*atmosphere;* see
  ere and *heir*)
  air base
  air·borne
  air brake
  air·brush
  air check
  air coach
  air com·mand
  air-con·di·tion
  air con·di·tion·er
  air-cool
  air-cooled
  air·craft
  air-dried
  air-drop *v.*
  air·drop *n.*
  air ex·press
  air·field
  air-filled
  air·flow
  air·foil
  air force
  air·frame
  air·freight
  air gun
  air·head
  air·i·ly
  air·i·ness
  air lane
  air·lift *n.* (*a supply line*)
  air·line *n.* (*transportation*)

air·lin·er
air·mail
air·man
air mass
air·mind·ed
air·plane
air pocket
air·port
air·proof
air pump
air raid
air ri·fle
air·screw
air shaft
air·ship
air·sick
air space n. (*space lying above nation*)
air space n. (*enclosed space for air*)
air·speed
air·stream
air·strip
air·tight
air·wave
air·way
air·wor·thi·ness
air·wor·thy
air·y
Aire·dale
aisle n. (*passage between seats; see isle*)
a·jar
a·kim·bo
a·kin
Al·a·bam·a
al·a·bas·ter
à la carte
a·lac·ri·ty
A·lad·din
à la king
à la mode
a·larm
a·larm·ist

A·las·ka
al·ba·tross
   pl. al·ba·tross *or* al·ba·tross·es
al·be·it
al·bi·no
   pl. al·bi·nos
al·bum
al·bu·men
al·bu·min
Al·bu·quer·que
al·che·my
   al·che·mist
al·co·hol
   al·co·hol·ic
   al·co·hol·ism
al·cove
al·der·man
   pl. al·der·men
ale n. (*beer; see ail*)
   ale·wife
A·leu·tian
al·fal·fa
al·fres·co
al·ga
   pl. al·gae *or* al·gas
al·ge·bra
   al·ge·bra·ic
   al·ge·bra·i·cal
Al·ger·i·a
al·go·rithm
a·li·as
al·i·bi
   pl. al·i·bis
   al·i·bied
   al·i·bi·ing
al·ien
al·ien·ate
   al·ien·at·ing
   al·ien·a·tion
   al·ien·ist
a·lign *or* a·line
   a·lign·ment
a·like

al·i·men·ta·ry
  al·i·men·ta·tion
al·i·mo·ny
al·i·quot
al·ka·li
  pl. al·ka·lies
  al·ka·line
  al·ka·lin·i·ty
al·ka·loid
al·ka·lo·sis
al·kyl
all *adj., adv. (whole amount; wholly; see awl)*
al·lay
al·lege
  al·le·ga·tion
  al·leg·ing
  al·leg·ed·ly
Al·le·ghe·ny *or* Al·le·gha·ny *or* Al·le·ga·ny
al·le·giance
al·le·go·ry
  pl. al·le·go·ries
  al·le·gor·i·cal
al·le·gret·to
al·le·gro
al·le·lu·ia *or* al·le·lu·jah *or* al·le·lu·ja
al·ler·gy
  pl. al·ler·gies
  al·ler·gen
  al·ler·gic
al·le·vi·ate
  al·le·vi·at·ing
  al·le·vi·a·tion
al·ley *n. (street; see ally)*
  pl. al·leys
al·li·ance
al·li·ga·tor
al·lit·er·a·tion
  al·lit·er·a·tive
al·lo·cate
  al·lo·ca·ble
  al·lo·cat·ing

al·lo·ca·tion
al·lo·cu·tion
al·lop·a·thy
  al·lo·path·ic
al·lot
  al·lot·ment
  al·lot·ted
  al·lot·ting
al·low
  al·low·a·ble
  al·low·ance
  al·lowed
  al·low·ed·ly
al·loy
all read·y *adj. (prepared; see already)*
all right
all·spice
al·lude *v. (to refer to; see elude)*
  al·lud·ing
al·lure
  al·lur·ing
al·lu·sion *n. (a reference to; see illusion)*
  al·lu·sive *adj. (suggestive; see elusive and illusive)*
al·lu·vi·al
al·ly *v., n. (to unite, associate; see alley)*
  pl. al·lies
  al·lied
  al·ly·ing
Al·ma Ma·ter
al·ma·nac
al·might·y
  al·might·i·ly
al·mond
al·most
alms
  alms·house
al·ni·co
al·oe
  pl. al·oes

a·loft
a·lo·ha
a·lone
a·long
  a·long·side
a·loof
a·loud
al·pac·a
al·pha
al·pha·bet
  al·pha·bet·ic
  al·pha·bet·ize
  al·pha·nu·mer·ic
al·read·y *adv.* (*previously*;
  see *all ready*)
Al·sace Lor·raine
Al·sa·tian
al·tar *n.* (*raised structure*;
  see *alter*)
  al·tar·piece
  al·tar rail
  al·tar stone
al·ter *v.* (*to change*; see *altar*)
  al·ter·a·ble
  al·ter·a·tion
  al·tered
al·ter·ca·tion
al·ter e·go
al·ter·nate
  al·ter·nat·ing
  al·ter·na·tion
  al·ter·na·tive
  al·ter·na·tive·ly
  al·ter·na·tor
al·though
al·tim·e·ter
al·ti·tude
al·to
al·to·geth·er
al·tru·ism
  al·tru·ist
  al·tru·is·tic
al·um
a·lu·mi·num

a·lum·na *n.*, *f.*
  pl. a·lum·nae
a·lum·nus
  pl. a·lum·ni
al·ve·o·lus
  pl. al·ve·o·li
al·ways
a·mal·gam
  a·mal·ga·mate
  a·mal·ga·mat·ing
  a·mal·ga·ma·tion
a·man·u·en·sis
a·mass
am·a·teur
  am·a·teur·ish
am·a·to·ry
a·maze
  a·maze·ment
  a·maz·ing
  a·maz·ing·ly
am·bas·sa·dor
am·ber·gris
am·bi·dex·trous
am·bi·ence
am·bi·ent
am·bi·gu·i·ty
  pl. am·bi·gu·i·ties
  am·big·u·ous
am·bi·tion
  am·bi·tious
am·biv·a·lence
am·bro·sia
am·bu·lance
am·bu·la·to·ry
am·bus·cade
am·bush
a·me·ba
  pl. a·me·bas *or* a·me·bae (*var.*
  of amoeba)
a·me·lio·rate
  a·me·lio·ra·tion
  a·me·lio·ra·tive
  a·me·lio·ra·tor

a·me·na·ble
a·mend v. (to improve; see
    emend)
    a·mend·ment
a·men·i·ty
    pl. a·men·i·ties
A·mer·i·can
    A·mer·i·ca·na
    A·mer·i·can·ism
    A·mer·i·can·i·za·tion
Am·er·ind
am·e·thyst
a·mi·a·ble
    a·mi·a·bil·i·ty
am·i·ca·ble
    am·i·ca·bil·i·ty
a·mid·ships
a·midst
a·miss
am·i·ty
am·me·ter
am·mo·nia
am·mu·ni·tion
am·ne·sia
am·nes·ty
a·moe·ba or a·me·ba
    pl. a·moe·bas or a·moe·bae
    (see ameba)
a·mok
a·mong or a·mongst
a·mor·al
a·mor·phous
am·or·tize
    am·or·ti·za·tion
    am·or·tiz·ing
a·mount
a·mour
    am·o·rous
am·pere
    am·per·age
am·per·sand
am·phet·a·mine
am·phib·i·an
am·phib·i·ous

am·phi·the·a·ter
am·pho·ra
am·ple
am·pli·fy
    am·pli·fi·ca·tion
    am·pli·fied
    am·pli·fi·er
    am·pli·fy·ing
am·pli·tude
am·ply
am·pu·tate
    am·pu·ta·tion
am·u·let
a·muse
    a·muse·ment
    a·mus·ing
am·y·lase
a·nach·ro·nism
    a·nach·ro·nis·tic
an·aer·o·bic
an·a·gram
an·al·ge·sia
    an·al·ge·sic
an·a·log
a·nal·o·gy
    pl. a·nal·o·gies
    an·a·log·i·cal
    a·nal·o·gous
an·a·lyze
    a·nal·y·sand
    a·nal·y·sis
    an·a·lyst n. (interpreter; see
    annalist)
    an·a·lyt·i·cal
an·a·phy·lax·is
an·ar·chy
    an·ar·chic
    an·ar·chism
    an·ar·chist
an·a·stig·mat·ic
a·nath·e·ma
a·nat·o·my
    an·a·tom·i·cal
    a·nat·o·mist

a·nat·o·mize

an·ces·tor
 an·ces·tral
 an·ces·try

an·chor
 an·chor·age

an·cho·vy
 pl. an·cho·vies

an·cient

an·cil·lar·y

and·i·ron

and/or

an·dro·gen

an·ec·dote n. (*short, amusing
 story; see* antidote)

a·ne·mi·a
 a·ne·mic *or* a·nae·mic

an·e·mom·e·ter

a·nem·o·ne

an·er·oid

an·es·the·sia *or* **an·aes·the·sia**
 an·es·the·si·ol·o·gist
 an·es·thet·ic *or* an·aes·thet·ic
 a·nes·the·tist *or* a·naes·the·tist
 a·nes·the·tize *or* a·naes·the·tize

an·cu·rysm *or* **an·eu·rism**

an·gel n. (*a heavenly being;
 see* angle)
 an·gel·ic

an·gel·fish

An·ge·lus

an·ger

an·gi·na

an·gle n., v. (*intersecting
 lines; see* angel)
 an·gling
 an·gle i·ron
 an·gler
 an·gle·worm

An·gli·can
 An·gli·can·ism

an·gli·cism
 an·gli·cize

An·glo-A·mer·i·can

an·glo·phile

an·glo·phobe

An·glo-Sax·on

An·go·la

an·go·ra

an·gry
 an·gri·ly

an·guish

an·gu·lar
 an·gu·lar·i·ty

an·i·line

an·i·mad·ver·sion

an·i·mal

an·i·mate
 an·i·mat·ed·ly
 an·i·ma·tion

an·i·mos·i·ty

an·i·mus

an·ise

an·i·seed

an·is·ette

an·kle
 an·kle·bone
 an·klet

an·nals
 an·nal·ist n. (*historian; see
 analyst*)

an·neal

an·nex
 an·nex·a·tion

an·ni·hi·late
 an·ni·hi·la·tion
 an·ni·hi·la·tor

an·ni·ver·sa·ry
 pl. an·ni·ver·sa·ries

an·no·tate
 an·no·ta·tion

an·nounce
 an·nounce·ment
 an·nounc·er
 an·nounc·ing

an·noy
 an·noy·ance
 an·noyed

an·noy·ing
an·nu·al
　an·nu·al·ly
an·nu·i·ty
　an·nu·i·tant
an·nul
　an·nu·lar
　an·nulled
　an·nul·ling
　an·nul·ment
an·nun·ci·a·tion
an·nun·ci·a·tor
an·od·ize
an·o·dyne
a·noint
a·nom·a·lous
a·nom·a·ly
a·non·y·mous
　an·o·nym·i·ty
a·noph·e·les
an·oth·er
an·swer
　an·swer·a·ble
ant *n. (small insect;* see *aunt)*
ant·ac·id
an·tag·o·nize
　an·tag·o·nism
　an·tag·o·nist
　an·tag·o·nis·tic
ant·arc·tic
Ant·arc·ti·ca
ant·eat·er
an·te·bel·lum
an·te·ced·ent
an·te·cham·ber
an·te·date
an·te·di·lu·vi·an
an·te·lope
an·te me·rid·i·em
an·ten·na
　pl. an·ten·nae *or* an·ten·nas
an·te·ri·or
an·te·room
an·them

an·ther
ant·hill
an·thol·o·gy
an·thra·cite
an·thrax
an·thro·poid
an·thro·pol·o·gy
an·thro·po·morph·ic
an·ti·air·craft
an·ti·bi·ot·ic
an·ti·bod·y
　pl. an·ti·bod·ies
an·tic
an·tic·i·pate
　an·tic·i·pat·ing
　an·tic·i·pa·tion
　an·tic·i·pa·tive
　an·tic·i·pa·to·ry
an·ti·cli·max
　an·ti·cli·mac·tic
an·ti·co·ag·u·lant
an·ti·dote *n. (a remedy;* see
　anecdote)
an·ti·freeze
an·ti·gen
An·ti·gua
an·ti·his·ta·mine
an·ti·ma·cas·sar
an·ti·ma·lar·i·al
an·ti·mo·ny
an·tip·a·thy
　an·ti·pa·thet·ic
an·ti·per·son·nel
an·tiph·o·nal
an·ti·po·de
　pl. an·ti·po·des
an·ti·py·ret·ic
an·ti·quate
　an·ti·quat·ed
an·tique
　an·ti·quar·i·an
　an·ti·quar·y
　an·tiq·ui·ty

an·ti-Se·mit·ic
an·ti·sep·tic
  an·ti·sep·sis
an·ti·so·cial
an·ti·spas·mod·ic
an·tith·e·sis
  an·ti·thet·ic
an·ti·tox·in
an·ti·trust
ant·ler
an·to·nym
an·trum
an·vil
anx·i·et·y
anx·ious
an·y
  an·y·bod·y
  an·y·how
  an·y·one
  an·y·thing
  an·y·way
  an·y·where
a·o·rist
a·or·ta
a·pace
a·part
a·part·heid
a·part·ment
ap·a·thy
  ap·a·thet·ic
a·pér·i·tif
ap·er·ture
a·pex
a·pha·sia
  a·pha·sic
aph·o·rism
Aph·ro·di·te
a·pi·ar·y
  pl. a·pi·ar·ies
ap·i·cal
a·pi·cul·ture
a·piece
a·plomb
a·poc·a·lypse

a·poc·ry·pha
a·poc·ry·phal
ap·o·gee
ap·o·logue
a·pol·o·gy
  pl. a·pol·o·gies
  a·pol·o·get·ic
  a·pol·o·get·i·cal·ly
  a·pol·o·get·ics
  a·pol·o·gize
  a·pol·o·giz·ing
ap·o·plex·y
  ap·o·plec·tic
a·pos·ta·sy
  a·pos·tate
a·pos·te·ri·o·ri
a·pos·tle
  a·pos·to·late
  ap·os·tol·ic
a·pos·tro·phe
  a·pos·tro·phize
a·poth·e·car·y
  pl. a·poth·e·car·ies
a·poth·e·o·sis
Ap·pa·la·chian
ap·pall
  ap·palled
  ap·pall·ing
ap·pa·ra·tus
ap·par·el
  ap·par·eled
ap·par·ent
ap·pa·ri·tion
ap·peal
  ap·peal·ing·ly
ap·pear
ap·pear·ance
ap·pease
  ap·pease·ment
ap·pel·lant
ap·pel·late
ap·pel·la·tion
ap·pel·lee

ap·pend
  ap·pend·age
ap·pen·dix
  pl. ap·pen·dix·es *or*
  ap·pen·di·ces
  ap·pen·dec·to·my
  ap·pen·di·ci·tis
ap·per·ceive
  ap·per·cep·tion
ap·per·tain
ap·pe·tite
  ap·pe·tiz·er
  ap·pe·tiz·ing
ap·plaud
ap·plause
ap·ple
  ap·ple·jack
ap·pli·ance
ap·pli·qué
ap·ply
  ap·pli·ca·ble
  ap·pli·cant
  ap·pli·ca·tion
  ap·plied
  ap·ply·ing
ap·point
  ap·poin·tee
  ap·point·ive
ap·por·tion
ap·po·site *adj.* (*relevant*; see
  opposite)
ap·po·si·tion
ap·praise *v.* (*set a value on*;
  see *apprise*)
  ap·prais·al
  ap·prais·ing
ap·pre·ci·ate
  ap·pre·cia·ble
  ap·pre·ci·a·tion
  ap·pre·cia·tive
ap·pre·hend
  ap·pre·hen·si·ble
  ap·pre·hen·sion
  ap·pre·hen·sive

ap·pren·tice
  ap·pren·ticed
  ap·pren·tice·ship
ap·prise *v.* (*notify*; see
  appraise)
ap·proach
ap·pro·ba·tion
ap·pro·ba·to·ry
ap·pro·pri·ate
  ap·pro·pri·ate·ness
  ap·pro·pri·a·tion
ap·prove
  ap·prov·al
  ap·prov·ing
ap·prox·i·mate
  ap·prox·i·ma·tion
ap·pur·te·nance
ap·pur·te·nant
a·pri·cot
A·pril Fool
a pri·o·ri
a·pron
ap·ro·pos
ap·ti·tude
apt·ly
apt·ness
aq·ua·cade
Aq·ua·lung (*trademark*)
aq·ua·ma·rine
aq·ua·plane
aq·ua·relle
a·quar·i·um
  pl. a·quar·i·ums *or* a·quar·i·a
a·quat·ic
aq·ua·tint
aq·ue·duct
a·que·ous
aq·ui·line
ar·a·besque
A·ra·bi·an
Ar·a·bic
ar·a·ble
ar·bi·ter
ar·bi·trage

ar·bi·trar·y
  ar·bi·trar·i·ly
ar·bi·trate
  ar·bi·tra·ble
  ar·bit·ra·ment
  ar·bi·tra·tion
  ar·bi·tra·tive
  ar·bi·tra·tor
ar·bor
  ar·bo·re·al
  ar·bo·re·tum
  ar·bor·vi·tae
ar·bu·tus
arc *n., v. (a curve*; see *ark*)
  arc·ing
ar·cade
ar·chae·ol·o·gy *or*
  ar·che·ol·o·gy
  ar·chae·o·log·i·cal *or*
  ar·che·o·log·i·cal
  ar·chae·ol·o·gist *or*
  ar·che·ol·o·gist
ar·cha·ic
arch·an·gel
arch·bish·op
arch·dea·con
arch·di·o·cese
arch·duch·ess
arch·duch·y
arch·duke
  arch·du·cal
arch·en·e·my
arch·er
  arch·er·y
ar·che·type
arch·fiend
ar·chi·e·pis·co·pal
ar·chi·pel·a·go
  pl. ar·chi·pel·a·goes
ar·chi·tect
  ar·chi·tec·tur·al
  ar·chi·tec·ture
ar·chi·trave
ar·chives

arch·ness
arch·way
arc·tic
Arc·tic Cir·cle
ar·dent
ar·dor
ar·du·ous
ar·e·a *n., adj. (place*; see *aria*)
  ar·e·a·way
a·re·na
a·re·o·la
Ar·gen·ti·na
ar·gon
ar·go·naut
ar·go·sy
ar·got
ar·gue
  ar·gued
  ar·gu·ing
ar·gu·ment
  ar·gu·men·ta·tion
  ar·gu·men·ta·tive
ar·gyle
a·ri·a *n. (song*; see *area*)
ar·id
  a·rid·i·ty
a·ri·o·so
ar·is·toc·ra·cy
  a·ris·to·crat
  a·ris·to·crat·ic
Ar·is·to·te·lian
a·rith·me·tic
  ar·ith·met·i·cal
  a·rith·me·ti·cian
Ar·i·zo·na
ark *n. (boat*; see *arc*)
Ar·kan·sas
ar·ma·da
ar·ma·dil·lo
ar·ma·ment
ar·ma·ture
arm·chair
arm·ful
arm·hole

ar·mi·stice
arm·let
ar·mor
  ar·mor·er
  ar·mo·ri·al
  ar·mo·ry
arm·pit
arm·rest
ar·my
  pl. ar·mies
  ar·my ant
  ar·my·worm
ar·ni·ca
a·ro·ma
  ar·o·mat·ic
ar·peg·gi·o
  pl. ar·peg·gi·os
ar·raign
  ar·raign·ment
ar·range
  ar·range·ment
  ar·rang·ing
ar·rant
ar·ras
ar·ray
  ar·rayed
  ar·ray·ing
ar·rear
ar·rest
ar·rhyth·mi·a
ar·rive
  ar·riv·al
  ar·riv·ing
ar·ro·gant
  ar·ro·gance
ar·ro·gate
ar·row
  ar·row·head
  ar·row·root
ar·roy·o
ar·se·nal
ar·se·nate
ar·se·nic
ar·son

ar·te·ri·al
ar·te·ri·ole
ar·te·ri·o·scle·ro·sis
ar·ter·y
  pl. ar·ter·ies
ar·te·sian
art·ful
  art·ful·ly
ar·thri·tis
ar·ti·choke
ar·ti·cle
  ar·ti·cled
ar·tic·u·late
  ar·tic·u·la·tion
ar·ti·fact
ar·ti·fice
  ar·tif·i·cer
  ar·ti·fi·cial
  ar·ti·fi·ci·al·i·ty
ar·til·ler·y
ar·ti·san
art·ist
  ar·tis·tic
  art·ist·ry
art·less
as·bes·tos
as·cend
  as·cend·an·cy
  as·cend·ant
  as·cend·er
  as·cend·ing
  as·cen·sion
as·cent *n (a rise;* see *assent)*
as·cer·tain
  as·cer·tain·a·ble
as·cet·ic *n. (a recluse;* see
  acetic, aesthetic, and *esthetic)*
  as·cet·i·cism *n. (see aesthet-*
  icism or *estheticism)*
as·cribe
  as·crib·ing
  as·crip·tion
a·sep·tic
  a·sep·sis

a·sep·ti·cal·ly
a·shamed
ash·en
ash·tray
ash·y
A·sia
A·sian
A·si·at·ic
a·side
as·i·nine
as·i·nin·i·ty
a·skance
a·skew
a·sleep
as·par·a·gus
as·pect
as·pen
as·per·i·ty
as·perse
as·per·sion
as·phalt
as·phyx·i·ate
as·phyx·i·a
as·phyx·i·at·ing
as·phyx·i·a·tion
as·pic
as·pi·rate
as·pi·ra·tion
as·pi·ra·tor
as·pire
as·pi·rant
as·pir·ing
as·pi·rin
as·sail
as·sail·ant
as·sas·sin
as·sas·si·nate
as·sas·si·na·tion
as·sault
as·say *n., v. (to attempt; see essay)*
as·sayed
as·say·ing

as·sem·ble
as·sem·blage
as·sem·bling
as·sem·bly
as·sem·bly·man
as·sent *v., n. (to agree; see ascent)*
as·sert
as·ser·tion
as·ser·tive
as·sess
as·sess·a·ble
as·sess·ment
as·ses·sor
as·set
as·sev·er·ate
as·sev·er·a·tion
as·sid·u·ous
as·si·du·i·ty
as·sign
as·sign·a·ble
as·sign·ee
as·sign·er
as·sim·i·late
as·sim·i·la·ble
as·sim·i·lat·ing
as·sim·i·la·tion
as·sim·i·la·tive
as·sim·i·la·to·ry
as·sist
as·sist·ance
as·sist·ant
as·size
as·so·ciate *adj.*
as·so·ci·ate *v.*
as·so·ci·at·ing
as·so·ci·a·tion
as·so·cia·tive
as·so·nance
as·so·nant
as·sort
as·suage
as·suag·ing

as·sume
 as·sum·ing
 as·sump·tion
as·sure
 as·sur·ance
 as·sured
 as·sur·ing
as·ter
as·ter·isk
as·ter·oid
as·the·ni·a
asth·ma
a·stig·ma·tism
 as·tig·mat·ic
as·ton·ish
as·tound
as·tra·khan *or* as·tra·chan
as·tral
a·stride
as·trin·gent
 as·trin·gen·cy
as·tro·dome
as·tro·labe
as·trol·o·gy
 as·trol·o·ger
as·tro·nau·tics
 as·tro·naut
 as·tro·nau·ti·cal
as·tron·o·my
 as·tron·o·mer
 as·tro·nom·ic
 as·tro·nom·i·cal
as·tute
a·sun·der
a·sy·lum
a·sym·met·ric *or*
 a·sym·met·ri·cal
a·syn·chro·nous
at·a·rac·tic
at·a·vism
a·te·lier
a·the·ism
 a·the·ist
 a·the·is·tic

ath·e·nae·um *or* ath·e·ne·um
ath·lete
 ath·let·ic
a·thwart
At·lan·tic
at·las
at·mo·sphere
 at·mo·spher·ic
at·om
 at·om·ic
at·om·ize
 at·om·iz·er
a·ton·al
a·tone·ment
a·ton·ing
a·tri·um
a·troc·i·ty
 a·tro·cious
at·ro·phy
 at·ro·phied
at·tach
 at·tached
at·ta·ché
at·ta·ché case
at·tack
at·tain
 at·tain·a·ble
at·tain·der
at·taint
at·tar
at·tempt
at·tend
 at·tend·ance
 at·tend·ant
at·ten·tion
at·ten·tive
at·ten·u·ate
 at·ten·u·a·tion
at·test
 at·tes·ta·tion
at·tic
at·tire
at·ti·tude
at·tor·ney

at·tract
  at·trac·tion
  at·tract·ive
at·tri·bute *n., v.*
  at·trib·ut·a·ble
  at·tri·bu·tion
  at·trib·u·tive
at·tri·tion
at·tune
a·typ·i·cal
au·burn
au con·traire
au cou·rant
auc·tion
  auc·tion·eer
au·dac·i·ty
  au·da·cious
au·di·ble
  au·di·bil·i·ty
  au·di·bly
au·di·ence
au·di·o·phile
au·di·o·vi·su·al
au·dit
  au·di·tor
au·di·tion
au·di·to·ri·um
au·di·to·ry
au fait
Auf Wie·der·seh·en
au·ger *n. (a tool; see augur)*
aught *n., adv. (zero; see ought)*
aug·ment
  aug·men·ta·tion
au gra·tin
au·gur *n., v. (to predict; see auger)*
  au·gu·ry
au·gust *adj.*
Au·gust *n.*
au jus
auk
au lait

au na·tu·rel
aunt *n. (relative; see ant)*
au·ra
au·ral *adj. (relating to hearing; see oral)*
au·re·ate
au·re·ole
au re·voir
au·ri·cle
au·ric·u·lar
au·rif·er·ous
au·ro·ra
  au·ro·ra bo·re·al·is
aus·cul·ta·tion
  aus·cul·tate
aus·pice
  aus·pi·cious
aus·tere
  aus·ter·i·ty
Aus·tra·lia
  Aus·tra·lian
Aus·tri·a
au·then·tic
  au·then·ti·cate
  au·then·tic·i·ty
au·thor
  au·thor·ship
au·thor·i·ty
  au·thor·i·tar·i·an
  au·thor·i·ta·tive
au·tho·rize
  au·tho·ri·za·tion
  au·tho·riz·ing
Au·to·bahn
au·to·bi·og·ra·phy
au·toch·tho·nous
au·tom·a·tism
  au·tom·a·ti·za·tion
  au·tom·a·tize
au·tom·a·ton
au·to·mo·bile
au·to·mo·tive
au·ton·o·my
  au·to·nom·ic

au·ton·o·mous
au·top·sy
au·to·sug·ges·tion
au·tumn
　au·tum·nal
aux·il·ia·ry
a·vail
　a·vail·a·bil·i·ty
　a·vail·a·ble
av·a·lanche
a·vant-garde
av·a·rice
　av·a·ri·cious
a·venge
av·e·nue
a·ver
　a·verred
　a·ver·ring
av·er·age
a·verse *adj.* (*reluctant*; see
　adverse)
a·ver·sion
a·vert
a·vi·ar·y
a·vi·a·tion
a·vi·a·tor
av·id
　a·vid·i·ty
av·o·ca·do
　pl. av·o·ca·dos *or* av·o·ca·does
av·o·ca·tion
a·void
　a·void·a·ble
　a·void·ance
av·oir·du·pois
a·vow
　a·vow·al
　a·vowed
a·vun·cu·lar
a·wait
a·wake
　a·wak·en
a·ward

a·ware
　a·ware·ness
a·wash
a·way *adv.* (*not near*; see
　aweigh)
a·weigh *adj.* (*raised*; see
　away)
awe·some
aw·ful *adj.*, *adv.* (*terrible*; see
　offal)
a·while
awk·ward
awl *n.* (*pointed tool*; see *all*)
aw·ning
awol
a·wry
ax *or* **axe**
ax·i·om
　ax·i·o·mat·ic
ax·is
　pl. ax·es
ax·le
ax·le·tree
aye *adv.*, *n.* (*affirmative*; see
　eye)
a·za·lea
az·i·muth
Az·tec
a·zure

B

bab·ble
　bab·bling
ba·boon
ba·bush·ka
ba·by
　pl. ba·bies
　ba·by·ing
　ba·by-sit
　ba·by-sit·ter
bac·ca·lau·re·ate
bac·ca·rat

bac·cha·nal
  bac·cha·na·lian
bac·chant
bach·e·lor
ba·cil·lus
  pl. ba·cil·li
back·ache
back·bite
back·board
back·bone
back·break·ing
back·cross
back door *n.*
back·drop
back·er
back·field
back·fire
back·gam·mon
back·ground
back·hand
  back·hand·ed
back·lash
back·log
back or·der
back·ped·aled
back·rest
back room
back·seat
back·slide
back·spac·er
back·stage
back·stairs
back·stitch
back·stop
back·stretch
back·stroke
back talk
back track *n.*
back·track *v.*
back up *v.*
back·up *n.*
back·ward
back·wash
back·wa·ter

back·woods
  back·woods·man
back·yard
ba·con
bac·te·ri·um *s.*
  pl. bac·te·ri·a
bac·te·ri·al
bac·te·ri·cide
bac·te·ri·ol·o·gy
bad *adj.* (*not good;* see *bade*)
bade *v.* (*pt. of bid;* see *bad*)
badg·er
bad·i·nage
bad·lands
bad·min·ton
baf·fle
  baf·fle·ment
  baf·fling
bag·a·telle
bag·gage
  bag·gage·mas·ter
bagged
bag·ging
bag·gy
bag·pipe
ba·guette
Ba·ha·mas
bail *v., n.* (*money;* see *bale*)
  bailed
  bail·ee
  bail·ment
  bail·or
bai·liff
bai·li·wick
bait *v., n.* (*a lure;* see *bate*)
Bak·e·lite (*trademark*)
bak·er's doz·en
bak·ing
bal·a·lai·ka
bal·ance
  bal·ance sheet
  bal·anc·ing
bal·co·ny
  pl. bal·co·nies

bald
bal·der·dash
bale *n., v.* (*tight bundle*; see
  bail)
  baled
  bal·ing
bale·ful
balk
  balk·y
Bal·kan·ize
  Bal·kan·i·za·tion
balk·line
bal·lad
  bal·lad·eer
  bal·lad·ry
bal·last
ball bear·ing
balled
bal·let
bal·lis·tic
bal·loon
  bal·loon·ist
bal·lot
ball park
ball-point pen
ball·room
bal·ly·hoo
balm
  balm·i·ness
  balm·y
bal·mor·al
bal·sa
bal·sam
Bal·tic
bal·us·trade
bam·boo
bam·boo·zle
ban *n.*
  pl. banns
ban *v.*
  banned *v.* (*forbidden*; see
  band)
ba·nal
  ba·nal·i·ty

ba·nan·a
band *n.* (*musicians*; see
  banned)
ban·dage
  ban·dag·ing
Band-Aid (*trademark*)
ban·dan·na
band·box
ban·deau
  pl. ban·deaux
ban·de·role
ban·dit
band·mas·ter
ban·do·lier
band saw
band shell
band·stand
ban·dy
  ban·dy-leg·ged
bane·ful
Ban·gla·desh
ban·gle
ban·ish
ban·is·ter *or* ban·nis·ter
ban·jo
bank·book
bank draft
bank·er
bank mon·ey
bank note
bank pa·per
bank rate
bank·roll
bank·rupt
  bank·rupt·cy
ban·ner
  ban·ner·et
ban·nock
banns
ban·quet
ban *v.*
ban·shee
ban·tam
ban·ter·ing·ly

ban·yan
ban·zai
ba·o·bab
bap·tize
  bap·tism
  bap·tist
  bap·tis·ter·y *or* bap·tis·try
bar *v.*
  barred (*past tense; see* bard)
  bar·ring
Bar·ba·dos
bar·ba·rism
  bar·bar·i·an
  bar·bar·ic
  bar·bar·i·ty
  bar·ba·rize
  bar·ba·rous
bar·be·cue
bar·bell
bar·ber
  bar·ber·shop
bar·bette
bar·bi·tu·rate
bar·ca·role
bar chart
bard *n.* (*poet; see* barred)
bard·ol·a·ter
bare *adj., v.* (*unclothed; see*
  bear)
  bare·back
  bare·faced
  bare·foot
  bare·hand·ed
  bare·head·ed
  bare·ly
bar·gain
barge·man
bar·i·tone
bar·i·um
bar·keep·er
bar·ken·tine
bark·er
bar·ley
  bar·ley·corn

bar·maid
bar·na·cle
barn·storm·er
barn·yard
bar·o·graph
ba·rom·e·ter
  bar·o·met·ric
bar·on *n.* (*a royal title; see*
  barren)
  bar·on·age
  bar·on·ess
  ba·ro·ni·al
  bar·o·ny
bar·on·et
  bar·on·et·cy
ba·roque
ba·rouche
bar·rack
bar·ra·cu·da
bar·rage
bar·rel
bar·ren *adj.* (*infertile; see*
  baron)
bar·ri·cade
bar·ri·er
bar·ris·ter
bar·room
bar·row
bar·tend·er
bar·ter
ba·sal
ba·salt
bas·cule
base *n.* (*foundation; see* bass)
  pl. bas·es
base·ball
base·board
base·born
base burn·er
base·less
base·ment
base·ness
base pay
bash·ful

BA·SIC
ba·sic
  ba·si·cal·ly
bas·il
ba·sil·i·ca
bas·i·lisk
ba·sin
ba·sis
  pl. ba·ses
bas·ket
  bas·ket·ball
  bas·ket·work
bas-re·lief
bass *n., adj. (musical tone;*
  see *base)*
bas·si·net
bas·soon
bass·wood
bas·tion
batch
bate *v. (to reduce;* see *bait)*
bat·fish
bath *n.*
  bath·house
  bath·mat
  bath·robe
  bath·room
  bath·tub
bathe *v.*
  bath·ing
ba·thet·ic
Bath·i·nette *(trademark)*
ba·thos
bath·y·sphere
ba·tik
ba·tiste
ba·ton
bat·tal·ion
bat·ten
bat·ter
bat·ter·y
  pl. bat·ter·ies
bat·tle
  bat·tle-ax *or* bat·tle-axe

  bat·tle cry
  bat·tle·field
  bat·tle·ground
  bat·tle·ment
  bat·tle roy·al
  pl. bat·tles roy·al *or* bat·tle
  roy·als
  bat·tle-scarred
  bat·tle·ship
bau·ble
baud
baux·ite
bawd·ry *n.*
bawd·y *adj.*
bawl
  bawled
bay·ber·ry
bay·o·net
bay·ou
bay rum
ba·zaar *n. (market;* see
  bizarre)
ba·zoo·ka
beach *n., v. (sand;* see *beech)*
  beach·comb·er
  beach·head
bea·con
bea·dle
bead·work
bead·y
bea·gle
beak·er
bean·ie
bear *n., v., adj. (animal;* see
  bare)
bear·a·ble
beard·ed
bear·er
bear·skin
beat *v., n., adj. (to pound;*
  see *beet)*
be·a·tif·ic
be·at·i·fy
  be·at·i·fi·ca·tion

be·at·i·tude
beau *n.* (*suitor*; see *bow*)
beau·te·ous
beau·ti·cian
beau·ti·fy
  beau·ti·fied
  beau·ti·fy·ing
beau·ty
  pl. beau·ties
  beau·ti·ful
bea·ver
be·calm
be·cause
beck·on
be·cloud
be·come
be·com·ing·ly
be·daub
bed board
bed·bug
bed·clothes
bed·ding
be·dev·il
bed·fast
bed·fel·low
be·dight
be·di·zen
bed·lam
Bed·ou·in
bed·post
be·drag·gled
bed rest
bed·rid·den
bed·rock
bed·room
bed·side
bed·sore
bed·spread
bed·stead
bed·time
beech *n.* (*tree*; see *beach*)
  beech·nut
beef·eat·er
beef·steak

bee·hive
bee·keep·er
bee·line
beer *n.* (*a beverage*; see *bier*)
bees·wax
beet *n.* (*a vegetable*; see *beat*)
bee·tle
be·fall
be·fit
  be·fit·ted
  be·fit·ting
be·fog
be·fool
be·fore
  be·fore·hand
  be·fore·time
be·friend
be·fud·dle
beg·gar
  beg·gar·li·ness
  beg·gar·ly
  beg·gar·y
be·gin
  be·gin·ning
  be·gun
be·grime
be·grudge
be·guile
  be·guiled
  be·guil·er
be·guine
be·gum
be·half
be·have
  be·hav·ing
  be·hav·ior
  be·hav·ior·ism
be·head
be·he·moth
be·hest
be·hind
  be·hind·hand
be·hold
  be·held

be·hoove
beige
be·jew·el
be·la·bor
be·lat·ed·ly
be·lay
bel can·to
be·lea·guer
bel·fry
Bel·gium
  Bel·gian
be·lie v. (lie; see belly)
  be·lied
  be·ly·ing
be·lief
be·lieve
  be·liev·a·ble
  be·liev·ing
be·lit·tle
  be·lit·tling
Be·lize
bell n., v. (ringing device; see belle)
bel·la·don·na
bell-bot·tom
bell·boy
belle n. (beautiful woman; see bell)
belles let·tres
bell·flow·er
bell·hop
bel·li·cose
bel·lig·er·ent
  bel·lig·er·ence
bell jar
bell met·al
bel·lows
bell rope
bell tow·er
bell·weth·er
bel·ly n., v. (stomach; see belie)
  bel·ly·ache
  bel·ly·band

bel·ly-land·ing
be·long
be·lov·ed
be·low
belt·ing
bel·ve·dere
be·moan
bench mark
bench war·rant
ben·day
be·neath
ben·e·dict
ben·e·dic·tion
ben·e·fac·tion
ben·e·fac·tor
ben·e·fice
be·nef·i·cence
  be·nef·i·cent
  be·nef·i·cent·ly
ben·e·fi·cial
ben·e·fi·cia·ry
  pl. ben·e·fi·cia·ries
ben·e·fit
  ben·e·fit·ed
  ben·e·fit·ing
be·nev·o·lent
  be·nev·o·lence
be·night·ed
be·nign
  be·nign·ly
be·nig·nant·ly
be·nig·ni·ty
ben·i·son
be·queath
  be·quest
ber·ceuse
be·reave
  be·reave·ment
ber·i·ber·i
Ber·lin
Ber·mu·da
ber·ry n. (fruit; see bury)
  pl. ber·ries n. (see buries)

ber·serk
berth *n., v.* (*bed*; see *birth*)
ber·yl
be·ryl·li·um
be·seech
be·set·ting
be·side *prep., adv.* (*at the side of; on par with*)
be·sides *prep., adv.* (*in addition to; other than*)
be·siege
be·smear
be·smirch
be·speak
bes·tial
   bes·ti·al·i·ty
best man
be·stow
best sell·er
be·ta
be·tide
be·times
be·to·ken·ing
be·tray
   be·tray·al
be·troth
   be·troth·al
bet·ting
bet·tor *n.* (*one who bets*)
be·tween
be·twixt
bev·el
   bev·eled *or* bev·elled
   bev·el·ing *or* bev·el·ling
bev·er·age
bev·y
   pl. bev·ies
be·wail
be·ware
be·wil·der
   be·wil·dered
be·witch
be·wray
be·yond

be·zant
bez·el *or* be·zil
bi·an·nu·al *adj.* (*occurring twice a year*; see *biennial*)
bi·as
   bi·ased
bi·be·lot
Bi·ble
   bib·li·cal
bib·li·og·ra·phy
   bib·li·og·ra·pher
bib·li·o·phile
bib·u·lous
bi·cam·er·al
bi·car·bon·ate
bi·cen·te·na·ry
   bi·cen·ten·ni·al
bi·ceps
bi·chlo·ride
bi·chro·mate
bi·cus·pid
bi·cy·cle
   bi·cy·clist
bi·en·ni·al *adj., n.* (*occurring once in two years*; see *biannual*)
bier *n.* (*coffin stand*; see *beer*)
bi·fo·cal
bi·fur·cate
big
   big·ger
   big·gest
big·a·my
   big·a·mist
   big·a·mous
Big Ben
big·head·ed
big·heart·ed
big·horn
bight *n., v.* (*bend in rope or river*; see *bite* and *byte*)
big·mouthed
big·ot·ed

big·ot·ry
big shot
big time *n*.
big top
big·wig
bi·jou
bi·ki·ni
bi·la·bi·al
bi·lat·er·al
bilge
  bilge wa·ter
bi·lin·gual
bil·ious
bill·board
billed
bil·let
bil·let-doux
  pl. bil·lets-doux
bill·fish
bill·fold
bill·head
bill·hook
bil·liards
bil·lings·gate
bil·lion
  bil·lion·aire
  bil·lionth
bill of fare
bill of health
bill of lad·ing
bill of rights
bill of sale
bil·low
  bil·low·y
bil·ly goat
bi·met·al·lism
  bi·me·tal·lic
  bi·met·al·list
bi·month·ly
bi·na·ry
bind·er
bind·er·y
bind·ing
bin·na·cle

bin·oc·u·lar
bi·no·mi·al
bi·o·chem·is·try
bi·og·ra·phy
  bi·og·ra·pher
  bi·o·graph·ic
  bi·o·graph·i·cal
bi·ol·o·gy
  bi·o·log·i·cal
bi·op·sy
bi·par·ti·san
bi·par·tite
bi·ped
bi·plane
bi·po·lar
bird·bath
bird·brain
bird·call
bird dog *n*.
bird-dog *v*.
bird·house
bird·seed
bird's-eye
birth *n*. (*born*; see *berth*)
  birth·day
  birth·mark
  birth·place
  birth·rate
  birth·right
  birth·stone
bis·cuit
bi·sect
bish·op
  bish·op·ric
bis·muth
bi·son
bisque
bis·sex·tile
bite *n*., *v*. (*to chew*; see *bight*
  and *byte*)
bi·tem·po·ral
bit·stock
bit·ter
  bit·ter end

bit·ter·root
bit·ter·sweet
bit·tern
bi·tu·men
bi·tu·mi·nous
bi·va·lent
bi·valve
biv·ouac
biv·ouacked
bi·week·ly
bi·zarre *adj.* (*strange*; see *bazaar*)
black-and-blue
black·ball
black·ber·ry
black·bird
black·board
black·ened
black·guard
black·head
black·jack
black lead *n.*
black·leg
black·list
black·mail
black mar·ket
black·ness
black out *v.*
black·out *n.*
black sheep
black·smith
black snake *n.*
black·snake *v.*
black·thorn
black·top
blad·der
blam·a·ble
blame·ful
blame·less
blame·wor·thy
blam·ing
blanc·mange
blan·dish
blank·book

blan·ket
blar·ney
bla·sé
blas·pheme
blas·phem·ing
blas·phe·mous
blas·phe·my
blast
bla·tant
bla·tan·cy
blath·er
blaze
blaz·er
blaz·ing
bla·zon
bla·zon·ry
bleach·er
bleak
blem·ish
blend·ed
bless·ed·ness
blew *v.* (*past tense of blow*; see *blue*)
blind·er
blind·fish
blind·fold
blind·ing
blink·er
bliss·ful
blis·ter
blithe
blithe·some
blitz·krieg
bliz·zard
bloat
bloc *n.* (*political group*; see *block*)
block *n., v.* (*geometric form; obstruction*; see *bloc*)
block·ade
block·head
block·house
blond *m. or f.* (see *blonde*)
blonde *f.* (see *blond*)

blood bank
blood count
blood·cur·dling
blood·ed
blood·hound
blood·less
blood·let·ting
blood·mo·bile
blood mon·ey
blood pres·sure
blood·root
blood·shed
blood·shot
blood·stain
blood·stone
blood·suck·er
blood·thirst·y
   blood·thirst·i·ness
blood-type *v.*
blood type *n.*
blood ves·sel
blood·y
   blood·i·est
   blood·i·ly
   blood·i·ness
blos·som
blot·ter
blot·ting
blouse
blow·er
blow·fish
blow·fly
blow·gun
blow·hole
blow·out *n.*
blow out *v.*
blow·pipe
blow·torch
blow·tube
blow·up *n.*
blow up *v.*
blub·ber
   blub·ber·y
blu·cher

bludg·eon
bluc *adj., n., v.* (*color;* see
  blew)
blue·bell
blue·ber·ry
blue·bird
blue blood
blue book
blue chip *n.*
blue-chip *adj.*
blue-eyed
blue·fish
blue·grass
blue·jack
blue jay
blue law
blue moon
blue-pen·cil *v.*
blue·print
blue rib·bon *n.*
blue-rib·bon *adj.*
blue·stock·ing
blu·ing
blu·ish
blun·der
   blun·der·buss
blunt·ly
blunt·ness
blurb
blurred
blur·ring
blurt
blus·ter
   blus·ter·ous
bo·a con·stric·tor
   pl. bo·as
boar *n.* (*male pig;* see *boor*
  and *bore*)
board *n., v.* (see *bored*)
   board·er *n.* (*lodger;* see *border*)
   board foot
   board·ing·house
   board·ing school
   board·room

board·walk
boast·ful
boast·ing·ly
boat hook
boat·house
boat·load
boat·man
boat·yard
bob·bin
  bob·bi·net
bob·bing
bob·by·sock *or* **bob·by-socks**
bob·cat
bob·o·link
bob·sled
bob·stay
bob·tail
bob·white
bod·ice
bod·i·less
bod·i·ly
bod·y·guard
bo·gey *n., v. (golf term; goblin; see* bogie *and* bogy)
bo·gey·man
bog·gle
bo·gie *n. (goblin; see* bogey *and* bogy)
bo·gus
bo·gy *n. (goblin; see* bogey *and* bogie)
Bo·he·mi·a
  Bo·he·mi·an
Bo·he·mi·an·ism
boil·er
bois·ter·ous
bold·er
bold·face *n.*
bold-faced *adj.*
bold·ly
bold·ness
bole *n. (tree trunk; see* boll *and* bowl)
bo·le·ro

bo·li·var
Bo·liv·i·a
boll *n. (seed pod; see* bole *and* bowl)
  boll wee·vil
  boll·worm
bo·lo·gna
bol·she·vik
bol·ster
bolt·er
bolt·rope
bo·lus
bom·bard
  bom·bar·dier
bom·bast
  bom·bas·tic
bomb·proof
bomb·shell
bomb·sight
bo·na fide
bo·nan·za
bon·bon
  bon·bon·nière
bond·age
bond·hold·er
bond·maid
bonds·man
bone-dry
bone meal
bon·fire
bon·ho·mie
bo·ni·to
  pl. bo·ni·tos *or* bo·ni·to
bon jour
bon mot
bon·net
bon·ny
bo·nus
bon vi·vant
bon voy·age
bon·y *or* **bon·ey**
boo·by
  boo·by trap
boo·dle

boo·hoo
  boo·hooed
book
  book·bind·er
  book·case
  book club
  book·end
  book·fair
  book·ish
  book·keep·er
  book·let
  book list
  book·lov·er
  book·mak·er
  book·mark
  book·mo·bile
  book·plate
  book·rack
  book·sell·er
  book·shelf
  book·store
  book·work
  book·worm
boo·mer·ang
boon·dog·gle
boor *n.* (*rude person*; see *boar* and *bore*)
  boor·ish·ness
boost·er
boot·black
boot camp
boot·ed
boo·tee *or* **boo·tie** *n.* (*baby's knitted boot*; see *booty*)
booth
boot·ing
boot·jack
boot·leg
  boot·legged
  boot·leg·ger
boot·less
boo·ty *n.* (*plunder*; see *bootee*)

booze
  booz·y
bo·rax
  bo·rac·ic
  bo·rate
Bor·deaux
bor·del·lo
bor·der *n.*, *v.* (*boundary*; see *boarder*)
  bor·der line *n.*
  bor·der·line *adj.*
bore *v.*, *n.* (*weary*; *drill*; see *boar* and *boor*)
  bored *v.* (see *board*)
  bore·dom
  bor·ing
bo·re·al
born *v.*, *adj.* (*brought forth*; see *borne*)
borne *v.* (*pt. of bear*; see *born*)
bo·ron
bor·ough *n.* (*municipal corporation*; see *burro* and *burrow*)
bor·row
borsch *or* **borscht** *or* **borsht**
bos·om
boss·y
  boss·i·ness
bot·a·ny
  bo·tan·i·cal
  bot·a·nist
  bot·a·nize
botch
both
both·er
  both·er·some
Bot·swa·na
bot·tle
  bot·tle·neck
  bot·tler
  bot·tling

bot·tom
  bot·tom·less
bot·tom·ry
bot·u·lism
bou·doir
bouf·fant
bough *n.* (*tree branch;* see *bow*)
bought
bouil·la·baisse
bouil·lon *n.* (*clear soup;* see *bullion*)
boul·der
bou·le·vard
  bou·le·var·dier
bounce
  bounc·er
  bounc·ing
bound
bound·a·ry
  pl. bound·a·ries
bound·er
bound·less
boun·te·ous
boun·ty
  boun·ti·ful
bou·quet
bour·bon
bour·geois *m.* (*middle class citizen;* see *bourgeoise*)
  bour·geoise *f.*
  bour·geoi·sie (*the middle class;* see *bourgeois* and *bourgeoise*)
bourse
bou·tique
bou·ton·niere
bo·vine
bow *v.* (*bend forward;* see *bough*)
bow *n., v.* (*weapon;* see *beau*)
  bow·man
  bow·shot (*distance of arrow shot*)

bowd·ler·ize
bow·el
bow·er
bow·er·y
bow·fin
bow·knot
bowl *n., v.* (*dish;* see *bole* and *boll*)
  bowl·er *n.* (*one that bowls*)
  bowl·ing
bow·leg·ged
bow·ler *n.* (*hat*)
bow·line
bow·sprit
bow·string
bow tie
box·car
box·er
box·ing
box kite
box of·fice
box score
box spring
box·thorn
box·wood
boy
  boy·hood
  boy·ish
bo·yar
boy·cott
boy·sen·ber·ry
brace·let
brac·er
brack·et
  brack·et·ing
brack·ish
brad·awl
brag
  brag·gart
  bragged
  brag·ging
brag·ga·do·ci·o
braille
brain·child

brain·less
brain·pow·er
brain·sick
brain·storm
brain trust
brain·wash·ing
brain wave
braise v. (*to cook*; see *braze*)
brake n., v. (*to stop*; see
  break)
  brake·man
bram·ble
bran·dish
brand-new
bran·dy
  bran·died
bras·sard
brass hat
bras·siere n. (*garment*; see
  brazier)
brass·i·ness
bra·va·do
brav·er·y
brav·est
bra·vo
bra·vu·ra
brawl
brawn·y
  brawn·i·est
braze v. (*to solder*; see
  braise)
bra·zen
  bra·zen·faced
bra·zier n. (*hot-coal fire*; see
  brassiere)
Bra·zil
  Bra·zil·ian
breach n., v. (*to break*; see
  breech)
bread n., v. (*dough*; see
  bred)
bread·fruit
bread·stuff

breadth n. (*width*; see
  breath)
bread·win·ner
break v., n. (*to smash*; see
  brake)
  break·a·ble
  break·age
  break down v.
  break·down n.
  break e·ven v.
  break·er
  break·neck
  break·through n.
  break·wa·ter
break·fast
break·front
breast
  breast·bone
  breast·stroke
breath n. (*exhaled air*; see
  breathe)
  breath·less
  breath·tak·ing
breathe v. (*to inhale*; see
  breath)
  breath·er
  breath·ing
breech n. (*trousers; buttocks*;
  see *breach*)
  pl. breech·es
  breech·load·er
  breech-load·ing
breed v., n.
  bred v. (*pt. of breed*; see
  bread)
  breed·ing
breeze
  breeze·way
  breez·y
breth·ren
bre·vet
bre·vi·a·ry
brev·i·ty

brew
  brew·er·y
  brew·ing
bribe
  brib·er·y
  brib·ing
bric-a-brac
brick
  brick·bat
  brick·kiln
  brick·lay·er
  brick·mak·er
  brick·work
  brick·yard
brid·al *n., adj. (pertaining to a bride*; see *bridle)*
bride
bride·groom
brides·maid
bride·well
bridge
  bridge·head
  bridge·work
bri·dle *n., v. (horse's halter*; see *bridal)*
brief
brief·case
brief·less
bri·er *or* **bri·ar**
  bri·er·root
  bri·er·wood
bri·gade
brig·a·dier
brig·and
brig·an·tine
bright
  bright·en
  bright-eyed
  bright·work
bril·liant
  bril·liance
  bril·lian·cy
  bril·lian·tine

  bril·liant·ly
brim
  brim·ful
  brimmed
  brim·mer
  brim·ming
brim·stone
brin·dle
brink
  brink·man·ship
brin·y
bri·quette *or* **bri·quet**
brisk
bris·ket
bris·tle
  bris·tle·tail
  bris·tling
bris·tol board
Brit·ain *n. (country*; see *Briton)*
  Brit·on *n. (citizen of Great Britain*; see *Britain)*
  Bri·tan·nic
Brit·ish
  Brit·ish·er
brit·tle
broach *n., v. (to open*; see *brooch)*
broad
  broad·ax *or* broad·axe
  broad·cast
  broad·cloth
  broad·en
  broad jump
  broad·leaf *adj.*
  broad-leaved *or* broad-leafed *adj.*
  broad·loom
  broad·ly
  broad-mind·ed
  broad·side
bro·cade
broc·co·li *or* **broc·o·li**
bro·chette

bro·chure
brogue
broil
  broil·er
bro·ken
  bro·ken·heart·ed
bro·ker
  bro·ker·age
bro·mate
bro·mide
bro·mine
bron·chi·al
bron·chi·tis
bron·cho·scope
bron·co *or* bron·cho
  pl. bron·cos *or* bron·chos
bronze
brooch *n.* (*decorative pin;* see *broach*)
brood
  brood·er
brook
  brook·let
broom·stick
broth
broth·el
broth·er
  broth·er·hood
  broth·er-in-law
  broth·er·ly
brough·am
brought
brow
brow·beat
brown bread
brown·ie
brown·ish
brown·out *n.*
brown out *v.*
brown·stone *n.* (*sandstone*)
brown sug·ar
browse
bru·in

bruise
  bruis·er
brum·ma·gem
bru·net *or* bru·nette
brunt
brush
  brush-off
  brush up *v.*
  brush·up *n.*
  brush·work
brusque
bru·tal
  bru·tal·i·ty
  bru·tal·i·za·tion
  bru·tal·ize
brute
  brut·ish
bub·ble
  bub·bly
bu·bon·ic
buc·ca·neer
buck·et
buck·eye
buck·le
  buck·ler
  buck·ling
buck·ram
buck·saw
buck·shot
buck·skin
buck·wheat
bu·col·ic
Bud·dha
  Bud·dhism
bud·ding
bud·get
  bud·get·ar·y
buf·fa·lo
  pl. buffalo (*or* buffaloes)
buff·er
buf·fet
buf·foon
  buf·foon·er·y
bug·bear

bugged
bug·ging
bu·gle
  bu·gling
build
  build·er
  build·ing
  build-up n.
  build up v.
  built
bul·bous
Bul·gar·i·a
  Bul·gar·i·an
bulge
  bulg·ing
bulk·head
bulk·y
bull·dog
bull·doze
  bull·doz·er
bul·let
  bul·let·proof
bul·le·tin
bull·fight
bull·finch
bull·frog
bull·head
bull·horn
bul·lion n. (uncoined gold or silver; see bouillon)
bul·lock
bull·pen n.
bull's-eye
bull·ter·ri·er
bull·whip
bul·ly
  bul·ly·rag
bul·rush
bul·wark
bum·ble·bee
bum·bling
bump·er
bump·kin
bump·y

bunch
bun·dle
bun·ga·low
bun·gle
bun·gling
bun·ion
bunk
bun·ker
bun·kum or bun·combe
bun·ting
buoy
buoy·ant
  buoy·an·cy
bur n. (prickly growth; see burr)
bur·den
  bur·den·some
bur·dock
bu·reau
  pl. bu·reaus
bu·reau·cra·cy
  bu·reau·crat
bu·rette or bu·ret
burg
bur·geon
bur·ger n. (hamburger; see burgher)
bur·gher n. (inhabitant of a town; see burger)
bur·glar
  bur·glar·ize
  bur·glar·proof
  bur·glar·y
  pl. bur·glar·ies
Bur·gun·dy
bur·i·al
bur·ied
bur·ies
bur·lap
bur·lesque
bur·ly
Bur·ma
burn
  burned or burnt

burn·er
burned-out *or* burnt-out *adj.*
bur·nish
bur·noose
burn out *v.*
burn·out *n.*
burn·sides
burr *n.* (*tool*; see *bur*)
bur·ro *n.* (*donkey*; see
   borough and *burrow*)
   pl. bur·ros
bur·row *n., v.* (*hole; to dig;*
   see *borough* and *burro*)
bur·sa
bur·sar
   bur·sa·ry
bur·si·tis
burst
bur·y *v.* (*to place*
   underground; see *berry*)
   bur·i·al
   bur·ied
   bur·ies *v.* (see *berries*)
   bur·y·ing
bus·boy
bused
bus·es
bush·el
bush league *n.*
bush-league *adj.*
bush·whack·er
bus·i·ness
   bus·i·ness·like
   bus·i·ness·man
   bus·i·ness·wom·an
bus·kin
bus·tle
   bus·tling
bus·y
   bus·ied
   bus·i·er
   bus·i·est
   bus·i·ly
   bus·y·ness

   bus·y·work
but *adj., prep.* (*except;* see
   butt)
butch·er
   butch·er·y
butt *n.* (*end;* see *but*)
butte
but·ter
   but·ter·cup
   but·ter·fat
   but·ter·fish
   but·ter·fly
   but·ter·milk
   but·ter·nut
   but·ter·scotch
   but·ter·y
but·tock
but·ton
   but·ton·hole
   but·ton·hook
   but·ton·wood
but·tress
bux·om
buy·er
buy·ing
buzz
   buzz·er
buz·zard
buzz saw
buzz word
by-e·lec·tion *or* bye-e·lec·tion
by·gone
by·law *or* bye·law
by-line
by·pass
by·path
by·play
by-pro·duct
by·road
by·stand·er
byte *n.* (*computer digits;* see
   bight and *bite*)
by·way
by·word
By·zan·tine

C

ca·bal
  cab·a·la
ca·ban·a
cab·a·ret
cab·bage
cab·in
cab·i·net
  cab·i·net·mak·er
  cab·i·net·work
ca·ble
  ca·ble car
  ca·ble·gram
ca·bling
cab·man
cab·o·chon
ca·boose
cab·ri·o·let
cab·stand
ca·ca·o
cach·a·lot
cache *n., v. (hiding place; see cash)*
ca·chet *n., v. (stamp; see cache)*
cach·in·na·tion
ca·cique
cack·le
ca·coph·o·ny
cac·tus
  pl. cac·ti
ca·dav·er
  ca·dav·er·ous
ca·dence
ca·den·za
ca·det
cad·mi·um
ca·du·ce·us
Cae·sar
cae·su·ra
café au lait
caf·e·te·ri·a

caf·feine
cairn·gorm
cais·son
cai·tiff
ca·jole
  ca·jol·er·y
cake·walk
cal·a·bash
cal·a·boose
ca·lam·i·ty
  ca·lam·i·tous
cal·car·e·ous
cal·ci·mine
cal·cine
  cal·ci·na·tion
cal·ci·um
  cal·cif·er·ous
  cal·ci·fi·ca·tion
  cal·ci·fy
cal·cu·late
  cal·cu·la·ble
  cal·cu·lat·ing
  cal·cu·la·tion
  cal·cu·la·tor
cal·cu·lus
cal·dron
cal·en·dar *n. (time schedule; see calender)*
cal·en·der *n., v. (press; see calendar)*
cal·ends
calf
  calf·skin
cal·i·ber
cal·i·brate
cal·i·co
Cal·i·for·nia
cal·i·per *or* cal·li·per
ca·liph
cal·is·then·ics
calk *or* caulk
calk·er
call·a·ble

cal·lig·ra·phy
  cal·lig·ra·pher
call·ing
cal·lous *adj., n. (resistant;*
  see *callus*)
  cal·los·i·ty
cal·low
cal·lus *n. (hardened skin;*
  see *callous*)
calm
cal·o·mel
ca·lo·ric
  cal·o·rie
  pl. cal·o·ries
cal·o·rim·e·ter
cal·um·ny
  pl. cal·um·nies
  ca·lum·ni·ate
  ca·lum·ni·a·tion
  ca·lum·ni·a·tor
  ca·lum·ni·ous
Cal·va·ry *n. (mountain;* see
  cavalry)
Cal·vin·ism
  Cal·vin·ist
  Cal·vin·is·tic
ca·lyp·so
ca·lyx
ca·ma·ra·de·rie
cam·ber
cam·bi·um
Cam·bo·di·a
cam·bric
cam·el
ca·mel·li·a *or* ca·me·li·a
ca·mel·o·pard
Cam·em·bert
cam·e·o
  pl. cam·e·os
cam·er·a
  cam·er·a·man
Cam·er·oon
cam·i·sole
cam·ou·flage

cam·paign
cam·pa·ni·le
camp·er
camp·fire
camp·ground
cam·phor
cam·pus
cam·shaft
cam wheel
Can·a·da
  Ca·na·di·an
ca·naille
ca·nal
  ca·nal·boat
  can·a·li·za·tion
can·a·pé *n. (appetizer;* see
  canopy)
ca·nard
ca·nar·y
  pl. ca·nar·ies
can·cel
  can·celed *or* can·celled
  can·cel·er *or* can·cel·ler
  can·cel·ing *or* can·cel·ling
  can·cel·a·tion *or* can·cel·la·tion
can·cer
  can·cer·ous
can·de·la·bra
can·did
  can·did·ly
  can·did·ness
can·di·date
  can·di·da·cy
can·dle
  can·dle·light
  can·dle·pow·er
  can·dle·stick
  can·dle·wick
  can·dle·wood
can·dor
can·dy
  pl. can·dies
  can·died
cane·brake

ca·nine
can·is·ter
can·ker
  can·ker·ous
  can·ker·worm
can·na
can·na·bis
can·ner·y
can·ni·bal
  can·ni·bal·ism
  can·ni·bal·ize
can·ning
can·non *n., v.* (*large gun;* see
  canon)
  can·non·ade
  can·non·eer
can·not
can·ny
  can·ni·ly
  can·ni·ness
ca·noe
  pl. ca·noes
  ca·noe·ing
can·on *n., v.* (*church laws;*
  see *cannon*)
  ca·non·i·cal
  can·on·ize
can·o·py *n., v.* (*a covering;*
  see *canapé*)
  pl. can·o·pies
can·ta·bi·le
can·ta·loupe
can·tan·ker·ous
can·ta·ta
can·teen
can·ter *n., v.* (*slow gallop;*
  see *cantor*)
can·ti·cle
can·ti·le·ver
can·to
can·ton
  can·ton·al
Can·ton·ese
can·ton·ment

can·tor *n.* (*choir leader;* see
  canter)
can·vas *or* can·vass *n., v.*
  (*cloth;* see *canvass*)
can·vass *or* can·vas *v., n.* (*to
  solicit;* see *canvas*)
can·yon
ca·pa·ble
  ca·pa·bil·i·ty
  pl. ca·pa·bil·i·ties
  ca·pa·bly
ca·pa·cious
ca·pac·i·tor
ca·pac·i·ty
cap-a-pie
ca·par·i·son
ca·per
cap·il·lar·y
  cap·il·lar·i·ty
cap·i·tal *n., adj.* (*city; wealth;*
  see *capitol*)
  cap·i·tal·ism
  cap·i·tal·ist
  cap·i·tal·i·za·tion
  cap·i·tal·ize
cap·i·tol *n.* (*building;* see
  capital)
ca·pit·u·late
  ca·pit·u·la·tion
ca·price
  ca·pri·cious
cap·size
cap·stan
cap·stone
cap·sule
cap·tain
cap·tion
cap·tious
cap·ti·vate
  cap·ti·va·tion
cap·ture
  cap·tive
  cap·tiv·i·ty
  cap·tor

cap·tur·ing
car·a·cole
car·a·cul
car·a·mel
  car·a·mel·ize
car·at *or* kar·at *n.* (*weight*;
  see *caret* and *carrot*)
car·a·van
  car·a·van·sa·ry
car·a·vel
car·a·way
car·bide
car·bine
car·bol·ic
car·bon
  car·bo·na·ceous
  car·bon·ate
  car·bon·ic
  car·bon·if·er·ous
  car·bon·ize
Car·bo·run·dum (*trademark*)
car·box·yl
car·boy
car·bun·cle
car·bu·re·tor
car·cass
car·cin·o·gen
car·ci·no·ma
car·da·mom
card·board
card·hold·er
car·di·ac
car·di·gan
car·di·nal
  car·di·nal·ate
car·di·o·gram
car·di·o·graph
car·di·ol·o·gist
car·di·o·vas·cu·lar
car·di·o·ver·ter
car·di·tis
card·play·er
card ta·ble
ca·reen

ca·reer
care·ful
  care·ful·ly
care·less
ca·ress
car·et *n.* (*editor's mark*; see
  carat and *carrot*)
care·worn
car·go
  pl. car·goes *or* car·gos
Ca·rib·be·an
car·i·bou
car·i·ca·ture
car·ies *n.* (*decay*; see *carries*)
  pl. car·ies
car·il·lon
car·i·o·ca
car·load
car·min·a·tive
car·mine
car·nage
car·nal
  car·nal·i·ty
car·na·tion
car·ne·lian
car·ni·val
car·niv·o·rous
car·ol *n., v.* (*song*; see *carrel*)
car·om
car·o·tene
ca·rot·id
ca·rouse
  ca·rous·al *n.* (*drunken revel*;
  see *carrousel*)
car·pen·ter
  car·pen·try
car·pet
  car·pet·bag
  car·pet·bag·ger
  car·pet·ing
car·port
car·rel *n.* (*enclosed table*; see
  carol)
car·riage

car·ri·er
car·ri·on
car·rot n. (vegetable; see
  carat and caret)
car·rou·sel n.
  (merry-go-round; see
  carousal)
car·ry
  car·ries v. (to convey; see
    caries)
  car·ry·all
  car·ry-o·ver n.
  car·ry o·ver v.
cart·age
carte blanche
car·tel
car·ti·lage
  car·ti·lag·i·nous
car·tog·ra·phy
  car·tog·ra·pher
car·ton
car·toon
  car·toon·ist
car·touche
car·tridge
carve
car·y·at·id
ca·sa·ba
cas·cade
case hard·en
ca·sein
case knife
case·mate
case·ment
ca·sern
case·work
cash n., v. (money; see cache)
  cash·book
  cash·ier n.
  ca·shier v.
cash·ew
cash·mere
ca·si·no n. (gambling house;
  see cassino)

cas·ket
casque
cas·se·role
cas·sia
cas·si·no n. (card game; see
  casino)
cas·sock
cas·so·war·y
cast v., n. (to throw; actors;
  see caste)
cas·ta·net
cast·a·way
caste n. (social class; see cast)
cas·tel·lat·ed
cas·ter n. (wheel; see castor)
cas·ti·gate
  cas·ti·ga·tion
Cas·til·ian
cast-i·ron adj.
cast i·ron n.
cas·tle
cast-off adj.
cast off v.
cas·tor n. (oil; see caster)
ca·su·al
ca·su·al·ty
ca·su·ist·ry
  ca·su·ist
cat·a·clysm
cat·a·comb
cat·a·falque
Cat·a·lan
cat·a·lep·sy
  cat·a·lep·tic
cat·a·log or cat·a·logue
ca·tal·pa
ca·tal·y·sis
cat·a·lyst
  cat·a·lyt·ic
cat·a·ma·ran
cat·a·mount
cat·a·pult
cat·a·ract

ca·tarrh
  ca·tarrh·al
ca·tas·ta·sis
ca·tas·tro·phe
  cat·a·stroph·ic
Ca·taw·ba
cat·bird
cat·boat
cat·call
catch·all
catch·er
catch·pen·ny
catch·word
cat·e·che·sis
cat·e·chism
  cat·e·chist
cat·e·chu·men
cat·e·go·ry
  cat·e·gor·i·cal
  cat·e·go·rize
cat·e·nar·y
cat·er-cor·ner or
  cat·ty-cor·ner or
  kit·ty-cor·ner
ca·ter·er
cat·er·pil·lar
cat·er·waul
cat·fish
cat·gut
ca·thar·sis
  ca·thar·tic
ca·the·dral
cath·e·ter
cath·ode
cath·o·lic adj.
  cath·o·lic·i·ty
  ca·thol·i·cize
Cath·o·lic n.
  Ca·thol·i·cism
cat·like
cat·nip
cat-o'-nine-tails
cat's-eye
cat's-paw

cat·sup or ketch·up or kat·sup
cat·tail
cat·tle
cat·walk
Cau·ca·sian
cau·cus
cau·dal
cau·li·flow·er
cause
  caus·al
  cau·sal·i·ty
  cau·sa·tion
  caus·a·tive
  caused
  caus·ing
cau·se·rie
cause·way
caus·tic
cau·ter·ize
  cau·ter·i·za·tion
  cau·ter·y
cau·tion
  cau·tion·ar·y
  cau·tious
cav·al·cade
cav·a·lier
  cav·a·lier·ly
cav·al·ry n. (soldiers; see
  Calvary)
  pl. cav·al·ries
cav·a·ti·na
ca·ve·at emp·tor
cav·ern
  cav·ern·ous
cav·i·ar
cav·il
  cav·iled
cav·i·ty
  pl. cav·i·ties
ca·vort
cay·enne (pepper)
cease
  ceased
  cease·less

ce·dar
cede v. (*to relinquish*; see *seed*)
ce·dil·la
ceil
ceil·ing
cel·e·brate
  cel·e·brant
  cel·e·brat·ed
  cel·e·bra·tion
  cel·e·bra·tor
ce·leb·ri·ty
ce·ler·i·ty
cel·er·y
ce·les·ta
ce·les·tial
cel·i·bate
  cel·i·ba·cy
cell n. (*small room; proto-plasm*; see *sell*)
cel·lar n. (*basement*; see *seller*)
  cel·lar·age
  cel·lar·er
  cel·lar·ette or cel·lar·et
cel·lo
  cel·list
cel·lo·phane
cel·lu·lar
Cel·lu·loid (*trademark*)
cel·lu·lose
Cel·si·us
ce·ment
  ce·men·ta·tion
cem·e·ter·y
  pl. cem·e·ter·ies
cen·o·bite
cen·o·taph
cen·ser n. (*incense holder*; see *censor* and *censure*)
cen·sor n., v. (*to screen*; see *censer* and *censure*)
  cen·so·ri·al
  cen·so·ri·ous

  cen·sor·ship
cen·sure n., v. (*to reprimand*; see *censer* and *censor*)
  cen·sur·a·ble
  cen·sur·ing
cen·sus
cent n. (*penny*; see *scent* and *sent*)
cen·taur
cen·ta·vo
  pl. cen·ta·vos
cen·ten·a·ry
cen·ten·nial
cen·ter·board
cen·ter·piece
cen·ti·grade
cen·ti·gram
cen·ti·li·ter
cen·time
cen·ti·me·ter
cen·ti·pede
cen·tral
  cen·tral·i·za·tion
  cen·tral·ize
cen·tri·fuge
  cen·trif·u·gal
cen·trip·e·tal
cen·trist
cen·tu·ri·on
cen·tu·ry
  pl. centuries
ce·phal·ic
ce·ram·ic
Cer·ber·us
ce·re·al n., adj. (*grain*; see *serial*)
cer·e·bel·lum
ce·re·bral
ce·re·bro·spi·nal
ce·re·bro·vas·cu·lar
cer·e·mo·ny
  pl. cer·e·mo·nies
  cer·e·mo·ni·al
  cer·e·mo·ni·ous

Ce·res
ce·rise
ce·ri·um
cer·tain
cer·tain·ly
cer·tain·ty
  pl. cer·tain·ties
cer·tif·i·cate
cer·ti·fy
  cer·ti·fi·a·ble
  cer·ti·fi·ca·tion
  cer·ti·fies
cer·ti·o·ra·ri
cer·ti·tude
ce·ru·le·an
cer·vix
  cer·vi·cal
ce·si·um
ces·sa·tion
ces·sion *n.* (*a yielding;* see *session*)
cess·pit
cess·pool
Cey·lon
Chad
chafe *v.* (*to irritate;* see *chaff*)
chaff *n., v.* (*husks of grain;* see *chafe*)
chaf·finch
cha·grin
  cha·grined
chain gang
chain mail
chain saw
chain-smoke
chain stitch
chair·man
chaise longue
  pl. chaise longues *or* chaises longues
chal·ced·o·ny
cha·let
chal·ice
chalk·y

chal·lenge
chal·lis
cham·ber
  cham·ber·lain
  cham·ber·maid
cha·me·leon
cham·fer
cham·ois
  pl. cham·ois *or* cham·oix
cham·o·mile *or* cam·o·mile
cham·pagne *n.* (*wine;* see *champaign*)
cham·paign *n., adj.* (*open country;* see *champagne*)
cham·per·ty
cham·pi·on
  cham·pi·on·ship
chance·ful
chan·cel
chan·cel·lor
  chan·cel·ler·y *or* chan·cel·lor·y
chan·cer·y
  pl. chan·cer·ies
chan·cre
chan·de·lier
chan·dler
  chan·dler·y
change·a·ble
  change·a·bil·i·ty
change·less
change·ling
change o·ver *v.*
change·o·ver *n.*
chang·ing
chan·nel
  chan·neled *or* chan·nelled
  chan·nel·ing *or* chan·nel·ling
chan·son
chan·teuse
chan·tey *or* chan·ty *n.* (*song;* see *shanty*)
chan·ti·cleer
cha·os
  cha·ot·ic

chap·ar·ral
chap·book
cha·peau
chap·el
chap·er·on *or* chap·er·one
chap·fall·en
chap·lain
chap·ter
char *or* charr
char·ac·ter
  char·ac·ter·is·tic
  char·ac·ter·i·za·tion
  char·ac·ter·ize
cha·rade
char·coal
charge·a·ble
char·gé d'af·faires
charg·ing
char·i·ot
  char·i·o·teer
cha·ris·ma
char·i·ty
  pl. char·i·ties
  char·i·ta·ble
  char·i·ta·bly
char·la·tan
Charles·ton (*dance*)
Charles·town (*city*)
char·ley horse
char·nel
char·ter
char·treuse
char·wom·an
Cha·ryb·dis
chased
chasm
chas·sis
  pl. chas·sis
chaste
chas·ten
chas·tise
  chas·tise·ment
chas·ti·ty
chas·u·ble

châ·teau
  pl. châ·teaus *or* châ·teaux
cha·te·laine
chat·tel
chat·ter
  chat·ter·box
  chat·ter·er
  chat·ting
chauf·feur
chau·tau·qua
chau·vin·ism
cheap·en
  cheap·ened
cheap·skate
check·book
check·er·board
check·ered
check in *v*.
check-in *n*.
check·list
check mark
check·mate
check off *v*.
check-off *n*.
check out *v*.
check-out *n*.
check·point
check·rein
check·room
check up *v*.
check·up *n*.
check·writ·er
cheek·bone
cheek·y
  cheek·i·ly
  cheek·i·ness
cheer·ful
  cheer·ful·ness
cheer·y
  cheer·i·ly
  cheer·less
cheese·burg·er
cheese·cake
cheese·cloth

cheese·par·ing
chef
chef d'oeu·vre
chem·i·cal
che·mise
chem·is·try
  chem·ist
chem·o·ther·a·py
che·nille
cher·ish
Cher·o·kee
che·root
cher·ry
  pl. cher·ries
cher·ub
  pl. cher·ubs *or* cher·u·bim
chess·board
chess·man
ches·ter·field
chest·nut
chev·a·lier
chev·i·ot
chev·ron
Chi·an·ti
chic *n., adj.* (*stylish*; see *sheik*)
chi·ca·ner·y
chick·a·dee
chick·en
chick·en·heart·ed
chick·en-liv·ered
chick·en pox
chick-pea
chick·weed
chi·cle
chic·o·ry
chief·ly
chief·tain
chif·fon
chif·fo·nier
chi·gnon
chil·blain
child·bed
child·birth

child·hood
child·ish
child·less
child·like
chil·dren
Chil·e
chil·i con car·ne *n.* (*meat soup*; see *chilly*)
chill
  chill·i·ness
  chill·ing·ly
  chill·y *adj.* (*cold*; see *chili con carne*)
chi·me·ra
  pl. chi·me·ras
  chi·mer·i·cal
chim·ney
  pl. chim·neys
chim·pan·zee
Chi·na
chi·na·ber·ry
Chi·na·man
Chi·na·town
chi·na·ware
chin·chil·la
Chi·nese
chi·nook (*wind*)
chintz
chip
  chip·ping
chip·munk
chi·rog·ra·phy
chi·rop·o·dist
chi·ro·prac·tor
chis·el
  chis·eled
  chis·el·er
  chis·el·ing
chit·chat
chiv·al·ry
  chi·val·ric
  chiv·al·rous
chlo·ral
chlo·rate

chlor·dane
chlo·ride
chlo·rine
  chlo·ric
  chlo·rin·ate
  chlo·rous
chlo·rite
chlo·ro·form
chlo·ro·phyll
chock-full
choc·o·late
Choc·taw
choir n. (singers; see quire)
choke·ber·ry
choke·cher·ry
choke·damp
chok·er
chol·er n. (anger; see collar)
  chol·er·ic
chol·er·a
cho·les·ter·ol
cho·line
choose
  choos·ing
  chose v. (pt. of choose)
  cho·sen
chop·house
chop·per
chop·ping
chop·stick
chop su·ey
cho·ral n., adj. (pertaining to a choir; see coral)
cho·rale or cho·ral n. (hymn; see corral)
chord n. (musical notes; see cord)
chore
cho·re·a
cho·re·og·ra·phy
chor·tle
cho·rus
  cho·ris·ter

chow·der
chrism
chris·ten
Chris·ten·dom
Chris·tian
  Chris·ti·an·i·ty
  Chris·tian·ize
Christ·like
Christ·ly
Christ·mas
  Christ·mas·tide
chro·mate
chro·mat·ic
chrome
chro·mite
chro·mi·um
chro·mo·some
chron·ic
chron·i·cle
chron·o·graph
chro·nol·o·gy
  chron·o·log·i·cal
chro·nom·e·ter
  chron·o·met·ric
chrys·a·lis
chry·san·the·mum
chrys·o·ber·yl
chrys·o·lite
chrys·o·prase
chuck·le
  chuck·le·head
chuk·ka n. (boot; see chukker)
chuk·ker n. (polo period; see chukka)
chum
  chum·mi·ness
  chum·my
chump
chunk
church·go·er
church·man
church·ward·en
church·yard

churl
  churl·ish
churn
chute *n., v. (passageway; see shoot)*
chut·ney
chyle
ci·bo·ri·um
ci·ca·da *or* ci·ca·la
ci·ca·trix
ci·der
ci·de·vant
ci·gar
cig·a·rette
Cim·me·ri·an
cinc·ture
cin·der
Cin·der·el·la
cin·e·ma
  cin·e·ma·tog·ra·pher
  cin·e·ma·tog·ra·phy
cin·na·bar
cin·na·mon
cin·que·cen·to
cinque·foil
ci·pher
cir·ca
Cir·cas·sian
Cir·ce
cir·cle
  cir·clet
  cir·cling
cir·cuit
  cir·cuit·ry
cir·cu·i·tous
cir·cu·lar
  cir·cu·lar·i·za·tion
  cir·cu·lar·ize
cir·cu·late
  cir·cu·la·tion
  cir·cu·la·tive
  cir·cu·la·tor
  cir·cu·la·to·ry
cir·cum·am·bi·ent

cir·cum·cise
  cir·cum·ci·sion
cir·cum·fer·ence
cir·cum·flex
cir·cum·lo·cu·tion
cir·cum·nav·i·gate
cir·cum·scribe
  cir·cum·scrip·tion
cir·cum·spect
  cir·cum·spec·tion
cir·cum·stance
  cir·cum·stan·tial
  cir·cum·stan·tial·ly
  cir·cum·stan·ti·ate
cir·cum·vent
  cir·cum·ven·tion
cir·cus
cir·rho·sis
cir·ro·cu·mu·lus
cir·ro·stra·tus
cir·rus
cis·tern
cit·a·del
cite *v. (to summon; to quote; see sight and site)*
  ci·ta·tion
  cit·ing
cit·i·zen
  cit·i·zen·ry
  cit·i·zen·ship
cit·rate
cit·ron
cit·ro·nel·la
cit·rus
  cit·ric
civ·et *(cat)*
ci·vet *(stew)*
civ·ic
civ·il
  ci·vil·ian
  ci·vil·i·ty
  civ·i·li·za·tion
  civ·i·lize
  civ·il·ly

claim·ant
clair·voy·ance
  clair·voy·ant
clam·bake
clam·ber
clam·my
  clam·mi·ness
clam·or
  clam·or·ous
clam·shell
clan·des·tine
clang·or
  clang·or·ous·ly
clan·nish
clans·man
clap·board
clapped
clap·per
clap·ping
clap·trap
claque
clar·et
clar·i·fy
  clar·i·fi·ca·tion
  clar·i·fied
clar·i·net
  clar·i·net·ist
clar·i·on
clar·i·ty
clas·sic
  clas·si·cal
  clas·si·cism
  clas·si·cist
clas·si·fy
  clas·si·fi·a·ble
  clas·si·fi·ca·tion
  clas·si·fied
  clas·si·fy·ing
class·mate
class·room
clat·ter
clause (*word group*)
claus·tro·pho·bi·a
clav·i·chord

clav·i·cle
cla·vier
clay·bank
clay·more
clean-cut
clean·er
clean·hand·ed
clean-limbed
clean·ly
  clean·li·ness
clean·ness
cleanse
  cleans·er
  cleans·ing
clean·up *n.*
clean up *v.*
clear·ance
clear-cut
clear-eyed
clear·head·ed
clear·ing·house
clear-sight·ed
cleat
cleav·age
cleav·er
clem·a·tis
clem·en·cy
clem·ent
clench
clere·stor·y
cler·gy
  cler·gy·man
cler·ic
  cler·i·cal
  cler·i·cal·ism
clev·er
clew
cli·ché
cli·ent
  cli·en·tele
cliff dwell·er
cliff-hang·er
cli·mac·ter·ic *adj.*, *n.* (*crucial period*; see *climactic* and *climatic*)

cli·mate
  cli·mat·ic *adj.* (*climate;* see *climacteric* and *climactic*)
cli·max
  cli·mac·tic *adj.* (*climax;* see *climacteric* and *climactic*)
clin·ic
  clin·i·cal
  cli·ni·cian
clink·er
clip·board
clip-on *adj.*
clip on *v.*
clip·per
clip·ping
clique
clit·o·ris
cloak-and-dag·ger
clob·ber
cloche
clock·wise
clock·work
clod·hop·per
clogged
clog·ging
clois·ter
close call
close-cropped
closed-end
close·fist·ed
close-hauled
close or·der
close out *v.*
close out *n.*
clos·et
close-up *adj.*
close-up *n.*
close up *v.*
clo·sure
cloth *n.*
clothe *v.*
  cloth·ier
  cloth·ing
clothes·line

clothes·pin
clothes tree
clo·ture
cloud·burst
cloud·i·ly
cloud·i·ness
cloud·less
clout
clo·ven
  clo·ven-foot·ed
clo·ver
cloy·ing
club·bing
club car
club chair
club foot
club·house
club steak
clum·sy
  clum·si·er
  clum·si·est
  clum·si·ly
  clum·si·ness
clus·ter
clut·ter
coach·man
co·ad·ju·tor
co·ag·u·late
  co·ag·u·la·tion
co·a·lesce
  co·a·les·cence
  co·a·les·cent
coal·field
co·a·li·tion
coal tar
coarse *adj.* (*rough;* see *course*)
  coars·en
coast·al
coast·er
coast guard
coast·line
coat·tail
co·au·thor

coax
co·ax·i·al
co·balt
cob·bler
cob·ble·stone
co·bra
cob·web
co·caine
coc·cyx
coch·i·neal
cock·ade
cock·a·too
cock·a·trice
cock·crow
cock·le·bur
cock·le·shell
cock·ney
cock·pit
cock·roach
cock·sure
cock·tail
co·coa
co·co·nut *or* co·coa·nut
co·coon
cod·dle
co·de·fend·ant
co·deine
co·dex
  pl. co·di·ces
cod·fish
codg·er
cod·i·cil
cod·i·fy
  cod·i·fi·ca·tion
  cod·i·fied
co·ed *or* co·ed *n*. (*female student*; see *cooed*)
co·ed·u·ca·tion
co·ef·fi·cient
coe·la·canth
co·erce
  co·erc·i·ble
  co·er·cion
  co·er·cive

co·e·val
co·ex·is·tence
cof·fee
  cof·fee break
  cof·fee cake
  cof·fee·house
  cof·fee·pot
  cof·fee shop
cof·fer
  cof·fer·ed
  cof·fer·ing
cof·fer·dam
cof·fin
co·gent
  co·gen·cy
cog·i·tate
  cog·i·ta·tion
  cog·i·ta·tive
co·gnac
cog·nate
cog·ni·zance
  cog·ni·zant
cog·no·men
  pl. cog·no·mens
cog·wheel
co·hab·it
  co·hab·i·tant
co·here
  co·her·ence
  co·her·en·cy
  co·her·ent
  co·he·sion
  co·he·sive
co·hort
coif *or* coiffe
coif·feur *m*., *n*. (*hair stylist*; see *coiffure*)
coif·fure *n*. (*hair style*; see *coiffeur*)
coin
  coin·age
co·in·cide
  co·in·ci·dence
  co·in·ci·den·tal

co·in·sure
  co·in·sur·ance
co·i·tion
co·i·tus
col·an·der
cold·blood n.
  cold-blood·ed adj.
cold chis·el
cold cream
cold cuts
cold frame
cold front
cold pack
cold sore
cold sweat n.
cold-sweat v.
cold war
cold wave
cole·slaw
col·ic n.
  col·ick·y
col·i·se·um
co·li·tis
col·lab·o·rate
  col·lab·o·ra·tion
  col·lab·o·ra·tor
col·lage
col·la·gen
col·lapse
  col·lapsed
  col·laps·i·ble
col·lar n., v. (neck band; see choler)
col·lar·bone
col·late
  col·la·tion
col·lat·er·al
col·league
col·lect
  col·lect·ed
  col·lect·i·ble or col·lect·a·ble
  col·lec·tion
  col·lec·tor

col·lec·tive adj., n.
  col·lec·tive·ly
  col·lec·tiv·ism
  col·lec·tiv·ize
col·lege
  col·le·gi·al
  col·le·gi·al·i·ty
  col·le·gian
  col·le·giate
col·lide
col·lie
col·lier
  col·lier·y
col·li·sion
col·lo·ca·tion
col·lo·di·on
col·loid
col·lop
col·lo·qui·al
  col·lo·qui·al·ism
  col·lo·qui·al·ly
col·lo·quy
  pl. col·lo·quies
col·lu·sion
  col·lu·sive
co·logne
Co·lom·bi·a
co·lon
col·o·nel n. (military officer; see colonial and kernel)
  col·o·nel·cy
col·on·nade
col·o·ny
  pl. col·o·nies
  co·lo·ni·al adj., n. (colony dweller; see colonel)
  co·lo·ni·al·ism
  col·o·nist
  col·o·ni·za·tion
  col·o·nize
col·o·phon
col·or
  col·or·a·tion
col·or-blind

col·or blind·ness
col·or·fast
col·or·ful
col·or guard
col·or·less
Col·o·rad·o
col·or·a·tu·ra
col·os·sc·um
co·los·sus
  co·los·sal
co·los·to·my
col·umn
  co·lum·nar
  col·um·nist
co·ma *n.* (*unconscious*; see
  comma)
  co·ma·tose
com·bat
  com·bat·ant
  com·bat·ed
  com·bat·ing
  com·bat·ive
com·bine
  com·bi·na·tion
com·bus·tion
  com·bus·ti·ble
come back *v.*
come·back *n.*
com·e·dy
  co·me·di·an
  co·me·di·enne
come·ly
  come·li·ness
come on *v.*
come-on *n.*
co·mes·ti·ble
com·et
com·fit
com·fort
  com·fort·a·ble
  com·fort·er
com·ic
  com·i·cal
com·ing

com·i·ty
com·ma *n.* (*punctuation
  mark*; see *coma*)
com·mand
  com·man·dant
  com·mand·er *n.*
com·man·deer *v.*
com·man·do
  pl. com·man·dos *or*
  com·man·does
com·mem·o·rate
  com·mem·o·ra·tion
  com·mem·o·ra·tive
com·mence
  com·mence·ment
  com·menc·ing
com·mend
  com·mend·a·ble
  com·men·da·tion
  com·men·da·to·ry
com·men·su·ra·ble
  com·men·su·ra·bil·i·ty
com·men·su·rate
  com·men·su·rate·ly
com·ment
  com·men·tar·y
  com·men·ta·tor
com·merce
  com·mer·cial
  com·mer·cial·ism
  com·mer·cial·i·za·tion
  com·mer·cial·ize
com·min·gle
com·mis·er·ate
  com·mis·er·a·tion
com·mis·sar
  com·mis·sar·i·at
com·mis·sar·y
com·mis·sion
  com·mis·sion·er
com·mit
  com·mit·ment
  com·mit·ted
  com·mit·ting

com·mit·tee
com·mode
com·mo·di·ous
com·mod·i·ty
  pl. com·mod·i·ties
com·mo·dore
com·mon
com·mon·al·i·ty *or*
  com·mon·al·ty
com·mon·er
com·mon·place
com·mon sense *n.*
com·mon·sense *adj.*
com·mon·wealth
com·mo·tion
com·mune
  com·mu·nal
com·mu·ni·cate
  com·mu·ni·ca·ble
  com·mu·ni·cant
  com·mu·ni·ca·tion
  com·mu·ni·ca·tive
  com·mu·ni·ca·tor
com·mu·nion
com·mu·ni·qué
com·mu·nism
  com·mu·nist
com·mu·ni·ty
  pl. com·mu·ni·ties
com·mu·ta·tor
com·mute
  com·mu·ta·tion
  com·mut·er
com·pact
com·pac·tor *or* com·pac·ter
com·pan·ion
  com·pan·ion·a·ble
  com·pan·ion·ship
  com·pan·ion·way
com·pa·ny
  pl. com·pa·nies
com·pare
  com·pa·ra·ble
  com·par·a·tive

com·par·i·son
com·part·ment
com·pass
com·pas·sion
  com·pas·sion·ate
com·pat·i·ble
  com·pat·i·bil·i·ty
com·pa·tri·ot
com·peer
com·pel
  com·pelled
  com·pel·ling
com·pen·di·um
  com·pen·di·ous
com·pen·sate
  com·pen·sa·ble
  com·pen·sa·tion
  com·pen·sa·tive
  com·pen·sa·to·ry
com·pete
  com·pe·ti·tion
  com·pet·i·tive
  com·pet·i·tor
com·pe·tence
  com·pe·ten·cy
  com·pe·tent
com·pile
  com·pi·la·tion
  com·pil·er
com·pla·cent *adj.* (*satisfied;*
  see *complaisant*)
  com·pla·cence *n.* (*satisfac-*
  tion; see *complaisance*)
  com·pla·cen·cy
com·plain
  com·plain·ant
  com·plaint
com·plai·sant *adj.* (*obliging;*
  see *complacent*)
  com·plai·sance *n.* (*willingness;*
  see *complacence*)
com·ple·ment *n., v.* (*whole;*
  see *compliment*)
  com·ple·men·tal

com·ple·men·ta·ry *adj.*
(*completing;* see
complimentary)
com·plete
com·ple·tion
com·plex
com·plex·i·ty
com·plex·ion
com·plex·ioned
com·pli·ant
com·pli·an·cy
com·pli·cate
com·pli·cat·ed
com·pli·ca·tion
com·plic·i·ty
com·pli·ment *n., v.* (*praise;*
see *complement*)
com·pli·men·ta·ry *adj.* (*admir-
ing;* see *complementary*)
com·ply
com·plied
com·po·nent
com·port
com·port·ment
com·pose
com·posed
com·pos·er
com·po·si·tion
com·pos·ite
com·pos·i·tor
com·post
com·po·sure
com·pote
com·pound
com·pre·hend
com·pre·hen·si·ble
com·pre·hen·sion
com·pre·hen·sive
com·press
com·pressed
com·press·i·ble
com·pres·sion
com·pres·sor
com·prise

com·pro·mise
comp·trol·ler
com·pul·sion
com·pul·so·ry
com·punc·tion
com·pute
com·put·a·ble
com·pu·ta·tion
com·put·er
com·put·er·ize
com·rade
con·cat·e·na·tion
con·cave
con·cav·i·ty
con·ceal
con·cede
con·ced·ed·ly
con·ceit
con·ceit·ed
con·ceive
con·ceiv·a·ble
con·cen·trate
con·cen·tra·tion
con·cen·tra·tor
con·cen·tric
con·cept
con·cep·tu·al
con·cep·tion
con·cern
con·cert
con·cert·mas·ter
con·cer·ti·na
con·cer·to
con·ces·sion
con·ces·sion·aire
conch
con·cierge
con·cil·i·ate
con·cil·i·a·tion
con·cil·ia·to·ry
con·cise
con·clave
con·clude
con·clu·sion

con·clu·sive
con·coct
con·coc·tion
con·com·i·tant
con·cord *n.* (*agreement*; see
   Concorde)
con·cor·dance
con·cor·dant
con·cor·dat
Con·corde *n.* (*trademark*)
   (*airplane*; see *concord*)
con·course
con·crete
con·crete·ly
con·cu·bine
con·cur
con·curred
con·cur·rence
con·cur·rent
con·cur·ring
con·cus·sion
con·demn
con·dem·na·tion
con·dem·na·to·ry
con·demned
con·dense
con·den·sa·tion
con·dens·er
con·de·scend
con·de·scend·ing·ly
con·de·scen·sion
con·dign
con·di·ment
con·di·tion
con·di·tion·al
con·di·tioned
con·dole
con·do·lence
con·do·min·i·um
con·done
con·do·na·tion
con·dor
con·duce
con·du·cive

con·duct
con·duc·tion
con·duc·tor
con·duit
con·fec·tion
con·fec·tion·er
con·fec·tion·er·y
con·fed·er·a·cy
con·fed·er·ate
con·fed·er·a·tion
con·fer
con·fer·ee
con·fer·ence
con·ferred
con·fer·ring
con·fess
con·fess·ed·ly
con·fes·sion
con·fes·sion·al
con·fes·sor
con·fet·ti
con·fide
con·fi·dant *or* confidante *n.,m.*
   or f. (*close friend*; see
   confident)
con·fi·dence
con·fi·dent *adj., n.*
   (*self-assured*; see *confidant*)
con·fi·den·tial
con·fid·ing
con·fig·u·ra·tion
con·fine
con·fine·ment
con·firm
con·fir·ma·tion
con·fir·ma·to·ry
con·fis·cate
con·fis·ca·tion
con·fis·ca·to·ry
con·fi·ture
con·fla·gra·tion
con·flict
con·flic·tion
con·flu·ence

con·form
  con·form·a·ble
  con·for·ma·tion
  con·form·ist
  con·for·mi·ty
con·found
  con·found·ed·ly
con·fra·ter·ni·ty
con·front
  con·fron·ta·tion
Con·fu·cian
con·fuse
  con·fus·ed·ly
  con·fus·ing
  con·fu·sion
con·fute
  con·fu·ta·tion
con·ga
con·gé
con·geal
con·ge·ner
con·ge·nial
  con·ge·nial·i·ty
con·gen·i·tal
con·ger eel
con·gest
  con·ges·tion
con·glom·er·ate
  con·glom·er·a·tion
Con·go
con·grat·u·late
  con·grat·u·la·tion
  con·grat·u·la·to·ry
con·gre·gate
  con·gre·ga·tion
  con·gre·ga·tion·al
con·gress
  con·gres·sio·nal
  con·gress·man
con·gru·ent
  con·gru·ence
  con·gru·i·ty
  con·gru·ous

con·ic
  con·i·cal
con·i·fer
  co·nif·er·ous
con·jec·ture
  con·jec·tur·al
con·ju·gal
con·ju·gate
  con·ju·ga·tion
con·junc·ti·va
  pl. con·junc·ti·vas *or*
  con·junc·ti·vae
con·junc·tive
con·junc·ture
con·jure
  con·jur·er *or* con·jur·or
con·nect
  con·nect·ed·ly
  con·nec·tion
  con·nec·tive
Con·nect·i·cut
conned
con·nip·tion
con·nive
  con·niv·ance
con·nois·seur
con·note
  con·no·ta·tion
  con·no·ta·tive
con·nu·bi·al
con·quer
  con·quered
  con·quer·ing
  con·quer·or
  con·quest
con·san·guin·eous
  con·san·guin·i·ty
con·science
  con·sci·en·tious
con·scious
con·script
  con·scrip·tion
con·se·crate
  con·se·cra·tion

con·sec·u·tive
con·sen·sus
con·sent
con·se·quence
con·se·quent
  con·se·quen·tial
con·serve
  con·ser·va·tion
  con·serv·a·tism
  con·serv·a·tive
  con·serv·a·to·ry
con·sid·er
  con·sid·er·a·ble
  con·sid·er·ate
  con·sid·er·a·tion
con·sign
  con·sign·ee
  con·sign·ment
  con·sign·or
con·sist
  con·sist·en·cy
con·sist·ent
con·sis·to·ry
con·sole *v.*
  con·sol·a·ble
  con·so·la·tion
  con·sol·a·to·ry
con·sol·i·date
  con·sol·i·da·tion
con·som·mé *or* con·som·me
con·so·nance
con·so·nant
con·sort
con·spec·tus
con·spic·u·ous
con·spire
  con·spir·a·cy
  con·spir·a·tor
con·sta·ble
  con·stab·u·lar·y
con·stant
  con·stan·cy
con·stel·la·tion
con·ster·na·tion

con·sti·pate
con·stit·u·ent
  con·stit·u·en·cy
con·sti·tute
  con·sti·tu·tion
  con·sti·tu·tion·al
con·strain *v.*
  con·straint *n.*
con·strict
  con·stric·tion
  con·stric·tor
con·struct
  con·struc·tion
  con·struc·tive
con·strue
  con·strued
  con·stru·ing
con·sul *n.* (*ambassador*; see *council* and *counsel*)
  con·sul·ar
  con·sul·ate
con·sult
  con·sul·tant
  con·sul·ta·tion
  con·sul·ta·tive
con·sume
  con·sum·a·ble
  con·sum·ed·ly
  con·sump·tion
  con·sump·tive
con·sum·mate
  con·sum·ma·tion
con·tact
con·ta·gion
  con·ta·gious
con·tain·er
con·tam·i·nate
  con·tam·i·na·tion
con·tem·plate
  con·tem·pla·tion
  con·tem·pla·tive
con·tem·po·rar·y
  con·tem·po·ra·ne·ous

con·tempt
  con·tempt·i·ble
  con·temp·tu·ous
con·tend
  con·ten·tion
con·ten·tious
con·tent·ment
con·test
  con·test·a·ble
  con·tes·tant
  con·tes·ta·tion
con·text
  con·tex·tu·al
  con·tex·ture
con·tig·u·ous
  con·ti·gu·i·ty
con·ti·nence
con·ti·nent
  con·ti·nen·tal
con·tin·gent
  con·tin·gen·cy
con·tin·ue
  con·tin·u·al
  con·tin·u·ance
  con·tin·u·a·tion
  con·tin·u·ing
  con·ti·nu·i·ty
  con·tin·u·ous
con·tort
  con·tor·tion
  con·tor·tion·ist
con·tour
con·tra·band
con·tra·bass
con·tra·cep·tion
con·tract
  con·trac·tion
  con·trac·tor
con·tra·dict
  con·tra·dic·tion
  con·tra·dic·to·ry
con·tra·in·di·cate
con·tral·to
con·trap·tion

con·tra·pun·tal
con·trar·y
  con·trar·i·ly
  con·trar·i·ness
  con·trar·i·wise
con·trast
con·tra·vene
  con·tra·ven·tion
con·tre·danse
con·tre·temps
con·trib·ute
  con·tri·bu·tion
  con·trib·u·tor
  con·trib·u·to·ry
con·trite
  con·tri·tion
con·trive
  con·triv·ance
con·trol
  con·trolled
  con·trol·ler
  con·trol·ling
con·tro·ver·sy
  con·tro·ver·sial
con·tro·vert
con·tu·ma·cy
  con·tu·ma·cious
con·tu·me·ly
  con·tu·me·li·ous
con·tuse
  con·tu·sion
co·nun·drum
con·va·lesce
  con·va·les·cence
  con·va·les·cent
  con·va·lesc·ing
con·vec·tion
con·vene
con·ve·nient
  con·ve·nience
con·vent
  con·ven·tu·al
con·ven·ti·cle

con·ven·tion
  con·ven·tion·al
  con·ven·tion·al·i·ty
con·verge
  con·ver·gence
con·verse
  con·ver·sant
  con·ver·sa·tion
  con·ver·sa·tion·al
con·vert
  con·ver·sion
  con·vert·er
  con·vert·i·bil·i·ty
  con·vert·i·ble
con·vex
  con·vex·i·ty
con·vey
  con·vey·ance
  con·vey·er *or* con·vey·or
con·vict
  con·vic·tion
con·vince
  con·vinc·ing·ly
con·viv·i·al
  con·viv·i·al·i·ty
con·voke
  con·vo·ca·tion
con·vo·lu·tion
con·vol·vu·lus
con·voy
con·vulse
  con·vul·sion
  con·vul·sive
coo
  cooed *v. (pt. of coo; see co-ed)*
cook·er·y
cook·out
cool·er
coo·lie *or* coo·ly *n. (worker;*
  see coolly)
  pl. coo·lies
cool·ly *adv. (cold; see coolie)*
co-op *or* co·op *n. (organiza-*
  tion; see coop)

coop *n. (chicken house; see*
  co-op and coupé and coup)
coop·er
  coo·per·age
  coop·ered
co·op·er·ate
  co·op·er·a·tion
  co·op·er·a·tive
co-opt
co·or·di·nate
cop·i·er
co·pi·lot
co·pi·ous
cop·per
  cop·per·plate
  cop·per·smith
cop·per·as
cop·per·head
cop·pice
co·pra
cop·u·late
cop·y·book
cop·y·hold·er
cop·y·ing
cop·y·ist
cop·y·read·er
cop·y·right
co·quet·ry
  co·quette
cor·al *n. (marine formations;*
  see choral)
  cor·al·line
cord *n., v. (rope; see chord)*
  cord·age
cor·dial
  cor·dial·i·ty
cord·ite
cor·don
cor·do·van
cor·du·roy
core *n., v. (center; see corps)*
co·re·spon·dent *n. (adulterer;*
  see correspondent)
co·ri·an·der

Co·rin·thi·an
cork·screw
cork·wood
cor·mo·rant
corn bor·er
corn bread
corn·cob
corn·crib
cor·ne·a
cor·ner
  cor·ner·stone
  cor·ner·wise *or* cor·ner·ways
cor·net *or* cor·nett
  cor·net·ist *or* cor·net·tist
corn-fed
corn·field
corn·flakes
corn·flow·er
cor·nice
corn·meal
corn pone
corn·stalk
corn·starch
corn sug·ar
cor·nu·co·pi·a
co·rol·la
cor·ol·lar·y
co·ro·na
cor·o·nach
cor·o·nar·y
cor·o·na·tion
cor·o·ner
cor·o·net
cor·po·ral
cor·po·rate
  · cor·po·ra·tion
  cor·po·ra·tive
cor·po·re·al
corps *n.* (*military unit*; see
  core and *corpse*)
corpse *n.* (*dead body*; see
  corps)
cor·pu·lent
  cor·pu·lence

cor·pus
cor·pus·cle
cor·ral *n., v.* (*arena*; see
  chorale)
cor·rect
  cor·rec·tion
  cor·rec·tive
  cor·rec·tor
cor·re·late
  cor·re·la·tion
  cor·rel·a·tive
cor·re·spond
  cor·re·spon·dence
  cor·re·spon·dent *adj., n.*
  (*writer; reporter*; see
  corespondent)
cor·ri·dor
cor·rob·o·rate
  cor·rob·o·ra·tion
  cor·rob·o·ra·tive
cor·rode
  cor·ro·sion
  cor·ro·sive
cor·ru·gate
  cor·ru·ga·tion
cor·rupt
  cor·rupt·i·ble
  cor·rup·tion
cor·sage
cor·sair
cor·set
cor·tege *or* cor·tège
cor·ti·sone
co·run·dum
cor·us·cate
  cor·us·ca·tion
cor·vette
co·ry·za
cos·met·ic
cos·mic
cos·mog·o·ny
cos·mol·o·gy
cos·mo·pol·i·tan
cos·mop·o·lite

cos·mos
cos·sack
Cos·ta Ri·ca
cost·li·ness
cos·tume
  cos·tum·er
co·tan·gent
co·te·rie
co·ter·mi·nous
co·til·lion
cot·tage
cot·ton
  cot·ton·tail
  cot·ton·wood
cou·gar
cou·lomb
coun·cil n., v. (an assembly;
  see consul and counsel)
  coun·ciled or coun·cilled
  coun·cil·lor or coun·cil·or
  coun·cil·man
coun·sel n., v. (advice; see
  consul and council)
  coun·seled or coun·selled
  coun·sel·ing or coun·sel·ling
  coun·sel·or or coun·sel·lor
count·down
coun·te·nance
coun·ter
  coun·ter·act
  coun·ter·bal·ance
  coun·ter·claim
  coun·ter·clock·wise
  coun·ter·feit
  coun·ter·feit·er
  coun·ter·foil
  coun·ter·mand
  coun·ter·march
  coun·ter·mea·sure
  coun·ter·mine
  coun·ter·pane
  coun·ter·part
  coun·ter·point
  coun·ter·sign

  coun·ter·spy
  coun·ter·ten·or
  coun·ter·weight
count·ess
count·ing·house
coun·try
  coun·try·man
  coun·try·seat n. (country
  estate)
  coun·try·side
coun·ty
  coun·ty seat
coup n. (takeover; see coup
  d'état and coop and coupé)
coup d'é·tat
  pl. coups d'é·tat or copu d'é·tats
cou·pé or coupe n. (car; see
  coop and coup d'état)
cou·ple n., v.
  cou·pler
  cou·pling
cou·plet
cou·pon
cour·age
  cou·ra·geous
cou·ri·er
course n., v. (path; see
  coarse)
cour·te·ous
cour·te·san or cour·te·zan
cour·te·sy
  pl. cour·te·sies
court·house
court·ier
court·ly
  court·li·ness
court-mar·tial n.
  pl. courts-mar·tial or
  court-mar·tials
court-mar·tial v.
  court-mar·tialed or
  court-mar·tialled
court·room
court·ship

court·yard
cous·cous
cous·in
cous·in-ger·man *n.*
  pl. cous·ins-ger·man
cou·tu·ri·er
  cou·tu·ri·ere *f.*
co·va·lence
cov·e·nant
Cov·en·try
cov·er
  cov·er·age
  cov·er·all *n.*
  cov·er·all *adj.*
  cov·er charge
  cov·er·let
cov·ert
cov·er·ture
cov·e·tous
cov·ey
cow·ard
  cow·ard·ice
  cow·ard·li·ness
  cow·ard·ly
cow·bell
cow·boy
cow·catch·er
cow·ered
cow·girl
cow·hand
cow·herd
cow·hide
cow·lick
cowl·ing
co-work·er
cox·comb
cox·swain *or* cock·swain
coy·ly
coy·ote *or* coy·o·te
co·zy *or* co·sy
  co·zi·ly *or* co·si·ly
  co·zi·ness *or* co·si·ness
crab ap·ple
crabbed *adj.*

crab·bing
crab·grass
crack·brained
crack down *v.*
crack·down *n.*
crack·er·jack
crack·le
  crack·le·ware
crack·pot
cracks·man
cra·dle
craft·i·ly
crafts·man
cram
  crammed
  cram·ming
cran·ber·ry
cra·ni·um
  cra·ni·al
crank·shaft
crank·y
  crank·i·ness
cran·ny
  cran·nied *adj.*
cra·ter
cra·vat
cra·ven
craw·fish *or* cray·fish
cray·on
cra·zy
  cra·zi·ly
  cra·zi·ness
creak *v., n. (noise; see creek)*
cream·er·y
cream·i·ly
cream·i·ness
cream puff
cre·ate
  cre·a·tion
  cre·a·tive
  cre·a·tiv·i·ty
  cre·a·tor
crea·ture
cre·dence

cre·den·tial
cred·i·ble
  cred·i·bil·i·ty
cred·it
  cred·it·a·ble
  cred·i·tor
cre·do
cre·du·li·ty
  cred·u·lous
creek *n.* (*stream*; see *creak*)
creep·y
  creep·i·ness
cre·mate
  cre·ma·tion
  cre·ma·to·ri·um
  cre·ma·to·ry
crème de ca·ca·o
crème de la crème
crème de menthe
Cre·ole
cre·o·sote
crepe *or* crêpe
crepe su·zette
cre·pus·cu·lar
cre·scen·do
  pl. cre·scen·dos *or*
  cre·scen·does
cres·cent
crest·fall·en
cre·tin
cre·tonne
cre·vasse *or* cre·vass *n.* (*fis-sure*; see *crevice*)
crev·ice *n.* (*break*; see *crevasse*)
crew
crew·el *n.* (*yarn*; see *cruel*)
crib
  cribbed
  crib·bing
crib·bage
crick
crick·et
Cri·me·an

crim·i·nal
  crim·i·nal·i·ty
  crim·i·nal·ly
  crim·i·nol·o·gy
crim·son
cringe
  cring·ing
crin·kle
crin·o·line
crip·ple
  crip·pled
  crip·pling
cri·sis
  pl. cri·ses *or* cri·sis·es
criss·cross
cri·te·ri·on
crit·ic
  crit·i·cal
crit·i·cize
  crit·i·cism
cri·tique
Cro·a·tian
cro·chet
crock·er·y
croc·o·dile
cro·cus
  pl. cro·cus·es *or* cro·ci
crook·ed·ness
croon·er
crop
  cropped
  crop·ping
cro·quet *n.* (*game*; see *croquette*)
cro·quette *n.* (*food*; see *croquet*)
cro·sier *or* cro·zier
cross·bar
cross·bow
cross·cut
cross-ex·am·ine
cross-eyed
cross-grained
cross hair

cross·hatch n., v.
  cross-hatch·ing n.
cross·o·ver
cross-ques·tion
cross-ref·er·ence
cross·road
cross sec·tion n.
cross-sec·tion v.
cross-stitch
cross·walk
cross·wise
cross·word
crotch·et
  crotch·et·y
crou·pi·er
crou·ton
crow·bar
cru·cial
cru·ci·ble
cru·ci·fix
  cru·ci·fix·ion
cru·ci·form
cru·ci·fy
cru·di·ty
cru·el adj. (harsh; see crewel)
  cru·el·ly
  cru·el·ty
cru·et
cruise v., n. (travel; see
  cruse)
  cruis·er
crul·ler
crum·ble
  crum·bling
crum·pet
crum·ple
  crum·pling
crup·per
cru·sade
cruse n. (container; see
  cruise)
crus·ta·cean
  crus·ta·ceous
crux

cry
  cried
  cri·er
  cry·ing
crypt
cryp·tic
cryp·to·gram
  crypt·an·al·y·sis
crys·tal
  crys·tal·line
  crys·tal·li·za·tion
  crys·tal·lize
Cu·ba
cu·bic
  cu·bi·cal adj. (cube-shaped; see
  cubicle)
cu·bi·cle n. (small space; see
  cubical)
cu·bit
cuck·old
cuck·oo
cu·cum·ber
cud·dle
cud·gel
  cud·geled or cud·gelled
  cud·gel·ing or cud·gel·ling
cue n., v. (signal; see queue)
cui·rass
cui·sine
cul-de-sac
  pl. culs-de-sac
cul·i·nar·y
cul·mi·nate
  cul·mi·na·tion
cul·pa·ble
  cul·pa·bil·i·ty
cul·prit
cul·ti·vate
  cul·ti·va·tion
  cul·ti·va·tor
cul·ture
  cul·tur·al
cul·vert

cum·ber·some
  cum·brous
cum lau·de
cum·mer·bund
cu·mu·la·tive
cu·mu·lus
cu·ne·i·form
cun·ning
cup·bear·er
cup·board
cu·pel
cup·ful
cu·pid·i·ty
cu·po·la
cur·a·ble
cu·ra·çao
cu·ra·re
cu·rate
cu·ra·tive
cu·ra·tor
curb·stone
cur·dle
cu·rette *or* cu·ret
cur·few
cu·ri·o
cu·ri·ous
  cu·ri·os·i·ty
cur·li·cue
curl·i·ness
cur·rant *n.* (*fruit*; *see
  current*)
cur·ren·cy
cur·rent *adj., n.* (*present;
  electricity; see currant*)
cur·ric·u·lum
cur·ry
  cur·ried
cur·ry·comb
cur·sive
cur·sor
cur·so·ry
  cur·so·ri·ly
cur·tail

cur·tain
  cur·tain call
curt·sy *or* curt·sey
curve
  cur·va·ture
  cur·vi·lin·e·ar
cush·ion
cus·pi·dor *or* cus·pi·dore
cus·tard
cus·to·dy
  cus·to·di·an
cus·tom
  cus·tom·ar·y
cus·tom·er
cus·tom·house
cut·a·way
cu·ti·cle
cut·lass *or* cut·las
cut·ler
  cut·ler·y
cut·let
cut off *v.*
cut·off *n.*
cut·out *n.*
cut out *v., adj.*
cut·purse
cut-rate
cut·throat
cut·ting
cut·tle·fish
cut up *v.*
cut·up *n.*
cut·wa·ter
cut·worm
cy·an·a·mide
cy·an·ic
cy·a·nide
cy·an·o·gen
cy·a·no·sis
cy·ber·net·ics
cy·cle
cy·cloid
cy·clone

cy·clo·pe·di·a *or*
  cy·clo·pae·di·a
Cy·clops
  pl. Cy·clo·pes
cy·clo·ra·ma
cy·clo·tron
cyg·net *n.* (*young swan;* see
  signet)
cyl·in·der
  cy·lin·dri·cal
cym·bal *n.* (*instrument;* see
  symbol)
cyn·ic
  cyn·i·cal
  cyn·i·cism
cy·no·sure
cy·press
Cy·prus
cyst
  cys·to·scope
Czech·o·slo·va·ki·a

D

dab·ble
da ca·po
dachs·hund
Da·cron (*trademark*)
dac·tyl
daf·fo·dil
dag·ger
da·guerre·o·type
dahl·ia
dai·ly
  pl. dai·lies
dain·ty
  dain·ti·ly
  dain·ti·ness
dair·y
  dair·y·maid
  dair·y·man
dais

dai·sy
  dai·sy·wheel
dal·li·ance
dal·ma·tian
dam *n.* (*barrier;* see *damn*)
  dammed
  dam·ming
dam·age
  dam·age·a·ble
dam·a·scene
dam·ask
damn *v., n., adj.* (*curse, con-*
  demn; see *dam*)
  dam·na·ble
  dam·na·tion
  damned
  damned·est
  damn·ing
damp·en
damp·er
dam·sel
dance
dan·de·li·on
dan·dle
  dan·dling
dan·druff
dan·ger
  dan·ger·ous
dan·gle
Dan·ish
dan·seur *m* (see *danseuse*)
dan·seuse *f.*
  pl. dan·seuses (see *danseur*)
dap·ple
dare·dev·il
dark·en
dark horse
dark·ness
dark·room
dar·ling
Dar·win·i·an
dash·board
das·tard·ly

da·tum *s.*
  pl. da·ta
date
  dat·ing
daugh·ter
  daugh·ter-in-law
daunt·less·ly
dau·phin *n.* (*a lord*; see
  dolphin)
dav·en·port
da·vit
daw·dle
  daw·dling
day·bed
day·book
day·break
day camp
day coach
day·dream
day la·bor
day let·ter
day·light
day·room
day school
day·star
day·time
daz·zle
  daz·zling
dea·con
dead·beat
dead·en
dead·eye
dead·fall
dead·head
dead heat
dead·light
dead·line
dead·li·ness
dead·lock
dead·weight
dead·wood
deaf-mute
dear *adj., n., adv.* (*beloved*;
  see *deer*)

dearth
death·bed
death ben·e·fit
death·blow
death·less
death·ly
death mask
death's-head
death war·rant
death·watch
de·ba·cle
de·bar·ka·tion
de·base
de·bate
  de·bat·a·ble
de·bauch
  de·bauch·er·y
de·ben·ture
de·bil·i·tate
  de·bil·i·ty
deb·it
deb·o·nair *or* deb·o·naire
de·bris
debt
  debt·or
de·bug
de·but
  deb·u·tante
dec·ade
dec·a·dence
  dec·a·dent
dec·a·gon
de·cal·co·ma·ni·a
dec·a·logue *or* dec·a·log
de·camp
de·cant
  de·cant·er
de·cap·i·tate
de·cath·lon
de·cay
de·cease
  de·ceased
  de·ce·dent
de·ceit·ful

de·ceive
  de·ceiv·a·ble
  de·cep·tion
  de·cep·tive
de·cel·er·a·tion
de·cem·vir
  pl. de·cem·virs
de·cent *adj. (respectable; kind;*
  see *descent* and *dissent*)
  de·cen·cy
de·cen·tral·ize
dec·i·bel
de·cide
  de·cid·ed
  de·ci·sion
  de·ci·sive
de·cid·u·ous
dec·i·mal
dec·i·mate
de·ci·pher
  de·ci·pher·a·ble
deck chair
de·claim
  dec·la·ma·tion
  de·clam·a·to·ry
de·clare
  dec·la·ra·tion
  de·clar·a·tive
dec·li·na·tion
de·cline
  de·clen·sion
de·cliv·i·ty
de·coc·tion
de·code
dé·col·le·té *or* **de·col·le·te**
  dé·col·le·tage
de·com·pose
  de·com·po·si·tion
dec·o·rate
  dec·o·ra·tion
  dec·o·ra·tive
  dec·o·ra·tor
de·co·rum
  dec·o·rous

de·coy
  de·coyed
  de·coy·ing
de·crease
de·cree
  de·creed
  de·cree·ing
de·crep·it
de·cre·scen·do
de·cry
ded·i·cate
  ded·i·cat·ed
  ded·i·ca·tion
de·duce
  de·duc·i·ble
  de·duc·ing
de·duct·i·ble
de·duct·ing
de·duc·tion
de·duc·tive
deep·en
deep-root·ed
deep-sea *adj*.
deep sea *n*.
deep-seat·ed
deer *n*. *(animal;* see *dear)*
  deer·hound
  deer·skin
de·face
de fac·to
de·fal·cate
  de·fal·ca·tion
de·fame
  def·a·ma·tion
  de·fam·a·to·ry
de·fault·er
de·feat
de·fect
  de·fec·tion
  de·fec·tive
  de·fec·tor
de·fend
  de·fend·ant
  de·fense

de·fen·si·ble
de·fen·sive
de·fer
  def·er·ence *n.* (*respect*; see
  difference)
  def·er·en·tial
  de·fer·ment
  de·fer·ra·ble
  de·ferred
  de·fer·ring
de·fi·ance
de·fi·ant
de·fi·bril·la·tion
de·fi·cient
  de·fi·cien·cy
def·i·cit
de·fied
de·file
de·fine
  de·fin·a·ble
  de·fine·ment
def·i·nite
def·i·ni·tion
de·fin·i·tive
de·flate
de·flect
  de·flec·tion
de·form
  de·for·ma·tion
  de·for·mi·ty
de·fraud
de·fray
  de·frayed
de·funct
de·fy
  de·fi·ance
  de·fi·ant
  de·fied
  de·fy·ing
de·gen·er·ate
  de·gen·er·a·cy
  de·gen·er·a·tion
de·grade
  deg·ra·da·tion

de·gree
  de·gree-day
de·hu·mid·i·fy
de·hy·drate
  de·hy·dra·tion
de·i·fi·ca·tion
deign
de·ist
de·i·ty
de·ject·ed
de·jec·tion
de ju·re
Del·a·ware
de·lay
  de·layed
  de·lay·ing
de·lec·ta·ble
  de·lec·ta·tion
del·e·gate
  del·e·ga·tion
de·lete
  de·le·tion
del·e·te·ri·ous
delft·ware
de·lib·er·ate
  de·lib·er·a·tion
  de·lib·er·a·tive
del·i·ca·cy
  pl. del·i·ca·cies
del·i·cate
del·i·ca·tes·sen
de·li·cious
de·light
  de·light·ful
de·lin·e·ate
  de·lin·e·a·tion
  de·lin·e·a·tor
de·lin·quen·cy
del·i·ques·cent
de·lir·i·um
  de·lir·i·ous
de·liv·er
  de·liv·er·ance
  de·liv·er·y

pl. de·liv·er·ies
de·lude
  de·lu·sion
del·uge
de·luxe
delve
de·mag·net·ize
dem·a·gogue *or* **dem·a·gog**
de·mand
de·mar·ca·tion *or*
  de·mar·ka·tion
de·mean
de·mean·or
de·ment·ed
de·men·tia
de·mer·it
de·mesne
dem·i·god
dem·i·john
de·mil·i·ta·rize
dem·i·monde
de·mise
dem·i·tasse
de·mo·bi·lize
de·moc·ra·cy
  dem·o·crat
  dem·o·crat·ic
de·mol·ish
  dem·o·li·tion
de·mon
de·mon·e·tize
  de·mon·e·ti·za·tion
dem·on·strate
  de·mon·stra·ble
  dem·on·stra·tion
  de·mon·stra·tive
  dem·on·stra·tor
de·mor·al·ize
de·mount·a·ble
de·mur *v., n. (hesitate;* see
  demure)
  de·mur·rage
  de·murred
  de·mur·rer

  de·mur·ring
de·mure *adj. (modest;* see
  demur)
de·na·ture
den·im
den·i·zen
Den·mark
de·nom·i·na·tion
de·nom·i·na·tor
de·note
de·noue·ment
de·nounce
den·si·ty
den·tal
den·ti·frice
den·tist
  den·tis·try
den·ture
de·nude
de·nun·ci·a·tion
  de·nun·ci·a·to·ry
de·ny
  de·ni·al
  de·nied
de·o·dor·ant
de·o·dor·ize
de·part
  de·par·ture
de·part·ment
  de·part·men·tal
de·pend·a·ble
de·pen·dent *or* **de·pen·dant**
  de·pen·den·cy
de·pict
  de·pic·tion
de·pil·a·to·ry
de·plane
de·plete
  de·ple·tion
de·plore
  de·plor·a·ble
de·ploy
de·po·nent
de·pop·u·late

de·port·a·ble
de·por·ta·tion
de·port·ment
de·pose
de·pos·it
  de·pos·it·ed
dep·o·si·tion
de·pos·i·to·ry
de·pot
de·prave
  dep·ra·va·tion *n.* (*corruption*;
  see *deprivation*)
  de·prav·i·ty
dep·re·cate
  dep·re·ca·tion
  dep·re·ca·to·ry
de·pre·ci·ate
  de·pre·ci·a·tion
dep·re·da·tion
de·press
  de·pressed
  de·pres·sion
de·prive
  de·pri·va·tion *n.* (*withhold*; see
  depravation)
de·pute
  dep·u·tize
dep·u·ty
  dep·u·ta·tion
  dep·u·tize
de·rail
de·range
  de·range·ment
Der·by (*race*)
der·by (*hat*)
  pl. der·bies
der·e·lict
  der·e·lic·tion
de·ride
  de·ri·sion
  de·ri·sive
  de·ri·so·ry
de·rive
  der·i·va·tion

de·riv·a·tive
der·ma·tol·o·gy
  der·ma·tol·o·gist
der·o·ga·tion
de·rog·a·to·ry
der·rick
der·ri·ere *or* der·ri·ère
der·vish
des·cant
de·scend
  de·scend·ant *or* de·scend·ent
  de·scend·er
  de·scent *n.* (*decline*; see *decent*
  and *dissent*)
de·scribe
  de·scrib·a·ble
  de·scrip·tion
  de·scrip·tive
des·e·crate
  des·e·cra·tion
de·seg·re·gate
de·sen·si·tize
des·ert *n.* (*barren expanse*;
  see *dessert*)
de·sert *v.* (*to abandon*; see
  dessert)
  de·ser·tion
de·serve
  de·serv·ed·ly
  de·serv·ing
des·ic·cate
  des·ic·ca·tion
  des·ic·ca·tor
de·sid·er·a·tum
  pl. de·sid·er·a·ta
de·sign
  de·sign·ed·ly
  de·sign·er
des·ig·nate
  des·ig·na·tion
de·sire
  de·sir·a·bil·i·ty
  de·sir·a·ble
  de·sir·ous

de·sist
des·o·late
  des·o·la·tion
de·spair
des·per·a·do
  pl. des·per·a·does *or*
  des·per·a·dos
des·per·ate *adj.* (*frantic;* see
  disparate)
  des·per·a·tion
de·spise
  de·spic·a·ble
de·spite
de·spoil
de·spond
  de·spon·den·cy
  de·spon·dent
des·pot
  des·pot·ic
  des·pot·i·cal·ly
  des·po·tism
des·sert *n.* (*food;* see *desert*)
  des·sert·spoon
des·tine
  des·ti·na·tion
  des·ti·ny
  pl. des·ti·nies
des·ti·tute
  des·ti·tu·tion
de·stroy
  de·struc·ti·ble
  de·struc·tion
  de·struc·tive
des·ue·tude
des·ul·to·ry
de·tach
  de·tach·ment
de·tail
de·tain
  de·ten·tion
de·tect
  de·tec·tion
  de·tec·tive
  de·tec·tor

de·ter
  de·terred
  de·ter·rent
  de·ter·ring
de·ter·gent
de·te·ri·o·rate
  de·te·ri·o·ra·tion
de·ter·mi·nate
  de·ter·mi·na·tion
de·ter·mine
  de·ter·min·a·ble
  de·ter·mi·nant
  de·ter·mi·nism
de·test
  de·test·a·ble
  de·tes·ta·tion
de·throne
det·i·nue
det·o·nate
  det·o·na·tion
  det·o·na·tor
de·tour
de·tract
  de·trac·tion
det·ri·ment
  de·tri·men·tal
dev·as·tate
  dev·as·ta·tion
de·vel·op
  de·vel·oped
  de·vel·op·ing
  de·vel·op·ment
de·vi·ate
  de·vi·a·tion
de·vice *n.* (*contrivance;* see
  devise)
dev·il·fish
dev·il·ish
dev·il·ment
de·vi·ous
de·vise *v.* (*to make;* see
  device)
de·void
de·volve

de·vote
  dev·o·tee
  de·vo·tion
  de·vo·tion·al
  de·vout
de·vour
dew n. (*moisture*; see *do* and *due*)
  dew·y
dew·ber·ry
dew·drop
dew·lap
dew point
dex·ter
dex·ter·i·ty
  dex·ter·ous or dex·trous
dex·trose
dhow or **dow**
di·a·be·tes
  di·a·bet·ic
di·a·ble·rie
di·a·bol·ic
  di·a·bol·i·cal
di·ab·o·lism
di·a·crit·i·cal
di·a·dem
di·aer·e·sis
di·ag·nose
  di·ag·no·sis
  di·ag·nos·tic
  di·ag·nos·ti·cian
di·ag·o·nal
di·a·gram
di·al
  di·aled
  di·al·ing
di·a·lect
di·a·lec·tic
  di·a·lec·ti·cal
di·a·logue or **di·a·log**
di·am·e·ter
  di·a·met·ric
di·a·mond
di·a·per

di·aph·a·nous
di·a·phragm
di·ar·rhe·a or **di·ar·rhoe·a**
di·a·ry
di·a·sto·le
di·a·ther·my
di·a·ton·ic
di·a·tribe
dice n. (see *die*)
di·chot·o·my
Dic·ta·phone (*trademark*)
dic·tate
  dic·ta·tion
  dic·ta·tor
  dic·ta·to·ri·al
dic·tion
dic·tion·ar·y
  pl. dic·tion·ar·ies
dic·tum
  pl. dic·ta
di·dac·tic
die v. (*to cease living*; see *dye*)
  died v. (see *dyed*)
  dies v. (see *dice*)
  dy·ing v. (see *dyeing*)
die n. (*stamp; cube*; see *dye*)
  pl. dice or dies (see *dies, v.*)
die·hard n.
die-hard adj.
di·e·lec·tric
die·mak·er
die·sel
die·sink·er
di·et
  di·e·tar·y
  di·e·tet·ic
  di·e·tet·ics
dif·fer
  dif·fer·ence n. (*unlikeness*; see *deference*)
  dif·fer·ent
  dif·fer·en·tial
  dif·fer·en·ti·ate
  dif·fer·en·ti·a·tion

dif·fi·cult
  dif·fi·cul·ty
  pl. dif·fi·cul·ties
dif·fi·dent
  dif·fi·dence
dif·frac·tion
dif·fuse
  dif·fu·sion
di·gest
  di·gest·i·ble
  di·ges·tion
  di·ges·tive
dig·it
  dig·i·tal
dig·i·tal·is
dig·ni·fy
  dig·ni·fied
dig·ni·tar·y
dig·ni·ty
di·gress
  di·gres·sion
di·lap·i·date
  di·lap·i·dat·ed
  di·lap·i·da·tion
di·late
  dil·a·ta·tion
dil·a·to·ry
  dil·a·to·ri·ness
di·lem·ma
dil·et·tante
dil·i·gent
  dil·i·gence
di·lute
  di·lu·tion
di·lu·vi·al
di·men·sion
di·min·ish
  dim·i·nu·tion
di·min·u·en·do
di·min·u·tive
dim·i·ty
dim·ness
dim·ple

dim·wit
  dim-wit·ted *adj.*
din·er *n.* (*one who eats*; see *dinner*)
di·nette
dingh·y *n.* (*boat*; see *dingy*)
din·gy *adj.* (*drab*; see *dinghy*)
din·ner *n.* (*meal*; see *diner*)
  din·ner bell
  din·ner cloth
  din·ner fork
  din·ner ta·ble
  din·ner·ware
di·no·saur
di·o·cese
  di·oc·e·san
di·o·ram·a
diph·the·ri·a
diph·thong
di·plo·ma
di·plo·ma·cy
  dip·lo·mat
  dip·lo·mat·ic
dip·per
dip·so·ma·ni·a
di·rect
  di·rec·tion
  di·rec·tor
  di·rec·tor·ate
  di·rec·to·ry
dire·ful
dirge
dir·i·gi·ble
dirn·dl
dirt·y
  dirt·i·ly
  dirt·i·ness
dis·a·ble
  dis·a·bil·i·ty
dis·a·buse
dis·ad·van·tage
  dis·ad·van·ta·geous
dis·af·fect·ed

dis·af·fec·tion
dis·a·gree
  dis·a·gree·a·ble
dis·al·low
dis·ap·pear
  dis·ap·pear·ance
dis·ap·point
dis·ap·prove
  dis·ap·pro·ba·tion
  dis·ap·pro·val
dis·ar·ma·ment
dis·ar·range
dis·ar·tic·u·late
dis·as·sem·ble
dis·as·so·ci·ate
di·sas·ter
  di·sas·trous
dis·a·vow
  dis·a·vow·al
dis·band
dis·bar
  dis·bar·ring
dis·be·lieve
  dis·be·lief
  dis·be·liev·er
dis·burse *v.* (*to give out;* see
  disperse)
  dis·burse·ment
dis·card
dis·cern
  dis·cern·i·ble *or*
  dis·cern·a·ble
dis·charge
dis·ci·ple
dis·ci·pline
  dis·ci·pli·nar·i·an
  dis·ci·pli·na·ry
dis·claim
  dis·claim·er
dis·close
  dis·clo·sure
dis·cog·ra·phy
dis·col·or
  dis·col·or·a·tion

dis·com·fit
  dis·com·fi·ture
dis·com·fort
dis·com·pose
  dis·com·po·sure
dis·con·cert
dis·con·nect
dis·con·so·late
dis·con·tent
dis·con·tin·ue
  dis·con·tin·u·ance
  dis·con·tin·u·ous
dis·cord
  dis·cor·dance
  dis·cor·dant
dis·count
dis·cour·age
  dis·cour·age·ment
dis·course
dis·cour·te·sy
  dis·cour·te·ous
dis·cov·er
  dis·cov·er·er
  dis·cov·er·y
dis·cred·it
  dis·cred·it·a·ble
dis·creet *adj.* (*prudent;* see
  discrete)
  dis·cre·tion
  dis·cre·tion·ar·y
dis·crep·an·cy
dis·crete *adj.* (*separate;* see
  discreet)
dis·crim·i·nate
  dis·crim·i·na·tion
dis·cur·sive
dis·cus (*a disk;* see *discuss*)
  pl. dis·cus·ses, disci *n.*
dis·cuss *v.* (*to talk;* see
  discus)
  dis·cus·sion
dis·dain
  dis·dain·ful

dis·ease
  dis·eased
dis·em·bar·ka·tion
dis·em·bar·rass
dis·em·bow·el
dis·en·chant·ment
dis·en·gage
dis·en·tan·gle
dis·es·teem
dis·fa·vor
dis·fig·ure
dis·fran·chise
dis·gorge
dis·grace
  dis·grace·ful
dis·grun·tle
dis·guise
dis·gust
dis·ha·bille
dish·cloth
dis·heart·en
di·shev·el
dish·mop
dis·hon·est
dis·hon·or
  dis·hon·or·a·ble
dish·pan
dish·rag
dish tow·el
dish·wash·er
dish·wa·ter
dis·il·lu·sion
dis·in·cli·na·tion
dis·in·fect
  dis·in·fec·tant
dis·in·fes·ta·tion
dis·in·gen·u·ous
dis·in·her·it
dis·in·te·grate
  dis·in·te·gra·tion
dis·in·ter·est·ed
dis·join
dis·junc·tion
dis·junc·tive

disk *or* disc
dis·like
dis·lo·cate
  dis·lo·ca·tion
dis·lodge
dis·loy·al
  dis·loy·al·ty
dis·mal
dis·man·tle
  dis·man·tling
dis·mast
dis·may
dis·mem·ber
dis·miss
  dis·mis·sal
dis·mount
dis·o·bey
  dis·o·be·di·ence
  dis·o·be·di·ent
  dis·o·beyed
dis·ob·lige
dis·or·der
dis·or·ga·nize
  dis·or·ga·ni·za·tion
dis·own
dis·par·age
dis·par·ate *adj.* (*dissimilar;*
  see *desperate*)
  dis·par·i·ty
dis·pas·sion·ate
dis·patch
dis·pel
  dis·pelled
  dis·pel·ling
dis·pen·sa·tion
dis·pense
  dis·pens·a·ble
  dis·pen·sa·ry
dis·perse *v.* (*to scatter;* see
  disburse)
  dis·per·sal
  dis·pers·i·ble
  dis·per·sion
di·spir·it

dis·place
dis·play
dis·please
　dis·plea·sure
dis·port
dis·pose
　dis·pos·a·ble
　dis·pos·al
　dis·po·si·tion
dis·pos·sess
dis·pro·por·tion
　dis·pro·por·tion·ate
dis·prove
　dis·proof
dis·pute
　dis·put·a·ble
　dis·pu·tant
　dis·pu·ta·tion
　dis·pu·ta·tious
dis·qual·i·fy
dis·qui·si·tion
dis·re·gard
dis·re·pair
dis·re·pute
　dis·rep·u·ta·ble
dis·re·spect
　dis·re·spect·ful
dis·robe
dis·rupt
dis·sat·is·fac·tion
dis·sat·is·fied
dis·sect
　dis·sec·tion
dis·sem·ble
dis·sem·i·nate
dis·sent *v.*, *n.* (*disagreement*;
　see *decent* and *descent*)
　dis·sen·sion
　dis·sent·er
　dis·sen·tient
dis·ser·ta·tion
dis·ser·vice
dis·si·dent
　dis·si·dence

dis·sim·i·lar
　dis·sim·i·lar·i·ty
dis·sim·i·late *v.* (*to make dis-*
　similar; see *dissimulate*)
dis·sim·u·late *v.* (*to dissemble*;
　see *dissimilate*)
dis·si·pate
　dis·si·pa·tion
dis·so·ci·ate
　dis·so·ci·a·tion
dis·so·lute
　dis·so·lu·tion
dis·solve
　dis·sol·u·ble
dis·so·nant
　dis·so·nance
dis·suade
　dis·sua·sion
dis·taff
dis·tant
　dis·tance
dis·taste
　dis·taste·ful
dis·tem·per
dis·tend
　dis·ten·sion *or* dis·ten·tion
dis·tich
dis·till
　dis·til·late
　dis·til·la·tion
　dis·till·er
　dis·till·er·y
dis·tinct
　dis·tinc·tion
　dis·tinc·tive
　dis·tinc·tive·ly
　dis·tinc·tive·ness
　dis·tinct·ly
dis·tin·guish
dis·tort
　dis·tor·tion
dis·tract
　dis·trac·tion
dis·traught

dis·tress

dis·trib·ute
  dis·tri·bu·tion
  dis·trib·u·tor

dis·trict

dis·trust
  dis·trust·ful

dis·turb
  dis·tur·bance

dis·un·ion

dis·use

dit·to
  pl. dit·tos *or* dit·toes

di·u·res·is

di·ur·nal

di·va
  pl. di·vas

di·va·gate

di·van

di·verge
  di·ver·gence
  di·ver·gent

di·vers *adj.* (*various;* see
  diverse)

di·verse *adj.* (*unlike;* see
  divers)

di·ver·si·fy

di·ver·si·ty

di·vert
  di·ver·sion

di·ver·tic·u·lum

di·vest

di·vide

div·i·dend

di·vine *v., adj.*
  div·i·na·tion
  di·vin·i·ty

di·vis·i·bil·i·ty

di·vi·sion

di·vorce

div·ot

di·vulge

diz·zy
  diz·zi·ly

diz·zi·ness

Dji·bou·ti

do *v., n.* (*to act;* see *dew*
  and *due*)

do *n.* (*musical tone;* see *doe*
  and *dough*)

doc·ile
  do·cil·i·ty

dock·et

dock·hand

dock·side

dock·yard

doc·tor
  doc·tor·ate

doc·tri·naire

doc·trine
  doc·tri·nal

doc·u·ment
  doc·u·men·ta·ry
  doc·u·men·ta·tion

dodge

do·do

doe *n.* (*deer;* see *do* and
  dough)
  doe·skin

doff

dog·catch·er

dog days

doge

dog-eared

dog·fight

dog·fish

dog·ged

dog·ger·el

dog·house

dog·ma
  dog·mat·ic
  dog·mat·i·cal
  dog·ma·tism
  dog·ma·tize

do-good·er

dog pad·dle *n.*

dog-pad·dle *v.*

dog rose

dog tag
dog·tooth
dog·trot
dog·watch
dog·wood
doi·ly
  pl. doi·lies
Dol·by (*trademark*)
dol·drums
dole·ful
dol·lar
doll·house
dol·lop
doll·y
dol·man *n.* (*coat;* see
  dolmen)
dol·men *n.* (*monument;* see
  dolman)
do·lo·mite
do·lor
  do·lo·rous
dol·phin *n., v.* (*sea animal;*
  see *dauphin*)
do·main
do·mes·tic
  do·mes·ti·cate
  do·mes·tic·i·ty
dom·i·cile
dom·i·nate
  dom·i·nant
  dom·i·na·tion
dom·i·neer·ing
Do·min·i·can
do·mi·nie
do·min·ion
dom·i·no
  pl. dom·i·noes *or* dom·i·nos
do·nate
  do·na·tion
done *adj.* (*completed;* see *dun*)
don·jon
Don Juan
don·key
  don·key·work

do·nor
dooms·day
door·jamb
door·keep·er
door·knob
door·man
door·mat
door·nail
door·plate
door prize
door·sill
door·step
door·way
door·yard
dor·mant
dor·mer
dor·mi·to·ry
dor·mouse
dor·sal
dos·age
dos·sier
dot·age
  dot·ard
dot-ma·trix
dou·ble
dou·ble cross *n.*
dou·ble-cross *v.*
dou·ble-deal·er
  dou·ble-deal·ing
dou·ble-deck·er
dou·ble edge *n.*
dou·ble-edged *adj.*
dou·ble-faced
dou·ble-park
dou·ble-quick
dou·blet
dou·ble take
dou·ble-talk
dou·ble-think
dou·ble time *n.*
dou·ble-time *v.*
dou·bloon
doubt·ful
doubt·less

dough n. (*bread*; see *do* and
  doe)
  dough·boy
  dough·nut
dove·cote
dove·tail
dow·a·ger
dow·dy
  dowd·i·ness
dow·el
  dow·eled
  dow·el·ing
dow·er
down·beat
down·cast
down·draft
down·fall
down·grade
down·heart·ed
down·hill
down·pour
down·range
down·right
Down's syn·drome
down·stage
down·stairs
down·state
down·stream
down·stroke
down·swing
down·time
down-to-earth
down·town
down·trend
down·trod·den
down·turn
down·ward
down·y
dow·ry
dox·ol·o·gy
doy·en m.
  doy·enne f.
doz·en

drab
  drab·ber
  drab·best
drach·ma
  pl. drach·mas
dra·co·ni·an
draft n. (*version*; see *draught*)
draft horse
drafts·man
drag
  dragged
  drag·ging
drag·line
drag·net
drag·o·man
drag·on
drag·on·et
drag·on·fly
dra·goon
drag·rope
drain·age
drain·er
drain·pipe
dra·mat·ic
dra·ma·tize
  dra·ma·tist
dra·ma·tur·gy
drap·er·y
dras·tic
draught n. (*drink*; see *draft*)
draw·back
draw·bar
draw·bridge
draw·er
draw·string
dray·age
dray·man
dread·ful
dread·nought
dream·land
dream·y
  dream·i·ly
  dream·i·ness

drear·y
  drear·i·ly
  drear·i·ness
dredge
dress·er
dress·i·ness
dress·ing room
dress·mak·er
drib·ble
  drib·bling
drift·wood
drill
  drill·ing
  drill·mas·ter
  drill press
drink·a·ble
drip
  drip-dry
  dripped
  drip·ping
drive-in
driv·el
driv·er
drive·way
driz·zle
droll·er·y
drom·e·dar·y
drop
  drop cur·tain
  drop·head
  drop-kick n.
  drop-kick v.
  drop leaf
  drop let·ter
  drop·light
  drop·out n.
  drop out v.
  dropped
  drop·per
  drop·ping
drop·sy
drought
drow·sy
drudg·er·y

drug n., v.
  drugged
  drug·ging
  drug·gist
  drug·store
drum
  drum·beat
  drum·fire
  drum·head
  drum ma·jor·ette
  drummed
  drum·mer
  drum·ming
  drum·stick
drunk·ard
drunk·en
dry
  dry·ly or dri·ly
dry·ad
dry cell
dry-clean
  dry clean·ing n.
dry dock n.
dry-dock v.
dry goods
dry ice
dry·ness
dry·point
dry rot n.
dry-rot v.
dry run
dry-shod
du·al adj., n. (two; see duel)
du·bi·e·ty
du·bi·ous
du·cal
duc·at
duch·ess
duch·y
duck·board
duck·ling
duck·pin
duck soup
duc·tile

dud·geon n. (ill-humor; see
　dungeon)
due adj., n., adv. (deserved;
　see dew and do)
du·el n., v. (combat; see dual)
　du·eled
　du·el·ing
　du·el·ist
du·ly adj. (in due manner;
　see dully)
du·et
du·gong
dug·out
duke·dom
dul·cet
dul·ci·mer
dul·lard
dul·ly adv. (not sharply; see
　duly)
dumb·bell
dumb·wait·er
dum·my
dump·ling
dun adj., n., v. (demand
　payment; see done)
dun·ga·ree
dun·geon n. (prison; see
　dudgeon)
dun·nage
du·o·dec·i·mal
du·o·dec·i·mo
du·o·de·num
　pl. du·o·de·na or du·o·de·nums
　du·o·de·nal
du·plex
du·pli·cate
　du·pli·ca·tion
　du·pli·ca·tor
du·plic·i·ty
du·ra·ble
du·rance
du·ra·tion
dur·bar
du·ress

dur·ing
dusk·y
dust·bin
dust bowl
dust cap
dust·cloth
dust cov·er
dust·heap
dust·i·ness
dust jack·et
dust·man
dust mop
dust·pan
dust·proof
dust·rag
dust storm
dust·up
du·ty
　du·te·ous
　du·ti·a·ble
　du·ti·ful
dwarf·ish
dwell·ing
dwin·dle
dye n., v. (to color; see die)
　dyed v. (see died)
　dye·ing v. (see dying)
　dye·stuff
　dye·wood
dy·nam·ic
dy·na·mite
dy·na·mo
dy·na·mom·e·ter
dy·nast
dys·en·ter·y
dys·lex·i·a
dys·pep·sia
　dys·pep·tic

E

ea·ger
ea·gle

ear·drop
ear·drum
ear·ly
  ear·li·er
  ear·li·est
ear·mark
earn *v.* (*gain;* see *urn*)
  earn·ings
ear·nest
ear·phone
ear·ring
ear·shot
ear·split·ting
earth·born
earth·bound
earth·en·ware
earth·ly
  earth·li·ness
earth·quake
earth·ward
earth·work
earth·worm
ear·wax
ear·wig
ea·sel
ease·ment
Eas·ter
east·ern
east·ward
eas·y
  eas·i·er
  eas·i·est
  eas·i·ly
  eas·y·go·ing
eat·a·ble
ebb
  ebbed
  ebb·ing
eb·o·ny
e·bul·lient
  eb·ul·li·tion
ec·cen·tric
  ec·cen·tric·i·ty
ec·chy·mo·sis

ec·cle·si·as·ti·cal
ech·e·lon
ech·o
  pl. ech·oes
e·clair
ec·lamp·sia
ec·lec·tic
e·clipse
e·con·o·my
  ec·o·nom·ic
  ec·o·nom·i·cal
  e·con·o·mist
  e·con·o·mize
e·co·sys·tem
ec·sta·sy
  ec·stat·ic
Ec·ua·dor
ec·u·men·i·cal
ec·ze·ma
ed·dy
e·del·weiss
e·de·ma
  pl. e·de·mas *or* e·dem·a·ta
edge·ways
edg·i·ness
edg·ing
ed·i·ble
e·dict
ed·i·fice
ed·i·fy
  ed·i·fi·ca·tion
ed·it
  e·di·tion *n.* (*book;* see *addition*)
  ed·i·tor
  ed·i·to·ri·al
  ed·i·to·ri·al·ize
ed·u·cate
  ed·u·ca·ble
  ed·u·ca·tion·al
  ed·u·ca·tive
  ed·u·ca·tor
ef·face
  ef·face·ment

ef·fect *adj., n.* (*the result; see affect*)
  ef·fec·tive
  ef·fec·tu·al
  ef·fec·tu·ate
ef·fem·i·nate
ef·fer·vesce
  ef·fer·ves·cent
ef·fete
ef·fi·ca·cy
  ef·fi·ca·cious
ef·fi·cient
  ef·fi·cien·cy
ef·fi·gy
ef·flo·res·cent
ef·flu·vi·um *or* ef·flu·vi·a
  pl. ef·flu·vi·a *or* ef·flu·vi·ums
  or ef·flu·vi·as
ef·fort
ef·fron·ter·y
ef·ful·gence
ef·fu·sion
ef·fu·sive
egg·head
egg·nog
egg·plant
e·go
  e·go·ism
  e·go·ist *n.* (*self-interest; see egotist*)
  e·go·tism
  e·go·tist *n.* (*self-importance; see egoist*)
e·gre·gious
e·gress
E·gypt
ei·der
ei·ther
e·jac·u·late
  e·jac·u·la·tion
  e·jac·u·la·to·ry
e·ject
  e·jec·tion

e·lab·o·rate
  e·lab·o·ra·tion
e·lapse
e·las·tic
  e·las·tic·i·ty
e·lat·ed·ly
e·la·tion
el·bow·room
el·der
el·der·ber·ry
el·dest
e·lect
  e·lec·tion
  e·lec·tion·eer
  e·lec·tive
  e·lec·tor
  e·lec·tor·al
  e·lec·tor·ate
e·lec·tric
  e·lec·tri·cal
  e·lec·tri·cian
  e·lec·tric·i·ty
e·lec·tri·fy
  e·lec·tri·fi·ca·tion
  e·lec·tri·fied
e·lec·tro·car·di·o·graph
e·lec·tro·cute
e·lec·trode
e·lec·trol·y·sis
e·lec·tro·lyte
e·lec·tro·mag·net
e·lec·tron
e·lec·tro·plate
e·lec·tro·scope
e·lec·tro·type
el·ee·mos·y·nar·y
el·e·gant
  el·e·gance
el·e·gy
  el·e·gi·ac
el·e·ment
  el·e·men·tal
  el·e·men·ta·ry

el·e·phant
  el·e·phan·ti·a·sis
  el·e·phan·tine
el·e·vate
  el·e·va·tor
elf
  pl. elves
e·lic·it *v.* (*draw forth;* see *illicit*)
e·lide
el·i·gi·ble
  el·i·gi·bil·i·ty
e·lim·i·nate
  e·lim·i·na·tion
e·li·sion
e·lite
e·lix·ir
E·liz·a·be·than
el·lipse
  el·lip·tic
  el·lip·ti·cal
el·lip·sis
  pl. el·lip·ses
el·o·cu·tion
  el·o·cu·tion·ist
e·lon·gate
  e·lon·ga·tion
e·lope
el·o·quent
  el·o·quence
El Sal·va·dor
else·where
e·lu·ci·date
  e·lu·ci·da·tion
e·lude *v.* (*to escape;* see *allude*)
  e·lu·sive *adj.* (*evasive;* see *allusive* and *illusive*)
e·ma·ci·ate
  e·ma·ci·a·tion
em·a·nate
  em·a·na·tion
e·man·ci·pate
  e·man·ci·pa·tion

  e·man·ci·pa·tor
e·mas·cu·late
em·balm
em·bank·ment
em·bar·go
  pl. em·bar·goes
em·bar·rass
em·bas·sy
em·bel·lish
em·bez·zle
em·bit·ter
em·bla·zon
em·blem
  em·blem·at·ic
em·bod·y
  em·bod·i·ment
em·bold·en
em·bo·lism
em·boss
em·bou·chure
em·brace
em·bra·sure
em·broi·der·y
em·broil
em·bry·o
  em·bry·on·ic
e·mend *v.* (*to correct;* see *amend*)
  e·men·da·tion
em·er·ald
e·merge
e·mer·gen·cy
e·mer·i·tus
  pl. e·mer·i·ti
e·met·ic
em·i·grate
  em·i·grant
  em·i·gra·tion
  em·i·gré
em·i·nent *adj.* (*important;* see *immanent* and *imminent*)
  em·i·nence
e·mir
em·is·sar·y

e·mis·sion
e·mit
　e·mit·ted
　e·mit·ting
e·mol·lient
e·mol·u·ment
e·mo·tion
　e·mo·tion·al
em·per·or
em·pha·size
　em·pha·sis
　pl. em·pha·ses
　em·phat·ic
em·pire
em·pir·ic
　em·pir·i·cal
em·ploy
　em·ploy·a·ble
　em·ploy·ee
　em·ploy·er
em·po·ri·um
　pl. em·po·ri·ums or em·po·ri·a
em·pow·er
em·press
emp·ty
em·py·re·an
e·mu
em·u·late
　em·u·la·tion
　em·u·lat·or
　em·u·lous
e·mul·si·fy
　e·mul·sion
en·a·ble
en·act
e·nam·el
　e·nam·eled
　e·nam·el·ing
　e·nam·el·ware
en·am·or
en·camp·ment
en·caus·tic
en·ceinte
en·ceph·a·lo·gram

en·chant·er
en·chant·ress
en·cir·cle
en·clave
en·clit·ic
en·close
　en·clo·sure
en·co·mi·um
　en·co·mi·as·tic
en·com·pass
en·core
en·coun·ter
en·cour·age
　en·cour·age·ment
　en·cour·ag·ing
en·croach
en·cum·ber
　en·cum·brance
en·cyc·li·cal
en·cy·clo·pe·di·a or
　en·cy·clo·pae·di·a
en·dan·ger
en·dear
en·deav·or
en·dem·ic
end·ing
en·dive
end·less
end·long
end man
end·most
en·do·crine
en·dorse
en·dorse·ment
en·dow
en·dow·ment
end ta·ble
en·dure
　en·dur·a·ble
　en·dur·ance
end·ways
en·e·ma
en·e·my
　pl. en·e·mies

en·er·gy
  en·er·get·ic
  en·er·gize
  en·er·giz·er
en·er·vate
  en·er·va·tion
en·fee·ble
en·fet·ter
en·fold
en·force
  en·force·a·ble
  en·forc·er
en·fran·chise
en·gage
  en·gaged
  en·gage·ment
  en·gag·ing
en·gen·der
en·gine
  en·gi·neer
En·gland
En·glish
  En·glish·man
  En·glish·wom·an
en·graft
en·grave
  en·grav·er
en·gross
en·gulf
en·hance
e·nig·ma
  e·nig·mat·ic
en·join
en·joy
  en·joy·a·bly
en·lace
en·large
en·light·en
en·list
en·liv·en
en·mi·ty
en·nui
e·nor·mous
  e·nor·mi·ty

e·nough
en·rage
en·rap·ture
en·rich
en·robe
en·roll *or* en·rol
  en·rolled
  en·roll·ing
  en·roll·ment
en route
en·sconce
en·shrine
en·shroud
en·sign
en·slave
en·snare
en·sue
en·sure
en·tab·la·ture
en·tail
en·tan·gle
en·ter
en·ter·prise
en·ter·tain
  en·ter·tain·er
en·thrall
en·throne
en·thuse
  en·thu·si·asm
  en·thu·si·ast
  en·thu·si·as·tic
en·tice
en·tire
  en·tire·ty
en·ti·tle
en·ti·ty
en·tomb
en·to·mol·o·gy
en·tou·rage
en·trail
en·train
en·trance
en·trant
en·trap

en·treat
  en·treat·y
  pl. en·treat·ies
en·trée
en·tre·pre·neur
en·tro·py
en·try·way
en·twine
e·nu·mer·ate
  e·nu·mer·a·tion
  e·nu·mer·a·tor
e·nun·ci·ate
  e·nun·ci·a·tion
  e·nun·ci·a·tor
en·vel·op *v.*
  en·vel·oped
  en·vel·op·ment
en·ve·lope *n.*
en·ven·om
en·vi·ron
  en·vi·ron·ment
en·vis·age
en·vi·sion
en·voy
en·vy
  en·vi·a·ble
  en·vi·a·bly
  en·vied
  en·vi·ous
en·zyme
E·o·lith·ic
e·on *or* ae·on
ep·au·let
e·phem·er·al
ep·ic
  ep·i·cal
ep·i·cure
  ep·i·cu·re·an
ep·i·dem·ic
ep·i·der·mis
  ep·i·der·mal
  ep·i·der·mic
ep·i·did·y·mis
ep·i·gas·tric

ep·i·gram
ep·i·graph
  ep·i·graph·ic
ep·i·lep·sy
  ep·i·lep·tic
ep·i·logue
e·piph·a·ny
e·pis·co·pal
E·pis·co·pa·lian
ep·i·sode
  ep·i·sod·ic
  ep·i·sod·i·cal
e·pis·tle
  e·pis·to·lar·y
ep·i·taph
ep·i·thet
e·pit·o·me
  e·pit·o·mize
ep·och
  ep·och·al
ep·ox·y
eq·ua·ble
  eq·ua·bil·i·ty
e·qual
  e·qualed
  e·qual·ing
  e·qual·ize
  e·qual·iz·er
  e·qual·ly
e·qua·nim·i·ty
e·qua·tion
e·qua·tor
  e·qua·to·ri·al
e·ques·tri·an
e·qui·an·gu·lar
e·qui·dis·tant
  e·qui·dis·tance
e·qui·lat·er·al
e·qui·lib·ri·um
e·qui·nox
  e·qui·noc·tial
e·quip
  e·quipped
  e·quip·ping

eq·ui·ty
  eq·ui·ta·ble
e·quiv·a·lent
  e·quiv·a·lence
e·quiv·o·cal
  e·quiv·o·cate
  e·quiv·o·ca·tion
  e·quiv·o·ca·tor
e·ra
e·rad·i·cate
  e·rad·i·ca·ble
  e·rad·i·ca·tion
  e·rad·i·ca·tive
  e·rad·i·ca·tor
e·rase
  e·ras·a·ble
  e·ras·er
  e·ra·sure
ere *conj., prep. (before*; see
  air and *heir*)
e·rect
e·rec·tile
e·rec·tion
er·go
er·mine
e·rode
e·ro·sion
e·ro·sive
e·rot·ic
err
er·rand
er·rant
  er·rant·ry
er·rat·ic
er·ra·tum
  pl. er·ra·ta
er·ror
  er·ro·ne·ous
erst·while
e·ruct
  e·ruc·ta·tion
er·u·di·tion
  er·u·dite

e·rupt
  e·rup·tion
  e·rup·tive
er·y·sip·e·las
es·ca·lade
es·ca·la·tor
es·ca·pade
es·cape
  es·ca·pism
es·cape·ment
es·ca·role
es·cheat
es·chew
  es·chew·al
es·cort
es·cri·toire
es·crow
es·cutch·eon
Es·ki·mo
e·soph·a·gus
  pl. e·soph·a·gi
es·o·ter·ic
es·pe·cial
Es·pe·ran·to
es·pi·o·nage
es·pla·nade
es·pouse
  es·pous·al
es·prit
es·py
es·quire
es·say *n., v. (writing*; see
  assay)
  es·say·ist
es·sence
es·sen·tial
  es·sen·ti·al·i·ty
es·tab·lish
es·tate
es·teem
  es·ti·ma·ble
es·thet·ic *or* aes·thet·ic *adj.*
  (referring to art; see
  ascetic)

es·thet·i·cism *or*
 aes·thet·i·cism *n.* (see
 asceticism)
es·ti·mate
 es·ti·ma·tion
es·top
 es·top·pel
es·trange
es·tro·gen
es·tu·ar·y
et cet·er·a
etch·ing
e·ter·nal
e·ter·ni·ty
e·ther
 e·ther·iz·a·tion
e·the·re·al
 e·the·re·al·ize
eth·ics
 eth·i·cal
E·thi·o·pi·a
 E·thi·o·pi·an
eth·nic
 eth·ni·cal
e·thos
eth·yl
eth·yl·ene
e·ti·ol·o·gy
et·i·quette
et·y·mol·o·gy
 et·y·mo·log·i·cal
eu·ca·lyp·tus
Eu·cha·rist
eu·chre
eu·clid·e·an
eu·gen·ics
eu·lo·gy
 pl. eu·lo·gies
 eu·lo·gize
eu·nuch
eu·phe·mism
 eu·phe·mis·tic
 eu·phe·mize

eu·phon·y
 eu·pho·ni·ous
Eu·rope
 Eu·ro·pe·an
eu·sta·chian tube
e·vac·u·ate
 e·vac·u·a·tion
e·vade
e·val·u·ate
 e·val·u·a·tion
ev·a·nes·cence
e·van·ge·lism
 e·van·gel·i·cal
 e·van·ge·list
 e·van·ge·lis·tic
 e·van·ge·lize
e·vap·o·rate
 e·vap·o·ra·tion
 e·vap·o·ra·tive
e·va·sion
e·va·sive
e·vec·tion
e·ven
e·ven·fall
e·ven·hand·ed
eve·ning *n.*
e·ven·ing *v.*
e·ven·ness
e·ven·song
e·vent
 e·vent·ful
e·ven·tide
e·ven·tu·al
 e·ven·tu·al·i·ty
 e·ven·tu·al·ly
 e·ven·tu·ate
ev·er·green
ev·er·last·ing
ev·er·more
e·vert
ev·ery·bod·y
ev·ery·day
ev·ery·thing
ev·ery·where

e·vict
 e·vic·tion
ev·i·dence
 ev·i·dent
 ev·i·den·tial
e·vil·ly
e·vince
e·vis·cer·ate
e·voke
 e·vo·ca·tion
 e·voc·a·tive
ev·o·lu·tion
 ev·o·lu·tion·ar·y
e·volve
e·vul·sion
ewe n. (sheep; see yew and you)
ex·ac·er·bate
 ex·ac·er·ba·tion
ex·act
 ex·act·ing
 ex·ac·ti·tude
ex·ag·ger·ate
 ex·ag·ger·a·tion
 ex·ag·ger·a·tor
ex·alt
 ex·al·ta·tion
ex·am·ine
 ex·am·i·na·tion
ex·am·ple
ex·as·per·ate
 ex·as·per·a·tion
Ex·cal·i·bur
ex·ca·vate
 ex·ca·va·tion
 ex·ca·va·tor
ex·ceed v. (to go beyond; see accede)
 ex·ceed·ing
ex·cel
 ex·celled
 ex·cel·lence
 ex·cel·len·cy
 ex·cel·lent

ex·cel·ling
ex·cel·si·or
ex·cept v., prep., conj. (to leave out; see accept)
 ex·cept·ing
 ex·cep·tion
 ex·cep·tion·a·ble
 ex·cep·tion·al
ex·cerpt
ex·cess n., adj. (too much; see access)
 ex·ces·sive
ex·change
ex·che·quer
ex·cise
 ex·cis·a·ble
 ex·ci·sion
ex·cit·a·ble
 ex·cit·a·bil·i·ty
ex·cite
 ex·ci·ta·tion
 ex·cite·ment
 ex·cit·ing
ex·claim
 ex·clam·a·to·ry
ex·clude
 ex·clu·sion
 ex·clu·sive
ex·com·mu·ni·cate
ex·co·ri·ate
ex·crete
 ex·cre·tion
ex·cru·ci·ate
 ex·cru·ci·a·tion
ex·cul·pate
 ex·cul·pa·tion
 ex·cul·pa·to·ry
ex·cur·sion
ex·cur·sive
ex·cuse
 ex·cus·a·ble
ex·e·crate
 ex·e·cra·tion

ex·e·cute
  ex·e·cu·tion
  ex·e·cu·tion·er
ex·ec·u·tive
ex·ec·u·tor
  ex·ec·u·trix *f.*
ex·e·ge·sis
  pl. ex·e·ge·ses
ex·em·plar
  ex·em·pla·ry
ex·em·pli·fy
ex·empt
  ex·emp·tion
ex·er·cise *v., n. (exertion;* see
  exorcise)
ex·ert
  ex·er·tion
ex·e·unt
ex·hale
  ex·hal·ant
  ex·ha·la·tion
ex·haust
  ex·haust·er
  ex·haust·i·ble
  ex·haus·tion
  ex·haus·tive
ex·hib·it
  ex·hi·bi·tion
  ex·hi·bi·tion·er
  ex·hib·i·tive
  ex·hib·i·tor
  ex·hib·i·to·ry
ex·hil·a·rate
  ex·hil·a·rant
  ex·hil·a·ra·tion
  ex·hil·a·ra·tive
ex·hort
  ex·hor·ta·tion
ex·hume
  ex·hu·ma·tion
ex·i·gen·cy
  pl. ex·i·gen·cies
ex·ile

ex·ist
  ex·is·tence
  ex·is·tent
  ex·is·ten·tial·ism
ex·it
ex·o·dus
ex·on·er·ate
  ex·on·er·a·tion
  ex·on·er·a·tive
ex·o·ra·ble
ex·or·bi·tant
ex·or·cise *v. (to expel;* see
  exercise)
ex·o·ter·ic
ex·ot·ic
ex·pand
  ex·panse
  ex·pan·si·ble
  ex·pan·sion
  ex·pan·sive
ex par·te
ex·pa·ti·ate
ex·pa·tri·ate
  ex·pa·tri·a·tion
ex·pect
  ex·pect·an·cy
  ex·pect·ant
  ex·pec·ta·tion
ex·pec·to·rate
  ex·pec·to·rant
  ex·pec·to·ra·tion
ex·pe·di·ent
  ex·pe·di·en·cy
ex·pe·dite
  ex·pe·di·tious
ex·pe·di·tion
  ex·pe·di·tion·ar·y
ex·pel
  ex·pelled
  ex·pel·ling
ex·pend·i·ture
ex·pense
ex·pen·sive
ex·pe·ri·ence

ex·per·i·ment
  ex·per·i·men·tal
ex·pi·ate
  ex·pi·a·ble
  ex·pi·a·tion
  ex·pi·a·to·ry
ex·pire
  ex·pi·ra·tion
ex·plain·a·ble
ex·plan·a·to·ry
ex·ple·tive
ex·plic·a·ble
ex·pli·cit
ex·plode
  ex·plo·sion
  ex·plo·sive
ex·ploit
  ex·ploi·ta·tion
ex·plore
  ex·plo·ra·tion
  ex·plor·a·to·ry
  ex·plor·er
ex·po·nent
  ex·po·nen·tial
ex·port
  ex·port·a·ble
  ex·por·ta·tion
  ex·port·er
ex·pose *v.*
  ex·po·se *n.*
  ex·pos·er
  ex·po·si·tion
  ex·pos·i·tive
  ex·pos·i·to·ry
  ex·po·sure
ex post fac·to
ex·pos·tu·la·tion
ex·pound
ex·press
  ex·press·age
  ex·press·i·ble
  ex·pres·sion
  ex·pres·sive
  ex·press·man

ex·pul·sion
ex·pul·sive
ex·punge
ex·pur·gate
  ex·pur·ga·tion
  ex·pur·ga·to·ry
ex·quis·ite
ex·sert
ex·tant *adj.* (*currently existing*; see *extent*)
ex·tem·po·rize
  ex·tem·po·ra·ne·ous
  ex·tem·po·rar·y
  ex·tem·po·re
ex·tend
  ex·ten·si·ble
  ex·ten·sion
  ex·ten·sive
ex·tent *n.* (*degree*; see *extant*)
ex·ten·u·ate
  ex·ten·u·a·tion
ex·te·ri·or
ex·ter·mi·nate
  ex·ter·mi·na·tion
  ex·ter·mi·na·tor
  ex·ter·mi·na·to·ry
ex·ter·nal
  ex·ter·nal·ize
  ex·ter·nal·ly
ex·tinct
  ex·tinc·tion
ex·tin·guish·a·ble
ex·tir·pate
ex·tol
  ex·tolled
  ex·tol·ling
ex·tort
  ex·tor·tion
ex·tra
ex·tract
  ex·tract·a·ble
  ex·trac·tion
  ex·trac·tive
  ex·trac·tor

ex·tra·cur·ric·u·lar
ex·tra·dite
 ex·tra·dit·a·ble
 ex·tra·di·tion
ex·tral·i·ty
ex·tra·mar·i·tal
ex·tra·mu·ral
ex·tra·ne·ous
ex·traor·di·nar·y
 ex·traor·di·nar·i·ly
ex·trap·o·late
ex·tra·sen·so·ry
ex·trav·a·gant
 ex·trav·a·gance
 ex·trav·a·gan·za
ex·trav·a·sa·tion
ex·treme
 ex·trem·ist
 ex·trem·i·ty
ex·tri·cate
 ex·tric·a·ble
 ex·tri·ca·tion
ex·trin·sic
ex·tro·vert
ex·trude
 ex·tru·sion
ex·u·ber·ant
 ex·u·ber·ance
ex·ude
 ex·u·da·tion
ex·ult
 ex·ul·ta·tion
eye n. (organ of sight; see
 aye)
 eye·ball
 eye·bright
 eye·brow
 eye·cup
 eye·drop·per
 eye·ful
 eye·glass
 eye·hole
 eye·lash
 eye·less

eye·let n. (small hole; see islet)
eye·lid
eye-o·pen·er
eye·piece
eye·sight
eye·sore
eye·spot
eye·strain
eye·strings
eye·tooth
 pl. eye·teeth
eye·wash
eye·wink
eye·wit·ness
eye v.
 eyed
 eye·ing
ey·rie

F

fa·ble
 fa·bled
fab·ric
fab·ri·cate
 fab·ri·ca·tion
fab·u·lous
fa·cade or fa·çade
face-hard·en
face-lift·ing
fac·er
fac·et
fa·ce·tious
fa·cial
fac·ile
 fa·cil·i·tate
 fa·cil·i·ty
 pl. fa·cil·i·ties
fac·ing
fac·sim·i·le
fac·tion
 fac·tion·al
 fac·tious

fac·ti·tious *adj*. (*artificial*; see
  fictitious)
fac·tor
  fac·to·ri·al
  fac·to·rize
fac·to·ry
fac·tu·al
fac·ul·ta·tive
fac·ul·ty
  pl. fac·ul·ties
fade
fag·ot
  fag·ot·ing
Fahr·en·heit
fa·ience
fail·ure
faint *adj*., *n*., *v*. (*unconscious*;
  see *feint*)
  faint·heart·ed
  faint·ish
fair *adj*., *adv*., *n*. (*beautiful*;
  just; *carnival*; see *fare*)
fair·ground
fair·mind·ed
fair-spok·en
fair trade *n*.
fair-trade *v*.
fair·way
fair-weath·er *adj*.
fair·y *n*., *adj*. (*spirit*; see
  ferry)
  fair·y·land
  fair·y tale *n*.
  fair·y-tale *adj*.
fait ac·com·pli
faith·ful
faith·less
fak·er *n*. (*pretender*; see
  fakir)
fa·kir *n*. (*ascetic*; see *faker*)
fal·con
Falk·land
fal·la·cy
  fal·la·cious

fall·en
fal·li·ble
  fal·li·bil·i·ty
fal·lo·pi·an tubes
fall out *v*.
fall·out *n*.
fal·low
false·hood
fal·set·to
fal·si·fy
  fal·si·fi·ca·tion
  fal·si·fi·er
fal·si·ty
fal·ter
fa·mil·ial
fa·mil·iar
  fa·mil·iar·i·ty
  fa·mil·iar·ize
fam·i·ly
  pl. fam·i·lies
fam·ine
fam·ish
fa·mous
fa·nat·ic
  fa·nat·i·cal
  fa·nat·i·cism
fan·cy
  fan·ci·er
  fan·ci·ful
  fan·cy-free
  fan·cy·work
fan·fare
fan·light
fanned
fan·ning
fan·tail
fan·ta·sia
fan·tas·tic
  fan·tas·ti·cal
fan·ta·sy
far·ad
far·a·day
far·a·way

farce
  far·ci·cal
fare *v., n.* (*fee; see fair*)
fare·well
far·fetched
fa·ri·na
  far·i·na·ceous
farm·er
  farm·er·ette
farm·hand
farm·house
farm·ing
farm·land
farm·stead
farm·yard
far-off
far·ra·go
far-reach·ing
far·row
far·see·ing
far·sight·ed
far·ther *adj., adv.* (*more distant; see further*)
  far·ther·most
  far·thest
far·thing
fas·ci·nate
  fas·ci·na·tion
  fas·ci·na·tor
fas·cism
fash·ion·a·ble
fas·ten·er
fas·tid·i·ous
fas·tig·i·ate
fast·ness
fa·tal·ist
  fa·tal·is·tic
fa·tal·i·ty
fa·tal·ly
fate
  fat·ed
  fate·ful
fa·ther
  fa·ther·hood

fa·ther-in-law
  pl. fa·thers-in-law
fa·ther·land
fa·ther·less
fa·ther·like
fath·om
  fath·om·a·ble
  fath·om·less
fa·tigue
fat·ten
fat·ty
fa·tu·i·ty
fat·u·ous
fau·cet
fault·less
fault·y
  fault·i·ly
  fault·i·ness
faun *n.* (*half-animal god; see fawn*)
fau·na
faux pas *s., pl.*
fa·vor·a·ble
fa·vored
fa·vor·er
fa·vor·ite
  fa·vor·it·ism
fawn *n., v.* (*young deer; see faun*)
fay *n.* (*fairy; see fey*)
faze *v.* (*to disturb; see phase*)
fe·al·ty
fear·ful
fear·less
fear·some
fea·si·ble
  fea·si·bil·i·ty
feat *n.* (*accomplishment; see feet and fete*)
feath·er·bed·ding
feath·er·brained
feath·er·edge
feath·er·stitch
feath·er·weight

feath·er·y
fea·ture
  fea·ture·less
feb·ri·fuge
Feb·ru·ar·y
fe·cal
fe·ces
fe·cund
  fe·cun·di·ty
fed·er·al·ism
  fed·er·al·ist
  fed·er·al·i·za·tion
  fed·er·al·ize
fed·er·ate
  fed·er·a·tion
fee·ble
  fee·ble·mind·ed
feed·back
feed·er
feed·stuff
feet *n.* (*plural of foot*; see *feat* and *fete*)
feign
  feigned
feint *n.*, *v.* (*trick*; see *faint*)
feld·spar
fe·lic·i·tate
  fe·lic·i·ta·tion
fe·lic·i·ty
  fe·lic·i·tous
fe·line
fel·low·ship
fel·on
  fe·lo·ni·ous
  fel·o·ny
felt·ing
fe·male
fem·i·nine
  fem·i·nin·i·ty
  fem·i·nism
  fem·i·ni·za·tion
fe·mur
fence
  fence·less

fenc·er
fenc·ing
fend·er
fen·es·tra·tion
fen·nel
fer·ment
  fer·ment·a·ble
  fer·men·ta·tion
fern·er·y
fe·ro·cious
  fe·roc·i·ty
fer·ret
Fer·ris wheel
fer·rous
fer·rule *n.* (*metal ring*; see *ferule*)
fer·ry *n.*, *v.* (*boat*; see *fairy*)
  fer·ried
  fer·ry·boat
fer·tile
  fer·til·i·ty
  fer·til·i·za·tion
  fer·til·ize
  fer·til·iz·er
fer·ule *n.* (*rod*; see *ferrule*)
fer·vent
fer·vid
fer·vor
fes·cue
fes·tal
fes·ter
fes·ti·val
  fes·tive
  fes·tiv·i·ty
fes·toon
fetch·ing
fete *or* fête *n.* (*celebration*; see *feat* and *feet*)
fe·tish·ism
fet·lock
fet·ter
fet·tle
fe·tus
  pl. fe·tus·es

feu·dal·ism
feu·dal·ize
feu·dal·ly
feu·da·to·ry
feud·ist
feuil·le·ton
fe·ver
  fe·ver·ish
  fe·ver·weed
fey *adj.* (*visionary*; see *fay*)
fi·an·cé *m.* (see *fiancée*)
  fi·an·cée *f.* (see *fiancé*)
fi·as·co
  pl. fi·as·coes *or* fi·as·cos
fi·at
fi·ber·board
Fi·ber·glas (*trademark*)
fi·ber glass
fib·ril·la·tion
fib·rin·o·gen
fi·brous
fib·u·la
  pl. fib·u·lae *or* fib·u·las
fick·le
fic·tion
  fic·tion·al
  fic·ti·tious *adj.* (*unreal*; see
    factitious)
fid·dle
  fid·dler
  fid·dle·stick
fi·del·i·ty
fid·get·y
fi·du·ci·ar·y
field corn
field day
field·er
field glass
field goal
field house
field·piece
fiend·ish
fierce
fi·er·y

fi·es·ta
fif·teen
fif·ty
  fif·ti·eth
fig·ment
fig·ure
  fig·u·ra·tive
  fig·ured
  fig·ure·head
fig·u·rine
Fi·ji
fil·a·ment
fil·a·ture
fil·bert
fil·i·al
fil·i·bus·ter
fil·i·gree
fil·ing
Fil·i·pi·no
fill·er
fil·let
fill·ing
film·strip
fil·ter *n.*, *v.* (*to purify*; see
  philter)
filth·y
  filth·i·ness
fi·nal
  fi·na·le
  fi·nal·ist
  fi·nal·i·ty
  fi·nal·ly
fi·nance
  fi·nan·cial
  fin·an·cier
find·er
find·ing
fine·ly
fine·ness
fin·er·y
fine·spun
fi·nesse
fin·ger
  fin·ger bowl

fin·ger·print
fin·ger·tip
fin·i·cal
fin·ick·y
fin·is
fin·ish
  fin·ished
  fin·ish·er
fi·nite
Fin·land
fir *n.* (*tree*; see *fur*)
fire ant
fire·arm
fire·ball
fire·bird
fire blight
fire·boat
fire·box
fire·brand
fire·break
fire·brick
fire·bug
fire·clay
fire·crack·er
fire-cured
fire·damp
fire·dog
fire-eat·er
fire·fly
fire·house
fire i·rons
fire·light
fire·men
fire·place
fire·plug
fire·pow·er
fire·proof
fire sale
fire screen
fire·side
fire·stone
fire·trap
fire wall
fire·wa·ter

fire·wood
fire·work
fir·ing
fir·kin
firm·ly
firm·ness
first·born
first class *n.*
  first-class *adj.*
first·hand
first-rate
fis·cal
fish·er *n.* (*one who fishes*; see *fissure*)
fish·er·man
fish·er·y
fish·hook
fish·i·ly
fish·mon·ger
fish·plate
fish stick
fish sto·ry
fish·tail
fish·wife
fish·y
fis·sion
  fis·sion·a·ble
fis·sure *n.* (*crack*; see *fisher*)
fist·ic
fist·i·cuffs
fis·tu·la
fit·ful
fit·ness
fit·ted
fit·ting
five·fold
fix·a·ble
fix·ate
  fix·a·tion
  fix·a·tive
fix·ture
fiz·zle
flab·ber·gast

flab·by
  flab·bi·ness
flac·cid
flac·on
flag·el·late
  flag·el·la·tion
flag·ging
flag·man
flag·on
flag·pole
fla·grant
  fla·gran·cy
flag·ship
flag·staff
flag·stone
flair *n.* (*aptitude*; see *flare*)
flak·y
flam·boy·ant
flame·out
flame·proof
fla·min·go
flam·ma·ble
fla·neur
flan·nel·ette
flap·jack
flapped
flap·ping
flare *n.*, *v.* (*signal*; see *flair*)
  flare-up
flash·back
flash·board
flash·bulb
flash card
flash·ing
flash·light
flash point
flash·y
  flash·i·ly
  flash·i·ness
flat·bed
flat·boat
flat·car
flat·foot *n.*
  flat·foot·ed *adj.*

flat·i·ron
flat·ten
flat·ter
  flat·ter·er
  flat·ter·y
flat·top
flat·u·lent
flat·ware
flat·work
flaunt
fla·vor·ful
flax·seed
flax·y
flea *n.* (*bug*; see *flee*)
  flea·bite
  flea-bit·ten
fledg·ling
flee *v.* (*run away*; see *flea*)
  flee·ing
flesh·ly
flesh·pot
flesh·y
  flesh·i·ness
fleur-de-lis
  pl. fleurs-de-lis
flew *v.* (*pt. of fly*; see *flu* and *flue*)
flex·i·ble
  flex·i·bil·i·ty
flick·er
fli·er (see *flyer*)
flight deck
flight·i·ness
flight pay
flim·flam
flim·sy
  flim·si·ly
  flim·si·ness
flin·ders
flint glass
flint·y
  flint·i·ness
flip-flop

flip·pant
flip·pan·cy
flipped
flip·per
flip·ping
flir·ta·tion
flir·ta·tious
flitch
flit·ter
fliv·ver
float·ing
floc·cu·lent
floe n. (ice; see flow)
flood·gate
flood·light
flood·wa·ter
floor·board
floor·ing
floor lamp
floor·walk·er
flop·house
flop·ping
flop·py
flop·py disk
flo·ral
flo·res·cence
flo·res·cent
flo·ri·cul·ture
flor·id
Flor·i·da
flor·in
flo·ta·tion
flo·til·la
flot·sam
flounce
flounc·ing
floun·der
flour n., v. (ground wheat; see flower)
flour·y
flour·ish
flow v., n. (circulate; see floe)
flow·chart

flow·er n., v. (plant; see flour)
flow·er·pot
flow·er·y
flown
flu n. (disease; see flew and flue)
fluc·tu·ate
fluc·tu·a·tion
flue n. (chimney; see flew and flu)
flu·ent
flu·en·cy
fluff·y
fluff·i·ness
flu·id
flu·id ex·tract
flu·id·i·ty
flu·id ounce
flu·o·res·cent
flu·o·ride
flu·o·ri·date
flu·o·ri·da·tion
flu·o·rine
flu·o·ro·scope
flur·ry
flut·ter
flut·ter·y
flux
fly·blown
fly-boy n. (pilot)
fly·by
fly-by-night
fly·catch·er
fly·er (see flier)
fly·ing
fly·leaf
fly·pa·per
fly·speck
fly·wheel
foam·y
fo·cal
fo·cal·ize
fo·cus
pl. fo·cus·es or fo·ci

fo·cused
fo·cus·ing
fod·der
foe·man
fog·bound
fog·gy *adj.* *(misty; see fogy)*
fog·horn
fo·gy *or* **fo·gey** *or* **fo·gie** *n.*
  (old-fashioned; see foggy)
fold·er
fo·li·age
fo·li·ate
  fo·li·a·tion
fol·ic ac·id
fo·li·o
folk·lore
folk·sy
  folks·i·ness
folk·tale
folk·way
fol·low
  fol·low·er
fol·low·ing
fol·low up *v.*
fol·low-up *n., adj.*
fol·ly
fo·ment
  fo·men·ta·tion
fon·dant
fon·dle
  fon·dler
fond·ly
fon·due *or* **fon·du**
font
fon·ta·nel *or* **fon·ta·nelle**
food·stuff
fool·er·y
fool·har·dy
  fool·har·di·ness
fool·ish
fool·proof
fools·cap *or* **fool's-cap** *n.*
foot·ball
foot·bath

foot·board
foot brake
foot·bridge
foot·can·dle
foot·ed
foot·fall
foot fault *n.*
  foot·fault *v.*
foot·gear
foot·hill
foot·hold
foot·ing
foot·less
foot·light
foot·lock·er
foot·loose
foot·man
foot·mark
foot·note
foot·pad
foot·path
foot-pound
foot·print
foot·race
foot·rest
foot rule
foot·step
foot·stool
foot-ton
foot·walk
foot·way
foot·wear
foot·work
fop·pish
for *prep., conj. (purpose; be-*
  cause; see fore and four)
for·age
for·ay
for·bear *v. (to endure; see*
  forebear)
  for·bear·ance
  for·bore
for·bid
  for·bade

for·bid·den
for·bid·der
for·bid·ding
forced
force·ful
for·ceps
forc·i·ble
fore *n., adj., adv.* (*front*; see *for* and *four*)
fore·arm
fore·bear *n.* (*ancestor*; see *forbear*)
fore·bode
fore·bod·ing
fore·cast
fore·cast·er
fore·cas·tle
fore·close
fore·clo·sure
fore·doom
fore·fa·ther
fore·fin·ger
fore·foot
fore·front
fore·go
fore·go·ing
fore·gone
fore·ground
fore·hand
fore·hand·ed
fore·head
for·eign
for·eign·er
fore·knowl·edge
fore·man
fore·mast
fore·most
fore·name
fore·noon
fo·ren·sic
fore·or·dain
fore·part
fore·quar·ter

fore·run
fore·run·ner
fore·see
fore·shad·ow
fore·short·en
fore·sight
for·est
for·est·a·tion
for·est·er
for·est·ry
fore·stall
fore·tell
fore·thought
for·ev·er
fore·warn
fore·word *n.* (*preface*; see *forward*)
for·feit
for·feit·ure
for·gave
for·ger·y
forg·er
for·get·ful
for·get-me-not
for·get·ta·ble
for·get·ting
for·give·ness
for·giv·ing
for·go *or* **fore·go**
for·got
for·lorn
for·mal
for·mal·i·ty
for·mal·ize
for·mal·ly
form·al·de·hyde
for·mat
for·ma·tion
for·ma·tive
for·mer *adj.*
form·er *n.*
For·mi·ca (*trademark*)
for·mi·da·ble
form·less

for·mu·la
  pl. for·mu·las *or* for·mu·lae
  for·mu·late
  for·mu·la·tion
for·sake
for·sooth
for·swear
  for·sworn
for·syth·i·a
fort *n.* (*fortified place; see forte*)
for·ta·lice
forte *n., adj., adv.* (*strong point; see fort*)
forth
  forth·com·ing
  forth·right
  forth·with
for·ti·fy
  for·ti·fi·ca·tion
  for·ti·fi·er
for·tis·si·mo
for·ti·tude
fort·night
FOR·TRAN
for·tress
for·tu·i·ty
  for·tu·i·tous
for·tu·nate
for·tune
  for·tune-tell·er
for·ty
  for·ti·eth
for·ty-nin·er
fo·rum
for·ward *adj., adv., n.* (*direction; see foreword*)
for·ward *v.*
  for·ward·er
for·wards *adv.*
fos·sil
  fos·sil·if·er·ous
fos·ter
foul *adj., v., n.* (*dirty; out of bounds; see fowl*)

foul·mouthed
foun·da·tion
found·er *n.*
foun·der *v.*
found·ling
found·ry
foun·tain
foun·tain·head
four *n., adj., prep.* (*number; see for and fore*)
  four-flush·er
  four-in-hand
  four·score
  four·some
  fourth
four·teen
  four·teenth
fowl *n., v.* (*bird; see foul*)
fox·hole
fox·hound
fox·i·ness
fox ter·ri·er
fox-trot
foy·er
fra·cas
frac·tion
  frac·tion·al
frac·tious
frac·ture
frag·ile
  fra·gil·i·ty
frag·ment
  frag·men·tar·y
fra·grant
  fra·grance
frail·ty
fram·er
frame-up
frame·work
franc *n.* (*coin; see frank*)
France
fran·chise
Fran·cis·can
frank *adj., v., n.* (*candid; see franc*)

frank·furt·er
frank·in·cense
fran·tic
fra·ter·nal
fra·ter·ni·ty
frat·er·nize
frat·ri·cide
Frau
fraud·u·lent
  fraud·u·lence
freak·ish
freck·le
free·board
free·born
freed·man
free·dom
free-for-all
free·hand
free·hold
free lance *n*.
free-lance *adj*., *v*.
free·ly
free·man
Free·ma·son
free·ma·son·ry
free·stone
free·think·er
free·way
freeze *v*., *n*. (*solidify*; see
  frieze)
  freeze-dry *v*.
  freez·er
  froze
  fro·zen
freight·er
fre·net·ic
fren·zy
Fre·on (*trademark*)
fre·quent
  fre·quen·cy
fres·co
  pl. fres·coes *or* fres·cos
fresh·en
fresh·wa·ter

fret·ful
fret·saw
fret·work
fri·a·ble
fri·ar *n*. (*monk*; see *fryer*)
fric·as·see
fric·tion
  fric·tion·al
Fri·day
friend·less
friend·ly
  friend·li·ness
friend·ship
frieze *n*. (*sculptured wall*; see
  freeze)
frig·ate
fright
  fright·en
  fright·ened
  fright·ful
frig·id
  fri·gid·i·ty
frip·per·y
Fris·bee (*trademark*)
frit·ter
friv·o·lous
  fri·vol·i·ty
frog·man
frol·ic
  frol·icked
  frol·ick·ing
  frol·ic·some
front·age
fron·tal
fron·tier
  fron·tiers·man
fron·tis·piece
front·less
front man
front mat·ter
frost·bite
frost·i·ness
frost·ing
fro·ward

fru·gal
  fru·gal·i·ty
  fru·gal·ly
fruit·cake
fruit fly
fruit·ful
fru·i·tion
fruit·less
frus·trate
  frus·tra·tion
fry·er n. (*chicken*; see *friar*)
fud·dy-dud·dy
fu·el
  fu·eled
  fu·el·ing
fu·gi·tive
ful·crum
ful·fill
  ful·fill·ing
  ful·fill·ment
full·back
full-blood·ed
full-blown
full-bod·ied
full dress n.
full·dress adj.
full-fledged
full-length
full·ness
full-scale
full time n.
full-time adj.
ful·ly
ful·mi·nate
ful·some
fum·ble
fu·mi·gate
  fu·mi·ga·tion
  fu·mi·ga·tor
func·tion
  func·tion·al
  func·tion·ar·y
fun·da·men·tal·ism

fu·ner·al
  fu·ne·re·al
fun·gi·ble
fun·gus
  pl. fun·gi or fun·gus·es
  fun·gi·cide
  fun·gous or fun·gus adj.
fu·nic·u·lar
fun·nel
  fun·neled
  fun·nel·ing
fun·ny
fur n., v. (*animal pelt*; see *fir*)
  fur·ri·er
  fur·ring
  fur·ry adj. (*with fur*; see *fury*)
fur·be·low
fur·bish
fu·ri·ous
fur·long
fur·lough
fur·nace
fur·nish
fur·ni·ture
fu·ror
fur·row
fur·ther adj., adv., v. (*in addition*; see *farther*)
  fur·thest adj., adv. (see *farthest*)
fur·ther·ance
fur·ther·more
fur·ther·most adj. (see *farthermost*)
fur·tive
fu·ry n. (*rage*; see *furry*)
furze
fu·se·lage
fu·si·ble
  fu·si·bil·i·ty
fu·sion
fuss·budg·et
fuss·y
  fuss·i·ly

fuss·i·ness
fu·tile
  fu·til·i·ty
fu·ture
  fu·tu·ri·ty
fuzz·y
  fuzz·i·ness

G

ga·ble
gad·a·bout
gad·fly
gad·get
ga·droon
Gael·ic
gag·man
gai·e·ty
gain·er
gain·ful
gain·say
gait *n.* (*walk*; see *gate*)
gai·ter
gal·ax·y
  ga·lac·tic
gal·lant
  gal·lant·ry
gal·le·on
gal·ler·y
  pl. gal·ler·ies
gal·ley
  pl. gal·leys
gal·li·cism
gal·lon
gal·lop
  gal·loped
  gal·lop·ing
gal·lows
gall·stone
gal·van·ic
gal·va·nize
  gal·va·ni·za·tion
gam·bit

gam·ble *v., n.* (*to bet*; see *gambol*)
  gam·bler
  gam·bling
gam·bol *n., v.* (*to frolic*; see *gamble*)
  gam·boled
  gam·bol·ing
gam·brel
game·keep·er
game·ness
games·man·ship
game·ster
gam·ma glob·u·lin
Gan·dhi·an
gan·gli·on
gang·plank
gan·grene
gang·ster
gang·way
gant·let
ga·rage
gar·bage
gar·den
  gar·den·er
gar·de·nia
gar·gle
gar·goyle
gar·land
gar·lic
gar·ment
gar·ner
gar·net
gar·nish
  gar·nish·ee
gar·ri·son
gar·ru·lous
  gar·ru·li·ty
gar·ter
gas·bag
gas cham·ber
gas·e·ous
gas·es
gas fit·ter

gas·house
gas·ket
gas·light
gas log
gas mask
gas·o·line
gassed
gas·sing
gas sta·tion
gas·sy
  gas·si·ness
gas·tight
gas·trec·to·my
gas·tric
gas·tri·tis
gas·tron·o·my
  gas·tro·nom·ic
gas·works
gate *n.* (*entrance*; see *gait*)
  gate·way
gath·er·ing
gauche *adj.* (*clumsy*; see
  gouache)
gauge
gaunt·let
gauze
gav·el
ga·votte
gay·ness
ga·ze·bo
ga·zelle
ga·zette
gear·ing
geck·o
ge·fil·te fish
gei·sha
gel *n., v.* (*jelly*; see *jell*)
gel·a·tin
  ge·la·ti·nize
  ge·lat·i·nous
geld·ing
Gem·i·ni
gen·darme
ge·ne·al·o·gy

gen·er·al
  gen·er·a·lis·si·mo
  gen·er·al·i·ty
  gen·er·al·i·za·tion
  gen·er·al·ize
  gen·er·al·ly
  gen·er·al·ship
gen·er·ate
  gen·er·a·tion
  gen·er·a·tive
  gen·er·a·tor
ge·ner·ic
gen·er·ous
  gen·er·os·i·ty
gen·e·sis
  pl. gen·e·ses
ge·net·ics
  ge·net·i·cist
Ge·ne·va
ge·nial
  ge·ni·al·i·ty
  ge·nial·ly
gen·i·tal
gen·i·tive
ge·nius
gen·o·cide
gen·re
gen·teel
gen·tile
gen·til·i·ty
gen·tle
  gen·tle·man
  gen·tle·ness
  gent·ly
gen·try
gen·u·flect
  gen·u·flec·tion
gen·u·ine
ge·nus
geo·cen·tric
geo·des·ic
geo·det·ic
ge·og·ra·phy
  ge·og·ra·pher

geo·graph·ic
geo·graph·i·cal
ge·ol·o·gy
  geo·log·ic
  geo·log·i·cal
  ge·ol·o·gist
ge·om·e·try
  ge·om·e·ter
  geo·met·ric
  geo·met·ri·cal
  geo·me·tri·cian
geo·mor·phic
geo·phys·ics
Geor·gia
geo·ther·mal
ge·ra·ni·um
ger·bil
ger·i·at·rics
ger·mane
Ger·man·y
  Ger·man
ger·mi·cide
ger·mi·nate
  ger·mi·na·tion
germ·proof
ger·on·tol·o·gy
ger·ry·man·der
ger·und
ge·stalt
Ge·sta·po n.
ges·tate
  ges·ta·tion
ges·tic·u·late
  ges·tic·u·la·tion
  ges·tic·u·la·to·ry
ges·ture
get·a·way
get·to·geth·er
gey·ser
Ghan·a
ghast·ly
  ghast·li·ness
gher·kin

ghet·to
  pl. ghet·tos or ghet·toes
ghost
  ghost·li·ness
  ghost·write
ghoul
gi·ant
gib·ber·ish
gibe n., v. (tease; see jibe)
gib·let
Gi·bral·tar
gid·dy
  gid·di·ly
  gid·di·ness
gi·gan·tic
gig·gle
gig·o·lo
gild v. (to overlay with gold;
  see guild)
gilt v., adj., n. (thin covering of gold; see guilt)
gilt-edged
gim·bals
gim·crack
gim·let
gim·mick
gin·ger
  gin·ger ale
  gin·ger·bread
  gin·ger·ly
  gin·ger·snap
ging·ham
gin·gi·vi·tis
gink·go or ging·ko
gi·raffe
gird·er
gir·dle
  gir·dling
girl·hood
girl·ish
girth
gist
giv·en
giv·ing

giz·zard
gla·cial
  gla·cial·ly
gla·ci·a·tion
gla·cier *n.* (*ice;* see *glazier*)
glad·den
glad·i·a·tor
  glad·i·a·to·ri·al
glad·i·o·lus
glad·ly
glam·our *or* glam·or
  glam·or·ize *or* glam·our·ize
  glam·or·ous *or* glam·our·ous
glance
  glanc·ing
glan·du·lar
glans
glar·ing
glass·blow·er
glass·ful
glass·ine
glass·ware
glass wool
glass·y
  glass·i·ly
  glass·i·ness
glau·co·ma
glaze
  gla·zier *n.* (*glassmaker;* see
  glacier)
gleam·y
glean
glee·ful
glid·er
glim·mer·ing
glimpse
glis·ten
glit·ter
  glit·ter·y
gloam·ing
glob·al·ly
glob·u·lar
glock·en·spiel

gloom·y
  gloom·i·ly
  gloom·i·ness
glo·ri·fy
  glo·ri·fi·ca·tion
  glo·ri·fi·er
glo·ry
  glo·ri·ous
glos·sa·ry
gloss·y
  gloss·i·ly
  gloss·i·ness
glow·er
glow·worm
glu·cose
glue
  glued
  glu·ey
  glu·i·er
  glu·i·est
  glu·ing
glum
  glum·ly
  glum·mer
  glum·mest
  glum·ness
glu·ten
  glu·ten·ous (*sticky;* see
  glutinous)
  glu·tin·ous (*like glue;* see
  glutenous)
glut·ton
  glut·ton·ous
  glut·ton·y
glyc·er·in *or* glyc·er·ine
gly·co·gen
gnarl
  gnarled
gnash
gnat
gnaw
gneiss
gnome
gno·mon

gnu *n.* (*animal;* see *knew* and *new*)
goal
  goal·post
gob·ble
  gob·bler
gob·let
gob·lin
go-cart
god·child
god·daugh·ter
god·dess
god·fa·ther
god·head
Go·di·va
god·less
god·like
god·ly
  god·li·ness
god·moth·er
god·par·ent
god·send
god·son
God·speed
Goe·the
gog·gle
go·ing
goi·ter
gold·brick
gold·en
gold·en·rod
gold·field
gold-filled
gold·fish
gold foil
gold leaf
gold·smith
Go·li·ath
gon·do·la
  gon·do·lier
goo
good-bye *or* good-by
good-heart·ed
good·hu·mored

good·ly
good-na·tured
good·ness
good-tem·pered
good·will
goo·ey
  goo·i·er
  goo·i·est
goof·i·ness
goo·gol
goose·ber·ry
goose·flesh
goose·neck
goose step *n.*
goose-step *v.*
go·pher
gorge
gor·geous
Gor·gon·zo·la
go·ril·la *n.* (*ape;* see *guerrilla*)
gor·man·dize
gos·pel
gos·sa·mer
gos·sip
  gos·sip·ing
Goth·ic
gouache *n.* (*painting;* see *gauche*)
gou·lash
gourd
gour·mand
gour·met
gout
gov·ern
  gov·ern·a·ble
  gov·er·ness
  gov·ern·ment
  gov·ern·men·tal
gov·er·nor·ship
grab
  grabbed
  grab·bing
grace·ful
grace·less

gra·cious
gra·da·tion
gra·di·ent
grad·u·al
grad·u·ate
  grad·u·a·tion
graft·er
gram·mar
  gram·mar·i·an
  gram·mat·i·cal
Gram·o·phone (*trademark*)
gra·na·ry
grand·aunt
grand·child
grand·daugh·ter
gran·deur
grand·fa·ther
gran·dil·o·quence
  gran·dil·o·quent
gran·di·ose
gran·di·o·so
grand·moth·er
grand·neph·ew
grand·niece
grand·sire
grand·son
grand·stand
grand·un·cle
grang·er
gran·ite
grant·ee
grant-in-aid
  pl. grants-in-aid
grant·or
gran·u·lar
gran·u·late
  gran·u·la·tion
  gran·u·la·tor
grape·fruit
grape·shot
grape·vine
graph·ic
  graph·i·cal
graph·ite

grap·nel
grap·ple
grasp·ing
grass·hop·per
grass·y
grate *v., n.* (*latticed frame;*
  see *great*)
  grat·ing
grate·ful
grat·i·fy
  grat·i·fi·ca·tion
  grat·i·fy·ing
grat·is
grat·i·tude
gra·tu·i·tous
gra·tu·i·ty
gra·va·men
  pl. gra·va·mens *or* gra·vam·i·na
grave·clothes
grav·el
grave·stone
grave·yard
grav·i·tate
  grav·i·ta·tion
  grav·i·ta·tive
grav·i·ty
gra·vy
gray·beard
gray·ish
gra·zier
greas·er
grease·wood
greas·y
  greas·i·ly
great *adj., adv., n.* (*large;*
  impressive; see *grate*)
  great·coat
  great·heart·ed
Gre·cian
Greece
  Greek
greed·y
  greed·i·ly
green·back

green·er·y
green-eyed
green·gage
green·gro·cer
green·horn
green·house
green·ing
green·ish
Green·land
green·room
greet·ing
gre·gar·i·ous
Gre·go·ri·an
grem·lin
Gren·a·da
gre·nade
   gren·a·dier
gren·a·din *or* gren·a·dine
grey·hound
grid·dle
   grid·dle cake
grid·i·ron
griev·ance
griev·ous
grif·fin *or* grif·fon
grill *n., v.* (*cooking device;*
   see *grille*)
   grill·room
grille *or* grill *n.* (*grating;* see
   grill)
   grill·work
grim·ace
grim·ly
grim·ness
grin
   grinned
   grin·ning
grind·stone
grip *n., v.* (*to hold;* see *gripe*
   and *grippe*)
   grip·ping
gripe *v., n.* (*to complain;* see
   grip and *grippe*)

grippe *n.* (*influenza;* see *grip*
   and *gripe*)
gris·ly *adj.* (*gruesome;* see
   grizzly and *gristly*)
gris·tle
   gris·tly *adj.* (*cartilage;* see
   grisly and *grizzly*)
grist·mill
grit
   grit·ted
   grit·ting
   grit·ty
griz·zle
   griz·zled
   griz·zly *adj., n.* (*gray; a bear;*
   see *grisly* and *gristly*)
groan *n., v.* (*moan;* see
   grown)
gro·cer·y
   pl. gro·cer·ies
grog·gy
groove
gross·ly
gro·tesque
grouch
ground·hog
ground·less
ground·ling
ground·wa·ter
ground·work
grove
grov·el
   grov·eled
   grov·el·ing
grow·er
growl·er
grown *v., adj.* (*mature;* see
   groan)
grub
   grubbed
   grub·bing
grub·stake
grudge
   grudg·ing·ly

gru·el
gru·el·ing
grue·some
grum·ble
grump·y
Guad·e·loupe
Guam
guar·an·tee *n., v. (to pledge security; see guaranty)*
guar·an·tor
guar·an·ty *n., v. (something given as security; see guarantee)*
guard·house
guard·i·an
  guard·i·an·ship
guards·man
Gua·te·ma·la
gu·ber·na·to·ri·al
Guern·sey
guer·ril·la *or* guerilla *n., adj. (soldier; see gorilla)*
guess·ti·mate
guess·work
guest·house
guest room
guid·a·ble
guid·ance
guild *n. (organization; see gild)*
  guild·hall
guile·less·ness
guil·lo·tine
guilt *n. (culpability; see gilt)*
guilt·y
  guilt·i·ly
  guilt·i·ness
  guilt·less
guimpe
Guin·ea
guise
gui·tar
gull·i·ble
  gull·i·bil·i·ty

gul·ly
  pl. gul·lies
gum·drop
gummed
gum·my
gump·tion
gun·boat
gun·cot·ton
gun·fire
gun·flint
gun·lock
gun·man
gun·met·al
gun·ner·y
gun·pow·der
gun room
gun·run·ner
gun·shot
gun·wale *or* gun·nel *or* gun·whale
gup·py
gur·gle
Gur·kha
  pl. Gur·kha *or* Gur·khas
gush·er
gus·to
gut·ta-per·cha
gut·ter
gut·ter·snipe
gut·tur·al
Guy·a·na
guz·zle
gym·na·si·um
  pl. gym·na·si·ums *or* gym·na·si·a
gym·nast
gym·nas·tic
gy·ne·col·o·gy
gyp·sy
gy·rate
  gy·ra·tion
gy·ro·com·pass
gy·ro·scope
gy·ro·sta·bi·liz·er

H

ha·be·as cor·pus
hab·er·dash·er
  hab·er·dash·er·y
ha·bil·i·tate
hab·it
  hab·i·tude
hab·it·a·ble
ha·bi·tant
hab·i·tat
hab·i·ta·tion
ha·bit·u·al
  ha·bit·u·ate
ha·ci·en·da
hack·man
hack·ney
  hack·neyed
hack·saw
had·dock
  pl. had·dock *or* had·docks
hag·gard
hag·gle
ha·gi·og·ra·phy
hail *n., v. (ice; to call; see*
  hale)
  hail·stone
  hail·storm
hair *n. (filaments; see hare*
  and heir)
  hair·breadth
  hair·brush
  hair·cut
  hair·do
  hair·dress·er
  hair·line
  hair·net
  hair·piece
  hair·pin
  hair-rais·ing
  hair shirt
  hair·split·ter
  hair·split·ting
  hair·spring

hair·y
  hair·i·ness
Hai·ti
  Hai·tian
hal·cy·on
hale *adj., v. (healthy; see*
  hail)
half
  pl. halves
half·back
half-baked
half-breed
half broth·er
half-du·plex
half·heart·ed
half-life
half-mast
half-moon
half note
half·pen·ny
half sole *n.*
half-sole *v.*
half step
half ti·tle
half·tone
half-track
half-truth
half·way
hal·i·but
  pl. hal·i·but *or* hal·i·buts
hal·i·to·sis
hall *n. (passageway; see haul)*
hall·mark
hal·low
Hal·low·een
hal·lu·ci·nate
  hal·lu·ci·na·tion
  hal·lu·ci·na·to·ry
hall·way
hal·ter
halve
ham·burg·er
ham·let
ham·mer

ham·mock
ham·per
ham·ster
ham·string
hand·bag
hand·ball
hand·bill
hand·book
hand·car
hand·cart
hand·clasp
hand·cuff
hand·ed·ness
hand·ful
hand·grip
hand·hold
hand·i·cap
  hand·i·capped
  hand·i·cap·ping
hand·i·craft
hand·i·ly
hand·i·work
hand·ker·chief
han·dle
  han·dled
  han·dler
  han·dling
han·dle·bar
hand let·ter *n.*
hand-let·ter *v.*
hand·line
hand·maid *n.* (*servant;* see *hand;* see *handmaid*)
hand·maid *n.* (*servant;* see *handmade*)
hand-me-down
hand or·gan
hand·out *n.*
hand out *v.*
hand·pick
hand·rail
hand·saw
hands down *adv.*
hands-down *adj.*

hand·set *n.*
hand-set *adj.*
hand·shake
hand·some
hand·spike
hand·spring
hand·stamp
hand·stand
hand truck
hand·work
hand·wo·ven
hand·writ·ing
han·dy·man
hang·ar *n.* (*airplane shelter;* see *hanger*)
hang·dog
hang·er *n.* (*that which hangs;* see *hangar*)
hang·ing
hang·man
hang·nail
hang out *v.*
hang·out *n.*
hang·o·ver
han·ker
han·ky-pan·ky
han·som
hap·haz·ard
hap·less
hap·ly
hap·pen
  hap·pen·ing
hap·pen·stance
hap·py
  hap·pi·ly
  hap·pi·ness
hap·py-go-luck·y
ha·rangue
ha·rass
  ha·rass·ing
har·bin·ger
har·bor
hard-bit·ten
hard-boiled

hard·bought
hard·en
hard·fist·ed
hard·head·ed
hard·heart·ed
hard·hit·ting
hard·ly
hard·ness
hard·pan
hard sauce
hard·ship
hard·tack
hard·top
hard·ware
hard·wood
hard·work·ing
har·dy
 har·di·hood
 har·di·ly
 har·di·ness
hare *n.* (*rabbit*; see *hair* and *heir*)
 hare·brained
 hare·lip
har·em
har·le·quin
 har·le·quin·ade
harm·ful
harm·less
har·mon·i·ca
har·mo·ny
 har·mon·ic
 har·mo·ni·ous
 har·mo·ni·za·tion
har·ness
harp·ist
har·poon
harp·si·chord
har·ried
har·ri·er
har·row
hart *n.* (*stag*; see *heart*)
har·um-scar·um

har·vest
 har·vest·er
has-been *n.*
has·sle
has·ten
hast·y
 hast·i·ly
 hast·i·ness
hat·band
hat·box
hatch·er·y
hatch·et
hatch·ing
hatch·way
hate·ful
hat·er
hat·ful
hat·pin
hat rack
ha·tred
hat·stand
hat·ter
haugh·ty
haul *v., n.* (*to carry*; see *hall*)
 haul·age
Ha·va·na
have
have·lock
ha·ven
have-not
hav·er·sack
hav·oc
Ha·wai·i
 Ha·wai·ian
haw·ser
haw·thorn
hay fe·ver
hay·rack
hay·seed
haz·ard
 haz·ard·ous
ha·zel
haz·ing

ha·zy
  ha·zi·ly
  ha·zi·ness
H-bomb
head·ache
head·band
head·board
head·cheese
head cold
head·dress
head·first
head·gear
head·hunt·er
head·i·ly
head·i·ness
head·ing
head·land
head·less
head·light
head·line
head·lock
head·long
head louse
head·man
head·mas·ter
head on *adv.*
head-on *adj.*
head·phone
head·piece
head·quar·ters
head·rest
head·set
head·spring
head·stone
head·strong
head·wait·er
head·wa·ter
head·way
head wind
head·work
heal *v.* (*cure*; see *heel*)
health·y
  health·ful
  health·i·ly
  health·i·ness

hear *v.* (*listen*; see *here*)
  heard *v.* (*pt. of hear*; see
  herd)
heark·en
hear·say
heart *n.* (*bodily organ*; see
  hart)
  heart·ache
  heart·beat
  heart block
  heart·break
  heart·bro·ken
  heart·burn
  heart·en
  heart·felt
hearth
  hearth·stone
heart·land
heart·less
heart·rend·ing
heart·sick
heart·string
heart·throb
heart·warm·ing
heart·y
  heart·i·ly
  heart·i·ness
heat·er
hea·then
heath·er
heav·en
  heav·en·ly
  heav·en·ward
heav·y
  heav·i·ly
  heav·i·ness
  heav·y-du·ty
  heav·y-foot·ed
  heav·y-hand·ed
  heav·y-heart·ed
  heav·y·set
  heav·y·weight
He·brew
  He·bra·ic

hec·tic
hec·to·graph
hedge·hog
hedge·row
hee·bie-jee·bies
heed·ful
heed·less
heel *n.*, *v.* (*foot*; see *heal*)
he·gem·o·ny
he·gi·ra
heif·er
height
  height·en
hei·nous
heir *n.* (*inheritor*; see *air*,
  ere, *hair*, and *hare*)
  heir·ess
  heir·loom
he·li·cop·ter
he·li·o·graph
he·li·o·trope
he·li·um
hell·hound
hel·lion
hel·met
helms·man
help·er
help·ful
help·less
help·mate
hel·ter-skel·ter
Hel·ve·tian
he·ma·tol·o·gy
hemi·sphere
hemi·spher·ic
  hemi·spher·i·cal
hem·lock
he·mo·di·al·y·sis
he·mo·glo·bin
he·mo·phil·i·a
hem·or·rhage
hem·or·rhoid
hem·stitch
hence·forth

hence·for·ward
hench·man
hen·peck
he·pat·ic
he·pat·i·ca
hep·a·ti·tis
hep·ta·gon
her·ald
  he·ral·dic
  her·ald·ry
herb·age
herb·al
her·biv·o·rous
Her·cu·les
  Her·cu·le·an
herd *n.*, *v.* (*animals*; see
  heard)
  herd·er
here *adv.*, *n.* (*present*; see
  hear)
here·a·bout
here·af·ter
he·red·i·ty
  he·red·i·tar·y
here·in
here·in·af·ter
here·in·be·fore
her·e·sy
  her·e·tic
  he·ret·i·cal
here·to·fore
here·with
her·i·ta·ble
her·i·tage
Her·mes
her·met·ic
her·mit
  her·mit·age
her·ni·a
  pl. her·ni·as *or* her·ni·ae
he·ro *n.*, *m.* (see *heroine*)
  pl. he·roes
  he·ro·ic
  he·ro·i·cal

her·o·ine *n., f. (female hero;*
see *hero* and *heroin)*
  her·o·ism
her·o·in *n. (narcotic;* see
heroine)
her·on
her·ring
  her·ring·bone
her·self
hertz *n. (unit of frequency)*
hes·i·tate
  hes·i·tan·cy
  hes·i·tant
  hes·i·tat·ing·ly
  hes·i·ta·tion
het·er·o·dox
het·er·o·ge·ne·ous
  het·er·o·ge·ne·i·ty
heu·ris·tic
hew *v. (to cut;* see *hue)*
hex·a·gon
  hex·ag·o·nal
hey·day
hi·a·tus
hi·ba·chi
hi·ber·nate
  hi·ber·na·tion
hi·bis·cus
hic·cup
hick·o·ry
hid·den
hide·a·way
hide·bound
hid·e·ous
hide·out
hi·er·ar·chy
  hi·er·arch
  hi·er·ar·chi·cal
hi·er·at·ic
hi·er·o·glyph·ic
high·ball
high·born
high·boy
high·bred

high·brow
high chair
high-class
high·er-up
high-flown
high grade *n.*
high-grade *adj., v.*
high-hand·ed
high·land
  high·land·er
high-lev·el
high·light
high-mind·ed
high·ness
high-pres·sure
high·road
high school
high sea
high-sound·ing
high-spir·it·ed
high strung
high-ten·sion
high-test
high-toned
high·way
  high·way·man
hi·lar·i·ous
  hi·lar·i·ty
hil·ding
hill·bil·ly
hil·lock
hill·side
hill·y
  hill·i·ness
him *pron. (see hymn)*
  him·self
Hi·ma·la·yan
hin·der *v.*
  hin·drance
hind·er *adj.*
hind·sight
hinge
  hing·ing
hin·ter·land

hip·bone
hip·po·drome
hip·po·pot·a·mus
  pl. hip·po·pot·a·mus·es *or*
  hip·po·pot·a·mi
hire·ling
hir·sute
hiss·ing
his·ta·mine
his·to·ry
  his·to·ri·an
  his·tor·ic
  his·tor·i·cal
his·tri·on·ic
hit-and-run
hith·er
hith·er·to
hoar *n.* (*frost; see* whore)
hoard *n., v.* (*to accumulate;*
  see horde)
hoard·ing
hoarse *adj.* (*harsh; see* horse)
hoar·y
  hoar·i·ness
hob·ble
hob·by·horse
hob·gob·lin
hob·nail
ho·bo
hock·ey
ho·cus-po·cus
hoe
  hoe·ing
hoe·cake
hoe·down
hog *v.*
  hogged
  hog·ging
hog *n.*
  hog·gish
  hogs·head
  hog·wash
hoi pol·loi
hoist·er

hold·back *n.*
hold back *v.*
hold·er
hold·fast
hold o·ver *v.*
hold·o·ver *n.*
hold up *v.*
hold·up *n.*
hole *n., v.* (*an opening; see*
  whole)
  hole·proof
  hole·y *adj.* (*full of holes; see*
    holly, holy, *and* wholly)
hol·i·day
Hol·land
hol·lan·daise
hol·low
hol·ly *n.* (*tree; see* holey, holy,
  and wholly)
ho·lo·caust
ho·lo·graph
hol·ster
ho·ly *adj.* (*sacred; see* holey,
  holly, *and* wholly)
  ho·li·ness
hom·age
hom·burg
home·bod·y
home·bound
home·bred
home·com·ing
home·grown
home·land
home·less
home·like
home·ly
  home·li·ness
home·made
home·mak·er
ho·me·op·a·thy
  ho·me·o·path
  ho·me·o·path·ic
ho·me·o·sta·sis
home·own·er

home plate
Ho·mer·ic
home·room
home rule
home run
home·sick
home·site
home·spun
home·stead
home·stretch
home·town
home·ward
home·work
hom·ey
hom·i·cide
hom·i·ly
   pl. hom·i·lies
ho·mo·ge·neous
   ho·mo·ge·ne·i·ty
ho·mog·e·nize
ho·mog·e·nous
ho·mol·o·gous
hom·o·nym
Hon·dur·as
hon·est
   hon·es·ty
hon·ey
   hon·ey·bee
   hon·ey·comb
   hon·ey·dew
   hon·eyed
   hon·ey·moon
   hon·ey·suck·le
honk·y-tonk
hon·or
   hon·or·a·ble
   hon·o·rar·i·um
   pl. hon·o·rar·i·ums *or*
   hon·o·rar·i·a
   hon·or·ar·y
   hon·or·if·ic
hood·ed
hood·lum
hoo·doo

hood·wink
hoof·print
hoo·kah *or* hoo·ka
hook up *v.*
hook·up *n.*
hook·worm
hoop·skirt
hoose·gow
Hoo·sier
hope·ful
hope·less
hop·per
hop·scotch
horde *n.* (*large group*; see *hoard*)
hore·hound
ho·ri·zon
   hor·i·zon·tal
hor·mone
hor·net
horn·pipe
horn·y
hor·o·scope
hor·ri·ble
hor·rid
hor·ri·fy
hor·ror
horse *n.* (*animal*; see *hoarse*)
   horse·back
   horse·car
   horse·flesh
   horse·fly
   horse·hair
   horse·hide
   horse·laugh
   horse·man
   horse·play
   horse·pow·er
   horse·rad·ish
   horse sense
   horse·shoe
   horse·whip
hor·ti·cul·ture
   hor·ti·cul·tur·al

ho·sier·y
hos·pice
hos·pi·ta·ble
hos·pi·tal
  hos·pi·tal·i·za·tion
  hos·pi·tal·ize
hos·pi·tal·i·ty
hos·tage
hos·tel *n.* (*inn; see* hostile)
  hos·tel·ry
host·ess
hos·tile *adj.* (*angry; see* hostel)
  hos·til·i·ty
hos·tler
hot air
hot·bed
hot-blood·ed
hot·box
hotch·potch
hot dog
ho·tel
hot·foot
hot·head
hot·head·ed
hot·house
hot plate
hot rod
hot·shot
hot spring
Hot·ten·tot
hot·ter
hot·test
hour *n.* (*time; see* our)
hour·glass
hour·ly
house·boat
house·break·ing
house·bro·ken
house·clean
house·coat
house·dress
house·fly
house·ful
house·hold

house·hold·er
house·keep·er
house·less
house·lights
house·maid
house·man
house·moth·er
house par·ty
house·room
house·warm·ing
house·wife
  pl. house·wives
house·work
hov·el
hov·er
how·ev·er
how·it·zer
howl·er
hoy·den
hua·ra·che
hub·bub
huck·le·ber·ry
huck·ster
hud·dle
hue *n.* (*color; see* hew)
huff·y
  huff·i·ly
  huff·i·ness
Hu·gue·not
hulk·ing
hul·la·ba·loo
hu·man
  hu·man·kind
  hu·man·ly
hu·mane
hu·man·ism
  hu·man·ist
  hu·man·is·tic
  hu·man·i·tar·i·an
hu·man·i·ty
hu·man·ize
hum·ble
  hum·bly
hum·bug

hum·drum
hu·mer·us *n.* *(upper arm; see humorous)*
hu·mid
  hu·mid·i·fy
  hu·mid·i·ty
hu·mi·dor
hu·mil·i·ate
  hu·mil·i·a·tion
hu·mil·i·ty
hummed
hum·ming
  hum·ming·bird
hum·mock
hu·mor
  hu·mor·ist
  hu·mor·ous *adj.* *(funny; see humerus)*
hump·back
hunch·back
hun·dred
  hun·dredth
  hun·dred·weight
Hun·gar·y
  Hun·gar·i·an
hun·ger
hun·gry
  hun·gri·er
  hun·gri·ly
hunt·er
hunts·man
hur·dle *n., v.* *(obstacle; see hurtle)*
hur·dy-gur·dy
hur·ly-bur·ly
Hu·ron
hur·rah
hur·ri·cane
hur·ry
  hur·ried
hurt·ful
hur·tle *v.* *(to fling; see hurdle)*
hus·band
  hus·band·man
  hus·band·ry

hus·ky *n.*
husk·y *adj.*
  husk·i·ly
  husk·i·ness
hus·sar
hus·sy
hus·tings
hus·tle
hy·a·cinth
hy·brid
Hy·dra
hy·dran·gea
hy·drant
hy·drate
hy·drau·lic
hy·dro·car·bon
hy·dro·chlo·ride
  hy·dro·chlo·ric
hy·dro·dy·nam·ics
hy·dro·e·lec·tric
hy·dro·gen
hy·drol·y·sis
hy·drom·e·ter
hy·dro·phane
hy·dro·pho·bi·a
hy·dro·phone
hy·dro·plane
hy·dro·pon·ics
hy·dro·scope
hy·dro·stat·ic
hy·drous
hy·e·na
hy·giene
  hy·gien·ic
hy·grom·e·ter
hy·gro·scope
  hy·gro·scop·ic
hy·men
  hy·me·ne·al
hymn *n.* *(religious song; see him)*
  hym·nol·o·gy
hy·per·bo·la *n.* *(geometric figure; see hyperbole)*

hy·per·bo·le *n*. (*exaggeration*;
  see *hyperbola*)
hy·per·crit·i·cal *adj*. (*overly*
  critical; see *hypocritical*)
hy·per·kin·e·sis
hy·per·phys·i·cal
hy·per·ten·sion
hy·per·thy·roid·ism
hy·per·tro·phy
hy·phen
  hy·phen·ate
  hy·phen·at·ed
hyp·no·sis
  pl. hyp·no·ses
  hyp·no·tic
  hyp·no·tism
  hyp·no·tist
  hyp·no·tize
hy·po·chon·dri·a
  hy·po·chon·dri·ac
hy·poc·ri·sy
  hyp·o·crite
  hyp·o·crit·i·cal *adj*.
  (*deceiving*; see *hypercritical*)
hy·po·der·mis
  hy·po·der·mal
  hy·po·der·mic
hy·po·gly·ce·mi·a
hy·pot·e·nuse
hy·poth·e·sis
  pl. hy·poth·e·ses
  hy·poth·e·cate
hy·po·thet·i·cal
  hy·po·thet·i·cal·ly
hy·po·thy·roid·ism
hys·sop
hys·ter·ec·to·my
hys·ter·e·sis
hys·te·ri·a
  hys·ter·i·cal
  hys·ter·ics

I

i·am·bus
  i·am·bic
I·be·ri·an
i·bex
i·bis
ice
  ice age
  ice bag
  ice·berg
  ice·boat
  ice·bound
  ice·box
  ice·break·er
  ice cap
  ice-cold
  ice cream *n*.
  ice-cream *adj*.
  ice field
  ice floe
  ice·house
  ice·man
  ice pack
  ice pick
  ice plant
  ice wa·ter
  ic·ing
Ice·land
i·ci·cle
i·con
  i·con·ic
i·con·o·clast
i·cy
  i·ci·ly
  i·ci·ness
I·da·ho
i·de·al
  i·de·al·ism
  i·de·al·ist
  i·de·al·is·tic
  i·de·al·i·za·tion
  i·de·al·ize

i·de·al·ly
i·den·ti·cal
i·den·ti·fy
  i·den·ti·fi·ca·tion
  i·den·ti·fied
id·e·o·gram
i·de·ol·o·gy
id·i·o·cy
id·i·om
  id·i·o·mat·ic
id·i·o·path·ic
id·i·o·syn·cra·sy
id·i·ot
  id·i·ot·ic
i·dle *adj.*, *v.* (*lazy*; see *idol* and *idyll*)
  i·dle·ness
  i·dly
i·dol *n.* (*object of adoration*; see *idle* and *idyll*)
  i·dol·a·trous
  i·dol·a·try
  i·dol·ize
i·dyll *or* i·dyl *n.* (*literary form*; see *idle* and *idol*)
  i·dyl·lic
ig·loo
ig·ne·ous
ig·nes·cent
ig·nis fat·u·us
ig·nite
  ig·nit·a·ble
  ig·ni·tion
ig·no·ble
ig·no·min·y
  ig·no·min·i·ous
ig·no·ra·mus
ig·no·rant
  ig·no·rance
ig·nore
i·gua·na
il·e·os·to·my
Il·i·ad

il·i·um
  il·i·ac
ilk
ill-ad·vised
ill-bred
il·le·gal
  il·le·gal·i·ty
il·leg·i·ble
  il·leg·i·bil·i·ty
il·le·git·i·mate
  il·le·git·i·ma·cy
ill-fat·ed
ill-fa·vored
il·lib·er·al
il·lic·it *adj.* (*unlawful*; see *elicit*)
il·lim·it·a·ble
Il·li·nois
il·lit·er·ate
  il·lit·er·a·cy
  il·lit·cr·ate·ness
ill-man·nered
ill-na·tured
ill·ness
il·log·i·cal
ill-starred
ill-treat
il·lu·mi·nate
  il·lu·mi·na·tion
  il·lu·mi·na·tor
il·lu·mine
il·lu·sion *n.* (*unreal*; see *allusion*)
  il·lu·sive *adj.* (*deceptive*; see *allusive* and *elusive*)
  il·lu·so·ry
il·lus·trate
  il·lus·tra·tion
  il·lus·tra·tive
il·lus·tri·ous
im·age
  im·age·ry
im·ag·ine
  im·ag·i·na·ble

im·ag·i·nar·y
im·ag·i·na·tion
im·ag·i·na·tive
im·bal·ance
im·be·cile
  im·be·cil·i·ty
im·bed
im·bibe
im·bri·cate
  im·bri·cat·ed
  im·bri·ca·tion
im·bro·glio
im·bue
im·i·tate
  im·i·ta·ble
  im·i·ta·tion
  im·i·ta·tor
im·mac·u·late
im·ma·nent *adj*. (*inherent;
  see* eminent *and* imminent)
im·ma·te·ri·al
  im·ma·te·ri·al·i·ty
im·ma·ture
im·mea·sur·a·ble
im·me·di·ate
  im·me·di·a·cy
  im·me·di·ate·ly
im·me·mo·ri·al
im·mense
  im·men·si·ty
im·merge
im·merse
  im·mer·sion
im·mi·grate
  im·mi·grant
  im·mi·gra·tion
im·mi·nent *adj*. (*impending;
  see* eminent *and* immanent)
  im·mi·nence
im·mis·ci·ble
im·mo·bile
  im·mo·bi·li·za·tion
  im·mo·bi·lize

im·mod·er·ate
  im·mod·er·a·tion
im·mod·est
im·mo·late
  im·mo·la·tion
im·mor·al
  im·mor·al·i·ty
im·mor·tal
  im·mor·tal·i·ty
  im·mor·tal·ize
im·mov·a·ble
  im·mov·a·bly
im·mune
  im·mu·ni·ty
  im·mu·nize
  im·mu·nol·o·gy
im·mure
im·mu·ta·ble
im·pact
im·pair
im·pal·pa·ble
im·pan·el
im·par·i·ty
im·park
im·part
im·par·tial
  im·par·tial·i·ty
im·par·ti·ble
im·pass·a·ble *adj*. (*not
  passable; see* impassible)
im·passe
im·pas·si·ble *adj*. (*unfeeling;
  see* impassable)
im·pas·sion
  im·pas·sioned
im·pas·sive
im·pa·tient
  im·pa·tience
im·peach
  im·peach·ment
im·pec·ca·ble
im·pe·cu·ni·ous
  im·pe·cu·ni·os·i·ty
im·ped·ance

im·pede
im·ped·i·ment
im·ped·i·men·ta
im·pel
im·pelled
im·pel·lent
im·pel·ling
im·pend
im·pen·e·tra·ble
im·per·a·tive
im·per·cep·ti·ble
im·per·fect
im·per·fec·tion
im·per·fo·rate
im·pe·ri·al
im·pe·ri·al·ism
im·pe·ri·al·ist
im·pe·ri·al·ly
im·per·il
im·pe·ri·ous
im·per·ish·a·ble
im·per·me·a·ble
im·per·son·al
im·per·son·ate
im·per·son·a·tion
im·per·son·a·tor
im·per·ti·nent
im·per·ti·nence
im·per·ti·nen·cy
im·per·turb·a·ble
im·per·vi·ous
im·pe·ti·go
im·pet·u·ous
im·pet·u·os·i·ty
im·pe·tus
im·pinge
im·pi·ous
im·pi·e·ty
imp·ish
im·pla·ca·ble
im·plant
im·ple·ment
im·pli·cate
im·pli·ca·tion

im·pli·ca·tive
im·plic·it
im·plore
im·plo·sion
im·ply
im·plied
im·po·lite
im·pol·i·tic
im·pon·der·a·ble
im·port
im·port·a·ble
im·por·ta·tion
im·por·tant
im·por·tance
im·por·tune
im·por·tu·nate
im·por·tu·ni·ty
im·pose
im·pos·ing
im·po·si·tion
im·pos·si·ble
im·pos·si·bil·i·ty
im·post
im·pos·tor or **im·pos·ter** *n.*
im·pos·ture *n., v.*
im·po·tence
im·po·ten·cy
im·po·tent
im·pound
im·pov·er·ish
im·prac·ti·ca·ble
im·prac·ti·cal
im·pre·cate
im·pre·ca·tion
im·pre·ca·to·ry
im·preg·nate
im·preg·na·bil·i·ty
im·preg·na·ble
im·preg·na·tion
im·pre·sar·i·o
im·press
im·press·i·ble
im·pres·sion
im·pres·sion·a·ble

im·pres·sive
im·pri·mis
im·print
im·pri·son
im·prob·a·ble
im·promp·tu
im·prop·er
  im·pro·pri·e·ty
im·prove
  im·prov·a·ble
  im·prov·er
im·prov·i·dent
  im·prov·i·dence
im·pro·vise
  im·pro·vi·sa·tion
im·pru·dent
  im·pru·dence
im·pugn
im·pulse
im·pul·sion
im·pul·sive
im·pu·ni·ty
im·pure
  im·pu·ri·ty
im·pute
  im·put·a·ble
  im·pu·ta·tive
in·a·bil·i·ty
in·ac·ces·si·ble
  in·ac·ces·si·bil·i·ty
in·ac·cu·rate
  in·ac·cu·ra·cy
in·ac·tion
in·ac·tive
  in·ac·tiv·i·ty
in·ad·e·quate
  in·ad·e·qua·cy
in·ad·mis·si·ble
in·ad·vert·ent
  in·ad·vert·ence
in·ad·vis·a·ble
in·al·ien·a·ble
in·al·ter·a·ble

in·ane
  in·an·i·ty
in·an·i·mate
in·ap·peas·a·ble
in·ap·pli·ca·ble
in·ap·po·site
in·ap·pre·ci·a·ble
in·ap·pre·ci·a·tive
in·ap·pro·pri·ate
in·apt *adj.* (*unsuitable*; see
  inept)
in·ar·tic·u·late
in·ar·tis·tic
in·as·much as
in·at·ten·tion
in·at·ten·tive
in·au·di·ble
in·au·gu·rate
  in·au·gu·ral
  in·au·gu·ra·tion
in·aus·pi·cious
in·born
in·bound
in·bred
in·cal·cu·la·ble
in·ca·les·cent
in·can·des·cent
  in·can·desce
  in·can·des·cence
in·can·ta·tion
in·ca·pa·ble
in·ca·pac·i·tate
  in·ca·pac·i·ta·tion
in·ca·pac·i·ty
in·car·cer·ate
  in·car·cer·a·tion
in·car·na·tion
in·cau·tious
in·cen·di·ar·y
in·cense
in·cen·tive
in·cep·tion
  in·cep·tive
in·ces·sant

in·cest
  in·ces·tu·ous
in·cho·ate
in·ci·dence
in·ci·dent
  in·ci·den·tal
  in·ci·den·tal·ly
in·cin·er·ate
  in·cin·er·a·tion
  in·cin·er·a·tor
in·cip·i·ent
in·cise
  in·ci·sion
  in·ci·sive
in·ci·sor
in·cite v., n. (to stir up; see
  insight)
  in·ci·ta·tion
in·cite·ment
  in·cit·er
in·ci·vil·i·ty
in·clem·ent
  in·clem·en·cy
in·cline
  in·cli·na·tion
  in·clined
  in·clin·ing
in·clude
  in·clud·ed
  in·clu·sion
  in·clu·sive
in·co·erc·i·ble
in·cog·ni·to
in·co·her·ent
  in·co·her·ence
in·com·bus·ti·ble
in·come
in·com·ing
in·com·mun·ni·ca·ble
in·com·mun·ni·ca·do or
  in·co·mu·ni·ca·do
in·com·pa·ra·ble
in·com·pat·i·ble

in·com·pe·tent
  in·com·pe·tence
in·com·plete
in·com·press·i·ble
in·com·put·a·ble
in·con·ceiv·a·ble
in·con·clu·sive
in·con·gru·ous
  in·con·gru·i·ty
in·con·se·quent
  in·con·se·quen·tial
in·con·sid·er·a·ble
in·con·sid·er·ate
in·con·sis·tent
in·con·sol·a·ble
in·con·spic·u·ous
in·con·stant
in·con·test·a·ble
in·con·ve·nient
  in·con·ve·nience
in·con·vert·i·ble
in·cor·po·rate
  in·cor·po·ra·tion
  in·cor·po·ra·tor
in·cor·po·re·al
in·cor·rect
in·cor·ri·gi·ble
in·cor·rupt
  in·cor·rupt·i·ble
in·crease
  in·creas·a·ble
  in·creas·ing·ly
in·cred·i·ble
  in·cred·i·bil·i·ty
in·cred·u·lous
  in·cre·du·li·ty
in·cre·ment
in·crim·i·nate
  in·crim·i·na·to·ry
in·crus·ta·tion
in·cu·bate
  in·cu·ba·tion
  in·cu·ba·tor

in·cu·bus
   pl. in·cu·bi *or* in·cu·bus·es
in·cul·cate
   in·cul·ca·tion
in·cul·pate
   in·cul·pa·tion
   in·cul·pa·to·ry
in·cum·bent
   in·cum·ben·cy
in·cur
   in·curred
   in·cur·ring
in·cur·a·ble
in·cu·ri·ous
in·cur·sion
in·cur·vate
   in·cur·va·tion
in·debt·ed·ness
in·de·cent
   in·de·cen·cy
in·de·ci·pher·a·ble
in·de·ci·sion
in·de·ci·sive
in·de·clin·a·ble
in·dec·o·rous
   in·de·co·rum
in·deed
in·de·fat·i·ga·ble
in·de·fen·si·ble
in·de·fin·a·ble
in·def·i·nite
in·del·i·ble
in·del·i·cate
   in·del·i·ca·cy
in·dem·ni·fy
   in·dem·ni·fi·ca·tion
   in·dem·ni·fied
in·dem·ni·ty
in·dent
   in·den·ta·tion
   in·den·tion
in·den·ture
in·de·pen·dent
   in·de·pen·dence

in·de·scrib·a·ble
in·de·struc·ti·ble
in·de·ter·min·a·ble
in·de·ter·mi·nate
in·dex
   pl. in·dex·es *or* in·di·ces
   in·dex·er
In·di·a
   In·di·an
In·di·an·a
in·di·cate
   in·di·ca·tion
   in·dic·a·tive
   in·di·ca·tor
   in·dic·a·to·ry
in·dict *v.* (*to accuse*; see *indite*)
   in·dict·a·ble
   in·dict·ment
in·dic·tion
In·dies
in·dif·fer·ent
   in·dif·fer·ence
in·dig·e·nous
in·di·gent
   in·di·gence
in·di·ges·tion
   in·di·gest·i·ble
in·dig·ni·ty
in·di·go
in·di·rect
   in·di·rec·tion
in·dis·cern·i·ble
in·dis·creet *adj.* (*imprudent*; see *indiscrete*)
   in·dis·cre·tion
in·dis·crete *adj.* (*not sepa-rated*; see *indiscreet*)
in·dis·crim·i·nate
in·dis·pens·a·ble
in·dis·posed
in·dis·po·si·tion
in·dis·put·a·ble
in·dis·sol·u·ble

in·dis·tinct
in·dite *v.* (*to compose;* see
  indict)
in·di·vert·i·ble
in·di·vid·u·al
  in·di·vid·u·al·ism
  in·di·vid·u·al·ist
  in·di·vid·u·al·i·ty
  in·di·vid·u·al·lize
  in·di·vid·u·al·ly
in·di·vis·i·ble
in·doc·ile
in·doc·tri·nate
in·do·lence
in·do·lent
in·dom·i·ta·ble
In·do·ne·sia
in·door *adj.*
in·doors *adv.*
in·drawn
in·du·bi·ta·ble
in·duce
  in·duce·ment
in·duct
  in·duc·tile
  in·duc·tion
  in·duc·tive
  in·duc·tor
in·dulge
  in·dul·gence
  in·dul·gent
in·du·rate
  In·du·ra·tion
in·dus·tri·al
  in·dus·tri·al·ism
  in·dus·tri·al·ist
  in·dus·tri·al·ize
in·dus·tri·ous
in·dus·try
in·e·bri·ate
  in·e·bri·ant
  in·e·bri·a·tion
  in·e·bri·e·ty
in·ed·i·ble

in·ef·fa·ble
in·ef·face·a·ble
in·ef·fec·tive
in·ef·fec·tu·al
in·ef·fi·ca·cy
  in·ef·fi·ca·cious
in·ef·fi·cient
  in·ef·fi·cien·cy
in·el·e·gant
  in·el·e·gance
in·el·i·gi·ble
  in·el·i·gi·bil·i·ty
in·el·o·quent
in·e·luc·ta·ble
in·ept *adj.* (*clumsy;* see *inapt*)
  in·ep·ti·tude
in·e·qual·i·ty
in·eq·ui·ty *n.* (*injustice;* see
  iniquity)
  in·eq·ui·ta·ble
in·e·rad·i·ca·ble
in·er·rant
in·ert
  in·er·tia
in·es·sen·tial
in·es·ti·ma·ble
in·ev·i·ta·ble
in·ex·act
  in·ex·ac·ti·tude
in·ex·cus·a·ble
in·ex·haust·i·ble
in·ex·o·ra·ble
in·ex·pe·di·ent
in·ex·pen·sive
in·ex·pe·ri·ence
in·ex·pert
in·ex·pi·a·ble
in·ex·plain·a·ble
in·ex·pli·ca·ble
in·ex·plic·it
in·ex·press·i·ble
in·ex·pres·sive
in·ex·pug·na·ble
in·ex·ten·si·ble

in·ex·tri·ca·ble
in·fal·li·ble
  in·fal·li·bil·i·ty
in·fa·mous
in·fa·my
in·fant
  in·fan·cy
  in·fan·tile
in·fan·ta *f.*
in·fan·te *m.*
in·fan·try
in·farc·tion
in·fat·u·ate
  in·fat·u·a·tion
in·fect
  in·fec·tion
  in·fec·tious
  in·fec·tive
  in·fec·tor
in·fe·lic·i·ty
  in·fe·lic·i·tous
in·fer
  in·fer·ence
  in·fer·en·tial
  in·ferred
  in·fer·ring
in·fe·ri·or
  in·fe·ri·or·i·ty
in·fer·nal
in·fer·no
in·fest
  in·fes·ta·tion
in·fi·del
  in·fi·del·i·ty
in·field
in·fil·trate
in·fi·nite
  in·fin·i·tes·i·mal
  in·fin·i·ty
in·fin·i·tive
in·firm
  in·fir·ma·ry
  in·fir·mi·ty

in·flame
  in·flam·ma·ble
  in·flam·ma·tion
  in·flam·ma·to·ry
in·flate
  in·fla·tion
in·flect
  in·flec·tion
in·flex·i·ble
in·flict
  in·flic·tion
in·flu·ence
  in·flu·en·tial
in·flu·en·za
in·flux
in·form
  in·for·mant
  in·for·ma·tion
  in·for·ma·tive
  in·form·er
in·for·mal
  in·for·mal·i·ty
in·frac·tion
in·fra·red
in·fra·struc·ture
in·fre·quent
in·fringe
in·fu·ri·ate
in·fuse
  in·fu·sion
in·ge·nious *adj.* (*clever*; see
  ingenuous)
  in·ge·nu·i·ty
in·ge·nue
in·gen·u·ous *adj.* (*naïve*; see
  ingenious)
in·ges·tion
in·glo·ri·ous
in·got
in·grained
in·gra·ti·ate
in·grat·i·tude
  in·grate
in·gre·di·ent

in·gress
in·grown
in·hab·it
  in·hab·i·tant
in·hale
in·har·mo·ni·ous
in·her·ent
  in·here
  in·her·ence
in·her·it
  in·her·i·tance
in·hib·it
  in·hi·bi·tion
in·hos·pi·ta·ble
in·hu·man
  in·hu·man·i·ty
in·hu·ma·tion
in·im·i·cal
in·im·i·ta·ble
in·iq·ui·ty *n.* (*wickedness*; see
  inequity)
  in·iq·ui·tous
in·i·tial
  in·i·tial·i·za·tion
in·i·ti·ate *v.*
in·i·ti·ate *n., adj.*
in·i·ti·a·tive
in·ject
  in·jec·tion
  in·jec·tor
in·ju·di·cious
in·junc·tion
in·jure
  in·ju·ri·ous
  in·ju·ry
  pl. in·ju·ries
in·jus·tice
in·kling
ink·stand
ink·well
in·laid *adj.*
in·land
in·lay *n., v.*
in·let

in-line
in·mate
in·most
in·nate
in·ning
inn·keep·er
in·no·cent
  in·no·cence
in·noc·u·ous
in·no·vate
  in·no·va·tion
in·nu·en·do
  pl. in·nu·en·dos *or*
  in·nu·en·does
in·nu·mer·a·ble
in·oc·u·late
  in·oc·u·la·tion
in·of·fen·sive
in·op·er·a·ble
in·op·por·tune
in·or·di·nate
in·or·gan·ic
in·os·i·tol
in·put
in·quest
in·qui·e·tude
in·quire
  in·qui·ry
  pl. in·qui·ries
  in·qui·si·tion
  in·quis·i·tive
  in·quis·i·tor
in·road
in·rush
in·sane
  in·san·i·ty
in·san·i·tar·y
in·sa·tia·ble
in·scribe
  in·scrip·tion
in·scru·ta·ble
in·sect
  in·sec·ti·cide

in·se·cure
  in·sc·cu·ri·ty
in·sem·i·nate
in·sen·sate
in·sen·si·ble
in·sen·si·tive
in·sep·a·ra·ble
in·sert
  in·ser·tion
in·side
in·sid·i·ous
in·sight n. (perception; see incite)
in·sig·ni·a s. and pl.
in·sig·nif·i·cant
  in·sig·nif·i·cance
in·sin·cere
in·sin·u·ate
  in·sin·u·a·tion
in·sip·id
in·sist
  in·sis·tence
  in·sis·tent
in·sole
in·so·lent
  in·so·lence
in·sol·u·ble
in·sol·vent
  in·sol·ven·cy
in·som·ni·a
in·sou·ci·ant
  in·sou·ci·ance
in·spect
  in·spec·tion
  in·spec·tor
in·spire
  in·spi·ra·tion
in·sta·bil·i·ty
in·stall
  in·stal·la·tion
  in·stalled
  in·stall·ing
  in·stall·ment
in·stance

in·stan·ta·ne·ous
in·stan·ter
in·stead
in·step
in·sti·gate
  in·sti·ga·tion
  in·sti·ga·tor
in·still
  in·stilled
  in·still·ing
in·stinct
  in·stinc·tive
in·sti·tute
  in·sti·tu·tion
  in·sti·tu·tion·al
in·struct
  in·struc·tion
  in·struc·tion·al
  in·struc·tive
  in·struc·tor
in·stru·ment
  in·stru·men·tal
  in·stru·men·tal·i·ty
in·sub·or·di·nate
  in·sub·or·di·na·tion
in·suf·fer·a·ble
in·suf·fi·cient
in·su·lar
in·su·late
  in·su·la·tion
  in·su·la·tor
in·su·lin
in·sult
in·su·per·a·ble
in·sup·port·a·ble
in·sup·press·i·ble
in·sur·ance
in·sure
  in·sur·a·ble
  in·sur·er
in·sur·gent
in·sur·rec·tion
in·tact
in·tagl·io

in·take
in·tan·gi·ble
in·te·ger
in·te·gral
in·te·grate
  in·te·gra·tion
in·teg·ri·ty
in·teg·u·ment
in·tel·lect
  in·tel·lec·tu·al
in·tel·li·gence
  in·tel·li·gent
in·tel·li·gi·ble
in·tem·per·ate
  in·tem·per·ance
in·tend
in·tend·ant
in·tense
  in·ten·si·fied
  in·ten·si·fy
  in·ten·si·ty
  in·ten·sive
in·tent
in·ten·tion
in·ter
  in·terred
  in·ter·ring
in·ter·ac·tion
  in·ter·ac·tive
in·ter·cede
  in·ter·ces·sion
in·ter·cept
in·ter·change·a·ble
in·ter·com
in·ter·course
in·ter·de·pen·dent
in·ter·dict
in·ter·est
in·ter·face
in·ter·fere
  in·ter·fered
  in·ter·fer·ence
  in·ter·fer·ing
in·ter·fe·ron

in·ter·fix
in·ter·im
in·te·ri·or
in·ter·ject
  in·ter·jec·tion
in·ter·leave
in·ter·lin·e·ar
in·ter·loc·u·tor
  in·ter·loc·u·to·ry
in·ter·lope
in·ter·lude
in·ter·mar·ry
  in·ter·mar·riage
in·ter·me·di·ate
  in·ter·me·di·ar·y
in·ter·ment
in·ter·mez·zo
  pl. in·ter·mez·zi *or*
  in·ter·mez·zos
in·ter·mi·na·ble
in·ter·min·gle
in·ter·mis·sion
in·ter·mit·tent
in·ter·nal
in·ter·na·tion·al
in·ter·ne·cine
in·ter·nist
in·tern·ment
in·ter·pel·late
in·ter·po·late
in·ter·pose
in·ter·pret
  in·ter·pre·ta·tion
  in·ter·pret·er
in·ter·reg·num
  pl. in·ter·reg·nums *or*
  in·ter·reg·na
in·ter·ro·gate
  in·ter·ro·ga·tive
  in·ter·rog·a·to·ry
in·ter·rupt
  in·ter·rup·tion
in·ter·sect
  in·ter·sec·tion

in·ter·sperse
in·ter·state *adj.* (*between
   states*; see *intrastate*)
in·ter·stice
   in·ter·sti·tial
in·ter·twine
in·ter·ur·ban
in·ter·val
in·ter·vene
   in·ter·ven·tion
in·ter·view
   in·ter·view·er
in·tes·tate
in·tes·tine
   in·tes·ti·nal
in·ti·mate
   in·ti·ma·cy
   in·ti·ma·tion
in·tim·i·date
   in·tim·i·da·tion
in·tol·er·a·ble
in·tol·er·ant
   in·tol·er·ance
in·tone
   in·to·na·tion
in·tox·i·cate
   in·tox·i·cant
in·trac·ta·ble
in·tra·mu·ral
in·tran·si·gent
in·tran·si·tive
in·tra·state *adj.* (*within a
   state*; see *interstate*)
in·trep·id
   in·tre·pid·i·ty
in·tri·cate
   in·tri·ca·cy
in·trigue
   in·trigued
   in·tri·guing
in·trin·sic
in·tro·duce
   in·tro·duc·tion
   in·tro·duc·to·ry

in·troit
in·tro·mis·sion
in·tro·spec·tion
in·tro·vert
in·trude
   in·tru·sion
in·tu·i·tion
in·tu·i·tive
in·unc·tion
in·un·date
   in·un·da·tion
in·ure
in·vade
   in·va·sion
in·val·id *adj.*
   in·val·i·date
in·val·id *n.*
in·val·u·a·ble
in·var·i·a·ble
in·vec·tive
in·veigh
in·vei·gle
in·vent
   in·ven·tion
   in·ven·tive
   in·ven·tor
in·ven·to·ry
   pl. in·ven·to·ries
in·verse
in·ver·sion
in·vert
in·vest
   in·vest·ment
   in·ves·tor
in·ves·ti·gate
   in·ves·ti·ga·tion
   in·ves·ti·ga·tor
in·ves·ti·ture
in·vet·er·ate
in·vid·i·ous
in·vig·o·rate
in·vin·ci·ble
in·vi·o·late
   in·vi·o·la·ble

in·vis·i·ble
in·vite
  in·vi·ta·tion
  in·vit·ing
in·voice
in·voke
  in·vo·ca·tion
in·vol·un·tar·i·ly
in·vol·un·tar·y
in·volve
in·vul·ner·a·ble
in·ward
i·o·dine
i·on·ize
  i·on·i·za·tion
i·on·o·sphere
i·o·ta
IOU
I·o·wa
ip·e·cac
ip·so fac·to
I·ran
Ir·aq
i·ras·ci·ble
i·rate
Ire·land
ir·i·des·cence
  ir·i·des·cent
i·rid·i·um
i·ris
irk·some
i·ron·clad
i·ron gray n.
i·ron lung
i·ron·mas·ter
i·ron·ware
i·ron·wood
i·ron·work
i·ro·ny
  i·ron·i·cal
ir·ra·di·ate
ir·ra·tion·al
ir·rec·on·cil·a·ble
ir·re·deem·a·ble

ir·re·duc·i·ble
ir·ref·ra·ga·ble
ir·re·fut·a·ble
ir·reg·u·lar
ir·rel·e·vant
  ir·rel·e·vance
ir·re·li·gious
ir·rep·a·ra·ble
ir·re·press·i·ble
ir·re·proach·a·ble
ir·re·sist·i·ble
ir·re·sol·u·ble
ir·res·o·lute
  ir·res·o·lu·tion
ir·re·spec·tive
ir·re·spon·si·ble
ir·re·triev·a·ble
ir·rev·er·ent
ir·re·vers·i·ble
ir·re·vo·ca·ble
ir·ri·gate
  ir·ri·ga·tion
ir·ri·tate
  ir·ri·ta·ble
  ir·ri·tant
  ir·ri·ta·tion
ir·rupt v. (*burst*; see *erupt*)
  ir·rup·tion n. (see *eruption*)
is·chi·um
  pl. is·chi·a
i·sin·glass
is·land
isle n. (*small island*; see *aisle*)
  is·let n. (*small island*; see
  eyelet)
i·so·bar
i·so·late
  i·so·la·tion
i·sos·ce·les
i·so·therm
i·so·tope
Is·ra·el
  Is·rae·li
  Is·ra·el·ite

is·sue
  is·su·ance
isth·mus
i·tal·ic
It·a·ly
i·tem·ize
i·tin·er·ant
i·tin·er·ar·y
its *possessive*
it's *contraction (it is)*
i·vo·ry

J

ja·bot
jack·al
jack·a·napes
jack·ass
jack·boot
jack·et
jack·ham·mer
jack-in-the-box
jack-in-the-pul·pit
jack·knife
jack-of-all-trades
jack-o'-lan·tern
jack·pot
jack·rab·bit
jack·screw
jack·straw
jack·tar
Jac·o·be·an
Jac·o·bin
jag·uar
jai·a·lai
jail·bird
jail·break
ja·lop·y
  pl. ja·lop·ies
jam *v., n. (to wedge in; jelly;*
  see jamb)
Ja·mai·ca
jamb *n. (door part; see jam)*

jam·bo·ree
jan·i·tor
Jan·u·ar·y
ja·pan *n., v.*
  ja·panned
  ja·pan·ning
Japan
  Jap·a·nese
jar
  jarred
  jar·ring
jar·gon
jas·mine
jas·per
jaun·dice
jaun·ty
  jaun·ti·ly
ja·va
jav·e·lin
jaw·bone
jaw·break·er
jay·walk
jeal·ous
  jeal·ou·sy
jeep
Je·ho·vah
je·june
jell *v. (to solidify; see gel)*
jel·lied
jel·li·fy
jel·ly·fish
jeop·ar·dy
  jeop·ar·dize
jer·e·mi·ad
jer·kin
jerk·y
  jerk·i·ly
jer·sey
jest
Je·su·it
jet-pro·pelled
jet·sam
jet stream
jet·ti·son

jet·ty
jeu d'es·prit
jew·el
  jew·eled
  jew·el·er
  jew·el·ry
jibe *v*. (*sailing term*; see *gibe*)
jig·gle
jig·saw
jin·go
jit·ney
jit·ter·bug
job
  job·ber
  job·bing
  job·less
  job lot
  job work
jock·ey
jo·cose
joc·u·lar
  joc·u·lar·i·ty
jo·cund
jodh·pur
jog
  jogged
  jog·ging
joie de vi·vre
join·der
join·er
joint·ly
join·turc
jok·er
jol·ly
  jol·li·ty
jon·quil
Jor·dan
josh
jos·tle
jour·nal
jour·nal·ism
  jour·nal·ist
  jour·nal·is·tic
  jour·nal·ize

jour·ney
jour·ney·man
joust
jo·vi·al
jowl
joy·ful
joy·ous
joy·ride
ju·bi·lant
  ju·bi·la·tion
ju·bi·lee
judge·ship
judg·ment *or* **judge·ment**
ju·di·ca·ture
  ju·di·ca·to·ry
ju·di·cial
ju·di·ci·ar·y
ju·di·cious
ju·do
jug·ger·naut
jug·gle
jug·u·lar
juic·i·ly
juic·i·ness
ju·jit·su
juke·box
ju·lep
ju·li·enne
jum·ble
jump·i·ness
junc·tion
junc·ture
jun·gle
jun·ior
ju·ni·per
jun·ket
jun·ta
ju·rid·i·cal
ju·ris·dic·tion
ju·ris·pru·dence
ju·ry
  pl. ju·ries
  ju·rist
  ju·ror
  ju·ry·man

jus·tice
jus·ti·fy
  jus·ti·fi·a·ble
  jus·ti·fi·ca·tion
ju·ve·nal
ju·ve·nile
jux·ta·po·si·tion

K

kaf·fee·klatsch
kai·ser
ka·lei·do·scope
ka·mi·ka·ze
Kam·pu·che·a
kan·ga·roo
Kan·sas
ka·o·lin
ka·pok
ka·put
kar·a·kul
ka·ra·te
kar·ma
ka·ty·did
kay·ak
keel
  keel·haul
  keel·son
keen·ness
keep·sake
ken·nel
Ken·tuck·y
Ken·ya
Ke·ogh
ker·a·to·sis
ker·nel n. (seed; see colonel)
ker·o·sene or ker·o·sine
ket·tle·drum
key n., v., adj. (lock device;
  see quay)
  key·board
  key·hole
  key·note

  key·pad
  key·stone
kha·ki
khan
kick back v.
kick·back n.
kick off v.
kick·off n.
kid·nap
  kid·napped
  kid·nap·ping
kid·ney
kill
  kill·er
  kill·ing
  kill·joy
kiln
kil·o·byte
kil·o·cy·cle
kil·o·gram
kil·o·me·ter
kil·o·watt
  kil·o·watt-hour
ki·mo·no
kin·der·gar·ten
kind·heart·ed
kind·li·ness
kin·dling
kind·ness
kin·dred
ki·net·ic
kin·folk or kins·folk
king·bird
king·bolt
king crab
king·dom
king·fish
king·ly
  king·li·ness
king·mak·er
king·pin
king·ship
kin·ship
kins·man

ki·osk
kis·met
kitch·en
  kitch·en·ette
  kitch·en·ware
kit·ten
knap·sack
knave n. (rogue; see nave)
  knav·er·y
knead v. (to press; see need)
knee·cap
knee-deep
knee-high
knew v. (pt. of know;
  see gnu and new)
knick·er n. (trousers; see
  nicker)
knick·knack
knife
  pl. knives
knight n., v. (soldier; see
  night)
  knight·hood
knit
  knit·ted
  knit·ting
knock·a·bout n.
knock a·bout v.
knock down v.
knock·down n.
knock out v.
knock·out n.
knoll
knot n., v. (slice; lump; see
  not)
  knot·hole
  knot·ted
  knot·ting
  knot·ty
know·a·ble
know-how
knowl·edge
  knowl·edge·a·ble or
  knowl·edg·a·ble

knuck·le
  knuck·le·bone
Ko·dak (trademark)
kohl·ra·bi
Kor·e·a
ko·sher
kow·tow
ku·do
  pl. ku·dos
ku·lak
küm·mel
kum·quat
Ku·wait

L

la·bel
  la·beled
  la·bel·ing
la·bi·al
la·bi·a ma·jor·a
la·bi·a mi·nor·a
la·bor
  la·bor·er
  la·bo·ri·ous
  la·bor·sav·ing
lab·o·ra·to·ry
la·bur·num
lab·y·rinth
  lab·y·rin·thine
lac·er·ate
  lac·er·a·tion
lach·ry·mal
  lach·ry·mose
lack·a·dai·si·cal
la·con·ic
lac·quer
la·crosse
lac·ta·tion
la·cu·na
  pl. la·cu·nae
lad·der
  lad·der-back

la·dy·bird
la·dy·bug
la·dy·fin·ger
la·dy·like
la·dy·ship
la·dy's slip·per
lag·gard
lag·ging
la·gniappe
la·goon
lain v.
lair n. (den; see layer)
lais·sez-faire n., adj.
la·it·y
la·ma n. (Tibetan priest; see
  llama)
La·maze
lamb·da
lam·bent
  lam·ben·cy
lam·bre·quin
lamb·skin
lame
la·mé
la·ment
  lam·en·ta·ble
  lam·en·ta·tion
lam·i·nate
lamp·black
lam·poon
lam·prey
lan·cet
lan·dau
land·fall
land·grave
land·hold·er
land·ing craft
land·ing field
land·ing gear
land·ing strip
land·la·dy
land·locked
land·lord
land·lub·ber

land·mark
land·own·er
land-poor
land·scape
land·slide
land·slip
lands·man
land·ward
lane
lan·guage
lan·guid
lan·guish
lan·guor·ous
lank·y
  lank·i·ness
lan·o·lin
lan·tern
lan·yard
La·os
lap·dog
la·pel
lap·i·dar·y
la·pis la·zu·li
lap·ping
lapse
lar·board
lar·ce·ny
  lar·ce·nous
large-scale
lar·ghet·to
lar·go
lar·i·at
lark·spur
lar·va
  pl. lar·vae or lar·vas
lar·yn·gi·tis
lar·ynx
  pl. la·ryn·ges or lar·ynx·es
las·civ·i·ous
la·ser
las·si·tude
latch·key
latch·string

la·tent
  la·ten·cy
lat·er
lat·er·al
lath *n., v. (building material; see lathe)*
lathe *n. (machine; see lath)*
lat·ish
lat·i·tude
lat·ter
lat·tice
  lat·tice·work
laud·a·ble
lau·da·num
lau·da·to·ry
laugh·a·ble
laugh·ing·stock
laugh·ter
laun·dry
  laun·dress
  laun·dry·man
lau·re·ate
lau·rel
la·va
lav·a·to·ry
lav·en·der
lav·ish
law-a·bid·ing
law·ful
law·giv·er
law·less
law·mak·er
law·mak·ing
law·suit
law·yer
lax·a·tive
lax·i·ty
lay·er *n., v. (one thickness; see lair)*
lay·man
lay off *v.*
lay·off *n.*
lay out *v.*
lay·out *n.*

lay over *v.*
lay·over *n.*
lay up *v.*
lay-up *n.*
la·zy
  la·zi·ly
  la·zi·ness
  la·zy·bones
  la·zy Su·san
  la·zy·tongs
lea *n. (grassland; see lee)*
lead *n. (graphite; see led)*
lead·en
  lead·work
lead *v., n. (to guide)*
  lead·er
  lead·er·ship
  lead-in *n.*
  lead off *v.*
  lead-off *n., adj.*
  leads·man
  lead up *v.*
  lead-up *n.*
leaf·let
leaf mold
league
leak *n., v. (hole; see leek)*
  leak·age
  leak·proof
lean *v., n., adj. (to incline; slender; see lien)*
  lean-to
leap·frog
leap year
lease·back
lease·hold
leath·er
  leath·er·work
leav·en
Leb·a·non
lec·tern
lec·ture
led *v. (pt. of lead; see lead, n.)*

ledg·er
lee *n.*, *adj.* (*protected side*; see *lea*)
leek *n.* (*herb*; see *leak*)
lee·ward
lee·way
left-hand·ed
left·o·ver
leg·a·cy
le·gal
  le·gal·ism
  le·gal·i·ty
  le·gal·ize
  le·gal·ly
leg·ate
  leg·a·tee
  le·ga·tion
le·ga·to
leg·end
  leg·en·dar·y
leg·er·de·main
leg·ging
leg·horn
leg·i·ble
  leg·i·bil·i·ty
le·gion
leg·is·late
  leg·is·la·tion
  leg·is·la·tive
  leg·is·la·tor
  leg·is·la·ture
le·git·i·mate
  le·git·i·ma·cy
  le·git·i·ma·tize
leg·man
le·gume
  le·gu·mi·nous
lei
lei·sure
  lei·sure·li·ness
  lei·sure·ly
leit·mo·tiv *or* leit·mo·tif
lem·ming
lem·on·ade

le·mur
length
  length·en
  length·i·ness
  length·wise
  length·y
le·nient
  le·nien·cy
Le·nin·ism
len·i·ty
len·tic·u·lar
len·til
leop·ard
le·o·tard
lep·ro·sy
  lep·rous
le·sion
les·see
less·en *v.* (*decrease*; see *lesson*)
less·er *adj.* (*smaller*; *inferior*; see *lessor*)
les·son *n.* (*instruction*; see *lessen*)
les·sor *n.* (*one who leases*; see *lesser*)
le·thal
leth·ar·gy
  le·thar·gic
lets *v.*
let's *contraction* (*let us*)
let·ter car·ri·er
let·tered
let·ter·head
let·ter-per·fect
let·ter·press
let·tuce
let up *v.*
let·up *n.*
leu·ke·mi·a
lev·ee *n.* (*dam*; see *levy*)
lev·el
  lev·eled
le·ver·age
le·vi·a·than

lev·i·ta·tion
lev·i·ty
lev·y *n., v.* (*tax;* see *levee*)
  lev·ied
  lev·y·ing
lex·i·cog·ra·pher
lex·i·con
li·a·ble *adj.* (*responsible;* see
  libel)
li·ai·son
li·ar *n.* (*one who lies;* see *lyre*)
li·ba·tion
li·bel *n., v.* (*defamation;* see
  liable)
  li·bel·ant
  li·bel·ee
  li·bel·ing *or* li·bel·ling
  li·bel·ous *or* li·bel·lous
lib·er·al
  lib·er·al·i·ty
  lib·er·al·ize
  lib·er·al·ly
lib·er·ate
  lib·er·a·tion
  lib·er·a·tor
Li·ber·i·a
lib·er·tine
lib·er·ty
li·bi·do
  li·bid·i·nous
li·brar·y
  li·brar·i·an
li·bret·to
  li·bret·tist
Lib·y·a
li·cense
li·cen·tious
li·chen *n.* (*fungus;* see *liken*)
lic·o·rice
lie *v.* (*horizontal; to deceive;*
  see *lye*)
  lied
  ly·ing
Liech·ten·stein

lien *n.* (*claim;* see *lean*)
lieu·ten·ant
  lieu·ten·an·cy
life belt
life·blood
life·boat
life buoy
life·guard
life·less
life·like
life·line
life·long
life net
life raft
life·sav·er
life·sav·ing
life·time
lig·a·ment
lig·a·ture
  li·ga·tion
light·en
  light·en·ing *v.* (*brightening;*
  see *lightning*)
ligh·ter·age
light·fast
light-fin·gered
light-head·ed
light-heart·ed
light·house
light-mind·ed
light·ning *n.* (*electrical flash;*
  see *lightening*)
light·proof
light·ship
light·some
light-struck
light·weight
light-year
lig·ne·ous
lig·nite
lik·a·ble
like·ly
  like·li·hood
like-mind·ed

lik·en v. (*to compare*; see
  lichen)
like·ness
like·wise
li·lac
lil·li·pu·tian
lil·y-liv·ered
lil·y-white
limb n. (*appendage*; see *limn*)
lim·ber
lim·bo
lime·ade
lime·kiln
lime·light
lim·er·ick
lime·stone
lime·wa·ter
li·min·al
lim·it
  lim·i·ta·tion
  lim·it·less
limn v. (*draw*; see *limb*)
lim·ou·sine
lim·pet
lim·pid
lin·age or line·age n. (*printed
  lines*; see *lineage*)
linch·pin
lin·e·age n. (*ancestry*; see
  linage)
lin·eal
lin·e·a·ment n. (*outline*; see
  liniment)
lin·e·ar
line·cut
line·man
lin·en
line up v.
line·up n.
lin·ger
lin·ge·rie
lin·go
  pl. lin·goes or lin·gos
lin·guist

lin·i·ment n. (*ointment*; see
  lineament)
lin·ing
link·age
li·no·le·um
Li·no·type (*trademark*)
lin·seed
lin·tel
li·on·ess
li·on·heart·ed
li·po·ma
lip-read v.
lip-read·er n.
lip·stick
liq·ue·fac·tion
liq·ue·fy or liq·ui·fy
  liq·ue·fi·a·ble
li·ques·cent
  li·ques·cence
li·queur n. (*flavored alcohol*;
  see *liquor*)
liq·uid
  li·quid·i·ty
liq·ui·date
  liq·ui·da·tion
li·quor n. (*liquid; alcohol*; see
  liqueur)
lis·ten
list·less
lit·er·a·cy
lit·er·al adj. (*exact*; see
  littoral)
  lit·er·al·ly
lit·er·ar·y
lit·er·ate
lit·er·a·tim
lit·er·a·ture
lith·i·um
lith·o·graph
  li·thog·ra·pher
  li·thog·ra·phy
lit·i·gate
  lit·i·gant
  lit·i·ga·tion
  li·ti·gious

lit·mus
lit·tle
lit·tle·neck clam
lit·to·ral *adj.*, *n.* (*coastal*; see *literal*)
  lit·ur·gy
  li·tur·gi·cal
liv·a·ble *or* live·a·ble
live·li·hood
live·long
liv·er·y
  liv·er·y·man
liv·ing room
liz·ard
lla·ma *n.* (*animal*; see *lama*)
  pl. lla·mas *or* lla·ma
load *n.*, *v.* (*a large mass*; see *lode*)
loan *n.*, *v.* (*to lend*; see *lone*)
loath *adj.* (*hesitant*; see *loathe*)
loathe *v.* (*to hate*; see *loath*)
loath·some
lob·by·ing
lob·ster
lo·cal *adj.*, *n.* (*nearby*; see *locale*)
  lo·cal·i·ty
  lo·cal·ize
lo·cale *n.* (*any area*; see *local*)
lo·cate
  lo·ca·tion
lock·jaw
lock·nut
lock·out *n.*
lock out *v.*
lock·smith
lock·step
lock·stitch
lock·up
lo·co·mo·tion
  lo·co·mo·tive
  lo·co·mo·tor
lo·cus *n.* (*place*; see *locust*)
  pl. lo·ci *or* lo·ca

lo·cust *n.* (*grasshopper*; see *locus*)
lo·cu·tion
lode *n.* (*mineral ore*; see *load*)
  lode·stone
lodg·ing
lodg·ment
log·a·rithm
log·gia
  pl. log·gias *or* log·gie
log·ging
log·i·cal
lo·gi·cian
lo·gis·tics
lo·go
  pl. logos
log·o·type
log·roll·ing
loi·ter
loll·ing
lol·li·pop
lone *adj.* (*solitary*; see *loan*)
  lone·some
lone·li·ness
long·boat
long·bow
lon·gev·i·ty
long·hand
long·head·ed
long·horn
lon·gi·tude
  lon·gi·tu·di·nal
long·shore·man
long shot
long-suf·fer·ing
long suit
long-wind·ed
look·ing glass
look out *v.*
look·out *n.*
loop
  loop code
  loop·hole
  loop·ing

loose *adj.*, *adv.* (*slack*; see *lose*)
  loose-joint·ed
  loose-leaf
  loose·ly
  loos·en
loot *v.*, *n.* (*booty*; see *lute*)
lop
  lopped
  lop·ping
  lop·sid·ed
lo·qua·cious
lo·ran
lord·li·ness
lor·do·sis
lor·gnette
lor·ry
lose *v.* (*to part with*; see *loose*)
lo·tion
lot·ter·y
loud·mouthed
loud·speak·er
Lou·i·si·an·a
lounge
lou·ver
lov·a·ble
love·less
love·lorn
love·ly
  love·li·ness
love·mak·ing
love seat
love-sick
low·born
low·bred
low·brow
low-down *adj.*
low·down *n.*
low·er·case
low·er·class·man
low·land
low-lev·el
low·li·ness
low-mind·ed

low-pres·sure
low-spir·it·ed
low-ten·sion
lox
loy·al·ty
loz·enge
lu·bri·cate
  lu·bri·cant
  lu·bri·ca·tion
lu·cid
  lu·cid·i·ty
Lu·ci·fer
luck·y
  luck·i·er
  luck·i·est
  luck·i·ly
lu·cra·tive
lu·cu·bra·tion
lu·di·crous
lug·gage
lu·gu·bri·ous
luke·warm
lul·la·by
lum·ba·go
lum·bar *adj.* (*loins*; see *lumber*)
lum·ber *n.*, *v.* (*wood*; see *lumbar*)
  lum·ber·yard
lu·mi·nar·y
lu·mi·nous
lu·na·cy
  lu·na·tic
lu·nar
lunch·eon
  lunch·eon·ette
  lunch·room
lu·nette
lu·pine
lurch
lu·rid
lus·cious
lus·ter *or* **lus·tre**
  lus·ter·ware

lust·ful
lus·trous
lust·y
  lust·i·ly
lute *n.* (*instrument; see loot*)
Lu·ther·an
Lux·em·bourg
lux·u·ri·ate
  lux·u·ri·ant
  lux·u·ri·ous
lux·u·ry
ly·ce·um
lych-gate
lye *n.* (*chemical; see lie*)
lymph
  lym·phat·ic
  lymph nodes
  lym·pho·cyte
lynch
lynx
ly·on·naise
lyre *n.* (*instrument; see liar*)
lyr·ic
  lyr·i·cal
  lyr·i·cism

M

ma·ca·bre
mac·ad·am
  mac·ad·am·ize
mac·a·da·mi·a
mac·a·ro·ni
mac·a·roon
Ma·cau
ma·ce·doine
mac·er·ate
  mac·er·a·tion
ma·chet·e
Mach·i·a·vel·li·an
ma·chic·o·la·tion
ma·chin·a·ble
mach·i·na·tion

ma·chine gun *n.*
ma·chine-gun *v.*
ma·chine·like
ma·chine-made
ma·chin·er·y
ma·chine-tooled
ma·chin·ist
mack·er·el
mack·i·naw
mack·in·tosh
mac·ra·me
mac·ro·bi·ot·ic
mac·ro·cosm
ma·cron
mac·ro-pro·gram·ming
Mad·a·gas·car
mad·am *n.*
  pl. mad·ams or mes·dames
ma·dame *n.*
  pl. mes·dames or ma·dames
mad·cap
mad·den·ing
made *v. adj.* (*pt. of make;*
  see maid)
ma·de·moi·selle
  pl. ma·de·moi·selles or
  mes·de·moi·selles
mad·house
mad·man
ma·don·na
mad·ri·gal
mael·strom
mae·stro
Ma·fi·a
mag·a·zine
ma·gen·ta
mag·got
mag·ic
  ma·gi·cian
mag·is·te·ri·al
mag·is·trate
  mag·is·tra·cy
  mag·is·tra·ture

Mag·na Char·ta *or* **Mag·na Car·ta**
mag·na cum lau·de
mag·nan·i·mous
  mag·na·nim·i·ty
mag·nate *n.* (*powerful person*; see *magnet*)
mag·ne·sia
mag·ne·si·um
mag·net *n.* (*lodestone*; see *magnate*)
  mag·net·ic
  mag·net·ism
  mag·ne·tize
mag·net·ite
mag·ne·to
mag·ne·ton
mag·nif·i·cent
  mag·nif·i·cence
mag·ni·fy
  mag·ni·fi·ca·tion
  mag·ni·fi·er
mag·nil·o·quent
mag·ni·tude
mag·no·lia
mag·num
mag·pie
mag·tape
ma·guey
Mag·yar
ma·ha·ra·ja *or* ma·ha·ra·jah
ma·ha·ra·ni *or* ma·ha·ra·nee
ma·hat·ma
Mah·ler
ma·hog·a·ny
maid *n.* (*servant*; see *made*)
  maid·en
  maid·en·hair
  maid·en·head
  maid·en·li·ness
  maid·en·ly
  maid·ser·vant
mail *n., v.* (*letters*; see *male*)
  mail·a·ble

mail·bag
mail·box
mail car·ri·er
mail clerk
mail·er
mail·man
mail or·der *n.*
mail-or·der *adj.*
maim
main *n., adj.* (*primary*; see *mane* and *Maine*)
main·frame
main·land
main line
main·ly
main·mast
main·sail
main·spring
main·stay
main stem
main·stream
Maine *n.* (*state*; see *main* and *mane*)
main·tain
  main·te·nance
mai·son
mai·tre d'
maize *n.* (*corn*; see *maze*)
maj·es·ty
  ma·jes·tic
ma·jol·i·ca
ma·jor
  ma·jor·do·mo
  ma·jor·i·ty
ma·jus·cule
make-be·lieve
make-o·ver *n.*
make o·ver *v.*
make·shift
make up *v.*
make·up *n.*
make·weight
mak·ing
mal·a·chite

mal·ad·just·ment
mal·ad·min·is·ter
mal·a·droit
mal·a·dy
mal·aise
mal·a·pert
mal·a·prop·ism
mal·ap·ro·pos
ma·lar·i·a
  ma·lar·i·al
Ma·lay
Ma·lay·sia
mal·con·tent
male *adj.*, *n.* (*masculine*; see *mail*)
mal·e·dic·tion
mal·e·fac·tor
  mal·e·fac·tion
ma·lef·ic
  ma·lef·i·cence
  ma·lef·i·cent
ma·lev·o·lent
  ma·lev·o·lence
mal·fea·sance
mal·for·ma·tion
mal·formed
mal·ice
  ma·li·cious
ma·lign
  ma·lig·ni·ty
ma·lig·nant
  ma·lig·nan·cy
ma·lin·ger
  ma·lin·ger·er
mall *n.* (*public area*; see *maul*)
mal·lard
mal·le·a·ble
  mal·le·a·bil·i·ty
mal·let
mal·nu·tri·tion
mal·oc·clu·sion
mal·o·dor
  mal·o·dor·ous
mal·po·si·tion

mal·prac·tice
Mal·ta
Mal·tese
Mal·thu·si·an
malt·ose
mal·treat
malt·ster
mal·ver·sa·tion
mam·mal
mam·mon
mam·moth
man
  man-a·bout-town
  man-child
  man-eat·er
  man-eat·ing
  man·ful
  man·han·dle
  man-hat·er
  man·hole
  man·hood
  man-hour
  man·hunt
  man hunt·er
  man-kill·er
  man·kind
  man·like
  man·li·ness
  man·ly
  man-made
  manned
  man·nish
  man-of-war
  man pow·er *n.*
  man·rope
  man·ser·vant
  man slaugh·ter
  man·trap
  man-year
man·a·cle
man·age *v.* (*handle*; see *manège* and *ménage*)
  man·age·a·ble
  man·age·ment

man·ag·er
man·a·ge·ri·al
man·a·tee
Man·chu
man·ci·ple
man·da·mus
man·da·rin
man·date
  man·da·tar·y *n.*
  man·da·to·ry *adj.*
man·di·ble
man·do·lin
man·drel *n.* (*spindle*; see
  mandrill)
man·drill *n.* (*baboon*; see
  mandrel)
mane *n.* (*horse hair*; see *main*
  and *Maine*)
ma·nège *or* ma·nege *n.*
  (*horsemanship*; see *manage*
  and *ménage*)
ma·neu·ver
man·ga·nese
man·gel-wur·zel
man·ger
man·gle
man·go
  pl. man·goes *or* man·gos
man·grove
man·gy
  man·gi·ly
ma·ni·a
  ma·ni·ac
  ma·ni·a·cal
man·i·cure
  man·i·cur·ist
man·i·fest
  man·i·fes·ta·tion
  man·i·fes·to
man·i·fold
man·i·kin *or* mannikin *n.*
  (*dwarf*; see *mannequin*)
ma·ni·la

ma·nip·u·late
  ma·nip·u·la·tion
  ma·nip·u·la·tive
  ma·nip·u·la·tor
  ma·nip·u·la·to·ry
man·i·tou
man·na
man·ne·quin *n.* (*tailor's
  dummy*; see *manikin and
  mannikin*)
man·ner *n.* (*behavior*; see
  manor)
  man·ner·ism
man-of-war
ma·nom·e·ter
man·or *n.* (*estate*; see *manner*)
  ma·no·ri·al
man·qué
man·sard
manse
man·sion
man·teau
man·tel *n.* (*fireplace beam*;
  see *mantle*)
  man·tel·piece
man·tel·et
man·til·la
man·tis
  pl. man·tis·es *or* man·tes
man·tle *n., v.* (*cloak*; see
  mantel)
man·tra
man·u·al
man·u·fac·ture
  man·u·fac·tur·er
man·u·mis·sion
ma·nure
man·u·script
man·y
  man·y-sid·ed
ma·ple
mapped
map·ping
mar·a·schi·no

mar·a·thon
ma·raud
mar·ble
  mar·ble·ize
  mar·bling
marc
mar·ca·site
mar·che·sa *f.*
  pl. mar·che·se
mar·che·se *m.*
  pl. mar·che·si
mar·chio·ness
Mar·co·ni
  mar·co·ni·gram
Mar·di Gras
mare's nest
mare's tail
mar·ga·rine
mar·ga·rite
mar·gin
  mar·gin·al
  mar·gi·na·li·a
mar·grave
mar·i·gold
mar·i·jua·na *or* mar·i·hua·na
mar·i·nade
ma·rine
  mar·i·ner
mar·i·o·nette
mar·i·tal
mar·i·time
mark down *v.*
mark·down *n.*
mar·ket
  mar·ket·a·ble
  mar·ket·ing
  mar·ket·place
marks·man
mark up *v.*
mark·up *n.*
mar·line·spike
mar·ma·lade
mar·mo·set
mar·mot

ma·roon
mar·quee *n.* (*canopy;* see *marquis*)
mar·que·try
mar·quis *n.* (*nobleman;* see *marquee*)
mar·quise
mar·riage
  mar·riage·a·ble
mar·row
  mar·row·bone
mar·ry *v.* (*to wed;* see *merry*)
Mar·seilles
mar·shal *n., v.* (*officer;* see *martial*)
  mar·shaled
  mar·shal·ing
marsh gas
marsh·mal·low
marsh·y
  marsh·i·ness
mar·su·pi·al
mar·ten *n.* (*weasel;* see *martin*)
mar·tial *adj.* (*military;* see *marshal*)
  mar·tial·ly
Mar·tian
mar·tin *n.* (*bird;* see *marten*)
mar·ti·net
Mar·tin·ique
Mar·tin·mas
mar·tyr
  mar·tyr·dom
  mar·tyr·ol·o·gy
mar·vel
  mar·veled
  mar·vel·ing
  mar·vel·ous
Marx·i·an
Mar·y·land
mas·cot
mas·cu·line
  mas·cu·lin·i·ty

mash·er
mash·ie
mask *n*., *v*. (*disguise*; see
  masque)
mask·er
mas·och·ism
ma·son
  ma·son·ry
Ma·son·ic
masque *n*. (*play*; see *mask*)
  mas·quer·ade
Mas·sa·chu·setts
mas·sa·cre
mas·sage
  mas·seur
  mas·seuse
mas·si·cot
mas·sive
  mass·y
mas·ter
  mas·ter-at-arms
  mas·ter·ful
  mas·ter-hand
  mas·ter key
  mas·ter·mind
  mas·ter·piece
  mas·ter plan
  mas·ter·ship
  mas·ter·stroke
  mas·ter·work
  mas·ter·y
mast·head
mas·ti·cate
  mas·ti·ca·tion
mas·tiff
mas·to·don
mas·toid
mat *or* matt *or* matte *n*., *v*.
mat·a·dor
match·board
match·book
match·less
match·lock
match·mak·er

match play
match·stick
match·wood
ma·te·ri·al *adj*., *n*. (*substance*;
  see *material*)
ma·te·ri·al·ism
ma·te·ri·al·ist
ma·te·ri·al·is·tic
ma·te·ri·al·i·ty
ma·te·ri·al·ize
ma·te·ri·al·ly
ma·té·ri·el *n*. (*equipment*; see
  material)
ma·ter·nal
ma·ter·ni·ty
math·e·mat·ics
  math·e·mat·i·cal
  math·e·ma·ti·cian
mat·i·nee
mat·ing *v*. (*to mate*; see
  matting)
ma·tri·arch
  ma·tri·ar·chate
  ma·tri·ar·chy
ma·tri·cide
ma·tric·u·late
  ma·tric·u·lant
  ma·tric·u·la·tion
mat·ri·mo·ny
  mat·ri·mo·ni·al
ma·trix
ma·tron
  ma·tron·ize
  ma·tron·ly
mat·ter
  mat·ter-of-fact *adj*.
mat·ting (*floor covering*; see
  mating)
mat·tock
mat·tress
ma·ture
  mat·u·rate
  mat·u·ra·tion
  ma·ture·ly

ma·ture·ness
ma·tu·ri·ty
ma·tu·ti·nal
mat·zo *or* **mat·zoh**
  pl. mat·zoth *or* mat·zos
maud·lin
maul *n., v. (to beat; see mall)*
maul·stick
mau·so·le·um
  pl. mau·so·le·ums *or*
  mau·so·le·a
mauve
mav·er·ick
mawk·ish
max·il·la
  pl. max·il·lae *or* max·il·las
  max·il·lar·y
max·im
max·i·mal
max·i·mize
max·i·mum
  pl. max·i·mums *or* max·i·ma
may·be
May Day
may·flow·er
may·hap
may·hem
may·on·naise
may·or
  may·or·al·ty
may·pole
maze *n. (network; see matze)*
ma·zur·ka
Mc·In·tosh
mead *n. (drink; see meed)*
mead·ow
  mead·ow·lark
mea·ger *or* **mea·gre**
meal·time
meal·worm
meal·y·mouthed
mean *v. (to intend; see mien)*
  mean·ing·less
me·an·der

mean·time
mean·while
mea·sles
mea·sly
mea·sure
  mea·sur·a·ble
  mea·sured
  mea·sure·less
  mea·sure·ment
  mea·sur·er
meat *n. (flesh; see meet and
  mete)*
me·a·tus
Mec·ca
me·chan·ic
  me·chan·i·cal
  mech·a·ni·cian
  me·chan·ics
  mech·a·nism
  mech·a·nist
med·al *n. (award; see meddle)*
  med·al·ist
  me·dal·lion
med·dle *v. (interfere; see
  medal)*
  med·dle·some
me·di·a
me·di·an
  me·di·al
me·di·ate
  me·di·ate·ly
  me·di·a·tion
  me·di·a·tive
  me·di·a·tor
  me·di·a·to·ry
med·i·cal
  med·i·ca·ble
med·i·cate
  me·di·ca·ment
  med·i·ca·tion
med·i·cine
  me·dic·i·na·ble
  me·dic·i·nal
  med·i·cine ball
  med·i·cine man

me·di·e·val
  me·di·e·val·ism
  me·di·e·val·ist
me·di·o·cre
  me·di·oc·ri·ty
med·i·tate
  med·i·ta·tion
  med·i·ta·tive
Med·i·ter·ra·nean
me·di·um *n.*
  pl. me·di·ums *or* me·di·a
  me·di·um·is·tic
med·lar
med·ley
Me·du·sa
meed *n.* (*a fitting return;* see
  mead)
meer·schaum
meet *v., n., adj.* (*to
  encounter;* see *meat* and
  mete*)
  meet·ing
  meet·ing·house
mega·byte
mega·cy·cle
mega·lith
meg·a·lo·ma·ni·a
mega·phone
mei·o·sis
Mei·ster·sing·er
mel·an·chol·y
  mel·an·cho·li·a
  mel·an·chol·ic
Mel·a·ne·sian
mé·lange *or* me·lange
mel·a·nin
  mel·a·nism
  mel·a·no·ma
me·lee
me·li·o·rate
  me·li·o·ra·tion
  me·li·o·ra·tive
  me·li·o·ra·tor
  me·li·o·rism

mel·lif·lu·ous
mel·low
me·lo·di·on *or* me·lo·de·on
melo·dra·ma
  melo·dra·mat·ic
  melo·dra·ma·tist
mel·o·dy
  me·lod·ic
  me·lo·di·ous
  mel·o·dist
  mel·o·dize
mel·on
melt·a·ble
melt·down
mem·ber
  mem·ber·ship
mem·brane
  mem·bra·nous
me·men·to
  pl. mo·men·tos *or*
  mo·men·toes
mem·oir
mem·o·ra·bil·i·a
mem·o·ra·ble
mem·o·ran·dum
  pl. mem·o·ran·dums *or*
  mem·o·ran·da
me·mo·ri·al
  me·mo·ri·al·ist
  me·mo·ri·al·ize
mem·o·ry
  mem·o·rize
men·ace
mé·nage *n.* (*household;* see
  manage and *manège*)
me·nag·er·ie
men·ar·che
men·da·cious
men·dac·i·ty
Men·de·li·an
men·di·cant
  men·di·can·cy
me·ni·al
men·in·gi·tis

me·nis·cus
  pl. me·nis·ci *or* me·nis·cus·es
Men·no·nite
men·o·pause
men·ses
men·stru·ate
  men·stru·al
  men·stru·a·tion
men·su·ral
  men·su·ra·ble
  men·su·ra·tion
men·tal
  men·tal·i·ty
  men·tal·ly
men·thol
men·tion
  men·tion·er
men·tor
men·u
me·phi·tis
mer·can·tile
  mer·can·til·ism
mer·ce·nar·y
mer·cer
  mer·cer·ize
mer·chan·dise
mer·chant
  mer·chant·a·ble
  mer·chant·man
mer·ci
mer·cu·ry
  mer·cu·ri·al
  mer·cu·ric
  mer·cu·rous
mer·cy
  mer·ci·ful
  mer·ci·less
mere·ly
mer·e·tri·cious
mer·gan·ser
merge
  mer·gence
  merg·er
me·rid·i·an

me·rid·i·o·nal
me·ringue
me·ri·no
mer·it
  mer·i·to·ri·ous
Mer·lin
mer·maid
mer·ry *adj.* (*joyous;* see
  marry)
  mer·ri·ly
  mer·ri·ment
  Mer·ry-An·drew
  mer·ry-go-round
  mer·ry·mak·ing
me·sa
mesh·work
mes·mer·ize
  mes·mer·ic
  mes·mer·ism
me·son
mes·quite
mes·sage
  mes·sen·ger
mes·si·ah
  mes·si·an·ic
Messrs.
mess·y
me·tab·o·lism
met·a·car·pus
  met·a·car·pal
met·al *n.* (*chemical element;*
  see *mettle*)
  me·tal·lic
  met·al·lif·er·ous
  met·al·log·ra·phy
  met·al·loid
  met·al·lur·gi·cal
  met·al·lur·gy
  met·al·smith
  met·al·ware
  met·al·work
meta·mor·phose
  meta·mor·phic
  meta·mor·phism

meta·mor·pho·sis
  pl. meta·mor·pho·ses
met·a·phor
  met·a·phor·i·cal
met·a·phys·ics
  met·a·phys·ic
  met·a·phy·si·cian
me·tas·ta·sis
  pl. me·tas·ta·ses
met·a·tar·sus
  met·a·tar·sal
mete *v.* (*to allot;* see *meat* and *meet*)
me·te·or
  me·te·or·ic
  me·te·or·ite
  me·te·or·o·graph
  me·te·or·oid
  me·te·o·ro·log·i·cal
  me·te·o·rol·o·gist
  me·te·o·rol·o·gy
me·ter
meth·a·done
meth·ane
meth·od
  me·thod·i·cal
  meth·od·ist
  meth·od·ize
  meth·od·ol·o·gy
me·tic·u·lous
  me·tic·u·los·i·ty
mé·tier
me·ton·y·my
met·ric
  met·ri·cal
me·trol·o·gy
met·ro·nome
me·trop·o·lis
  met·ro·pol·i·tan
met·tle *n.* (*ardor;* see *medal*)
  met·tle·some
mewl *v.* (*to whimper;* see *mule*)
mews *v., n.* (*back street;* see *muse*)

Mex·i·co
  Mex·i·can
mez·za·nine
mez·zo·so·pra·no
mi·as·ma
  pl. mi·as·mas *or* mi·as·ma·ta
mi·caw·ber
Mich·ael·mas
Mich·i·gan
mi·crobe
  mi·cro·bi·al
  mi·cro·bic
mi·cro·com·put·er
mi·cro·cosm
mi·cro·film
mi·cro·groove
mi·crom·e·ter
mi·cro·or·ga·nism
mi·cro·phone
mi·cro·proc·ess·or
mi·cro·scope
  mi·cro·scop·ic
  mi·cro·scop·i·cal·ly
mid·air
mid·brain
mid·day
mid·dle
  mid·dle-aged
  mid·dle·brow
  mid·dle class *n.*
  mid·dle-class *adj.*
  mid·dle·man
  mid·dle-sized
  mid·dle·weight
  mid·dling
midg·et
mid·i·ron
mid·land
mid·night
mid·riff
mid·ship·man
mid·sum·mer
mid·term
mid·way

mid·week
mid·west
  mid·west·ern·er
mid·wife
mid·win·ter
mid·year
micn *n.* (*demeanor;* see *mean*)
might *v., n.* (*possibly;*
  strength; see *mite*)
  might·i·ly
  might·i·ness
  might·y
mi·gnon·ette
mi·grate
  mi·gra·tion
  mi·gra·to·ry
mi·ka·do
mi·la·dy
milch
mil·dew
  mil·dew·proof
mild·ly
mile·age
mile·post
mile·stone
mi·lieu
mil·i·tant
  mil·i·tan·cy
mil·i·tar·y
  mil·i·ta·rism
  mil·i·ta·rist
  mil·i·ta·ris·tic
  mil·i·ta·rize
mil·i·tate
mi·li·tia
  mi·li·tia·man
milk
  milk·er
  milk glass
  milk house
  milk·i·ness
  milk leg
  milk-liv·ered
  milk·maid

milk·man
milk punch
milk shake
milk snake
milk·sop
milk sug·ar
milk toast *n.*
milk-toast *adj.*
milk tooth
milk·weed
milk·y
mill·board
mill·dam
mil·len·ni·um
  mil·le·nar·i·an
  mil·le·nar·y
  mil·len·ni·al
mill·er
mil·let
mil·li·gram
mil·li·me·ter
mil·li·ner·y
  mil·li·ner
mill·ing
mil·lion
  mil·lion·aire
  mil·lionth
mil·li·pede
mill·pond
mill·race
mill·stone
mill·stream
mill wheel
mill·wright
Milque·toast
mim·e·o·graph
mi·me·sis
  mi·met·ic
mim·ic
  mim·icked
  mim·ick·ing
  mim·ic·ry
mi·mo·sa
min·a·ret

min·a·to·ry
mince·meat
mince pie
minc·er
minc·ing·ly
mind n., v. (brain; see mined)
  mind·er
  mind·ful
  mind read·er
mined v. (to mine; see mind)
min·er n. (one who mines;
  see minor)
min·er·al
  min·er·al·ize
  min·er·al·og·i·cal
  min·er·al·o·gist
  min·er·al·o·gy
Mi·ner·va
min·e·stro·ne
min·gle
  min·gling
min·i·a·ture
min·i·com·put·er
min·i·mal
min·i·mize
  min·i·mi·za·tion
min·i·mum
min·ing
min·ion
min·is·ter
  min·is·te·ri·al
  min·is·trant
  min·is·tra·tion
  min·is·try
min·i·um
min·i·ver
min·ne·sing·er
Min·ne·so·ta
min·now
Mi·no·an
mi·nor adj., n., v. (lesser; see
  miner)
  mi·nor·i·ty
Mi·no·taur

min·ster
min·strel·sy
mint·age
min·u·end
min·u·et
mi·nus
min·ute n.
  min·ute hand
  min·ute·ly
  min·ute·man
mi·nute adj.
  mi·nute·ly
mir·a·cle
  mi·rac·u·lous
mi·rage
mir·ror
mirth·less
mis·ad·ven·ture
mis·al·li·ance
mis·an·thrope
  mis·an·throp·ic
  mis·an·thro·py
mis·ap·pli·ca·tion
mis·ap·pre·hen·sion
mis·ap·pro·pri·ate
mis·be·got·ten
mis·be·have
mis·be·lief
mis·cal·cu·late
mis·car·ry
  mis·car·riage
mis·ce·ge·na·tion
mis·cel·la·ny
  pl. mis·cel·la·ne·a n.
  mis·cel·la·neous
mis·chance
mis·chief
  mis·chie·vous
mis·con·cep·tion
mis·con·duct
mis·con·strue
  mis·con·struc·tion
mis·cre·ant
mis·cue

mis·deal
mis·de·mean·or
mis·di·rect
mi·ser
  mi·ser·li·ness
  mi·ser·ly
mis·er·a·ble
mi·se·re·re
mis·er·y
mis·fea·sance
mis·file
mis·fire
mis·fit
mis·for·tune
mis·giv·ing
mis·gov·ern
mis·guide
mis·hap
mis·in·form
mis·in·ter·pret
mis·join·der
mis·judge
mis·lay
mis·lead
mis·man·age
mis·no·mer
mi·sog·a·my
mi·sog·y·nist
mi·sol·o·gy
mis·place
mis·print
mis·pri·sion
mis·pro·nounce
mis·quo·ta·tion
mis·read
mis·reck·on
mis·rule
mis·sal *n.* (*prayer book*; see *missile*)
mis·sile *n.* (*weapon*; see *missal*)
miss·ing
mis·sion
  mis·sion·ar·y

Mis·sis·sip·pi
  Mis·sis·sip·pi·an
mis·sive
Mis·sour·i
mis·spell
mis·state
mis·take
  mis·tak·a·ble
  mis·tak·en
mis·tle·toe
mis·took
mis·tral
mis·treat
  mis·treat·ment
mis·tress
mis·tri·al
mis·trust
mist·y
  mist·i·ness
mis·un·der·stand
mis·use
  mis·us·age
mite *n.* (*small object*; see *might*)
mi·ter
mit·i·gate
  mit·i·ga·ble
  mit·i·ga·tion
  mit·i·ga·tive
  mit·i·ga·tor
mi·tral
mit·ten
mit·ti·mus
mix·er
mix·ture
mix up *v.*
mix-up *n.*
miz·zen·mast
mne·mon·ic *adj.*
mne·mon·ics *n.*
Mo·ab·ite
moat *n.* (*barrier*; see *mote*)
mob·cap

mo·bile
  mo·bil·i·ty
  mo·bi·li·za·tion
  mo·bi·lize
mob·oc·ra·cy
  mob·o·crat·ic
moc·ca·sin
mo·cha
mock·er
mock·er·y
mock·ing·bird
mock·ing·ly
mock-up *n.*
mode
  mod·al *adj., n. (of a mode;*
  see model)
mod·el *n., v., adj. (type;*
  example; see modal)
  mod·eled
  mod·el·ing
mod·em
mod·er·ate *adj.*
  mod·er·a·tion
mod·er·ate *v.*
  mod·er·a·tor
mod·ern
  mod·ern·ism
  mod·ern·ist
  mo·der·ni·ty
  mod·ern·ize
mod·est
  mod·es·ty
mod·i·cum
mod·i·fy
  mod·i·fi·a·ble
  mod·i·fi·ca·tion
  mod·i·fi·er
mod·ish
mo·diste
mod·u·late
  mod·u·la·tion
  mod·u·la·tor
mod·u·lus
  mod·u·lar

mo·dus vi·ven·di
mo·hair
Mo·ham·med·an
Mo·hawk
moi·e·ty
moist
  moist·en
  moist·en·er
mois·ture
  mois·ture·proof
mo·lar
mo·las·ses
mold *v.*
  mold·a·ble
  mold·er
mold *n.*
  mold·i·ness
  mold·ing
  mold·y
mol·e·cule
  mo·lec·u·lar
mole·hill
mole·skin
mo·lest
  mo·les·ta·tion
mol·li·fy
  mol·li·fi·ca·tion
mol·lusk
mol·ly·cod·dle
mol·ten
mo·lyb·de·num
mo·ment
  mo·men·tar·i·ly
  mo·men·tar·y
  mo·ment·ly
  mo·men·tous
  mo·men·tum
Mon·a·co
mon·arch
  mon·ar·chism
  mon·ar·chy
mon·as·ter·y
  mon·as·te·ri·al

mo·nas·tic
  mo·nas·ti·cism
mon·au·ral
mon·e·tar·y
mon·e·tize
mon·ey
  pl. mon·eys *or* mon·ies
  mon·ey·bags
  mon·eyed
  mon·ey·lend·er
  mon·ey-mak·er
mon·ger
Mon·gol
  mon·gol·i·an
mon·gol·oid
mon·grel
mo·ni·tion
mon·i·tor
  mon·i·tor·ship
  mon·i·tress
mon·i·to·ry
monk·er·y
mon·key
  mon·key·shine
monk·ish
mono·chrome
  mono·chro·mat·ic
mon·o·cle
mo·noc·ra·cy
mon·oc·u·lar
mon·o·dy
mo·nog·a·my
  mo·nog·a·mist
  mo·nog·a·mous
mono·gram
mono·graph
mono·lith
mono·logue
  mo·nol·o·gist
mono·ma·ni·a
mono·met·al·lism
  mono·me·tal·lic
Mo·non·ga·he·la
mono·plane

mo·nop·o·ly
  mo·nop·o·list
  mo·nop·o·lis·tic
  mo·nop·o·li·za·tion
  mo·nop·o·lize
mono·rail
mon·o·spac·ing
mono·syl·la·ble
  mono·syl·lab·ic
mono·tone
  mo·not·o·nous
  mo·not·o·ny
Mono·type (*trademark*)
mon·ox·ide
mon·sei·gneur
  pl. mes·sei·gneurs
mon·sieur
  pl. mes·sieurs
mon·si·gnor
  pl. mon·si·gnors
mon·soon
mon·ster
  mon·stros·i·ty
  mon·strous
mon·strance
mon·tage
Mon·tan·a
month·ly
mon·u·ment
  mon·u·men·tal
mood·y
  mood·i·ly
  mood·i·ness
moon·beam
moon-blind
moon·calf
moon·fish
moon·light
  moon·light·er
  moon·lit
moon·rise
moon·shine
  moon·shin·er
moon·stone

moon·struck
moor·age
moor·ing
Moor·ish
moose n. (*animal*; see *mousse*)
moot
mop·board
mop·ping
mop up v.
mop-up n.
mo·raine
mor·al
  mor·al·ism
  mor·al·ist
  mo·ral·i·ty
  mor·al·i·za·tion
  mor·al·ize
mo·rale
mo·rass
mor·a·to·ri·um
Mo·ra·vi·an
mor·bid
  mor·bid·i·ty
mor·dant n., adj. (*chemical*;
  see *mordent*)
mor·dent n. (*musical
  ornament*; see *mordant*)
more·o·ver
mo·res
mor·ga·nat·ic
mor·i·bund
Mor·mon
morn n. (*morning*; see *mourn*)
morn·ing
  morn·ing glo·ry
Mo·roc·co
mo·ron
mo·rose
  mo·rose·ness
Mor·phe·us
mor·phine
mor·row
Morse code
mor·sel

mor·tal
  mor·tal·i·ty
mor·tar
  mor·tar·board
mort·gage
  mort·gag·ee
  mort·gag·or
mor·ti·fy
  mor·ti·fi·ca·tion
mor·tise
mor·tu·ar·y
mo·sa·ic
Mo·ses
mo·sey
Mos·lem
mos·qui·to
moss·back
moss-grown
most·ly
mote n. (*particle*; see *moat*)
mo·tel
mo·tet
moth·ball
moth-eat·en
moth·er
  moth·er·hood
  moth·er-in-law
  moth·er·land
  moth·er·less
  moth·er·li·ness
  moth·er·ly
  moth·er-of-pearl
moth·proof
mo·tif
mo·tion
  mo·tion·less
mo·ti·vate
mo·tive
mot·ley
mo·tor
  mo·tor·boat
  mo·tor bus
  mo·tor·cade
  mo·tor·car

mo·tor·cy·cle
mo·tor·drome
mo·tor·ist
mo·tor·ize
mo·tor·man
mo·tor·truck
mot·tle
mot·to
mount·a·ble
moun·tain
  moun·tain·eer
  moun·tain·ous
  moun·tain·side
moun·te·bank
mount·er
mount·ing
mourn v. (*to grieve*; see *morn*)
  mourn·ful
  mourn·ing
mouse n. (*rodent*; see *mousse*)
  mouse-ear
  mous·er
  mouse·trap
mousse n. (*dessert*; see
  moose and *mouse*)
mous·tache or **mus·tache**
mouth·ful
mouth·piece
mov·a·ble
  mov·a·ble·ness
move·ment
mov·ie
  pl. mov·ies
mov·ing
mow·er
mown
Mo·zam·bique
moz·za·rel·la
moz·zet·ta
mu·ci·lage
  mu·ci·lag·i·nous
muck·rake
mu·cous adj. (see *mucus*)
mu·cus n. (see *mucous*)

mud·dle
mud·dy
  mud·di·ly
  mud·di·ness
mud·guard
mud·sling·er
muen·ster
muf·fin
muf·fle
  muf·fler
muf·ti
mugged
mug·ger
mug·gi·ness
mug·ging
mug·wump
mu·lat·to
  pl. mu·lat·toes
mul·ber·ry
mulct
mule n. (*animal*; see *mewl*)
  mu·le·teer
  mul·ish
mu·li·eb·ri·ty
mull·er
mul·lion
mul·ti·far·i·ous
mul·ti·form
Mul·ti·graph (*trademark*)
mul·ti·lat·er·al
mul·ti·mil·lion·aire
mul·ti·na·tion·al
mul·ti·ped
mul·ti·plex
  mul·ti·plex·or
mul·ti·ply
  mul·ti·pli·a·ble
  mul·ti·pli·cand
  mul·ti·pli·ca·tion
  mul·ti·pli·ca·tive
  mul·ti·plic·i·ty
  mul·ti·pli·er
mul·ti·ra·cial
mul·ti·stage

mul·ti·tude
  mul·ti·tu·di·nous
mum·bo jum·bo
mum·mer·y
mum·my
  mum·mi·fy
mun·dane
mu·nic·i·pal
  mu·nic·i·pal·i·ty
  mu·nic·i·pal·ize
mu·nif·i·cent
  mu·nif·i·cence
mu·ni·ment
mu·ni·tion
mu·ral
mur·der
  mur·der·er
  mur·der·ous
murk·y
  murk·i·ly
  murk·i·ness
mur·mur
  mur·mur·ing
  mur·mur·ous
mus·ca·dine
mus·ca·tel
mus·cle *n., v. (tissue;* see
  mussel)
  mus·cle-bound
  mus·cu·lar
  mus·cu·la·ture
muse *v., n. (to meditate;* see
  mews)
  mus·ing
Muse *n.* (goddess; see *mews*
  and *muse)*
mu·se·um
mush·room
mush·y
mu·sic
  mu·si·cal *adj., n. (musically
  inclined; a show;* see *musicale)*
  mu·si·cale *n. (concert;* see
  musical)

  mu·si·cian
  mu·si·col·o·gist
musk deer
mus·ket
  mus·ke·teer
  mus·ket·ry
musk·mel·on
musk-ox
musk·rat
musk·y
Mus·lim
mus·lin
mus·sel *n. (shellfish;* see
  muscle)
mus·tang
mus·tard
mus·tered
must·y
  must·i·ness
mu·ta·ble
mu·tate
  mu·tant
  mu·ta·tion
  mu·ta·tive
mute·ness
mu·ti·late
  mu·ti·la·tion
mu·ti·ny
  mu·ti·neer
  mu·ti·nous
mut·ism
mut·ter
mut·ton
  mut·ton·chops
mu·tu·al
  mu·tu·al·i·ty
  mu·tu·al·ly
muz·zle
my·col·o·gy
my·lar
my·o·car·di·al in·farc·tion
my·o·pi·a
  my·o·pic
myr·i·ad

myr·mi·don
myrrh
my·self
mys·ter·y
  mys·te·ri·ous
mys·tic
  mys·ti·cal
  mys·ti·cism
mys·ti·fy
  mys·ti·fi·ca·tion
mys·tique
myth·i·cal
my·thol·o·gy
  myth·o·log·i·cal

N

na·cre
  na·cre·ous
na·dir
nain·sook
nais·sance
nais·sant
na·ïve *or* na·ive
na·ïve·té *or* na·ive·te
na·ked
nam·by-pam·by
name·a·ble *or* nam·a·ble
name·less
name·ly
name·plate
nam·er
name·sake
Na·mib·i·a
nand gate
nan·keen *or* nan·kin
na·palm
na·per·y
naph·tha
nap·kin
Na·po·le·on·ic
nap·per
nap·ping

nar·cis·sus
  nar·cis·sism
nar·co·sis
nar·cot·ic
  nar·co·tize
nar·rate
  nar·ra·tion
  nar·ra·tive
  nar·ra·tor
nar·row
  nar·row-mind·ed
na·sal
  na·sal·i·ty
  na·sal·ize
  na·sal·ly
na·scent
na·so·phar·ynx
nas·tur·tium
nas·ty
  nas·ti·ly
  nas·ti·ness
na·tal
na·ta·tion
  na·tant
  na·ta·to·ri·al
  na·ta·to·ri·um
  na·ta·to·ry
na·tion
  na·tion·al
  na·tion·al·ism
  na·tion·al·i·ty
  na·tion·al·ize
  na·tion·al·iz·er
  na·tion·al·ly
  na·tion·wide
na·tive
  na·tive·ly
  na·tive·ness
  na·tiv·ism
na·tiv·i·ty
nat·ty
nat·u·ral
  nat·u·ral·ism
  nat·u·ral·ist

nat·u·ral·is·tic
nat·u·ral·i·za·tion
nat·u·ral·ize
nat·u·ral·ly
nat·u·ral·ness
na·ture
naugh·ty
naugh·ti·ly
naugh·ti·ness
nau·se·a
nau·se·ate
nau·seous
nau·ti·cal
nau·ti·lus
na·val *adj.* (*of the navy*; see *navel*)
nave *n.* (*church area*; see *knave*)
na·vel *n.* (*belly button*; see *naval*)
nav·i·gate
nav·i·ga·ble
nav·i·ga·tion
nav·i·ga·tor
na·vy
na·vy yard
nay *n., adj.* (*no*; see *née* and *neigh*)
Naz·a·rene
Ne·an·der·thal
Ne·a·pol·i·tan
near·sight·ed
neat·herd
Ne·bras·ka
neb·u·la
pl. neb·u·las *or* neb·u·lae
neb·u·lar
neb·u·lize
neb·u·los·i·ty
neb·u·lous
nec·es·sar·y
nec·es·sar·i·ly
ne·ces·si·tate
ne·ces·si·tous

ne·ces·si·ty
neck·band
neck·cloth
neck·er·chief
neck·ing
neck·lace
neck·line
neck·piece
neck·tie
neck·wear
ne·crol·o·gy
nec·ro·log·i·cal
ne·crol·o·gist
nec·ro·man·cy
ne·crop·o·lis
pl. ne·crop·o·lis·es
ne·cro·sis
pl. ne·cro·ses
nec·tar
nec·tar·ine
née *or* **nee** *adj.* (*born as*; see *nay* and *neigh*)
need *n., v.* (*a lack*; see *kneed*)
need·ful
need·i·est
need·i·ness
need·less
nee·dle
nee·dle·point
nee·dle·work
ne'er-do-well
ne·far·i·ous
ne·ga·tion
neg·a·tive
ne·glect
ne·glect·ful
neg·li·gee *or* **neg·li·gée**
neg·li·gent
neg·li·gence
neg·li·gi·ble
ne·go·ti·ate
ne·go·ti·a·bil·i·ty
ne·go·ti·a·ble
ne·go·ti·a·tion
ne·go·ti·a·tor

Ne·gro
  pl. Ne·groes
neigh *v., n. (horse's cry;* see
  nay and *née)*
neigh·bor
  neigh·bor·hood
nei·ther
nem·a·tode
nem·e·sis
  pl. nem·e·ses *or* nem·e·sis·es
ne·o·clas·sic
ne·o·lith·ic
ne·ol·o·gism
ne·ol·o·gy
  ne·ol·o·gist
ne·on
ne·o·phyte
ne·o·plasm
ne·o·ter·ic
Ne·pal
ne·pen·the
neph·ew
ne·phri·tis
ne plus ul·tra
nep·o·tism
Nep·tune
nerve
  nerve·less
  ner·vous
  nerv·y
ne·science
  ne·scient
nest egg
nes·tle
  nest·ling
Neth·er·lands
neth·er·most
net·ting
net·tle
net·work
neu·ral
  neu·ral·gi·a
neur·as·the·ni·a
neu·ri·tis

neu·rol·o·gy
  neu·rol·o·gist
neu·ron *or* **neu·rone**
neu·ro·sis
  pl. neu·ro·ses
  neu·rot·ic
neu·ro·sur·ger·y
neu·ter
neu·tral·i·ty
neu·tral·ize
  neu·tral·i·za·tion
neu·tral·ly
Nev·a·da
nev·er
  nev·er·the·less
new *adj., adv. (recent;* see
  gnu and *knew)*
  new·born
  new·com·er
  new·fan·gled
  new-fash·ioned
  new·ly
  new·mar·ket
  new·ness
new·el
New·found·land
New Hamp·shire
New Jer·sey
New Mex·i·co
news·boy
news·break
news·cast
  news·cast·er
news·hawk
news·hound
news·let·ter
news·man
news·mon·ger
news·pa·per
  news·pa·per·man
news·print
news·reel
news·stand
news·wor·thy

news·y
New Year
New York
New Zea·land
nib·ble
nib·lick
Nic·a·ra·gua
nice·ly
Ni·cene
nice·ness
ni·ce·ty
niche
nick
nick·el
   nick·el·if·er·ous
   nick·el·o·de·on
nick·er *v.* (*neigh gently*; see
   knicker)
nick·name
nic·o·tine
niece
Ni·ger
Ni·ge·ri·a
nig·gard
   nig·gard·ly
nig·gling
night *n.* (*evening*; see *knight*)
   night·cap
   night·clothes
   night·club
   night·dress
   night·fall
   night·gown
   night·hawk
   night·in·gale
   night key
   night latch
   night let·ter
   night·long
   night·ly
   night·mare
   night owl
   night rid·er
   night-robe

   night·shade
   night shift
   night shirt
   night·stick
   night table
   night·time
   night·walk·er
ni·gres·cent
ni·gri·tude
ni·hi·lism
   ni·hi·list
   ni·hi·lis·tic
Ni·ke (*trademark*)
nim·ble
nim·bus
Nim·rod
nin·com·poop
nine·pin
nine·teen
   nine·teenth
nine·ti·eth
nip·per
nip·ping
nip·ple
Nip·pon·ese
nir·va·na
ni·trate
ni·tric
ni·tride
ni·tri·fy
   ni·tri·fi·ca·tion
ni·trite
ni·tro·gen
   ni·trog·e·nous
ni·tro·glyc·er·in *or*
   ni·tro·glyc·er·ine
ni·trous
No·ah
no·bil·i·ty
no·ble·man
no·blesse o·blige
no·ble·wom·an
no·bly
no·bod·y

noct·am·bu·list
noc·tur·nal
noc·turne
nod·ded
nod·ding
node
  nod·u·lar
  nod·ule
noise·less
noi·some
nois·y
  nois·i·ly
no·mad
  no·mad·ic
  no·mad·ism
nom de guerre
nom de plume
no·men·cla·ture
nom·i·nal
  nom·i·nal·ly
nom·i·nate
  nom·i·na·tion
  nom·i·na·tor
  nom·i·nee
nom·i·na·tive
non·cha·lant
  non·cha·lance
non·com·bat·ant
non·com·mis·sioned
non·com·mit·tal
non com·pos men·tis
non·con·duc·tor
non·con·form·i·ty
  non·con·form·ist
non·co·op·er·a·tion
non·de·script
non·en·ti·ty
none·such
non·fea·sance
non·flam·ma·ble
non·in·ter·ven·tion
non·join·der
non·me·tal·lic
non·pa·reil

non·par·ti·san
non·pro·fit
non·re·sis·tance
  non·re·sis·tant
non·re·stric·tive
non·sched·uled
non·sense
  non·sen·si·cal
non se·qui·tur
non·skid
non·stop
non·suit
non·sup·port
non·un·ion
non·vi·o·lence
  non·vi·o·lent
non·vol·a·tile
noo·dle
noon·day
noon·tide
noon·time
nor gate
nor·mal
  nor·mal·i·ty
  nor·mal·i·za·tion
  nor·mal·ize
  nor·mal·ly
Norse·man
north
  north·er·ly
  north·ern
  North·ern·er
  north·land
  north·ward
North Car·o·lin·a
North Da·ko·ta
north·east
  north·east·er·ly
  north·east·ern
  north·east·ward
north·west
  north·west·er·ly
  north·west·ern

Nor·way
  Nor·we·gian
nose·bleed
nose cone
nose dive *n.*
nose-dive *v.*
nose drops
nose·gay
nose-heav·y
nose·piece
nose·print
nose ring
nose·wheel
no-show
no·sol·o·gy
nos·tal·gia
nos·tril
nos·trum
not *adv.* (*negative*; see *knot*)
no·ta·ble
  no·ta·bly
no·ta·ry
  no·tar·i·al
  no·ta·ri·za·tion
  no·ta·rize
no·ta·tion
note·book
not·ed
note·pa·per
note·tak·er
note-tak·ing
note·wor·thy
  note·wor·thi·ness
noth·ing
  noth·ing·ness
no·tice
  no·tice·a·ble
no·ti·fy
  no·ti·fi·ca·tion
no·tion
no·to·ri·ous
  no·to·ri·e·ty
not·with·stand·ing
nour·ish

nou·veau
nou·veau riche
  pl. nou·veaux riches
Nov·a Sco·tia
no·va·tion
nov·el
  nov·el·ette
  nov·el·ist
  nov·el·is·tic
  nov·el·ize
  no·vel·la
  pl. no·vel·las *or* no·vel·le
  nov·el·ty
no·ve·na
nov·ice
  no·vi·tiate
No·vo·cain (*trademark*)
now·a·days
no·way *adv.*
no·ways *adj.*
no·where
no·wise
nox·ious
noz·zle
nu·ance
nu·cle·us
  pl. nu·cle·i *or* nu·cle·us·es
  nu·cle·ar
  nu·cle·ate
  nu·cle·a·tion
  nu·cle·ic
  nu·cle·o·lus
  pl. nu·cle·o·li
nu·di·ty
nu·ga·to·ry
nug·get
nui·sance
null
  nul·li·fi·ca·tion
  nul·li·fi·er
  nul·li·fy
num·ber
  num·ber·less
numb·ness

nu·mer·al
  nu·mer·ate
  nu·mer·a·tion
  nu·mer·a·tor
  nu·mer·ic
  nu·mer·i·cal
  nu·mer·ous
nu·mis·mat·ic
nu·mis·ma·tist
num·skull *or* **numb·skull**
nun·cu·pa·tive
nun·ner·y
nup·tial
nurse·maid
nur·ser·y
  nur·ser·y·man
nurs·ling
nur·ture
nut·crack·er
nut·meg
nu·tri·ent
nu·tri·ment
nu·tri·tion
  nu·tri·tious
  nu·tri·tive
nut·shell
nuz·zle
ny·lon
nymph

O

oa·kum
oar *n.* (*paddle*; see *ore*)
  oar·lock
  oars·man
o·a·sis
  pl. o·a·ses
oat·cake
oat·meal
ob·bli·ga·to
ob·du·rate
  ob·du·ra·cy

o·be·di·ent
  o·be·di·ence
o·bei·sance
ob·e·lisk
o·bese
  o·be·si·ty
o·bey
ob·fus·cate
  ob·fus·ca·tion
ob·i·ter dic·tum
o·bit·u·ar·y
ob·ject
  ob·jec·tion
  ob·jec·tion·a·ble
  ob·jec·tive
  ob·jec·tive·ly
  ob·jec·tive·ness
  ob·jec·tiv·i·ty
ob·jet d'art
ob·jur·ga·tion
ob·la·tion
ob·li·gate
  ob·li·ga·tion
  ob·lig·a·to·ry
ob·lige
  ob·lig·ing
ob·lique
  ob·liq·ui·ty
ob·lit·er·ate
  ob·lit·er·a·tion
ob·liv·i·on
ob·liv·i·ous
ob·long
ob·lo·quy
ob·nox·ious
o·boe
  o·bo·ist
ob·scene
  ob·scen·i·ty
ob·scure
  ob·scu·rant
  ob·scu·ra·tion
  ob·scure·ness
  ob·scu·ri·ty

ob·se·quy
  pl. ob·se·quies
  ob·se·qui·ous
ob·serve
  ob·serv·a·ble
  ob·serv·ance
  ob·serv·ant
  ob·ser·va·tion
  ob·ser·va·tion·al
  ob·serv·a·to·ry
  ob·serv·er
ob·sess
  ob·ses·sion
  ob·ses·sive
ob·so·lesce
  ob·so·les·cence
ob·so·lete
ob·sta·cle
ob·stet·rics
  ob·stet·ric
  ob·stet·ri·cal
  ob·ste·tri·cian
ob·sti·nate
  ob·sti·na·cy
ob·strep·er·ous
ob·struct
  ob·struc·tion
  ob·struc·tion·ist
  ob·struc·tive
ob·tain
  ob·tain·a·ble
ob·trud·er
ob·tru·sion
ob·tru·sive
ob·tu·rate
ob·tuse
ob·verse
ob·vi·ate
ob·vi·ous
oc·a·ri·na
oc·ca·sion
  oc·ca·sion·al
  oc·ca·sion·al·ly

Oc·ci·dent
  Oc·ci·den·tal·ism
oc·ci·den·tal·ize
oc·cip·i·tal
oc·ci·put
oc·clude
  oc·clu·sion
oc·cult
  oc·cul·ta·tion
  oc·cult·ism
  oc·cult·ist
oc·cu·pa·tion·al
oc·cu·py
  oc·cu·pan·cy
  oc·cu·pant
oc·cur
  oc·curred
  oc·cur·rence
  oc·cur·ring
o·cean·go·ing
o·ce·an·ic
o·cean·og·ra·pher
o'·clock
oc·ta·gon
  oc·tag·o·nal
oc·tan·gu·lar
oc·tave
oc·ta·vo
oc·to·ge·nar·i·an
oc·to·pus
  pl. oc·to·pus·es *or* oc·to·pi
oc·u·lar
oc·u·list
odd·i·ty
odd·ly
ode *n.* (*poem;* see *owed*)
o·di·um
  o·di·ous
o·dor
  o·dor·if·er·ous
  o·dor·less
  o·dor·ous
O·dys·se·us
od·ys·sey

of·fal *n.* (*waste material*; see
  awful)
off-bal·ance
off·beat
off·cast
off-cen·ter
off-col·or
of·fend
  of·fend·er
of·fense
  of·fen·sive
of·fer
  of·fer·ing
  of·fer·to·ry
off·hand
of·fice
  of·fice·hold·er
  of·fi·cer
of·fi·cial
  of·fi·cial·ism
  of·fi·cial·ly
of·fi·ci·ate
  of·fi·ci·ar·y
  of·fi·ci·a·tion
of·fi·ci·nal·ly
of·fi·cious
off·ing
off-key
off-line
off·print
off-scour·ing
off-sea·son
off·set
off·shoot
off·shore
off side *adv.*
off·side *n.*
off·spring
off·stage
off-white
off year
of·ten
  of·ten·times
oft·times

O·hi·o
ohm
  ohm·me·ter
oil cake
oil·cloth
oil·er
oil field
oil·i·ness
oil pan
oil·proof
oil·skin
oil slick
oil·stone
oil·tight
oil well
oil·y
oint·ment
Ok·la·ho·ma
old age *n.*
old-age *adj.*
old·en
old-fash·ioned
old·ish
old-line
Old Nick
old·ster
old-time *adj.*
old-tim·er *n.*
old-world *adj.*
old world *n.*
o·le·o·graph
o·le·o·mar·ga·rine
ol·fac·to·ry
  ol·fac·tion
ol·i·garch
  ol·i·gar·chy
ol·ive
o·lym·pi·ad
O·lym·pi·an
O·lym·pic
O·lym·pus
om·e·let *or* om·e·lette
om·i·nous

o·mis·sion
  o·mis·si·ble
o·mit
  o·mit·ted
  o·mit·ting
om·ni·bus
om·ni·di·rec·tion·al
om·nip·o·tent
  om·nip·o·tence
om·ni·pres·ent
om·ni·scient
  om·ni·science
om·niv·o·rous
once-o·ver
one *adj.*, *n.* (*single*; see *won*)
  one-horse
  one·ness
  one·self *or* one's self
  one-sid·ed
  one-step
  one·time
  one-track
  one-up·man·ship
  one-way
on·er·ous
on·ion
  on·ion·skin
on-line
on·look·er
on·ly
on·rush
on·set
on·slaught
On·tar·i·o
on·to
on·tog·e·ny
on·tol·o·gy
  on·to·log·i·cal
o·nus
on·ward
on·yx
ooz·y
o·pal·es·cent

o·paque
  o·pac·i·ty
o·pen
  o·pen air *n.*
  o·pen-air *adj.*
  o·pen-and-shut
  o·pen-end *adj.*
  o·pen·er
  o·pen-eyed
  o·pen·hand·ed
  o·pen·heart·ed
  o·pen hearth
  o·pen house
  o·pen·ing
  o·pen·ly
  o·pen mar·ket *n.*
  o·pen-mar·ket *adj.*
  o·pen-mind·ed
  o·pen-mouthed
  o·pen·ness
  o·pen·work
op·er·a
  op·er·at·ic
  op·er·et·ta
op·er·ate
  op·er·a·ble
  op·er·a·tion·al
  op·er·a·tive
  op·er·a·tor
op·er·ose
oph·thal·mic
oph·thal·mol·o·gy
oph·thal·mo·scope
o·pine
  o·pin·ion
  o·pin·ion·at·ed
o·pi·um
  o·pi·ate
op·po·nent
op·por·tune
  op·por·tun·ism
  op·por·tun·ist
  op·por·tu·ni·ty
op·pose

op·pos·a·ble
op·po·site *adj., n., prep.*
(*radically different*; see
apposite)
  op·po·si·tion
op·press
  op·pres·sion
  op·pres·sive
  op·pres·sor
op·pro·bri·um
  op·pro·bri·ous
op·ta·tive
op·tics
  op·ti·cal
  op·ti·cian
op·ti·mism
  op·ti·mist
  op·ti·mis·tic
op·ti·mum
  pl. op·ti·ma *or* op·ti·mums
op·tion
  op·tion·al
op·tom·e·try
  op·tom·e·trist
op·u·lent
  op·u·lence
or·a·cle
  o·rac·u·lar
o·ral *adj., n.* (see
aural)
or·ange
  or·ange·ade
  or·ange·wood
or·a·tor
  o·ra·tion
  or·a·to·ri·cal
  or·a·to·ry
or·a·to·ri·o
or·bic·u·lar
or·bit
or·chard
or·ches·tra
  or·ches·tral

or·ches·trate
or·ches·tra·tion
or·chid
or·dain
or·deal
or·der
  or·der·li·ness
  or·der·ly
or·di·nal
or·di·nance *n.* (*regulation*;
see *ordnance*)
or·di·nar·y
  or·di·nar·i·ly
or·di·nate
  or·di·na·tion
ord·nance *n.* (*military
supplies*; see *ordinance*)
ore *n.* (*mineral*; see *oar*)
Or·e·gon
or·gan
  or·gan·ic
  or·ga·nism
  or·gan·ist
or·ga·nize
  or·ga·niz·a·ble
  or·ga·ni·za·tion
or·gy
o·ri·ent
  o·ri·en·tal
  o·ri·en·tal·ism
  o·ri·en·tal·ize
o·ri·en·tate
  o·ri·en·ta·tion
or·i·fice
o·ri·ga·mi
or·i·gin
  o·rig·i·nal
  o·rig·i·nal·ly
  o·rig·i·nate
  o·rig·i·na·tion
  o·rig·i·na·tive
  o·rig·i·na·tor
o·ri·ole
O·ri·on

or·i·son
or·na·ment
  or·na·men·tal
  or·na·men·ta·tion
or·nate
or·ner·y
or·ni·thol·o·gy
o·ro·tund
or·phan
  or·phan·age
Or·phe·us
or·tho·don·tist
or·tho·dox
or·thog·ra·phy
  or·tho·graph·ic
or·tho·pe·dic
or·tho·pe·dist
os·cil·late
  os·cil·la·tion
  os·cil·la·tor
os·cu·late
  os·cu·la·tion
  os·cu·la·to·ry
O·si·ris
os·mi·um
os·mo·sis
os·prey
os·si·fy
  os·si·fi·ca·tion
os·su·ar·y
os·ten·si·ble
os·ten·sive
  os·ten·sive·ly
os·ten·ta·tion
  os·ten·ta·cious
os·te·op·a·thy
  os·te·o·path
  os·te·o·path·ic
os·tra·cize
  os·tra·cism
os·trich
oth·er
  oth·er·wise
Ot·ta·wa

ot·to·man
ought v. (*should*; see *aught*)
our adj. (*poss. of we*; see
  hour)
our·self
  pl. our·selves
oust·er
out-and-out
out·bal·ance
out·bid
out·board
out·bound
out·build·ing
out·burst
out·cast
out·class
out·come
out·crop
out·cry
out·dat·ed
out·dis·tance
out·do
out·door
out·er
out·er·most
out·face
out·field
out·fit
  out·fit·ter
out·flank
out·fox
out·go·ing
out·grow
  out·growth
out·guess
out·house
out·ing
out·land·er
out·land·ish
out·last
out·law
  out·law·ry
out·lay
out·let

out·line
out·live
out·look
out·ly·ing
out·ma·neu·ver
out·match
out·mod·ed
out·num·ber
out-of-door
out·pa·tient
out·play
out·point
out·post
out·pour·ing
out·put
out·rage
  out·ra·geous
out·reach
out·rid·er
out·rig·ger
out·right
out·run
out·sell
out·set
out·side
  out·sid·er
out·skirt
out·smart
out·soar
out·speak
  out·spo·ken
out·spread
out·stand·ing
out·stay
out·stretch
out·ward *adj.*
out·ward *or* out·wards *adv.*
  out·ward·ly
out·wear
out·weigh
out·wit
out·work
o·val
  o·val·ly

o·va·ry
o·va·tion
ov·en
over
over·a·bun·dance
over·all
over·arm
over·awe
over·bal·ance
over·bear·ing·ly
over·board
over·build
over·bur·den
over·cast
over·charge
over·coat
over·come
over·do *v.* (*do too much;* see *overdue*)
over·draft
over·draw
  over·drawn
over·due *adj.* (*past due;* see *overdo*)
over·em·pha·sis
over·flow
over·grow
over·hand
over·hang
over·haul
over·head
over·hear
over·land
over·lay
over·look
over·lord
over·ly
over·night
over·pass
over·pow·er
over·pro·duc·tion
over·reach
over·ride
over·rule

over·run
over·seas
over·shad·ow
over·shoe
over·sight
over·size *v., n., adj.*
over·sized
over·sleep
over·spread
over·stay
over·step
over·sub·scribe
over·sup·ply
overt
overt·ly
over·take
over-the-count·er
over·throw
over·time
over·tone
over·ture
over·turn
over·weigh
over·weight
over·whelm·ing·ly
over·work
o·vu·la·tion
o·vum
pl. o·va
owed *v.* (*indebted*; see *ode*)
owl·et
owl·ish
own·er·ship
ox·eye
ox·ford
ox·heart
ox·ide
ox·i·dize
ox·i·da·tion
ox·tail
ox·tongue
ox·y·gen
ox·y·gen·ate
ox·y·gen·a·tion

oys·ter
oys·ter bed
oys·ter·man
o·zone

P

pace·mak·er
pac·er
pach·y·derm
pach·y·san·dra
pa·cif·ic
pac·i·fi·ca·tion
pa·cif·i·ca·tor
pa·cif·i·ca·to·ry
pa·cif·i·cist
pac·i·fy
pac·i·fi·er
pac·i·fism
pack·age
pack·er
pack·et
pack·horse
pack·ing
pack·ing·house
pack·man
pack rat
pack·sack
pack·sad·dle
pack·thread
pad·ding
pad·dle
pad·dler
pad·dock
pad·lock
pa·dre
pae·an *n.* (*song*; see *peon*)
pa·gan
pa·gan·ism
pa·gan·ize
pag·eant
pag·eant·ry
pag·i·na·tion

pa·go·da
pail n. (*bucket*; see *pale*)
pain n., v. (*hurt*; see *pane*)
  pain·ful
  pain·less
  pains·tak·ing
paint box
paint·brush
paint·er
paint·ing
paint·pot
pair n., v. (*couple*; see *pare* and *pear*)
pa·ja·mas
Pa·ki·stan
pal·ace
  pa·la·tial
pal·an·quin
pal·at·a·ble
pal·ate n. (*roof of the mouth*; see *pallet* and *palette*)
  pal·a·tal
  pal·a·tal·i·za·tion
  pal·a·tal·ize
pal·a·tine
pa·lav·er
pale adj., v., n. (*light colored*; see *pail*)
  pale·face
pa·le·ol·o·gy
pa·le·on·tol·o·gy
pal·ette n. (*painter's board*; see *palate* and *pallet*)
pal·frey
pal·ing
pal·i·sade
Pal·la·di·an
pal·la·di·um
pall·bear·er
pal·let n. (*mattress*; see *palate* and *palette*)
pal·li·ate
  pal·li·a·tion
  pal·li·a·tive

pal·lid
pal·lor
pal·met·to
  pl. pal·met·tos or pal·met·toes
palm·ist·ry
pal·o·mi·no
pal·pa·ble
pal·pate
pal·pi·tate
  pal·pi·ta·tion
pal·sy
  pal·sied
pal·try
pam·per
pamph·let
  pam·phle·teer
pan·a·ce·a
Pan·a·ma
Pan-A·mer·i·can
pan·a·tel·a
pan·cake
pan·cre·as
  pan·cre·a·tin
pan·dem·ic
pan·de·mo·ni·um
Pan·do·ra's box
pane n. (*glass sheet*; see *pain*)
pan·e·gyr·ic
  pan·e·gyr·i·cal
  pan·e·gyr·ist
pan·el
  pan·eled
  pan·el·ing
  pan·el·ist
pan·han·dle
pan·ic
  pan·icked
  pan·ic-strick·en
pan·ni·kin
pan·o·ply
pan·o·ra·ma
  pan·o·ram·ic
pan·sy
pan·ta·loon

pan·the·ism
  pan·the·ist
  pan·the·is·ti·cal
pan·the·on
pan·ther
pan·to·graph
pan·to·mime
pan·try
pa·pa·cy
pa·pal
pa·pa·ya
pa·per
  pa·per·back
  pa·per·board
  pa·per chase
  pa·per clip
  pa·per cut·ter
  pa·per·hang·er
  pa·per knife
  pa·per·weight
  pa·per work
pa·pier-mâ·ché
pa·pil·la
  pl. pa·pil·lae
  pap·il·lar·y
pa·pil·lo·ma
pa·poose
pa·pri·ka
Pap smear
pa·py·rus
  pl. pa·py·rus·es *or* pa·py·ri
par·a·ble
pa·rab·o·la
  par·a·bol·ic
par·a·chute
pa·rade
par·a·digm
par·a·dise
par·a·dox·i·cal
par·af·fin
par·a·gog·ic
par·a·gon
par·a·graph
Par·a·guay

par·al·lax
par·al·lel
  par·al·leled
  par·al·lel·ing
  par·al·lel·ism
  par·al·lel·o·gram
pa·ral·y·sis
par·a·lyze
  par·a·lyt·ic
pa·ram·e·ter *n.* (*key element*; see *perimeter*)
par·a·mount
par·a·noi·a
  par·a·noi·ac
  par·a·noid
par·a·pet
par·a·pher·na·lia
par·a·phrase
par·a·site
  par·a·sit·ic
  par·a·sit·i·cide
par·a·sol
par·a·troop·er
par·boil
par·cel
  par·celed
  par·cel·ing
parch·ment
par·don
  par·don·a·ble
  par·don·er
pare *v.* (*to trim*; see *pair* and *pear*)
par·e·gor·ic
par·ent
  par·ent·age
  par·ent·hood
par·en·ter·al
pa·ren·the·sis
  pl. pa·ren·the·ses
  par·en·thet·i·cal
pa·re·sis
  pl. pa·re·ses
par·fait

pa·ri·ah
pa·ri·e·tal
par·i·mu·tu·el
par·ish *n.* (*church district;*
   see *perish*)
  pa·rish·io·ner
Pa·ri·sian
par·i·ty
par·ka
park·way
par·lance
par·lay *n., v.* (*to exploit;* see
  parley)
par·ley *n., v.* (*to confer;* see
  parlay)
par·lia·ment
  par·lia·men·tar·i·an
  par·lia·men·ta·ry
par·lor
  par·lor car
  par·lor·maid
par·lous
pa·ro·chi·al
par·o·dy
pa·role
par·ox·ysm
  par·ox·ys·mal
par·quet
  par·que·try
par·ra·keet
par·ri·cide
par·rot
parse
Par·si·fal
par·si·mo·ny
  par·si·mo·ni·ous
pars·ley
pars·nip
par·son
  par·son·age
par·take
  par·tak·er
part·ed
par·terre

Par·the·non
par·tial
  par·tial·i·ty
  par·tial·ly
par·tic·i·pate
  par·tic·i·pant
  par·tic·i·pa·tion
  par·tic·i·pa·tor
par·ti·ci·ple
  par·ti·cip·i·al
par·ti·cle
par·tic·u·lar
  par·tic·u·lar·i·ty
  par·tic·u·lar·ize
  par·tic·u·lar·ly
par·ti·san
  par·ti·san·ship
par·ti·tion
part·ly
part·ner
  part·ner·ship
par·tridge
part time *n.*
part-time *adj.*
par·tu·ri·tion
par·ty
par·ve·nu
par·vis
PAS·CAL
pas·chal
pa·sha
pass·a·ble
pas·sage
  pas·sage·way
pass·book
pas·sé
passed *v.* (*pt. of pass;* see
  past)
pas·sen·ger
pas·ser·by
  pl. pas·sers·by
pass·ing
pas·sion
  pas·sion·ate

pas·sion·flow·er
pas·sion·less
pas·sive
pass·key
pass·port
pass·word
past *adj., n., prep., adv.*
  (*time*; see *passed*)
paste·board
pas·tel
pas·tern
pas·teur·ize
  pas·teur·i·za·tion
pas·tiche
pas·tille
pas·time
pas·tor
  pas·tor·ate
  pas·tor·ship
pas·to·ral
  pas·to·ral·ism
  pas·to·ral·ly
pas·tra·mi
pas·try
pas·ture
  pas·tur·age
pas·try
patch·ou·li
patch test
patch·work
patch·y
pate
pâ·té
pa·tel·la
  pl. pa·tel·lae
pat·ent
  pat·ent·a·ble
  pat·en·tee
pa·ter·fa·mil·i·as
pa·ter·nal
  pa·ter·nal·ism
  pa·ter·nal·ly
pa·ter·ni·ty
pa·thet·ic

path·find·er
path·o·gen
pa·thol·o·gy
  path·o·log·ic
  path·o·log·i·cal
pa·thos
path·way
pa·tient
  pa·tience
pa·ti·na
  pl. pa·ti·nas *or* pa·ti·nae
pa·ti·o
pâ·tis·se·rie
pa·tri·arch
  pa·tri·ar·chal
  pa·tri·ar·chy
pa·tri·cian
pat·ri·cide
pat·ri·mo·ny
pa·tri·ot
  pa·tri·ot·ic
  pa·tri·o·tism
pa·trol
  pa·trolled
  pa·trol·ling
  pa·trol·man
pa·tron
  pa·tron·age
  pa·tron·ize
pat·ro·nym·ic
pa·troon
pat·ten
pat·ter
pat·tern
pat·ty
pau·ci·ty
paunch·i·ness
pau·per
  pau·per·ism
  pau·per·ize
pave·ment
pa·vil·ion
pav·ing
pawn·bro·ker

pawn·bro·king
pawn·er
pawn·shop
pay·a·ble
pay·check
pay·day
pay dirt
pay·ee
pay·er
pay·load
pay·mas·ter
pay·ment
pay off *v.*
pay·off *n., adj.*
pay·roll
peace *n.* (*serenity; see piece*)
  peace·a·ble
  peace·ful
  peace·mak·er
  peace pipe
  peace·time
peach
  peach·blow
  peach·y
pea·cock
pea·hen
peak *n., v.* (*top; see peek and
  pique*)
peal *n., v.* (*to ring out; see
  peel*)
pea·nut
pear *n.* (*fruit, see pare and
  pair*)
  pear-shaped
pearl *n., v.* (*jewel; see purl*)
  pearl·y
peas·ant·ry
peb·ble
pec·ca·dil·lo
pec·cant
  pec·can·cy
pec·to·ral
pec·u·late
  pec·u·la·tion
  pec·u·la·tor

pe·cu·liar
  pe·cu·liar·i·ty
  pe·cu·liar·ly
pe·cu·ni·ar·y
ped·a·go·gy
  ped·a·gog·ic
  ped·a·gog·i·cal
  ped·a·gogue
ped·al *n., v., adj.* (*foot piece;
  see peddle*)
  ped·aled
  ped·al·ing
ped·ant
  pe·dan·tic
  ped·ant·ry
ped·dle *v.* (*to sell; see pedal*)
  ped·dler
  ped·dling
ped·es·tal
pe·des·tri·an
  pe·des·tri·an·ism
pe·di·at·rics
  pe·di·a·tri·cian
ped·i·cure
ped·i·gree
ped·i·ment
pe·dom·e·ter
peek *v., n.* (*to look; see peak
  and pique*)
peel *v., n.* (*to skin; see peal*)
peep·hole
peep show
peep sight
peer *n.* (*equal; see pier*)
  peer·age
  peer·ess
  peer·less
pee·vish
Peg·a·sus
pegged
peg·ging
pe·jo·ra·tive
pel·i·can
pe·lisse

pel·la·gra
pel·let
pell-mell
pel·lu·cid
pel·try
pel·vis
  pl. pel·vis·es *or* pel·ves
pe·nal
  pe·nal·i·za·tion
  pe·nal·ize
  pen·al·ty
pen·ance
pench·ant
pen·cil
  pen·ciled
  pen·cil·ler
pen·dant *n.* (*ornament*; see *pendent*)
pen·den·cy
pen·dent *adj.* (*suspended*; see *pendant*)
pend·ing
pen·drag·on
pen·du·lum
  pen·du·lous
pen·e·trate
  pen·e·tra·ble
  pen·e·tra·tion
  pen·e·tra·tive
pen·guin
pen·hold·er
pen·i·cil·lin
pen·in·su·la
  pen·in·su·lar
pen·i·tent
  pen·i·tence
  pen·i·ten·tial
  pen·i·tent·ly
pen·i·ten·tia·ry
pen·knife
pen·man
  pen·man·ship
pen name
pen·nant

Penn·syl·va·ni·a
pen·ny
  pl. pen·nies
  pen·ni·less
  pen·ny·weight
  pen·ny-wise
  pen·ny·worth
pe·nol·o·gy
  pe·no·log·i·cal
  pe·nol·o·gist
pen·sile
pen·sion
  pen·sion·ar·y
  pen·sion·er
pen·sive
pen·stock
pen·ta·gon
  pen·tag·o·nal
pen·tath·lon
Pen·te·cost
pent·house
pe·nult
  pen·ul·ti·mate
pen·u·ry
  pe·nu·ri·ous
pe·on *n.* (*peasant*; see *paean*)
  pe·on·age
pe·o·ny
peo·ple
pep·per
  pep·per-and-salt
  pep·per·box
  pep·per·corn
  pep·per·mint
  pep·per·y
pep·sin
pep·tic
per·ad·ven·ture
per·am·bu·la·tion
per·am·bu·la·tor
per an·num
per·cale
per cap·i·ta

per·ceive
  per·ceiv·a·ble
per·cent
  per·cent·age
  per·cen·tile
per·cept *n.* (*impression;* see
  precept)
  per·cep·ti·ble
  per·cep·tion
  per·cep·tive
  per·cep·tu·al
per·chance
Per·che·ron
per·cip·i·ent
  per·cip·i·ence
per·co·late
  per·co·la·tor
per·cus·sion
  per·cus·sive
per di·em
per·di·tion
per·e·gri·na·tion
pe·remp·to·ry
  pe·remp·to·ri·ly
  pe·remp·to·ri·ness
pe·ren·ni·al
per·fect
  per·fect·i·ble
  per·fec·tion
  per·fec·tion·ism
per·fec·to
per·fi·dy
  per·fid·i·ous
per·fo·rate
  per·fo·ra·tion
  per·fo·ra·tor
per·force
per·form
  per·form·ance
  per·form·er
per·fume
  per·fum·er
  per·fum·er·y
per·func·to·ry

per·haps
per·i·car·di·um
per·il·ous
pe·rim·e·ter *n.* (*boundary;*
  see *parameter*)
pe·ri·od
  pe·ri·od·ic
  pe·ri·od·i·cal
per·i·o·don·tist
pe·riph·er·y
  pe·riph·er·al
pe·riph·ra·sis
  per·i·phras·tic
per·i·scope
  per·i·scop·ic
per·ish *v.* (*to die;* see *parish*)
  per·ish·a·ble
per·i·stal·sis
per·i·to·ne·um
per·i·to·ni·tis
per·i·win·kle
per·jure
  per·jur·er
  per·ju·ry
perk
per·ma·nence
  per·ma·nen·cy
  per·ma·nent
per·me·ate
  per·me·a·bil·i·ty
  per·me·a·ble
  per·me·a·tion
per·mit
  per·mis·si·ble
  per·mis·sion
  per·mis·sive
  per·mit·ted
  per·mit·ting
per·mu·ta·tion
per·ni·cious
per·nick·e·ty
per·o·ra·tion
per·ox·ide
per·pen·dic·u·lar

per·pe·trate
  per·pe·tra·tion
  per·pe·tra·tor
per·pet·u·al
  per·pet·u·al·ly
per·pet·u·ate
  per·pet·u·a·tion
  per·pet·u·a·tor
  per·pe·tu·i·ty
per·plex
  per·plexed
  per·plex·ed·ly
  per·plex·i·ty
per·qui·site *n.* (*privilege*; see *prerequisite*)
per·ry
per se
per·se·cute *v.* (*to harass*; see *prosecute*)
  per·se·cu·tion *n.* (*see prosecution*)
  per·se·cu·tor *n.* (*see prosecutor*)
per·se·vere
  per·se·ver·ance
Per·sia
  Per·sian
per·si·flage
per·sim·mon
per·sist
  per·sist·ence
  per·sist·en·cy
  per·sist·ent
per·son
  per·son·a
  pl. per·son·ae *or* per·son·as
  per·son·a·ble
  per·son·age
  per·son·al *adj., n.* (*private*; see *personnel*)
  per·son·al·i·ty *n.* (*personal being*; see *personalty*)
  per·son·al·ize
  per·son·al·ly

per·son·al·ty *n.* (*personal property*; see *personality*)
  per·son·i·fi·ca·tion
  per·son·i·fy
  per·son·nel *n.* (*employees*; see *personal*)
per·spec·tive *n.* (*angle of vision*; see *prospective*)
per·spi·cac·i·ty
  per·spi·ca·cious
per·spi·cu·i·ty
  per·spic·u·ous
per·spire
  per·spi·ra·tion
  per·spi·ra·to·ry
per·suade
  per·sua·si·ble
  per·sua·sion
  per·sua·sive
per·tain
per·ti·na·cious
  per·ti·nac·i·ty
per·ti·nent
  per·ti·nence
  per·ti·nen·cy
per·turb
  per·turb·a·ble
  per·tur·ba·tion
Per·u
  Pe·ru·vi·an
pe·ruse
  pe·rus·al
  pe·rus·er
per·vade
  per·va·sive
per·verse
  per·ver·sion
  per·ver·si·ty
  per·ver·sive
per·vert
  per·vert·ed
  per·vert·er
per·vi·ous
pe·so

pes·si·mism
  pes·si·mist
  pes·si·mis·tic
pes·ter
pest·hole
pest·house
pes·ti·cide
pes·tif·er·ous
pes·ti·lent
  pes·ti·lence
  pes·ti·len·tial
pes·tle
pet·al
pet·cock
pet·it adj. (legal term; see petite and petty)
pe·tite adj., n. (small; see petit and petty)
pet·it four
pe·ti·tion
  pe·ti·tion·er
pet·it point
pet·ri·fy
  pet·ri·fac·tion
  pet·ri·fac·tive
pet·rol
pe·tro·le·um
  pet·ro·la·tum
pe·trol·o·gy
  pet·ro·log·ic
pet·ti·coat
pet·ti·fog
  pet·ti·fog·ger·y
pet·ty adj. (trivial; see petit and petite)
  pet·ti·ly
  pet·ti·ness
pet·u·lant
  pet·u·lance
  pet·u·lan·cy
pe·tu·ni·a
pew
pew·ter
  pew·ter·er

pha·lanx
  pl. pha·lanx·es or pha·lan·ges
phan·tasm
  phan·tas·ma·go·ri·a
phan·tom
phar·aoh
phar·i·see
phar·ma·cy
  phar·ma·ceu·ti·cal
  phar·ma·cist
  phar·ma·co·poe·ia
phase n., v. (period of time; see faze)
pheas·ant
phe·nom·e·non
  pl. phe·nom·e·na
  phe·nom·e·nal·ly
  phe·nom·e·nol·o·gy
phi·al
phi·lan·der
  phi·lan·der·er
phi·lan·thro·py
  phil·an·throp·ic
  phil·an·throp·i·cal
  phi·lan·thro·pist
phi·lat·e·ly
  phil·a·tel·ic
phil·har·mon·ic
phi·lip·pic
Phil·ip·pines
phi·lis·tine
phi·lol·o·gy
  phil·o·log·i·cal
  phi·lol·o·gist
phi·los·o·phy
  phi·los·o·pher
  phil·o·soph·ic
  phil·o·soph·i·cal
phil·ter n. (love potion; see filter)
phle·bi·tis
phlegm
  phleg·mat·ic
Phoe·ni·cian

phoe·nix
pho·net·ic
pho·ne·ti·cian
pho·nics
pho·no·graph
phos·phate
phos·pho·res·cence
  phos·pho·resce
  phos·pho·res·cent
phos·pho·rus *n.*
  phos·pho·ric
  phos·pho·rous *adj.*
pho·to·cop·y
pho·to·e·lec·tric
pho·to·en·grav·ing
pho·to·gen·ic
pho·tog·ra·phy
  pho·to·graph
  pho·tog·ra·pher
  pho·to·graph·ic
pho·to·gra·vure
pho·to·mu·ral
pho·ton
pho·to-off·set
pho·to·play
Pho·to·stat (*trademark*)
phra·se·ol·o·gy
phre·net·ic
phre·nol·o·gy
  phre·nol·o·gist
phys·ics
  phys·ic
  phys·i·cal
  phy·si·cian
  phys·i·cist
phys·i·og·no·my
phys·i·og·ra·phy
phys·i·ol·o·gy
  phys·i·ol·o·gist
phys·io·ther·a·py
phy·sique
pi·a·nis·si·mo
pi·an·o
  pl. pi·an·os
  pi·an·ist

pi·as·ter
pi·az·za
pi·ca
pic·a·dor
pi·ca·resque
pic·a·yune
pic·ca·lil·li
pic·co·lo
  pic·co·lo·ist
pick n., v. (*tool; choice; see
  pique*)
pick·a·nin·ny *or* pic·a·nin·ny
pick·ax *or* pick·axe
pick·er·el
pick·et
pick·le
pick·lock
pick·pock·et
pick·up *n.*
pick up *v.*
pic·nic
  pic·nicked
  pic·nick·ing
pi·cot
pic·tog·ra·phy
  pic·to·graph
pic·to·ri·al
pic·ture n., v. (*image; see
  pitcher*)
  pic·tur·esque
pid·gin n. (*language; see
  pigeon*)
pie·bald
piece n., v. (*portion; see
  peace*)
  piece goods
  piece·meal
  piece·work
pièce de ré·sist·ance
pie chart
pie·plant
pier n. (*dock; see peer*)
pi·e·ty
pi·geon n. (*bird; see pidgin*)
  pi·geon·hole

pi·geon-toed
pi·geon·wing
pig·fish
pig·ger·y
pig·gish
pig·gy·back
pig·head·ed
pig i·ron
pig·ment
  pig·men·ta·tion
pig·my
pig·pen
pig·skin
pig·sty
pig·tail
  pig-tailed
pig·weed
pike·man
pike perch
pik·er
pike·staff
pi·las·ter
pil·chard
pil·fer
pil·grim
  pil·grim·age
pil·ing
pil·lage
pil·lar
pill·box
pil·lion
pil·lo·ry
pil·low
  pil·low·case
pi·lot
  pi·lot·house
pi·men·to
  pl. pi·men·tos *or* pi·men·to
pim·ple
pin·a·fore
pi·ña·ta
pince-nez
pin·cer
pinch·beck

pinch-hit *v.*
pinch hit *n.*
pin curl
pin·cush·ion
pine·ap·ple
pin·feath·er
pin·fold
Ping-Pong (*trademark*)
pin·head
  pin·head·ed
pin·hole
pin·ion
pink·eye
pin·na·cle
pi·noch·le
pin·point
pin·prick
pin·stripe
pin·up
pin·wheel
pi·o·neer
pi·ous
pipe clay *n.*
pipe-clay *v.*
pipe dream
pipe·line
pip·er
pipe·stone
pipe wrench
pi·quant
  pi·quan·cy
pique *n., v.* (*anger; see peak
  and peek*)
pi·ra·cy
pi·ra·nha
pi·rate
  pi·rat·i·cal
pir·ou·ette
pis·ca·to·ry
pis·ces
pis·ta·chi·o
pis·til *n.* (*plant section; see
  pistol and pistole*)

pis·tol *n.* (*gun;* see *pistil* and
  pistole)
  pis·tol-whip
pis·tole *n.* (*gold coin;* see
  pistil and *pistol*)
pis·ton
pitch black *n.*
pitch-black *adj.*
pitch-dark
pitch·er *n.* (*vessel;* see *picture*)
pitch·fork
pitch·man
pitch pipe
pitch·stone
pit·e·ous
pit·fall
pit·head
pith·y
  pith·i·ly
  pith·i·ness
pit·man
pit saw
pit·tance
pit·ter-pat·ter
pi·tu·i·tar·y
pit·y
  pit·i·a·ble
  pit·i·ful
  pit·i·less
piv·ot
  piv·ot·al
pix·el
pix·ie
piz·za
  piz·ze·ri·a
piz·zi·ca·to
pla·ca·ble
  pla·ca·bil·i·ty
pla·card
pla·cate
  pla·ca·to·ry
pla·ce·bo
place-kick
place·ment

plac·id
  pla·cid·i·ty
pla·gia·ry
  pla·gia·rism
  pla·gia·rist
  pla·gia·rize
plague
plain *adj., adv., n.*
  (*undecorated; flat land;*
  see *plane*)
  plain·clothes·man
  plain·ness
  plains·man
  plain·spo·ken
plaint
plain·tiff *n.*
plain·tive *adj.*
plait *n., v.* (*to braid;* see *plate*)
plane *n., v.* (*airplane;*
  geometric figure; see *plain*)
plan·et
  plan·e·tar·i·um
  plan·e·tar·y
plan·gent
plank·ing
plank·ton
plan·ner
plan·tain
plan·tar *adj.* (*of the sole of
  the foot;* see *planter*)
plan·ta·tion
plant·er *n.* (*one who plants;*
  see *plantar*)
plaque
plas·ma
plas·ter
  plas·ter·board
  plas·ter·er
  plas·ter·work
plas·tic
  plas·tic·i·ty
plat
plate *n., v.* (*dish;* see *plait*)
  plate·ful

plate glass
plat·er
plat·ing
pla·teau
 pl. pla·teaus *or* pla·teaux
plat·en
plat·form
plat·i·num
plat·i·tude
 plat·i·tu·di·nous
Pla·to·nism
 pla·ton·ic
pla·toon
plat·ter
plau·dit
plau·si·ble
 plau·si·bil·i·ty
play·act·ing
play back *v.*
play·back *n.*
play·bill
play·boy
play·clothes
play·er
play·fel·low
play·ful
play·go·er
play·ground
play·house
play·let
play off *v.*
play-off *n.*
play·pen
play·room
play school
play·suit
play·thing
play·time
play·wright
pla·za
plea
plead·a·ble
plead·er
plead·ing

pleas·ant
 pleas·ant·ry
pleas·ing
plea·sure
 plea·sur·a·ble
pleat
ple·be·ian
pleb·i·scite
plec·trum
 pl. plec·tra *or* plec·trums
pledge
 pledg·ee
pled·get
ple·na·ry
plen·i·po·ten·ti·a·ry
plen·i·tude
plen·ty
 plen·te·ous
 plen·ti·ful
ple·num
 pl. ple·nums *or* ple·na
ple·o·nasm
pleth·o·ra
pleu·ri·sy
pli·a·ble
pli·ant
 pli·an·cy
pli·ers
plod·ded
plod·der
plod·ding
plot·ted
plot·ter
plot·ting
plow·boy
plow·man
plow·share
plug
 plugged
 plug·ging
 plug-ug·ly
plum *n.* (*fruit*; see *plumb*)
plu·mage

plumb *n., adj., adv., v.*
  (*weight*; see *plum*)
  plumb bob
  plumb·ing
  plumb line
plumb·er
plum·met
plump·ness
plun·der
  plun·der·er
plung·er
plu·per·fect
plu·ral
  plu·ral·ism
  plu·ral·is·tic
  plu·ral·i·ty
  plu·ral·i·za·tion
  plu·ral·ize
plu·toc·ra·cy
  plu·to·crat
  plu·to·crat·ic
plu·to·ni·um
ply·wood
pneu·mat·ics
  pneu·mat·ic
pneu·mo·nia
pneu·mon·ic
poach·er
pock·et
  pock·et·book
  pock·et·ful
  pock·et·knife
pock·mark
po·di·a·trist
po·di·a·try
po·di·um
  pl. po·di·ums *or* po·di·a
po·em
po·e·sy
po·et
  po·et·as·ter
  po·et·ic
  po·et·i·cal
  po·et·ry

po·grom
poi·gnant
  poi·gnan·cy
poin·set·tia
point-blank
point·ed
point·er
point·less
poi·son
  poi·son·ous
  poi·son-pen
pok·er
Po·land
po·lar
po·lar·i·ty
po·lar·ize
  po·lar·i·za·tion
Po·lar·oid (*trademark*)
pole *n., v.* (*shaft*; see *poll*)
  pole·ax *or* pole·axe
  pole·cat
  pole·star
  pole vault *n.*
  pole-vault *v.*
  pole-vault·er *n.*
po·lem·ic
  po·lem·i·cal
po·lice·man
pol·i·clin·ic *n.* (*outpatient
  department*; see *polyclinic*)
pol·i·cy
  pol·i·cy·hold·er
pol·ish *v., n.* (*to smooth*; see
  Polish)
  pol·ish·er
Polish *adj., n.* (*language*; see
  polish)
Po·lit·bu·ro
po·lite
  po·lite·ness
pol·i·tics
  pol·i·tic
  po·lit·i·cal
  po·lit·i·cal·ly
  pol·i·ti·cian

pol·i·ty
pol·ka
pol·ka dot *n.*
pol·ka-dot *v.*
poll *n., v.* (*voting place;* see
   pole)
pol·len
   pol·li·nate
pol·li·wog
poll tax
pol·lute
   pol·lu·tion
po·lo·naise
pol·ter·geist
pol·troon
poly·an·dry
poly·an·thus
poly·cen·trism
poly·chrome
   poly·chro·mat·ic
poly·clin·ic *n.* (*hospital;* see
   policlinic)
po·lyg·a·my
   po·lyg·a·mist
   po·lyg·a·mous
poly·glot
poly·gon
poly·graph
   poly·graph·ic
poly·mer
polyp
poly·phon·ic
poly·syl·la·ble
   poly·syl·lab·ic
poly·tech·nic
po·made
pome·gran·ate
pom·mel
pom·pa·dour
pom·pa·no
pom·pom
pomp·ous
   pom·pos·i·ty

pon·cho
   pl. pon·chos
pon·der
   pon·der·ous
pon·der·a·ble
pon·gee
pon·iard
pon·tiff
   pon·tif·i·cal
   pon·tif·i·cate
pon·toon
po·ny
   po·ny·tail
poo·dle
pooh-pooh
pool·room
poor *adj., n.* (see *pore* and
   pour)
   poor box
   poor farm
   poor·house
   poor·ly
   poor-spir·it·ed
pop·corn
pop·eyed
pop·gun
pop·in·jay
pop·lar *n.* (*tree;* see *popular*)
pop·lin
pop·o·ver
pop·py
pop·py·cock
pop·u·lace *n.* (*inhabitants;*
   see *populous*)
pop·u·lar *adj.* (*well-liked;* see
   poplar)
   pop·u·lar·i·ty
   pop·u·lar·i·za·tion
   pop·u·lar·ize
pop·u·late
   pop·u·la·tion
pop·u·lous *adj.* (*densely
   populated;* see *populace*)
por·ce·lain

por·cu·pine
pore *n., v. (opening;* see
  poor and *pour*)
pork·er
pork·pie hat
por·nog·ra·phy
po·rous
por·phy·ry
por·poise
por·ridge
por·rin·ger
por·ta·ble
por·tage
por·tal
por·tend
por·tent
  por·ten·tous
por·ter
  por·ter·house
port·fo·li·o
port·hole
por·ti·co
  pl. por·ti·co·es *or* por·ti·cos
por·tiere
por·tion
port·ly
  port·li·ness
port·man·teau
  pl. port·man·teaus *or*
  port·man·teaux
por·trait
  por·trai·ture
por·tray
  por·tray·al
Por·tu·gal
  Por·tu·guese
pos·it
po·si·tion
pos·i·tive
pos·i·tron
pos·se
pos·sess
  pos·sessed
  pos·ses·sion

pos·ses·sive
pos·ses·sor
pos·si·ble
  pos·si·bil·i·ty
post·age
post·al
post·box
post·boy
post·card
post·clas·si·cal
post·date
post·doc·tor·al
post·er
pos·te·ri·or
pos·ter·i·ty
pos·tern
post·grad·u·ate
post·haste
post·hole
post horn
post-horse
post·hu·mous
post·hyp·not·ic
pos·til·ion *or* pos·til·lion
post·lude
post·man
post·mark
post·mas·ter
post·mis·tress
post·mor·tem
post·na·sal
post-o·bit
post of·fice *n.*
post-of·fice *adj.*
post-of·fice box
post·paid
post·par·tum
post·pone
  post·pone·ment
post·pran·di·al
post·script
pos·tu·lant
pos·tu·late
pos·ture

post·war
po·ta·ble
pot·ash
po·tas·si·um
po·ta·tion
po·ta·to
  pl. po·ta·toes
pot·bel·ly
  pot·bel·lied
pot·boil·er
pot·boy
pot cheese
po·ten·cy
po·ten·tate
po·ten·tial
  po·ten·ti·al·i·ty
po·tent·ly
pot·hole
pot·hook
pot·house
po·tion
pot·latch
pot·luck
pot·pie
pot roast
pot·sherd
pot·shot
pot still
pot·tage
pot·ter
  pot·ter·y
poul·tice
poul·try
  poul·try·man
pound·age
pound cake
pour *v.* (*to flow*; see *poor* and *pore*)
pov·er·ty-strick·en
pow·der
  pow·der·y
pow·er·boat
pow·er·ful
pow·er·less

pow·wow
prac·ti·ca·ble
  prac·ti·ca·bil·i·ty
prac·ti·cal
  prac·ti·cal·i·ty
  prac·ti·cal·ly
prac·tice
  prac·ticed
  prac·tic·er
  prac·ti·tion·er
prag·ma·tism
  prag·mat·ic
  prag·mat·i·cal
  prag·ma·tist
prai·rie
praise·wor·thy
  praise·worth·i·ness
pra·line
prance
prank·ish
prat·tle
pray *v.* (*entreat*; see *prey*)
  prayer *n.* (*request*)
  pray·er *n.* (*one who prays*)
  prayer book
  prayer·ful
preach·er
preach·ment
pre·am·ble
pre·can·cel
pre·car·i·ous
pre·cau·tion
  pre·cau·tion·ar·y
pre·cede *v.* (*to come before*; see *proceed*)
  prec·e·dence
  prec·e·den·cy (see *presidency*)
  pre·ced·ent *adj.*
  prec·e·dent *n., v.* (*that which comes before*; see *president*)
  pre·ced·ing
pre·cept *n.* (*law*; see *percept*)
  pre·cep·tive *adj.* (see *perceptive*)

pre·cep·tor
pre·cep·to·ry
pre·ces·sion *n.* (*rotation*; see
  procession)
pre·ces·sion·al *adj.* (see
  processional)
pre·cinct
pre·cious
prec·i·pice
pre·cip·i·tan·cy
  pre·cip·i·tance
pre·cip·i·tate
  pre·cip·i·tant
  pre·cip·i·tate·ly
  pre·cip·i·tate·ness
  pre·cip·i·ta·tion
  pre·cip·i·ta·tor
  pre·cip·i·tous
pre·cise
  pre·ci·sion
pre·clude
  pre·clu·sion
  pre·clu·sive
pre·co·cious
  pre·coc·i·ty
pre·con·ceive
  pre·con·cep·tion
pre·con·cert
pre·cook
pre·cur·sor
  pre·cur·so·ry
pred·a·to·ry
pre·de·cease
  pred·e·ces·sor
pre·des·tine
  pre·des·ti·nar·i·an
  pre·des·ti·na·tion
pre·de·ter·mine
pre·dic·a·ment
pred·i·cate
  pred·i·ca·tion
  pred·i·ca·tive
pre·dict
  pre·dict·a·ble

pre·dic·tion
pre·dic·tive
pre·dic·tor
pre·di·lec·tion
pre·dis·pose
  pre·dis·po·si·tion
pre·dom·i·nate
  pre·dom·i·nance
  pre·dom·i·nant
  pre·dom·i·na·tion
pre·em·i·nent
  pre·em·i·nence
pre·empt
  pre·emp·tive
pre·fab·ri·cate
  pre·fab
pref·ace
  pref·a·to·ry
pre·fect
  pre·fec·ture
pre·fer
  pref·er·a·ble
  pref·er·ence
  pref·er·en·tial
  pre·ferred
  pre·fer·ring
pre·fix
pre·flight
preg·nant
  preg·nan·cy
pre·heat
pre·his·tor·ic
pre·judge
prej·u·dice
  prej·u·di·cial
prel·ate
  prel·a·cy
pre·lim·i·nar·y
prel·ude
pre·ma·ture
  pre·ma·tu·ri·ty
pre·med·i·tate
  pre·med·i·ta·tion

pre·mier *adj., n. (first in rank;*
  see premiere)
pre·miere *n., v. (first*
  performance; see premier)
prem·ise
  pl. prem·is·es
pre·mi·um
pre·mo·ni·tion
  pre·mon·i·to·ry
pre·na·tal
pre·oc·cu·py
  pre·oc·cu·pan·cy
  pre·oc·cu·pa·tion
  pre·oc·cu·pied
pre·or·dain
pre·pare
  prep·a·ra·tion
  pre·par·a·tive
  pre·par·a·to·ry
  pre·pared
  pre·par·ed·ness
pre·pay
  pre·paid
  pre·pay·ment
pre·pon·der·ate
  pre·pon·der·ance
  per·pon·der·ant
prep·o·si·tion
  prep·o·si·tion·al
pre·pos·sess
  pre·pos·sess·ing
  pre·pos·ses·sion
pre·pos·ter·ous
pre·po·ten·cy
pre·re·cord
pre·req·ui·site *adj., n.*
  (requirement; see
  perquisite)
pre·rog·a·tive
pres·age
Pres·by·te·ri·an
pre·sci·ent
pre·scribe *v. (to dictate; see*
  proscribe)

pre·scrip·ti·ble
pre·scrip·tion
pre·scrip·tive
pres·ence
pre·sent *v.*
  pre·sent·a·ble
  pre·sen·ta·tion
  pre·sen·ta·tive
pres·ent *adj., n.*
  pres·ent-day
  pres·ent·ly
pres·en·tee
pre·sen·ti·ment *n.*
  (premonition; see
  presentment)
pre·sent·ment *n. (act of*
  presenting; see
  presentiment)
pre·serve
  pre·serv·a·ble
  pres·er·va·tion
  pre·serv·a·tive
pre·side
  pre·sid·er
pres·i·dent *n. (chief; see*
  precedent)
  pres·i·den·cy *n. (see*
  precedency)
  pres·i·den·tial
press a·gent
press·board
press box
pressed
press·er
press-gang
press·ing
press·man
press·mark
press·room
press·run
pres·sure
  pres·sur·ize
press·work
pres·ti·dig·i·ta·tor

pres·tige
  pres·tig·i·ous
pres·tis·si·mo
pre·sume
  pre·sum·a·ble
  pre·sump·tion
  pre·sump·tive
  pre·sump·tu·ous
pre·sup·pose
pre·tend
  pre·tend·ed
  pre·tend·er
  pre·tense
pre·ten·sion
pre·ten·tious
pret·er·it *or* pret·er·ite
pre·ter·nat·u·ral
pre·text
pret·ty
  pret·ti·ly
  pret·ti·ness
pret·zel
pre·vail
  pre·vail·ing
prev·a·lent
  prev·a·lence
pre·var·i·cate
  pre·var·i·ca·tion
  pre·var·i·ca·tor
pre·vent
  pre·vent·a·ble
  pre·ven·tion
  pre·ven·tive
pre·view
pre·vi·ous
pre·vi·sion
prey *n., v. (victim; see pray)*
price-cut·ter
price·less
price tag
prick·er
prick·le
  prick·li·ness
  prick·ly

priest·ess
priest·hood
priest·ly
pri·ma·cy
pri·ma don·na
pri·ma fa·ci·e
pri·ma·ry
  pri·mar·i·ly
pri·mate
prim·er
pri·me·val
prim·i·tive
pri·mo·gen·i·ture
pri·mor·di·al
prim·rose
prince·ly
prin·cess
prin·ci·pal *adj., n. (first; most important; see principle)*
  prin·ci·pal·i·ty
  prin·ci·pal·ly
prin·ci·ple *n. (law; see principal)*
print·a·ble
print·er
print·er·y
print·ing
print·out
pri·or
  pri·or·ess
  pri·or·ship
pri·or·i·ty
prism
  pris·mat·ic
pris·on
  pris·on·er
pris·tine
pri·vate
  pri·va·cy
  pri·va·teer
  pri·vate·ly
pri·va·tion
priv·et
priv·i·lege

priv·y
  priv·i·ly
  priv·i·ty
prize fight
prize ring
prob·a·ble
prob·a·bly
pro·bate
  pro·ba·tion
  pro·ba·tion·ar·y
  pro·ba·tion·er
  pro·ba·tive
  pro·ba·to·ry
pro·bi·ty
prob·lem
  prob·lem·at·ic
  prob·lem·at·i·cal
pro·bos·cis
  pl. pro·bos·cis *or*
  pro·bos·ci·des
pro·ca·the·dral
pro·ce·dure
  pro·ce·dur·al
pro·ceed *v.* (*to continue*; see
  precede)
  pro·ceed·ing
pro·cess
  pro·ces·sor
pro·ces·sion *n.* (*parade*; see
  precession)
  pro·ces·sion·al *adj.* (see
  precessional)
pro·claim
  proc·la·ma·tion
pro·cliv·i·ty
pro·con·sul
pro·cras·ti·nate
  pro·cras·ti·na·tion
  pro·cras·ti·na·tor
pro·cre·a·tion
pro·cre·a·tive
pro·crus·te·an
proc·ti·tis

proc·tor
  proc·to·ri·al
proc·to·scope
pro·cure
  pro·cur·a·ble
  proc·u·ra·tion
  proc·u·ra·tor
  pro·cure·ment
prod·i·gal
  prod·i·gal·i·ty
prod·i·gy
  pro·di·gious
pro·duce *v.*
  pro·duc·er
  prod·uct
  pro·duc·tion
  pro·duc·tive
  pro·duc·tiv·i·ty
pro·fane
  prof·a·na·tion
  pro·fa·na·to·ry
  pro·fan·i·ty
pro·fess
  pro·fess·ed·ly
pro·fes·sion
  pro·fes·sion·al
  pro·fes·sion·al·ism
  pro·fes·sion·al·ly
pro·fes·sor
  pro·fes·so·ri·al
  pro·fes·sor·ship
prof·fer
  prof·fer·ing
pro·fi·cient
  pro·fi·cien·cy
pro·file
prof·it *n.*, *v.* (*gain*; see
  prophet)
  prof·it·a·ble
  prof·i·teer
  prof·it·less
prof·li·gate
  prof·li·ga·cy
pro for·ma

pro·found
  pro·fun·di·ty
pro·fuse
  pro·fu·sion
pro·gen·i·tor
prog·e·ny
pro·ges·ter·one
prog·no·sis
  pl. prog·no·ses
prog·nos·ti·cate
  prog·nos·tic
  prog·nos·ti·ca·tion
pro·gram
prog·ress *n.*
pro·gress *v.*
  pro·gres·sive
pro·hib·it
  pro·hi·bi·tion
  pro·hi·bi·tion·ist
  pro·hib·i·tive
  pro·hib·i·to·ry
proj·ect *n.*
  pro·jec·tile
  pro·jec·tion
  pro·jec·tion·ist
  pro·jec·tive
  pro·jec·tor
pro·le·tar·i·at
  pro·le·tar·i·an
pro·lif·er·ate
pro·lif·ic
pro·lix
  pro·lix·i·ty
pro·logue
pro·long
  pro·lon·gate
prom·e·nade
Pro·me·the·us
prom·i·nent
  prom·i·nence
pro·mis·cu·ous
  pro·mis·cu·i·ty
prom·ise
  pl. prom·is·es

  prom·i·sor
  prom·is·so·ry
prom·on·to·ry
pro·mote
  pro·mot·er
  pro·mo·tion
  pro·mo·tion·al
prompt
  prompt·book
  prompt·er
  promp·ti·tude
pro·mul·gate
  pro·mul·ga·tion
pro·noun
  pro·nom·i·nal
pro·nounce
  pro·nounce·a·ble
  pro·nounced
  pro·nounce·ment
  pro·nounc·ing
  pro·nun·ci·a·men·to
  pro·nun·ci·a·tion
proof·read·er
proof·room
prop·a·gan·da
  prop·a·gan·dist
  prop·a·gan·dize
prop·a·gate
  prop·a·ga·ble
  prop·a·ga·tion
  prop·a·ga·tive
pro·pel
  pro·pelled
  pro·pel·ler
  pro·pel·ling
pro·pense
  pro·pen·si·ty
prop·er·ly
prop·er·ty
  prop·er·tied
proph·e·cy *n.* (*prediction*; see *prophesy*)
proph·e·sy *v.* (*to predict*; see *prophecy*)
  proph·e·si·er

proph·et *n.* (*soothsayer*; see
  profit)
  pro·phet·ic
  pro·phet·i·cal
pro·phy·lac·tic
  pro·phy·lax·is
  pl. pro·phy·lax·es
pro·pin·qui·ty
pro·pi·ti·ate
  pro·pi·ti·a·tion
  pro·pi·ti·a·tor
  pro·pi·ti·a·to·ry
pro·pi·tious
pro·po·nent
pro·por·tion
  pro·por·tion·al
  pro·por·tion·ate
pro·pose
  pro·pos·al
  prop·o·si·tion
pro·pound
pro·pri·e·tor
  pro·pri·e·tar·y
pro·pri·e·ty
pro·pul·sion
  pro·pul·sive
pro ra·ta
pro·rate
pro·rogue
pro·sa·ic
pro·sce·ni·um
pro·scribe *v.* (*to forbid*; see
  prescribe)
  pro·scrip·tion
  pro·scrip·tive
prose
pros·e·cute *v.* (*try for a crime*;
  see *persecute*)
  pros·e·cu·tion *n.* (see
  persecution)
  pros·e·cu·tor *n.* (*see persecutor*)
pros·e·lyte
pro·sit
pros·o·dy

pros·pect
  pro·spec·tive *adj.* (*expectant*;
  see *perspective*)
  pro·spec·tus
pros·per
  pros·per·i·ty
  pros·per·ous
pros·tate *n.* (*gland*; see
  prostrate)
pros·the·sis
  pros·thet·ics
pros·ti·tute
  pros·ti·tu·tion
pros·trate *v., adj.* (*to lie flat*;
  see *prostate*)
  pros·tra·tion
pros·y
pro·tag·o·nist
pro·te·an
pro·tect
  pro·tec·tion
  pro·tec·tion·ism
  pro·tec·tion·ist
  pro·tec·tive
  pro·tec·tor
  pro·tec·tor·ate
pro·té·gé *n.*
pro·tein
pro tem
pro·test
  prot·es·tant
  Prot·es·tant·ism
  pro·tes·ta·tion
pro·throm·bin
pro·to·col
pro·to·plasm
pro·to·type
pro·tract
  pro·trac·tile
  pro·trac·tion
  pro·trac·tor
pro·trude
  pro·tru·sion
  pro·tru·sive

pro·tu·ber·ant
  pro·tu·ber·ance
prov·a·ble
proved
prov·en
prov·e·nance
prov·en·der
pro·verb
  pro·ver·bi·al
pro·vide
  pro·vid·ed
  pro·vid·er
prov·i·dent
  prov·i·dence
  prov·i·den·tial
prov·ince
  pro·vin·cial
  pro·vin·cial·ism
pro·vi·sion
  pro·vi·sion·al
  pro·vi·sion·ar·y
  pro·vi·sion·er
pro·vi·so
  pro·vi·so·ry
prov·o·ca·tion
  pro·voc·a·tive
pro·voke
  pro·vok·ing
prow·ess
prox·i·mate
  prox·i·mal
  prox·im·i·ty
prox·y
prude
  prud·ish
pru·dent
  pru·dence
  pru·den·tial
pru·ri·ent
  pru·ri·ence
pry·ing
psalm
  psalm·book
  psalm·ist
  psal·mo·dy

pseu·do·nym
  pseu·don·y·mous
psit·ta·co·sis
pso·ri·a·sis
  pl. pso·ri·a·ses
psy·che
psy·chi·a·try
  psy·chi·at·ric
  psy·chi·a·trist
psy·chic
psy·cho·a·nal·y·sis
  psy·cho·an·a·lyst
  psy·cho·an·a·lyze
psy·cho·gen·ic
psy·cho·graph·ics
psy·chol·o·gy
  psy·cho·log·i·cal
  psy·chol·o·gist
  psy·chol·o·gize
psy·cho·neu·ro·sis
psy·cho·path
  psy·cho·path·ic
psy·cho·sis
  pl. psy·cho·ses
psy·cho·so·mat·ic
psy·cho·ther·a·py
psy·chot·ic
pu·ber·ty
pub·lic
  pub·lic·ly
  pub·lic-spir·it·ed
pub·li·ca·tion
pub·lic·i·ty
  pub·li·cist
  pub·li·cize
pub·lish
  pub·lish·er
puck·er
pud·ding
pud·dle
  pud·dling
pu·den·cy
pudg·i·ness
pueb·lo

pu·er·ile
Puer·to Ri·co
puff·y
　puff·i·ness
pu·gi·list
　pu·gi·lism
　pu·gi·lis·tic
pug·na·cious
　pug·nac·i·ty
pug nose n.
pug-nosed adj.
pu·is·sance
　pu·is·sant
pul·chri·tude
　pul·chri·tu·di·nous
pul·let
pul·ley
Pull·man (trademark)
pull o·ver v.
pull o·ver adj., n.
pul·mo·nar·y
Pul·mo·tor (trademark)
pul·pit
pulp·wood
pulp·y
　pulp·i·ness
pul·sar
pul·sate
　pul·sa·tion
pul·ver·ize
pum·ice
pum·mel
　pum·meled
　pum·mel·ing
pum·per·nick·el
pump·kin
punch·board
punch-drunk
pun·cheon
punc·til·i·o
　punc·til·i·ous
punc·tu·al
　punc·tu·al·i·ty
　punc·tu·al·ly

punc·tu·ate
　punc·tu·a·tion
　punc·tu·a·tor
punc·ture
pun·dit
pun·gent
　pun·gen·cy
pun·ish
　pun·ish·a·ble
　pun·ish·er
　pun·ish·ment
pu·ni·tive
pun·ster
punt·er
pu·ny
pu·pil
pup·pet
　pup·pet·ry
pup·py
pup tent
pur·blind
pur·chase
　pur·chas·a·ble
pur·dah
pu·ree
pure·ly
pur·ga·to·ry
　pur·ga·to·ri·al
purge
　pur·ga·tion
　pur·ga·tive
pu·ri·fy
　pu·ri·fi·ca·tion
　pu·ri·fi·er
pur·ist
pu·ri·tan
　pu·ri·tan·i·cal
pu·ri·ty
purl n., v. (knitting term; see
　pearl)
pur·lieu
pur·loin
pur·ple
　pur·plish

pur·port
  pur·port·ed·ly
pur·pose
  pur·pose·ly
  pur·pos·ive
purr
purs·er
pur·sue
  pur·su·ance
  pur·su·ant
  pur·suit
pu·ru·lent
pur·vey
  pur·vey·ance
  pur·vey·or
pur·view
push·ball
push broom
push but·ton *n*.
push-but·ton *adj*.
push·cart
push·i·ness
push·ing
push·o·ver
push·pin
push-pull
push-up
pu·sil·lan·i·mous
  pu·sil·la·nim·i·ty
pus·tu·late
  pus·tu·lant
  pus·tu·lar
  pus·tu·la·tion
  pus·tule
pu·ta·tive
put-on *adj*., *n*.
put on *v*.
pu·tre·fy
  pu·tre·fac·tion
  pu·tre·fac·tive
  pu·tres·cence
  pu·tres·cent
pu·trid
putt

put·ter
put·ty
put up *v*.
put-up *adj*., *n*.
puz·zle
  puz·zle·ment
  puz·zler
pyg·my
py·lon
py·lo·rus
  pl. py·lo·ri
py·or·rhe·a
pyr·a·mid
  py·ram·i·dal
pyre
py·ro·ma·ni·a
  py·ro·ma·ni·ac
py·rox·y·lin
pyr·rhic
py·thon

Q

quack·er·y
quad·ran·gle
  qua·dran·gu·lar
quad·rant
  qua·dran·tal
qua·drat·ic
qua·dren·ni·um
  qua·dren·ni·al
quad·ri·lat·er·al
qua·drille
qua·dril·lion
quad·ru·ped
  qua·dru·pe·dal
qua·dru·ple
  qua·dru·pli·cate
qua·dru·plet
quaff
quag·mire
quail

qual·i·fy
  qual·i·fi·ca·tion
  qual·i·fied
qual·i·ty
  qual·i·ta·tive
qualm
quan·da·ry
quan·ti·ty
  quan·ti·ta·tive
quan·tum
quar·an·tine
quar·rel
  quar·reled
  quar·rel·ing
  quar·rel·some
quar·ry
  quar·ry·ing
quart
quar·ter
  quar·ter·back
  quar·ter·deck
  quar·ter·ly
  quar·ter·mas·ter
quar·tet
quar·to
quartz
qua·sar
qua·si
  qua·si·ju·di·cial
  qua·si·pub·lic
qua·train
qua·tre·foil
qua·ver·ing·ly
quay *n.* (*wharf*; see *key*)
quea·sy
  quea·si·ness
Que·bec
queer
quench·less
quer·u·lous
que·ry
ques·tion
  ques·tion·a·ble
  ques·tion·er
  ques·tion·naire

queue *n.*, *v.* (*line of people*;
  see *cue*)
quib·ble
  quib·bling
quick·en
quick fire *n.*
quick-fire *adj.*
quick-freeze
quick·ie
quick·lime
quick-lunch
quick·sand
quick·sil·ver
quick·step
quick-tem·pered
quick-wit·ted
quid·di·ty
quid·nunc
quid pro quo
qui·es·cent
  qui·es·cence
qui·et
  qui·et·ness
  qui·e·tude
  qui·e·tus
qui·nine
quin·sy
quin·tes·sence
quin·tet
quin·tu·plet
quin·tu·pli·cate
quip
  quipped
  quip·ping
quire *n.* (*paper*; see *choir*)
quit
  quit·claim
  quit·tance
  quit·ter
quite
quiv·er
qui vive
quix·ot·ic
quiz
  quizzed

quiz·zi·cal
quiz·zing
quoin *n., v.*
quoit
quon·dam
quo·rum
quo·ta
quote
quot·a·ble
quo·ta·tion
quo·tid·i·an
quo·tient

R

rab·bet *n. (a groove; see
rabbit)*
rab·bi
rab·bit *n., v. (bunny; see
rabbet)*
rab·bit·ry
rab·ble
rab·ble-rous·er
ra·bies
rab·id
rac·coon
race·course
race·horse
rac·er
race·track
race·way
ra·cial
rac·i·ly
rac·i·ness
rac·ing
rac·ism
rack *n., v. (shelf; see wrack)*
rack·et
rack·e·teer
rac·on·teur
ra·dar
ra·dar·scope
ra·di·al

ra·di·ant
ra·di·ance
ra·di·an·cy
ra·di·ate
ra·di·a·tion
ra·di·a·tor
rad·i·cal
rad·i·cal·ism
rad·i·cal·ly
ra·di·o
ra·di·o·ac·tive
ra·di·o·gram
ra·di·o·graph
ra·di·og·ra·phy
ra·di·o·i·so·tope
ra·di·om·e·ter
ra·di·o·phone
ra·di·o·sonde
ra·di·o·tel·e·graph
ra·di·o·tel·e·phone
ra·di·o·ther·a·py
rad·ish
ra·di·um
ra·di·us
pl. ra·di·i *or* ra·di·us·es
ra·dix
raf·fle
raft·er
rafts·man
rag·a·muf·fin
rag·ged
rag·ing
rag·lan
rag·man
ra·gout
rag·pick·er
rag·time
rag·weed
rail·bird
rail fence
rail·head
rail·ing
rail·ler·y
rail·road

rail-split·ter
rail·way
rai·ment
rain *n., v. (precipitation;* see
  reign and *rein*)
  rain·bow
  rain check
  rain cloud
  rain·coat
  rain dance
  rain·drop
  rain·fall
  rain gage
  rain·mak·ing
  rain·proof
  rain·spout
  rain·squall
  rain·storm
  rain·wa·ter
  rain·wear
  rain·y
raise *v., n. (to lift;* see *raze)*
rai·sin
rai·son d'être
ra·ja *or* ra·jah
rake·hell
rake-off
rak·ish
rale
ral·ly
ram·ble
  ram·bler
  ram·bling
ram·e·kin
ram·i·fy
  ram·i·fi·ca·tion
ram·pant
ram·part
ram·rod
ram·shack·le
ranch·man
ran·cid
ran·cor
  ran·cor·ous

ran·dom
  ran·dom ac·cess
rang·y
ran·kle
ran·sack
ran·som
ra·pa·cious
  ra·pac·i·ty
rap·id
  ra·pid·i·ty
  rap·id·ly
ra·pi·er
rap·ine
rapped
rap·port
rapt
rap·ture
  rap·tur·ous
rare·bit
rar·e·fy
  rar·e·fac·tion
  rar·e·fied
rare·ly
rare·ness
rar·i·ty
ras·cal
  ras·cal·i·ty
rash·ly
rash·ness
rasp·ber·ry
rasp·ing·ly
ra·sta·far·i·an
ras·ter scan
rat·a·ble
ratch·et
rath·er
raths·kel·ler
rat·i·fy
  rat·i·fi·ca·tion
rat·ing
ra·ti·o
ra·ti·oc·i·na·tion
ra·tion

ra·tio·nal *adj.* (*reasonable*;
  see *rationale*)
ra·tio·nale *n.* (*rational basis*;
  see *rational*)
ra·tio·nal·ize
  ra·tion·al·i·za·tion
rat·like
rat·line
rat·proof
rat race
rat·tail
rat·tan
rat·tle
  rat·tle·brained
  rat·tler
  rat·tle·snake
  rat·tle·trap
rat·trap
rau·cous
rav·age
rav·el
  rav·eled
  rav·el·ing
ra·ven
rav·en·ing
rav·en·ous
ra·vine
rav·i·o·li
rav·ish·ing·ly
raw·boned
raw·hide
ray
ray·on
raze *v.* (*tear down*; see *raise*)
ra·zor
  ra·zor·back
re·act
  re·ac·tion
  re·ac·tion·ar·y
  re·ac·tor
re·ac·ti·vate
read·a·ble
read·er·ship
read·i·ly

read·i·ness
re·ad·just·ment
read-out
read·y-made
read·y-to-wear
re·af·firm
Rea·gan·om·ics
re·a·gent
re·al *adj., adv.* (*true*; see *reel*)
  re·al·ism
  re·al·ist
  re·al·is·tic
  re·al·i·ty
  re·al·i·za·tion
  re·al·ize
  re·al·ly
realm
Re·al·tor (*trademark*)
re·al·ty
re·ap·point
re·ap·prais·al
rear guard
re·arm
re·ar·range
rea·son
  rea·son·a·ble
  rea·son·ing
re·as·sem·ble
re·as·sure
  re·as·sur·ance
reb·el *adj., n.*
re·bel *v.*
  rebelled
  re·bel·ling
  re·bel·lion
  re·bel·lious
re·birth
re·buff
re·buke
re·bus
re·but·tal
re·cal·ci·trant
  re·cal·ci·tran·cy
re·cant

re·ca·pit·u·late
  re·ca·pit·u·la·tion
re·cap·ture
re·cede
re·ceipt
re·ceive
  re·ceiv·a·ble
  re·ceiv·er·ship
re·cent
re·cep·ta·cle
re·cep·tion
re·cep·tive
re·cess
re·ces·sion
  re·ces·sion·al
re·ces·sive
re·cher·ché
re·cid·i·vism
rec·i·pe
re·cip·i·ent
re·cip·ro·cate
  re·cip·ro·cal
  re·cip·ro·ca·tion
  rec·i·proc·i·ty
re·cite
  re·cit·al
  rec·i·ta·tion
  rec·i·ta·tive
reck v. (to regard; see wreck)
reck·less
reck·on
re·claim v. (to reform; see
  re-claim)
  rec·la·ma·tion
re-claim v. (to claim again;
  see reclaim)
re·cline
rec·luse
rec·og·nize
  rec·og·ni·tion
  rec·og·niz·a·ble
  re·cog·ni·zance
re·coil

re-col·lect v. (to rally; see
  recollect)
rec·ol·lect v. (to remember;
  see re-collect)
  rec·ol·lec·tion
rec·om·mend
  rec·om·men·da·tion
re·com·mit
rec·om·pense
rec·on·cile
  rec·on·cil·i·a·tion
re·con·dite
re·con·di·tion
re·con·firm
  re·con·fir·ma·tion
re·con·nais·sance
re·con·noi·ter
re·con·sid·er
re·con·struc·tion
re·cord v.
  re·cord·er
rec·ord n.
re-count v. (to count again;
  see recount)
re·count v. (to tell; see
  re-count)
re·course
re·cov·er v. (to get back; see
  re-cover)
  re·cov·er·y
re-cov·er v. (to cover again;
  see recover)
rec·re·ant
re-cre·ate v. (to create again;
  see recreate)
rec·re·ate v. (refresh; see
  re-create)
  rec·re·a·tion
re·crim·i·na·tion
re·cru·des·cence
re·cruit
rect·an·gle
  rect·an·gu·lar

rec·ti·fy
  rec·ti·fi·ca·tion
  rec·ti·fi·er
rec·ti·lin·e·ar
rec·ti·tude
rec·to·ry
rec·tum
re·cum·bent
re·cu·per·ate
  re·cu·per·a·tion
re·cur
  re·curred
  re·cur·rence
  re·cur·rent
  re·cur·ring
red-bait·ing
red·bird
red-blood·ed
red·breast
red·bud
red·cap
red-car·pet
red·coat
Red Cross
re·dec·o·rate
re·deem
  re·deem·a·ble
  re·deem·er
  re·demp·tion
re·de·vel·op·ment
red-hand·ed
red·head
red-hot
re·dis·count
re·dis·trib·ute
re·dis·trict
red lead
red-let·ter
red·o·lent
  red·o·lence
re·dou·ble
re·doubt·a·ble
re·dound
red-pen·cil

re·dress
red·skin
red tape
re·duce
  re·duc·tion
re·dun·dant
  re·dun·dan·cy
red·wing
red·wood
re·ech·o
re·ed·u·cate
reek *n., v.* (odor; see *wreak*)
reel *n., v.* (spin; see *real*)
re·e·lect
re·em·pha·size
re·em·ploy
re·en·act
re·en·grave
re·en·list
re·en·trance
re·en·try
re·es·tab·lish
re·ex·am·ine
  re·ex·am·i·na·tion
re·ex·port
re·fer
  ref·er·ee
  ref·er·ence
  ref·er·en·dum
  pl. ref·er·en·da *or*
  ref·er·en·dums
  re·ferred
  re·fer·ring
re·fine
  re·fined
  re·fine·ment
  re·fin·er
  re·fin·er·y
re·flect
  re·flec·tion
  re·flec·tive
  re·flec·tor
re·flex
  re·flex·ive

re·for·est·a·tion
re-form v. (to form again; see reform)
re-form v., n., adj. (to improve; see re-form)
  ref·or·ma·tion
  re·for·ma·to·ry
  re·formed
re·frac·tion
re·frac·to·ry
rc·frain
re·fresh
  re·fresh·ment
re·frig·er·ate
  re·frig·er·ant
  re·frig·er·a·tion
  re·frig·er·a·tor
ref·uge
  ref·u·gee
re·ful·gent
re·fur·bish
re·fuse v.
  re·fus·al
ref·use n.
re·fute
  re·fut·a·ble
  ref·u·ta·tion
re·gain
re·gal adj. (royal; see regale)
re·gale v. (to entertain; see regal)
re·ga·li·a
re·gard
  re·gard·ful
  re·gard·less
re·gat·ta
re·gen·cy
re·gen·er·ate
  re·gen·er·a·tive
re·gent
reg·i·cide
re·gime
reg·i·men

reg·i·ment
  reg·i·men·tal
  reg·i·men·ta·tion
re·gion
  re·gion·al
re·gis·seur
reg·is·ter
  reg·is·tered
  reg·is·trar
  reg·is·tra·tion
  reg·is·try
reg·nant
re·gress
  re·gres·sion
  re·gres·sive
re·gret
  re·gret·ful
  re·gret·ta·ble
  re·gret·ted
  re·gret·ting
reg·u·lar
  reg·u·lar·i·ty
  reg·u·lar·ize
reg·u·late
  reg·u·la·tion
  reg·u·la·to·ry
re·gur·gi·tate
re·hash
re·hear·ing
re·hearse
  re·hears·al
reign n., v. (to rule; see rain and rein)
re·im·burse
  re·im·burs·a·ble
rein n., v. (strap; see rain and reign)
re·in·car·na·tion
rein·deer
re·in·force
  re·in·force·ment
re·in·sert
re·in·state

re·in·sure
  re·in·sur·ance
re·in·vest
re·in·vig·o·rate
re·it·er·ate
  re·it·er·a·tion
re·ject
  re·jec·tion
re·joice
re·join
  re·join·der
re·ju·ve·nate
re·kin·dle
re·lapse
re·late
  re·la·tion·ship
rel·a·tive
  rel·a·tiv·i·ty
re·lax
  re·lax·a·tion
  re·laxed
re·lay
re-lease v. (to lease again; see release)
re·lease v., n. (to set free; see re-lease)
rel·e·gate
re·lent
  re·lent·less
rel·e·vant
  rel·e·vance
rel·ic
re·lict
re·lief
re·lieve
re·li·gion
  re·li·gious
re·lin·quish
rel·i·quar·y
rel·ish
re·luc·tant
  re·luc·tance
re·ly
  re·li·a·ble

re·li·ance
re·li·ant
re·main
  re·main·der
re·mand
re·mark
  re·mark·a·ble
re·mar·riage
rem·e·dy
  re·me·di·a·ble
  re·me·di·al
re·mem·ber
  re·mem·brance
re·mind
  re·mind·er
rem·i·nisce
  rem·i·nis·cence
  rem·i·nis·cent
re·mis·sion
re·mit·tance
re·mit·tent
rem·nant
re·mon·e·tize
re·mon·strate
  re·mon·strance
  re·mon·stra·tion
re·morse
  re·morse·less
re·mote
re·move
  re·mov·a·ble
  re·mov·al
re·mu·ner·ate
  re·mu·ner·a·tion
  re·mu·ner·a·tive
ren·ais·sance
ren·der
ren·dez·vous
ren·di·tion
ren·e·gade
re·nege
re·ne·go·ti·ate
  re·ne·go·ti·a·ble
re·new·a·ble

re·new·al
ren·net
re·nom·i·nate
re·nounce
ren·o·vate
　ren·o·va·tion
re·nown
rent·al
re·nun·ci·a·tion
re·o·pen
re·or·der
re·or·ga·ni·za·tion
re·pair
　re·pair·man
　rep·a·ra·tion
rep·ar·tee
re·past
re·pa·tri·ate
　re·pa·tri·a·tion
re·pay
re·peal
re·peat
　re·peat·er
　rep·e·ti·tion
　rep·e·ti·tious
　re·pet·i·tive
re·pel
　re·pelled
　re·pel·lent
　re·pel·ling
re·pent
　re·pent·ance
　re·pent·ant
re·per·cus·sion
rep·er·toire
rep·er·to·ry
re·pine
re·place
　re·place·a·ble
　re·place·ment
re·plen·ish·ment
re·plete
re·plev·in
rep·li·ca

re·ply
re·port
　re·port·er
re·pose
　re·pos·i·to·ry
re·pos·sess
re·pous·sé
rep·re·hend
　rep·re·hen·si·ble
rep·re·sent
　rep·re·sen·ta·tion
　rep·re·sent·a·tive
re·press
　re·pressed
　re·pres·sion
re·prieve
rep·ri·mand
re·print
re·pri·sal
re·proach
　re·proach·ful
rep·ro·bate
re·pro·duce
　re·pro·duc·tion
　re·pro·duc·tive
re·proof
re·prove
rep·tile
　rep·til·i·an
re·pub·lic
　re·pub·li·can
re·pu·di·ate
　re·pu·di·a·tion
re·pug·nant
　re·pug·nance
re·pulse
　re·pul·sion
　re·pul·sive
re·pur·chase
re·pute
　rep·u·ta·ble
　rep·u·ta·tion
re·quest
re·qui·em

re·quire
  re·quire·ment
req·ui·site
req·ui·si·tion
re·quite
  re·quit·al
re·run
re·sal·a·ble
re·scind
  re·scis·sion
re·script
res·cue
re·search
re·sem·ble
  re·sem·blance
re·sent
  re·sent·ful
  re·sent·ment
re·serve
  res·er·va·tion
  re·served
res·er·voir
re·shuf·fle
re·side
  res·i·dence
  res·i·dent
  res·i·den·tial
res·i·due
  re·sid·u·al
  re·sid·u·ar·y
  re·sid·u·um
re·sign v. (to sign again; see resign)
re·sign v. (to withdraw; see re-sign)
  res·ig·na·tion
re·sil·ient
  re·sil·ience
res·in
  res·in·ous
re·sist
  re·sist·ance
  re·sist·ant

re·sist·er n. (one who resists; see resistor)
re·sis·tiv·i·ty
re·sis·tor n. (electrical device; see resister)
res·o·lute
re·solve
  res·o·lu·tion
res·o·nant
  res·o·nance
  res·o·na·tor
re·sort v. (to sort again; see resort)
re·sort v., n. (vacation spa; see re-sort)
re·sound
re·source
  re·source·ful
re·spect
  re·spect·a·bil·i·ty
  re·spect·a·ble
  re·spect·ful·ly
re·spec·tive
  re·spec·tive·ly
res·pi·ra·tion
  res·pi·ra·tor
  re·spi·ra·to·ry
re·spite
re·splen·dent
re·spond
  re·spon·dent
  re·sponse
  re·spon·sive
re·spon·si·bil·i·ty
re·spon·si·ble
rest n., v. (state of inactivity; see wrest)
  rest home
  rest house
  rest·less
res·tau·rant
  res·tau·ra·teur
res·ti·tu·tion
res·tive

re·store
  res·to·ra·tion
  re·stor·a·tive
re·strain
  re·straint
re·strict
  re·stric·tion
  re·stric·tive
re·sult
  re·sult·ant
re·sume v. (to begin again; see résumé)
  re·sump·tion
ré·su·mé or re·su·me or re·su·mé n. (summary; see resume)
re·sur·gence
res·ur·rect
  res·ur·rec·tion
re·sus·ci·tate
  re·sus·ci·ta·tion
re·tail
re·tain
  re·tain·er
re·tal·i·ate
  re·tal·i·a·tion
  re·tal·i·a·to·ry
re·tard
  re·tar·da·tion
retch v. (to vomit; see wretch)
re·ten·tion
re·ten·tive
re·ten·tiv·i·ty
ret·i·cent
  ret·i·cence
ret·i·cule
ret·i·na
  pl. ret·i·nas or ret·i·nae
ret·i·no·path·y
re·tire
  re·tire·ment
re·tool
re·tort
re·touch

re·trace
re·tract
  re·trac·tile
  re·trac·tion
re·treat
re·trench
ret·ri·bu·tion
re·trieve
  re·triev·a·ble
  re·triev·er
re·tro·ac·tive
re·tro·ces·sion
ret·ro·grade
  re·tro·gres·sion
re·tro·spect
  re·tro·spec·tive
re·turn
  re·turn·a·ble
re·u·nite
  re·un·ion
re·use
  re·us·a·ble
re·val·ue
re·vamp
re·veal
rev·eil·le
rev·el
  rev·eled
  rev·el·ing
rev·e·la·tion
re·venge
rev·e·nue
re·ver·ber·ate
  re·ver·ber·a·tion
  re·ver·ber·a·to·ry
re·vere
  rev·er·ence
rev·er·end
rev·er·ent
  rev·er·en·tial
rev·er·ie
re·verse
  re·ver·sal
  re·vers·i·ble

re·ver·sion
  re·ver·sion·ar·y
re·vert
  re·vert·ed
re·view *n., v. (to inspect; see*
  revue)
  re·view·er
re·vile
re·vise
  re·vi·sion
re·vi·tal·ize
re·vive
  re·viv·al
re·viv·i·fy
re·voke
  re·vo·ca·ble
  rev·o·ca·tion
re·volt
rev·o·lu·tion
  rev·o·lu·tion·ar·y
  rev·o·lu·tion·ist
  rev·o·lu·tion·ize
re·volve
  re·volv·er
re·vue *n. (theatrical*
  production; see review)
re·vul·sion
re·ward
re·wind
re·word
re·work
re·write
rhap·so·dy
  rhap·sod·ic
  rhap·so·dist
  rhap·so·dize
rhe·o·stat
rhe·sus
rhet·o·ric
  rhe·tor·i·cal
rheum *n. (watery discharge;*
  see room)
  rheu·mat·ic
  rheu·ma·tism

RH fac·tor
rhine·stone
rhi·noc·er·os
  pl. rhi·noc·er·os·es *or*
  rhi·noc·er·os *or* rhi·noc·er·i
rho *n. (Greek letter; see roe*
  and row)
Rhode Is·land
Rho·de·sia
rhom·boid
rhu·barb
rhyme *n., v. (corresponding*
  sounds; see rime)
rhythm
  rhyth·mic
rib·ald
  rib·al·dry
rib·bon
rice bowl
rick·ets
ric·o·chet
rid·dle
rid·er·less
ridge·pole
rid·i·cule
  ri·dic·u·lous
rif·fle *n., v. (ripple; see rifle)*
riff·raff
ri·fle *v., n. (gun; see riffle)*
  ri·fle·man
  ri·fling
right *adj., adv., n., v.*
  (correct; see rite and write)
  righ·teous·ness
  right·ful
  right hand *n.*
  right-hand *adj.*
  right-hand·ed
  right-of-way
  right wing *n.*
  right-wing *adj.*
rig·id
  ri·gid·i·ty
rig·or·ous

rik·sha
rime *n., v.* (*frost; see* *rhyme*)
ring *n., v.* (*circle; sound; see*
  wring)
  ring·bolt
  ring·bone
  ring·dove
  ring·lead·er
  ring·mas·ter
  ring·side
  ring·worm
rinse
ri·ot·ous
ri·par·i·an
rip·en
ri·poste
rip·ple
rip·rap
rip-roar·ing
rip·saw
rip·snort·er
rip·tide
ris·i·bil·i·ty
risk·i·ness
ris·qué
rite *n.* (*ceremony; see* *right*
  and *write*)
rit·u·al
ri·val
  ri·valed
  ri·val·ing
  ri·val·ry
riv·er·bed
riv·er·boat
riv·er·side
riv·et
riv·u·let
road *n.* (*way; see* *rode and*
  rowed)
  road·bed
  road·block
  road hog
  road·house
  road·stead

road·ster
road test
road·way
road·work
rob
  robbed
  rob·ber·y
  rob·bing
rob·in
ro·bot
  ro·bot·ics
ro·bust
  ro·bus·tious
rock·bot·tom *n.*
rock-bot·tom *adj.*
rock·bound
rock·et
  rock·et·ry
rock-ribbed
rock salt
rock·slide
rock snake
rock wool
rock·work
ro·co·co
rode *v.* (*pt. of ride; see* *road*
  and *rowed*)
ro·dent
ro·de·o
rod·man
roe *n.* (*fish eggs; see* *rho and*
  row)
Roent·gen
rogue
  rogu·ish
roil *v.* (*stir up; see* *royal*)
role *or* rôle *n.* (*actor's part;*
  see *roll*)
roll *v., n.* (*cylinder; see* *role*)
  roll·back *n.*
  roll back *v.*
  roll call
roll·er coast·er
ro·maine

ro·mance
  ro·man·tic
  ro·man·ti·cism
Ro·ma·ni·a
rood *n.* (*crucifix*; see *rude*
  and *rued*)
roof·less
roof·top
roof·tree
rook·er·y
rook·ie
room *n., v.* (*dwelling*; see
  rheum)
  room·er *n.* (*lodger*; see *rumor*)
  room·ette
  room·ful
  room·i·ness
  room·mate
roost·er
root *n., v.* (*plant part*; see
  rout and *route*)
  root beer
  root·less
  root·let
rope·danc·er
rope·walk
ro·sa·ry
ro·sé *n.* (*wine*; see *rose*)
rose *n.* (*flower*; see *rosé*)
  rose·bud
  rose·bush
  rose-col·ored
  rose wa·ter *n.*
  rose-wa·ter *adj.*
  rose·wood
ro·se·ate
rose·mar·y
ro·se·o·la
ro·sette
ros·in
ros·ter
ros·trum
ro·ta·ry

ro·tate
  ro·ta·tion
rote *n.* (*routine*; see *wrote*)
ro·tis·ser·ie
ro·to·gra·vure
rot·ten·stone
ro·tund
  ro·tun·da
  ro·tun·di·ty
rough *adj., n.* (*not smooth*;
  see *ruff*)
  rough·age
  rough-and-rea·dy
  rough-and-tum·ble
  rough·cast
  rough·dry
  rough·en
  rough·hew
  rough·house
  rough·neck
  rough·rid·er
  rough·shod
rou·lade
rou·leau
  pl. rou·leaux *or* rou·leaus
rou·lette
round·a·bout *n.*
roun·de·lay
round·house
round-shoul·dered
rounds·man
round up *v.*
round·up *n.*
roust·a·bout
rout *n., v.* (*defeat*; see *root*
  and *route*)
route *n., v.* (*highway*; see
  root and *rout*)
  route·man
rou·tine
  rou·tin·ize
row *n., v.* (*line*; see *rho* and
  roe)
  row·boat

rowed v. (pt. of row; see road
and rode)
row house
row·lock
row ma·trix
row·di·ness
row·dy
row·el
roy·al adj. (kingly; see roil)
roy·al·ist
roy·al·ty
ru·ba·to
pl. ru·ba·ti or ru·ba·tos
rubbed
rub·ber
rub·ber·ize
rub·ber·neck
rub·ber stamp n.
rub·ber-stamp v.
rub·bing
rub·bish
rub·ble
rub·ble·work
rub down v.
rub·down n.
Ru·bi·con
ru·bi·cund
ru·bric
ruck·sack
ruck·us
rud·der
rud·dy
rude adj. (impolite; see rood
and rued)
ru·di·ment
ru·di·men·ta·ry
rued v. (regretted; see rood
and rude)
rue·ful
ruff n., v. (stiff collar; see
rough)
ruf·fi·an
ruf·fle

rug·ged
rug·ged·i·za·tion
ru·in n., v. (to destroy; see
rune)
ru·in·ous
Ru·man·i·a
rum·ba
rum·ble
ru·mi·nate
ru·mi·nant
ru·mi·na·tion
rum·mage
ru·mor n., v. (hearsay; see
roomer)
ru·mor·mon·ger
rum·ple
rum·pus
rum·run·ner
run·a·bout
run·a·round n.
run a·round v.
run a·way v.
run·a·way adj., n.
run down v.
run-down n., adj.
rune n. (runic alphabet
character; see ruin)
rung v., n. (past participle of
rang; see wrung)
run in v.
run-in n.
run·ner
run·ner-up
run off v.
run·off n.
run-of-the-mill
run-of-the-mine
run on v.
run-on adj., n.
run o·ver v.
run-o·ver adj.
run·o·ver n.
run·proof
run through v.

run-through *n.*
run·way
ru·pee
rup·ture
ru·ral
  ru·ral·ly
rus·set
rus·tic
  rus·ti·cate
rus·tle
rust·proof *adj.*
rust-proof *v.*
ru·ta·ba·ga
ruth·less
rye *n. (cereal grass; see wry)*

S

Sab·bath
  sab·bat·i·cal
sa·ber
sa·ble
sab·o·tage
  sab·o·teur
sa·bra
sac *n. (pouch within animal or plant; see sack)*
sac·cha·rin *n.*
sac·cha·rine *adj.*
sac·er·do·tal
sa·chem
sa·chet *n. (see sashay)*
sack *n., v. (a bag; see sac)*
  sack·cloth
  sack coat
  sack·ful
  sack race
sac·ra·ment
  sac·ra·men·tal
sa·cred
sac·ri·fice
  sac·ri·fi·cial

sac·ri·lege
  sac·ri·le·gious
sac·ris·ty
  sac·ris·tan
sac·ro·sanct
sad·den
sad·der
sad·dest
sad·dle
  sad·dle·bag
  sad·dle·bow
  sad·dle·cloth
  sad·dler
sad·i·ron
sa·dism
  sa·dist
  sa·dis·tic
sad·ness
safe-con·duct
safe·crack·er
safe-de·pos·it
safe·guard
safe·keep·ing
safe·ty
saf·fron
sa·ga
sa·ga·cious
  sa·gac·i·ty
sag·a·more
sage·brush
sa·hib
sail *n., v. (canvas sheet; see sale)*
  sail·boat
  sail·cloth
  sail·fish
  sail·or
saint·ly
  saint·li·ness
sake *n. (purpose)*
sa·ke *n. (rice wine)*
sa·laam
sal·a·ble
  sal·a·bil·i·ty

sa·la·cious
sal·ad
sal·a·man·der
sa·la·mi
sal·a·ry
  sal·a·ried
sale *n.* (*transfer of ownership; see sail*)
sal·e·ra·tus
sales check
sales·clerk
sales·man
  sales·man·ship
sales·room
sales·wom·an
sal·i·cyl·ic
sa·li·ent
  sa·li·ence
sa·line
sa·li·va
  sal·i·var·y
sal·low
sal·ma·gun·di
salm·on
Sal·mo·nel·la
sa·lon *n.* (*elegant living room; see saloon*)
sa·loon *n.* (*barroom; see salon*)
sal·ta·to·ry
salt·box
salt·cel·lar
sal·tine
salt marsh
salt·pe·ter
salt·shak·er
salt wa·ter *n.*
salt·wa·ter *adj.*
salt·works
salt·y
  salt·i·ness
sa·lu·bri·ous
sal·u·ta·tion
  sal·u·tar·y
  sa·lu·ta·to·ri·an

sa·lute
sal·vage
  sal·va·tion
Sa·mar·i·tan
same·ness
sa·mite
sam·o·var
sam·pan
sam·ple
  sam·pler
  sam·pling
sa·mu·rai
san·a·to·ry
sanc·ti·fy
  sanc·ti·fi·ca·tion
sanc·ti·mo·ni·ous
sanc·tion
sanc·ti·ty
sanc·tu·ar·y
sanc·tum
san·dal
san·dal·wood
sand·bag
sand·bank
sand·bar
sand·blast
sand·box
sand·bur
sand·er
sand·glass
sand·hog
sand·lot
sand·man
sand·pa·per
sand pile *n.*
sand·pip·er
sand·stone
sand·storm
sand ta·ble
sand trap
sand·wich
sand·worm
San Fran·cis·co

sang·froid
san·gri·a
san·guine
  san·gui·nar·y
san·i·tar·i·um *or*
  san·a·to·ri·um
  pl. san·i·tar·i·ums *or*
  san·i·tar·i·a
san·i·tar·y
  san·i·ta·tion
san·i·ty
sans·cu·lotte
sa·pi·ent
sap·ling
sa·pon·i·fy
sap·phire
sap·suck·er
sap·wood
sar·a·band
sar·casm
  sar·cas·tic
sar·co·ma
sar·coph·a·gus
  pl. sar·coph·a·gi *or*
  sar·coph·a·gus·es
sar·dine
sar·don·ic
sar·don·yx
sar·gas·so
sa·rong
sar·sa·pa·ril·la
sar·to·ri·al
sa·shay *v.* (*to strut;* see *sachet*)
Sas·katch·e·wan
sas·sa·fras
Sa·tan·ic
satch·el
sa·teen
sat·el·lite
sa·ti·ate
  sa·ti·a·ble
  sa·ti·e·ty
sat·in
sat·in·wood

sat·ire
  sa·tir·ic
  sa·tir·i·cal
  sat·i·rize
sat·is·fy
  sat·is·fac·tion
  sat·is·fac·to·ri·ly
  sat·is·fac·to·ry
sa·trap
sat·u·rate
  sat·u·rat·ed
  sat·u·ra·tion
Sat·ur·day
sat·ur·nine
sa·tyr
sauce·pan
sau·cer
Sa·u·di A·ra·bi·a
sau·er·bra·ten
sau·er·kraut
sau·na
saun·ter
sau·sage
sau·té
sau·terne
sav·age
  sav·age·ry
sa·van·na
sa·vant
sav·er *n.* (*one who saves;* see
  savor)
sav·ior
sa·voir faire
sa·vor *n., v.* (*to enjoy;* see
  saver)
  sa·vor·y
saw·dust
sawed-off
saw·horse
saw·mill
saw-toothed *adj.*
saw·yer
sax·o·phone
scab·bard

scaf·fold
  scaf·fold·ing
scal·a·wag
scal·lion
scal·lop
scal·pel
scam·per
scan
scan·dal
  scan·dal·ize
  scan·dal·ous
scan·ner
scan·ning
scan·sion
scant·ling
scant·y
  scant·i·ly
scape·goat
scap·u·la
  pl. scap·u·lae or scap·u·las
  scap·u·lar
scar·ab
scarce·ly
scar·ci·ty
scare·crow
scar·i·fy
scar·la·ti·na
scar·let
scath·ing
scat·ter
  scat·ter·brain
scav·eng·er
sce·nar·i·o
scene n. (setting; see seen)
  sce·ner·y
  scene·shift·er
  sce·nic
scent v., n. (aroma; see cent
  and sent)
scep·ter
sched·ule
sche·mat·ic
scheme

scher·zo
  pl. scher·zos or scher·zi
schism
schist
schol·ar
  schol·ar·ly
  schol·ar·ship
scho·las·ti·cism
  scho·las·tic
school·bag
school board
school·book
school·boy
school bus
school·child
school·fel·low
school·girl
school·house
school·marm
school·mas·ter
school·mate
school·room
school·teach·er
school·work
school·yard
schoo·ner
sci·at·i·ca
  sci·at·ic
sci·ence
  sci·en·tif·ic
  sci·en·tist
scim·i·tar
scin·til·late
  scin·til·la
  pl. scin·til·las or scin·til·lae
sci·on
scis·sors
scle·ro·sis
  pl. scle·ro·ses
scoff·law
sco·li·o·sis
scone
scorch
score·board

score·card
score·keep·er
scorn·ful
scor·pi·on
scot-free
Scot·land
scoun·drel
scourge
scout·mas·ter
scrap·book
scrap·per
scrap·ple
scratch
  scratch·i·ness
  scratch·y
screech
screed
screen
  screen·play
screw·ball
screw·driv·er
scrib·ble
scrim·mage
scrim·shaw
scrip n. (temporary paper
  currency; see script)
script n. (text of a drama; see
  scrip)
scrip·ture
  scrip·tur·al
scriv·en·er
scrof·u·la
scroll·work
scrubbed
scrub·bing
scrump·tious
scru·ple
  scru·pu·lous
scru·ti·ny
  scru·ti·nize
scuf·fle
  scuf·fling
scull n. (boat; see skull)
scul·ler·y

scul·lion
sculp·ture
  sculp·tor
  sculp·tur·al
scur·ri·lous
  scur·ril·i·ty
scur·vy
scut·tle·butt
scut·tling
scythe
sea n., adj. (body of water;
  see see)
  sea·bag
  sea bass
  sea·beach
  sea·bird
  sea·board
  sea·boot
  sea-born adj. (born in the sea;
  see seaborne)
  sea·borne adj. (carried by the
  sea; see sea-born)
  sea breeze
  sea chest
  sea·coast
  sea dog
  sea·drome
  sea·far·er
  sea·far·ing
  sea fight
  sea·food
  sea·fowl
  sea·front
  sea·girt
  sea·go·ing
  sea green n.
  sea-green adj.
  sea gull
  sea horse
  sea·lane
  sea legs
  sea·man n. (sailor; see semen)
  sea·man·like
  sea·man·ship

sea·plane
sea·port
sea·room
sea·scape
sea·shell
sea·shore
sea·sick
sea·side
sea·wall
sea·ward
sea·wa·ter
sea·way
sea·weed
sea·wor·thi·ness
sea·wor·thy
seal ring
seal·skin
seam *n., v. (to join by stitching; see seem)*
seam·stress
sé·ance
scar *v., adj., n. (to burn; see seer and sere)*
search·light
sea·son
  sea·son·a·ble
  sea·son·al
seat·mate
se·ba·ceous
se·cant
se·cede
  se·ces·sion
se·clude
  se·clu·sion
Sec·o·nal *(trademark)*
sec·ond
  sec·on·dar·i·ly
  sec·on·dar·y
  sec·on·dar·y da·ta
  sec·ond class *n.*
  sec·ond-class *adj.*
  sec·ond-guess *v.*
  sec·ond·hand *adj.*
  sec·ond-rate *adj.*

se·cret
  se·cre·cy
sec·re·tar·y
  sec·re·tar·i·al
se·crete
  se·cre·tion
  se·cre·tive
  se·cre·to·ry
sec·tar·i·an
sec·ta·ry
sec·tion
  sec·tion·al·ly
sec·tor
sec·u·lar
  sec·u·lar·ism
se·cure
  se·cu·ri·ty
se·dan
se·date
  se·da·tion
  sed·a·tive
sed·en·tar·y
sed·i·ment
  sed·i·men·ta·ry
se·di·tion
  sc·di·tious
se·duce
  se·duc·er
  se·duc·tion
  se·duc·tive
sed·u·lous
sec *v., n. (to perceive; see sea)*
seed *n., v. (kernel; see cede)*
  seed·i·ness
  seed·ling
  seed·pod
  seed·y
seem *v. (to appear; see seam)*
  seem·li·ness
  seem·ly
seen *v. (past participle of see; see scene)*
seep·age

seer *n.* (*predictor of future*;
  see *sear* and *sere*)
seer·suck·er
see·saw
seg·ment
seg·re·gate
  seg·re·gat·ed
  seg·re·ga·tion
  seg·re·ga·tion·ist
sei·del
sei·gneur *n.* (*lord or*
  gentleman; see *senior* and
  señor)
seis·mic
seis·mo·graph
seize
  seiz·ing
  sei·zure
sel·dom
se·lect
  se·lec·tion
  se·lec·tive
  se·lect·man
se·le·ni·um
self-a·base·ment
self-ad·dressed
self-as·sured
self-cen·tered
self-com·posed
self-con·fi·dence
self-con·scious
self-con·tained
self-con·trol
self-de·fense
self-de·struc·tion
self-dis·ci·pline
self-ed·u·ca·ted
self-ef·face·ment
self-em·ployed
self-es·teem
self-ex·e·cut·ing
self-ex·pres·sion
self-gov·ern·ment
self-im·por·tance

self-im·posed
self-im·prove·ment
self-in·dul·gence
self-in·sured
self-in·ter·est
self·ish
self·less
self-liq·ui·dat·ing
self-made
self-pit·y
self-pos·sessed
self-pos·ses·sion
self-pro·tec·tion
self-re·gard
self-re·li·ance
self-re·spect
self-right·eous
self-ris·ing
self-sac·ri·fice
self·same
self-sat·is·fied
self-start·er
self-suf·fi·cien·cy
self-suf·fi·cient
self-taught
self-wind·ing
sell *n., v.* (*to exchange for*
  money; see *cell*)
  sell·er *n.* (*one who sells*; see
  cellar)
Selt·zer
sel·vage
se·man·tic
sem·a·phore
sem·blance
se·men *n.* (*male reproductive*
  fluid; see *seaman*)
se·mes·ter
semi·an·nu·al
semi·ar·id
semi·au·to·mat·ic
semi·au·ton·o·mous
semi·cir·cle
semi·civ·i·lized

semi·co·lon
semi·con·duc·tor
semi·con·scious
semi·crys·tal·line
semi·dark·ness
semi·de·tached
semi·di·vine
semi·fi·nal
semi·month·ly
sem·i·nal
sem·i·nar
sem·i·nar·y
se·mi·ot·ic
semi·per·me·a·ble
semi·pre·cious
semi·pri·vate
semi·pro
semi·pub·lic
Sem·ite
Sem·it·ic
semi·trans·lu·cent
semi·trans·par·ent
semi·vow·el
semi·week·ly
sem·pi·ter·nal
sen·ate
　　sen·a·tor
　　sen·a·to·ri·al
send-off n.
send off v.
Sen·e·gal
se·nes·cent
se·nile
　　se·nil·i·ty
sen·ior adj., n. (older; see
　　seigneur and señor)
　　se·nior·i·ty
señ·or n. (Spanish for mister;
　　see seigneur and senior)
se·ño·ra
se·ño·ri·ta
sen·sa·tion
　　sen·sa·tion·al
sense·less

sens·es
sen·si·ble
　　sen·si·bil·i·ty
sen·si·tive
　　sen·si·tiv·i·ty
　　sen·si·tize
sen·so·ry
sen·su·al
sen·su·ous
sent v. (pt. of send; see cent
　　and scent)
sen·tence
sen·ten·tious
sen·tient
sen·ti·ment
　　sen·ti·men·tal
　　sen·ti·men·tal·ism
　　sen·ti·men·tal·i·ty
sen·ti·nel
sen·try
sep·a·rate
　　sep·a·ra·ble
　　sep·a·ra·tion
　　sep·a·rat·ist
　　sep·a·ra·tor
se·pi·a
sep·sis
　　pl. sep·ses
sep·tet
sep·tic
sep·ti·ce·mi·a
sep·tu·a·ge·nar·i·an
sep·ul·cher
　　se·pul·chral
　　sep·ul·ture
se·quel
se·quence
　　se·quen·tial
　　se·quen·tial ac·cess
se·ques·ter
　　se·que·strate
se·quin
se·quoi·a
se·ra·gli·o

ser·aph
  se·raph·ic
sere *adj.* (*withered*; see *sear*
  and *seer*)
ser·e·nade
ser·en·dip·i·ty
se·rene
  se·ren·i·ty
serf *n.* (*peasant*; see *surf*)
serge *n.* (*twill fabric*; see
  surge)
ser·geant
se·ri·al *adj., n.* (*arranged in
  a series*; see *cereal*)
  se·ri·al·i·za·tion
  se·ri·al·ize
se·ri·a·tim
se·ries
ser·if
ser·i·graph
se·ri·o·com·ic
se·ri·ous
  se·ri·ous-mind·ed
ser·mon
  ser·mon·ize
se·rous
ser·pent
  ser·pen·tine
ser·ra·tion
se·rum
  pl. se·rums *or* se·ra
ser·vant
ser·vice
  ser·vice·a·ble
ser·vile
  ser·vil·i·ty
ser·vi·tor
ser·vi·tude
ser·vo·mech·a·nism
ser·vo·mo·tor
ses·a·me
ses·sion *n.* (*meeting*; see
  cession)
set·back *n.*
set back *v.*

set off *v.*
set·off *n.*
set out *v.*
set·out *n.*
set piece
set·screw
set·tee
set·ter
set·tle·ment
set·tling
set to *v.*
set-to *n.*
  pl. set-tos
set up *v.*
set·up *n.*
sev·en·teenth
sev·en-up
sev·er
sev·er·al
  sev·er·al·fold
  sev·er·al·ty
sev·er·ance
se·vere
  se·ver·i·ty
sew *v.* (*to stitch*; see *so* and
  sow)
  sew·er *n.* (*one who sews*)
sew·age
sew·er *n.* (*pipe*)
  sew·er·age
sex·tant
sex·tet
sex·ton
shab·by
  shab·bi·ness
shack·le
shad·ow
  shad·ow box *n.*
  shad·ow·box *v.*
  shad·ow·y
shag·bark
shag·gi·ness
sha·green
shake·down *adj., n.*

shake-out *n.*
shake up *v.*
shake-up *n.*
shak·i·ly
shal·lop
shal·lot
shal·low
sham
  sham·ming
sham·ble
shame
  shame·faced
  shame·ful
  shame·less
sham·poo
sham·rock
shang·hai
  shang·haied
shan·ty *n.* (*shack*; see *chantey*)
  shan·ty·town
shape·less
shape·ly
  shape·li·ness
shape-up *n.*
share·crop·per
share·hold·er
shark·skin
sharp·en·er
sharp·er
sharp-eyed
sharp·shoot·er
sharp-sight·ed
sharp-tongued
sharp-wit·ted
shat·ter·proof
shawl
sheaf
  pl. sheaves *or* sheafs
shear *v., n.* (*to cut*; see *sheer*)
sheath *n.*
  sheath knife
sheathe *v.*
  sheath·ing
sheen

sheep·cote
sheep-dip
sheep dog
sheep·fold
sheep·herd·er
sheep·ish
sheep·skin
sheep·walk
sheer *adj., adv., v., n.*
  (*transparent; perpendicular;*
  see *shear*)
Sheet·rock (*trademark*)
sheik *or* sheikh *n.* (*Arab*
  ruler; see *chic*)
shel·lac
  shel·lacked
  shel·lack·ing
shell·back
shell·fire
shell·fish
shell game
shell·proof
shell shock *n.*
shell-shock *v.*
shel·ter
she·nan·i·gan
shep·herd
sher·bet
sher·iff
sher·ry
shib·bo·leth
shield
shift·less
shift·y
  shift·i·ly
  shift·i·ness
shil·ling
shim·mer
shin·gle
shin·plas·ter
ship·board
ship·fit·ter
ship·mas·ter
ship·mate

ship·ment
ship·pa·ble
shipped
ship·per
ship·ping
ship·shape
ship·wreck
ship·wright
ship·yard
shire
shir·ring
shirt·ing
shirt·mak·er
shirt·tail
shirt·waist
shish ke·bab
shiv·er
shock·proof
shod·dy
  shod·di·ly
  shod·di·ness
shoe
  shod
  shoed
  shoe·horn
  shoe·ing
  shoe·lace
  shoe·mak·er
  shoe·string
  shoe tree
sho·gun
shone
shoot *v., n.* (*to fire a weapon;*
  see *chute*)
shop·keep·er
shop·lift·er
shop·lift·ing
shop·per
shop·talk
shop·worm
short·age
short·bread
short·cake
short·change *v.*

short cir·cuit *n.*
short-cir·cuit *v.*
short·com·ing
short·cut *n.*
short-cut *v.*
short·en·ing
short·hand
  short·hand·ed
short haul *n.*
short-haul *adj.*
short·horn *n.*
short-lived
short-range *adj.*
short ribs
short·sight·ed
short-spo·ken
short·stop
short-tem·pered
short-term
short·wave
short weight *n.*
short-weight *v.*
short-wind·ed
shot·gun
shot put
  shot-put·ter
shoul·der
shov·el
  shov·eled
  shov·el·ful
  shov·el·ing
show·boat
show·case
show·down
show·er
show·man
shown
show off *v.*
show-off *n.*
show·piece
show·place
show·room
show·y
  show·i·er

show·i·est
show·i·ly
show·i·ness
shrap·nel
shrewd
shrew·ish
shriek
shrimp
shrink·age
shriv·el
shriv·eled
shriv·el·ing
shroud
shrub·ber·y
shud·der
shuf·fle
shuf·fle·board
shut down v.
shut·down n.
shut-eye
shut-in adj., n.
shut in v.
shut·off n.
shut off v.
shut out v.
shut·out n.
shut·ter
shut·ter·bug
shut·tle·cock
shy·ster
Si·a·mese
pl. Si·a·mese
Si·be·ri·a
sib·i·lant
sib·ling
sib·yl
sib·yl·line
sic adv., v. (as written; attack; see sick)
sick adj., n. (ill; see sic)
sick bay
sick·bed
sick call
sick·en·ing

sick·ish
sick leave
sick·li·ness
sick·ness
sick·room
sic·kle
side band
side·board
side·burns
side·car
side·light
side·line
side·long
si·de·re·al
side·sad·dle
side·show
side·slip
side·spin
side·split·ting
side step n.
side·step v.
side·swipe
side·track
side·walk
side·wall
side·ways
side·wise
si·dle
siege
si·en·na
si·es·ta
sieve
sight n. (faculty of seeing; see cite and site)
sight·less
sight·li·ness
sight·ly
sight-read v.
sight-see·ing
sig·moid
sign n., v. (marker; see sine)
sig·nal
sig·naled
sig·nal·ing

sig·nal·ize
sig·nal·man
sig·na·to·ry
sig·na·ture
sign·board
sig·net *n.* (*seal; see cygnet*)
sig·nif·i·cant
sig·nif·i·cance
sig·ni·fy
sig·ni·fi·ca·tion
sign·post
si·lage
si·lent
si·lence
si·lenc·er
si·le·sia
si·lex
sil·hou·ette
sil·i·ca
sil·i·cate
sil·i·con *n.* (*nonmetallic element; see silicone*)
sil·i·cone *n.* (*compound used as insulator; see silicon*)
sil·i·co·sis
pl. sil·i·co·ses
silk·en
silk-stock·ing *adj.*
silk stock·ing *n.*
silk·weed
silk·worm
silk·y
silk·i·ness
sil·ly
si·lo
pl. si·los
sil·ver
sil·ver·smith
sil·ver-tongue *n.*
sil·ver tongued *adj.*
sil·ver·ware
sil·ver·y
sim·i·an

sim·i·lar
sim·i·lar·i·ty
sim·i·le
si·mil·i·tude
sim·mer
si·mon-pure *n., adj.*
sim·per
sim·ple
sim·ple·mind·ed
sim·ple·ton
sim·plex
sim·plic·i·ty
sim·pli·fy
sim·pli·fi·ca·tion
sim·ply
sim·u·la·crum
pl. sim·u·la·cra *or* sim·u·la·crums
sim·u·late
sim·u·la·tion
si·mul·ta·ne·ous
sin·cere
sin·cer·i·ty
sine *n.* (*trigonometry function; see sign*)
si·ne·cure
sin·ew
sin·ew·y
sin·ful
Sing·a·pore
singe
singed
singe·ing
sin·gle
sin·gle-breast·ed
sin·gle-hand·ed
sin·gle-mind·ed
sin·gle·ness
sin·gle-space
sin·gle·ton
sin·gle-track
sin·gly
sing·song

sin·gu·lar
  sin·gu·lar·i·ty
sin·is·ter
sink·age
sink·er
sink·hole
sin·u·ous
  sin·u·os·i·ty
si·nus
Sioux
si·phon
si·ren
sir·loin
si·roc·co
sis·ter-in-law
  pl. sis·ters-in-law
sit-down *n.*, *adj.*
site *n.*, *v.* (*place*; see *cite* and *sight*)
sit-in *n.*
sit·u·at·ed
sit·u·a·tion
six-pack *n.*
sixth
six·ti·eth
siz·a·ble
siz·zle
  siz·zling
skat·er
skein
skel·e·ton
skep·tic *or* scep·tic
  skep·ti·cal *or* scep·ti·cal
  skep·ti·cism
sketch
  sketch·book
  sketch·i·ly
  sketch·y
skew·er
ski
  ski·ing
  ski jump
  ski·lift

skid
  skid·ded
  skid·ding
  skid row
skilled
skil·let
skill·ful
skimp·y
skin
  skin·flint
  skinned
  skin·ning
  skin·tight
skip
  skipped
  skip·per
  skip·ping
skir·mish
skit·tish
skiv·er
skul·dug·ger·y
skulk
skull *n.* (*skeleton of the head*; see *scull*)
  skull·cap
skunk
sky blue *n.*
sky-blue *adj.*
sky·cap
sky·coach
sky-high *adj.*, *adv.*
sky·lark
sky·light
sky·line
sky·rock·et
sky·scrap·er
sky·ward
sky wave
sky·way
sky·writ·er
  sky·writ·ing
slack·en
sla·lom

slam
  slammed
  slam·ming
slan·der
  slan·der·ous
slap·dash
slap·hap·py
slap·jack
slapped
slap·ping
slap·stick
slat·tern
  slat·tern·li·ness
slaugh·ter
  slaugh·ter·house
slav·er·y
slav·ish
slay *v.* (*to kill;* see *sleigh*)
slea·zy
  slea·zi·ness
sledge
  sledge·ham·mer
sleep·er
sleep·less
sleep·walk·er
sleep·y
  sleep·i·ness
sleeve·less
sleigh *n.* (*large sled;* see *slay*)
  sleigh bell
sleight *n.* (*deceitful craftiness;*
  see *slight*)
slen·der
sleuth
slide rule
slight *adj., v., n.* (*small;* see
  sleight)
slime
sling·shot
slip
  slip·case
  slip·cov·er
  slip·knot
  slip noose
  slip-on *n.*

slip·o·ver
slip·page
slipped
slip·ping
slip sheet *n.*
slip-sheet *v.*
slip·shod
slip up *v.*
slip-up *n.*
slip·per
slip·per·y
  slip·per·i·ness
slith·er
sliv·er
sloe *n.* (*dark blue fruit;* see
  slow)
  sloe-eyed
slo·gan
sloop
slope
slop·py
  slop·pi·ness
sloth·ful
slouch
  slouch·i·ness
  slouch·y
slov·en·ly
  slov·en·li·ness
slow *adj., adv., v.* (*not quick;*
  see *sloe*)
  slow·down *n.*
  slow·poke *n.*
  slow-wit·ted
sloyd
sludge
slug·gard
slug·gish
sluice
  sluice·way
slum·ber
slush
small·pox
smart·en
smash·up *n.*

smat·ter·ing
smear
smi·lax
smith·er·eens
smoke·house
smoke·jack
smoke·less
smok·er
smoke·stack
smok·ing room *n.*
smok·ing-room *adj*
smok·y
smol·der *or* smoul·der
smooth
  smooth·bore
  smooth-tongued *adj.*
smor·gas·bord
smoth·er
smudge
smug·gle
smut·ty
snaf·fle
sna·fu
snag
  snagged
  snag·ging
snail-paced
snake pit
snake·root
snake·skin
snak·y
snap·drag·on
snap·shot
snare drum
sneak·er
sneak thief
sneeze
snick·er
snif·ter
snip
  snipped
  snip·pet·y
  snip·pi·ness
  snip·ping
  snip·py

sniv·el
  sniv·eled
snob
  snob·ber·y
  snob·bish
snor·kel
snow·ball
snow·bank
snow-blind *adj.*
snow·blow·er
snow·bound
snow·capped *adj.*
snow·drift
snow·drop
snow·fall
snow·flake
snow line
snow·man
snow·mo·bile
snow·plow
snow·shed
snow·shoe
snow·storm
snow·suit
snow tire
snow-white *adj.*
snow·y
snub
  snubbed
  snub·bing
  snub nose *n.*
  snub-nosed *adj.*
snuff·box
snuff·er
snuf·fle
so *adv., conj., n.*
  (*subsequently; extremely;*
  therefore; see *sew* and
  sow)
soap·box
soap·mak·ing
soap·stone
soap·suds
soap·y
  soap·i·ness

soar *v.* (*to fly aloft*; see *sore*)
  soared
so·ber
so·bri·e·ty
so·bri·quet
so-called
soc·cer
so·cia·ble
  so·cia·bil·i·ty
so·cial
  so·cial·ism
  so·cial·ist
  so·cial·ite
  so·cial·ize
  so·cial·ly
  so·cial-mind·ed
so·ci·e·ty
so·ci·o·ec·o·nom·ic
so·ci·ol·o·gy
so·ci·o·path
sock·et
Soc·ra·tes
so·da
so·dal·i·ty
sod·den
so·di·um
sod·o·mize
soft·ball
soft-boiled
soft·en
soft·head·ed
soft·heart·ed
soft-shoe
soft soap *n.*
soft-soap *v.*
soft-spo·ken
soft·wood
sog·gy
  sog·gi·ness
soi-di·sant
soi·ree
so·journ
sol·ace
so·lar

sol·der
sol·dier
sole *n., v., adj.* (*bottom of shoe, foot; single*; see *soul*)
  sole·ly
sol·e·cism
sol·emn
  so·lem·ni·ty
  sol·em·ni·za·tion
  sol·em·nize
so·le·noid
so·lic·it
  so·lic·i·ta·tion
  so·lic·i·tor
  so·lic·i·tous
  so·lic·i·tude
sol·id
  sol·i·dar·i·ty
  so·lid·i·fi·ca·tion
  so·lid·i·fy
  so·lid·i·ty
so·lil·o·quy
  pl. so·lil·o·quies
  so·lil·o·quize
sol·i·taire
sol·i·tar·y
sol·i·tude
so·lo
  pl. so·los *or* so·li
sol·stice
sol·u·ble
  sol·u·bil·i·ty
so·lu·tion
solv·a·ble
sol·vent
  sol·ven·cy
So·mal·i·a
som·ber *or* **som·bre**
som·bre·ro
some
  some·bod·y
  some·day
  some·how
  some·one

some·place
some·thing
some·time
some·times
some·what
some·where
som·er·sault
som·me·lier
som·nam·bu·lism
som·no·lent
so·na·ta
song·bird
song·book
song·fest
song·writ·er
son-in-law
son·net
  son·ne·teer
so·no·rous
  so·nor·i·ty
sooth *n.* (*truth*; see *soothe*)
  sooth·say·er
soothe *v.* (*to comfort*; see
  sooth)
  sooth·ing·ly
soot·y
  soot·i·ness
soph·ism
  soph·ist·ry
so·phis·ti·cate
  so·phis·ti·ca·ted
  so·phis·ti·ca·tion
soph·o·more
so·po·rif·ic
so·pra·no
sor·cer·y
  sor·cer·er
sor·did
sore *adj., n.* (*painful; open
  wound*; see *soar*)
  sore·head
sor·ghum
so·ror·i·ty
sor·rel

sor·row
  sor·row·ful
sor·ry
  sor·ri·ly
sou·brette
souf·flé
soul *n.* (*spirit*; see *sole*)
  soul·ful
  soul·less
  soul mate
sound·proof
soup·çon
sour·dough
sour grapes
South Car·o·li·na
South Da·ko·ta
south·east
south·er·ly
south·ern
South·ern·er
south·land
south·paw
South Pole
south·west
sou·ve·nir
sov·er·eign
  sov·er·eign·ty
so·vi·et
So·vi·et Un·ion
sow *n., v.* (*to plant*; see *sew*
  and *so*)
soy
  soy·a
  soy·bean
space·craft
space flight
space·man
space·ship
space suit
spa·cious
spade·work
spa·ghet·ti
Spain
span·drel

span·gle
span·iel
span·ner
spare·ribs
spar·kle
spark plug *n*.
spar·row
Spar·tan
spas·mod·ic
spas·tic
spa·tial
spat·ter
spat·u·la
spav·ined
speak·eas·y
speak·er
spear·fish
spear·head
spear·mint
spe·cial
  spe·cial·ist
  spe·cial·ize
  spe·cial·ty
spe·cie *n*. (*money*; see *species*)
spe·cies *n*. (*kind*; see *specie*)
  pl. spe·cies
spe·cif·ic
spec·i·fy
  spec·i·fi·ca·tion
spec·i·men
spe·cious
spec·ta·cle
  spec·tac·u·lar
spec·ta·tor
spec·ter
  spec·tral
spec·tro·scope
spec·trum
  pl. spec·tra *or* spec·trums
spec·u·late
  spec·u·la·tion
  spec·u·la·tive
spec·u·lum
  pl. spec·u·la *or* spec·u·lums

speech
  speech·less
speed·boat
speed·i·ly
speed·om·e·ter
speed·up *n*.
speed·way
spe·le·ol·o·gy
spell·bind·er
spell·bound
spe·lunk·er
spend·thrift
sphag·num
spher·i·cal
sphinx
spick-and-span
spic·ule
spic·y
spi·der
spig·ot
spike·nard
spill·way
spin·ach
spi·nal
spin·dle
spine·less
spin·et
spin·off
spin·ster
spi·ral
  spi·raled
  spi·ral·ing
  spi·ral·ly
spir·it
  spir·it·ed
  spir·it·less
  spir·i·tu·al
  spir·i·tu·al·ism
  spir·i·tu·al·i·ty
  spir·i·tu·ous
spit·ball
spit curl
spite·ful
spit·fire

spit·toon
splash·board
splash guard
splen·did
splen·dor
sple·net·ic
splin·ter
split-lev·el
splotch
splurge
spoil·age
spoils·man
spoil·sport
spoke·shave
spokes·man
spo·li·a·tion
spon·dee
sponge
  spon·gy
spon·sor
spon·ta·ne·ous
  spon·ta·ne·i·ty
spoon-feed
spoon·ful
spoor n. (*trail, esp. of a wild animal; see* spore)
spo·rad·ic
spore n., v. (*seed; see* spoor)
spor·tive
sports·cast
sport shirt
sports·man
  sports·man·ship
sports·wear
sports·writ·er
spot-check v.
spot·less
spot·light
spot·ted
spot·ter
sprawl
spread ea·gle n.
spread-ea·gle v.

spright·ly
  spright·li·ness
spring·board
spring·bok
spring-clean·ing
spring·house
spring·i·ness
spring·time
sprin·kle
  sprin·kling
sprock·et
sprout
spruce
spu·mo·ni
spur
  spurred
  spur·ring
spu·ri·ous
spurn
spurt
spur track
sput·nik
sput·ter
spu·tum
spy·glass
squab
squab·ble
squad·ron
squad room
squal·id
  squal·or
squall
squan·der
square dance
square deal
square knot
square-rigged *adj.*
square root
squash
squat·ter
squaw
squawk
squeak
squea·mish

squee·gee
squir·rel
squirt
Sri Lan·ka
sta·bi·lize
  sta·bil·i·ty
  sta·bi·li·za·tion
  sta·bi·liz·er
sta·ble
stac·ca·to
sta·di·um
  pl. sta·di·a *or* sta·di·ums
staff·er
stage·coach
stage·craft
stage fright
stage·hand
stage·struck
stag·fla·tion
stag·ger
stag·nate
  stag·nant
  stag·na·tion
staid
stain·less
stair *n.* (*steps; see* stare)
  stair·case
  stair·way
stake *n., v.* (*stick; post; see* steak)
  stake·hold·er
sta·lac·tite
sta·lag·mite
stale·mate
stalk·ing-horse
stal·lion
stal·wart
sta·men
  pl. sta·mens *or* stam·i·na
stam·i·na *n.* (*endurance*)
stam·mer
stam·pede
stamp·er

stanch *v.* (*to stop the flow; see* staunch)
stan·chion
stan·dard
  stan·dard-bear·er
  stan·dard·bred
  stan·dard·i·za·tion
  stan·dard·ize
stand by *v.*
stand·by *n., adj.*
stand·ee
stand in *v.*
stand-in *n.*
stand off *v.*
stand·off *adj., n.*
stand·off·ish
stand out *v.*
stand·out *n.*
stand·pat·ter
stand·pipe
stand·point
stand·still
stand up *v.*
stand-up *adj., n.*
stan·za
sta·pes
staph·y·lo·coc·cus
sta·ple
star·board
star-cham·ber *adj.*
starch·y
  starch·i·ness
star-crossed
star·dom
star·dust
stare *v., n.* (*to gaze intently; see* stair)
star·fish
star·gaz·er
star·let
star·light
  star·lit
star·ling
star·ry-eyed

star shell
star-span·gled
star·tle
 star·tling
starve
 star·va·tion
state·craft
state·hood
state·house
state·less
state·ly
 state·li·ness
state·ment
state·room
states·man
states' right·er
stat·ic
sta·tion
sta·tion·ar·y *adj.* (*not moving;*
 see *stationery*)
sta·tio·ner·y *n.* (*writing*
 paper; see *stationary*)
 sta·tio·ner
stat·ism
sta·tis·tics
 sta·tis·ti·cal
 stat·is·ti·cian
stat·ue
 stat·u·ar·y
 stat·u·esque
 stat·u·ette
stat·ure
sta·tus
stat·ute
 stat·u·to·ry
staunch *v.*, *adj.* (*steadfast;*
 see *stanch*)
stayed
stay·sail
stead·fast
stead·i·ly
steak *n.* (*meat;* see *stake*)
steal *v.*, *n.* (*to rob;* see *steel*)
stealth

steam·boat
steam·er
steam fit·ter
steam-heat·ed *adj.*
steam-rol·ler
steam·ship
steam ta·ble
steam·tight
steel *n.*, *v.* (*strong metal;* see
 steal)
 steel wool
 steel·work
 steel·yard
stee·ple
 stee·ple·chase
 stee·ple·jack
steer·age
 steer·age·way
steers·man
stel·lar
stem
 stemmed
 stem·ware
 stem·wind·er
sten·cil
 sten·ciled
 sten·cil·ing
ste·nog·ra·phy
 ste·nog·ra·pher
 sten·o·graph·ic
sten·to·ri·an
step *v.*, *n.* (*to move the foot;*
 see *steppe*)
 step·child
 step·daugh·ter
 step down *v.*
 step-down *n.*, *adj.*
 step·fa·ther
 step in *v.*
 step-in *n.*, *adj.*
 step·lad·der
 step·moth·er
 step·par·ent
 step·ping-off place

step·ping-stone
step·sis·ter
step·son
step stool
step up v.
step-up adj., n.
steppe n. (treeless plain; see
  step)
ste·re·o
  ste·re·o·pho·nic
ste·re·op·ti·con
ste·re·o·type
ster·ile
  ste·ril·i·ty
  ster·i·lize
ster·ling
ster·num
  pl. ster·nums or ster·na
ster·nu·ta·tion
ster·oid
ster·to·rous
steth·o·scope
stev·e·dore
stew·ard
stew·pan
stick·ful
stick·i·ness
stick·ler
stick·pin
stick·up n., adj.
stick up v.
stiff·en
stiff-necked adj.
sti·fle
stig·ma
  pl. stig·ma·ta or stig·mas
  stig·ma·tize
stile n. (steps over a fence;
  see style)
sti·let·to
still·birth
still·born
still hunt n.
still-hunt v.

still life
stilt·ed
Stil·ton cheese
stim·u·late
  stim·u·lant
  stim·u·la·tion
stim·u·lus
  pl. stim·u·li
stin·gy
  stin·gi·ness
stink·er
stink·weed
sti·pend
  sti·pen·di·ar·y
stip·ple
stip·u·late
  stip·u·la·tion
stir
  stirred
  stir·ring
stir·rup
sto·chas·tic
stock·ade
stock·bro·ker
stock car
stock clerk
stock·hold·er
stock·ing
stock-in-trade n.
stock·job·ber
stock·man
stock·pile
stock·pot
stock·proof
stock room
stock·yard
stodg·y
  stodg·i·ness
Sto·ic
stoke·hold
stok·er
stol·id
stom·ach
  stom·ach·ache

stone-blind
stone·boat
stone-broke
stone crush·er
stone·cut·ter
stone-deaf
Stone·henge
stone·ma·son
stone·ware
stone·work
ston·i·ly
ston·y·heart·ed
stoop *n., v. (to bend; see stoup)*
stop·cock
stop·gap
stop·light
stop off *v.*
stop-off *adj., n.*
stop·o·ver *n.*
stop·page
stop·per
stop street
stop·watch
stor·a·ble
stor·age
store·front
store·house
store·keep·er
store·room
store·wide
storm·bound
storm cloud
storm door
storm·proof
storm·y
sto·ry
  sto·ry·book
  sto·ry·tell·er
stoup *n. (container for beverages; see stoop)*
stout·heart·ed
stove·pipe
stow·age

stow a·way *v.*
stow·a·way *n.*
stra·bis·mus
strad·dle
  strad·dling
strag·gle
  strag·gly
straight *adj., adv., n. (without curves; see strait)*
  straight·a·way
  straight·edge
  straight·for·ward
  straight-line *adj.*
  straight man
strait *n. (narrow passage; see straight)*
  strait·jack·et
  strait·laced *or* straight·laced
strang·er
stran·gle·hold
stran·gu·late
strap·hang·er
strap·less
strapped
strap·ping
strat·e·gy
  strat·a·gem
  stra·te·gic
  strat·e·gist
strat·i·fy
strat·o·sphere
stra·tum
straw·ber·ry
straw·board
straw man
stream
  stream·lined
street·car
strength
  strength·en
stren·u·ous
strep·to·coc·cus
  pl. strep·to·coc·ci
stress·ful

stretch·er-bear·er
stretch-out *n*.
stri·a·tion
stric·ture
stri·dent
strike·bound
strike·break·er
strike out *v*.
strike·out *n*.
strike o·ver *v*.
strike·o·ver *n*.
strin·gent
string·i·ness
strip·ling
stro·bo·scope
strong-arm *v*., *adj*.
strong arm *n*.
strong·hold
strong-mind·ed
strong room
strong suit
stron·ti·um
stro·phe
struc·ture
  struc·tur·al
strug·gle
  strug·gling
strych·nine
stub
  stubbed
  stub·bing
  stub·by
stub·born
stuc·co
  pl. stuc·cos *or* stuc·coes
  stuc·co·work
stuck-up *adj*.
stud·book
stu·dent
stu·di·o
  pl. stu·di·os
stud·y
  stud·ied
  stu·di·ous

stuff
  stuff·i·ness
  stuff·ing
  stuff·y
stul·ti·fy
stum·ble·bum
stu·pe·fy
stu·pen·dous
stu·pid
  stu·pid·i·ty
stu·por
stur·dy
stur·geon
stut·ter
style *n*., *v*. (*prevailing mode;
  see* stile)
  style·book
  styl·ish
  styl·ist
  styl·i·za·tion
  styl·ize
sty·lo·graph·ic
sty·lus
  pl. sty·li *or* sty·lus·es
sty·mie
styp·tic
Sty·ro·foam (*trademark*)
sua·sion
suave
  suav·i·ty
sub·al·tern
sub·av·er·age
sub·base·ment
sub·cel·lar
sub·com·mit·tee
sub·con·scious
sub·con·ti·nent
sub·con·tract
  sub·con·trac·tor
sub·cul·ture
sub·cu·ta·ne·ous
sub·deb·u·tante
  sub·deb

sub·di·vide
  sub·di·vi·sion
sub·due
sub·ed·i·tor
sub·head
sub·ject
  sub·jec·tion
  sub·jec·tive
sub·ju·gate
sub·junc·tive
sub·lease
sub·li·mate
  sub·li·ma·tion
sub·lime
  sub·lim·i·ty
sub·li·mi·nal
sub·ma·rine
sub·merge
  sub·mer·gi·ble
sub·mers·i·ble
sub·mer·sion
sub·mit
  sub·mis·sion
  sub·mis·sive
sub·nor·mal
sub·or·di·nate
  sub·or·di·na·tion
sub·orn
sub·poe·na
sub·rou·tine
sub·scribe
  sub·scrip·tion
sub·script
sub·se·quent
sub·ser·vi·ent
sub·side
  sub·si·dence
sub·sid·i·ar·y
sub·si·dy
  sub·si·dize
sub·sist
  sub·sist·ence
sub·stance
sub·stan·dard

sub·stan·tial
sub·stan·ti·ate
sub·stan·tive
sub·sti·tute
sub·ter·fuge
sub·ter·ra·ne·an
sub·tle
  sub·tle·ty
  sub·tly
sub·tract
  sub·trac·tion
sub·tra·hend
sub·trea·sur·y
sub·trop·i·cal
sub·urb
  sub·ur·ban·ite
  sub·ur·bi·a
sub·ven·tion
sub·ver·sive
  sub·ver·sion
sub·way
suc·ceed
suc·cess
  suc·cess·ful
suc·ces·sion
suc·ces·sive
suc·ces·sor
suc·cinct
suc·cor *v., n. (to help;* see
  sucker)
suc·co·tash
suc·cu·lent
suc·cumb
suck·er *n. (something that
  sucks;* see *succor)*
suc·tion
Su·dan
sud·den
su·do·rif·ic
sue
  sued
  su·ing
suede
su·et

suf·fer
  suf·fer·ance
  suf·fer·ing
suf·fice
suf·fi·cient
  suf·fi·cien·cy
suf·fix
suf·fo·cate
  suf·fo·ca·tion
suf·frage
  suf·frag·ette
  suf·frag·ist
suf·fuse
  suf·fu·sion
sug·ar
  sug·ar beet
  sug·ar·cane
  sug·ar·coat
  sug·ar·house
  sug·ar·loaf
  sug·ar·plum
sug·gest
  sug·ges·tion
  sug·ges·tive
su·i·cide
  su·i·ci·dal
suit *n., v. (clothes; to fit*; see *suite)*
  suit·a·ble
  suit·case
  suit·or
suite *n. (group of rooms*; see *suit* and *sweet)*
sul·fur
sulk·y
  sulk·i·ness
sul·len
sul·tan
sul·tan·a
sul·try
sum
  sum·ma·tion
su·mac

sum·ma·ry *n., adj. (short restatement*; see *summery)*
  sum·ma·ri·ly
  sum·ma·rize
sum·mer house
sum·mer·time
sum·mer·y *adj. (like summer*; see *summary)*
sum·mit
sum·mons
sump·tu·ar·y
sump·tu·ous
sun·baked
sun·bath *n.*
sun·bathe *v.*
sun·beam
sun·bon·net
sun·burn
sun·burst
sun·dae *n. (ice cream dessert*; see *Sunday)*
Sun·day *n. (see sundae)*
sun deck
sun·di·al
sun·down
sun·dry
  pl. sun·dries
sun·fish
sun·flow·er
sun·glass·es
sun·glow
sun-god
sun hat
sunk·en
sun lamp
sun·light
  sun·lit
sun·ny
  sun·ni·ly
sun par·lor
sun porch
sun·proof
sun·rise
sun-room

sun·set
sun·shade
sun·shine
  sun·shin·y
sun·spot
sun·stroke
sun·suit
sun·tan
sun·up
su·per·a·bun·dant
su·per·an·nu·ate
su·perb
su·per·cal·en·der
su·per·car·go
su·per·cil·i·ous
su·per·e·go
su·per·e·rog·a·to·ry
  su·per·er·o·ga·tion
su·per·fi·cial
  su·per·fi·ci·al·i·ty
su·per·flu·ous
  su·per·flu·i·ty
su·per·heat
su·per·hu·man
su·per·im·pose
su·per·in·duce
su·per·in·tend
  su·per·in·tend·ent
su·pe·ri·or
  su·pe·ri·or·i·ty
su·per·la·tive
su·per·man
su·per·nal
su·per·nat·u·ral
su·per·nu·mer·ar·y
su·per·script
  su·per·scrip·tion
su·per·sede
su·per·son·ic
su·per·sti·tion
  su·per·sti·tious
su·per·struc·ture
su·per·tank·er
su·per·vene

su·per·vise
  su·per·vi·sion
  su·per·vi·sor
su·pi·nate
su·pine
sup·per
sup·plant
sup·ple
sup·ple·ment
  sup·ple·men·tal
  sup·ple·men·ta·ry
sup·pli·ant
  sup·pli·ance
sup·pli·cate
  sup·pli·cant
  sup·pli·ca·tion
sup·ply
  sup·pli·er
sup·port
  sup·port·er
sup·pose
  sup·po·si·tion
sup·pos·i·ti·tious
sup·press
  sup·pres·sion
sup·pu·ra·tion
su·pra
  su·pra·re·nal
su·prem·a·cy
  su·prem·a·cist
su·preme
  su·preme·ly
sur·base
sur·cease
sur·charge
sure·fire
sure·foot·ed
sure·ly *adv.* (*certainly*; see *surly*)
sure·ty
surf *n., v.* (*waves*; see *serf*)
  surf·board
  surf-rid·ing
sur·face

sur·feit
surge *n.*, *v.* (*sweeping
  forward*; see *serge*)
sur·ger·y
  sur·geon
  sur·gi·cal
Sur·i·name *or* Sur·i·nam
sur·ly *adj.* (*rude*; see *surely*)
  sur·li·ness
sur·mise
sur·mount
sur·name
sur·pass
sur·plice *n.* (*ecclesiastical
  garment*; see *surplus*)
sur·plus *n.*, *adj.*
  (*overabundance*; see
  surplice)
  sur·plus·age
sur·prise
sur·re·al·ism
sur·re·but·tal
sur·ren·der
sur·rep·ti·tious
sur·rey
sur·ro·gate
sur·round
sur·tax
sur·veil·lance
sur·vey
  sur·vey·or
sur·vive
  sur·viv·al
  sur·vi·vor
sus·cep·ti·ble
  sus·cep·ti·bil·i·ty
sus·pect
sus·pend
  sus·pen·sion
sus·pense
sus·pi·cion
  sus·pi·cious
sus·tain
  sus·te·nance

sut·tee
su·ture
su·ze·rain
svelte
swad·dle
swag·ger
swal·low
swamp
  swamp·i·ness
  swamp·land
swans·down
swan song
sward *n.* (*turf*; see *sword*)
swarth·y
  swarth·i·ness
swash·buck·ler
swas·ti·ka
swatch
swath *n.* (*a broad strip*; see
  swathe)
swathe *v.* (*to wrap*; see *swath*)
Swaz·i·land
swear·word
sweat·band
sweat·box
sweat·er
sweat pants
sweat shirt
sweat·shop
sweat·y
Swe·den
sweep·stakes
sweet *adj.*, *adv.*, *n.* (*like
  sugar*; see *suite*)
  sweet·bread
  sweet corn
  sweet·en
  sweet·heart
  sweet·meat
  sweet pea
  sweet·shop
  sweet talk *n.*
  sweet-talk *v.*
  sweet tooth
  sweet Wil·liam

swelled head·ed
swel·ter
  swel·ter·ing
swerve
swill
swim·ming·ly
swim·suit
swin·dle
  swin·dler
  swin·dling
swine·herd
swin·ish
switch·back
switch·blade knife
switch·board
switch·man
switch·yard
Swit·zer·land
swiv·el
swoon
swoop
sword n. (weapon; see sward)
  sword·fish
  sword grass
  sword knot
  sword·play
swords·man
syc·a·more
syc·o·phant
syl·la·ble
  syl·lab·ic
  syl·lab·i·cate
syl·la·bus
syl·lo·gism
sylph
syl·van
sym·bi·o·sis
sym·bol n. (representative object; see cymbal)
  sym·bol·ic
  sym·bol·ism
  sym·bol·ize
sym·me·try
  sym·met·ri·cal

sym·pa·thize
  sym·pa·thiz·er
sym·pa·thy
  sym·pa·thet·ic
sym·pho·ny
  sym·phon·ic
sym·po·si·um
  pl. sym·po·si·a or sym·po·si·ums
symp·tom
syn·a·gogue
syn·chro·mesh
syn·chro·nize
  syn·chro·ni·za·tion
  syn·chro·nous
syn·co·pate
  syn·co·pa·tion
syn·co·pe
syn·dic
syn·di·cal·ism
syn·di·cate
syn·ec·do·che
syn·er·gism
  syn·er·gis·tic
syn·od
syn·o·nym
  syn·on·y·mous
syn·op·sis
  pl. syn·op·ses
syn·tax
syn·the·size
  syn·the·sis
syn·thet·ic
syph·i·lis
Syr·i·a
sy·ringe
syr·up
sys·tem·at·ic
sys·tem·a·tize
sys·tem·ic
sys·to·le
  sys·tol·ic
syz·y·gy

T

Ta·bas·co (*trademark*)
tab·er·na·cle
ta·ble
tab·leau
　　pl. tab·leaux
ta·ble·cloth
ta·ble-hop
ta·ble·land
ta·ble·spoon·ful
　　pl. ta·ble·spoon·fuls *or*
　　ta·ble·spoons·ful
tab·let
ta·ble·ware
tab·loid
ta·boo *or* ta·bu
　　pl. ta·boos *or* ta·bus
　　ta·boed *or* ta·bued
ta·bor
tab·o·ret *or* tab·ou·ret
tab·u·late
　　tab·u·lar
　　tab·u·la·tor
ta·chis·to·scope
ta·chom·e·ter
tach·y·car·di·a
ta·chyg·ra·phy
tac·it
tac·i·turn
tack·le
ta·co
　　pl. ta·cos
tac·o·nite
tact·ful
tac·tics
　　tac·ti·cal
　　tac·ti·cian
tac·tile
tact·less
tad·pole
taf·fe·ta
taff·rail

tag·board
tag day
tag end
tagged
tag·ging
tag line
tail *n., v.* (*animal's rear
　　appendage;* see *tale*)
　　tail·board
　　tail·coat
　　tail·gate
　　tail·light
　　tail·piece
　　tail pipe
　　tail·race
　　tail·spin
　　tail·stock
　　tail wind
tai·lored
tai·lor-made
Tai·wan
take down *v.*
take-down *adj., n.*
take-home pay
take off *v.*
take·off *n.*
take o·ver *v.*
take-o·ver *n.*
take up *v.*
take-up *n.*
talc
tale *n.* (*story;* see *tail*)
　　tale·bear·er
tal·ent
tales·man *n.* (*person added
　　to a jury;* see *talisman*)
tal·is·man *n.* (*a charm;* see
　　talesman)
talk·a·tive
talk·ing-to *n.*
tal·low
tal·ly
Tal·mud
tal·on

ta·ma·le
tam·a·rind
tam·bou·rine
tam·per
tam·pon
tan·bark
tan·dem
tan·gent
tan·ger·ine
tan·gi·ble
tan·gle
tan·go
tan·kard
tan·ner·y
tan·nic
tans·du·cer
tan·ta·lize
tan·ta·lus
tan·ta·mount
Tan·za·ni·a
Tao·ism
tap dance *n*.
tap-dance *v*.
tape·line
ta·per *n*., *v*. (*candle; to narrow; see tapir*)
tape-re·cord *v*.
tape re·cord·er *n*.
tap·es·try
tape·worm
tap·i·o·ca
ta·pir *n*. (*horse-like animal; see taper*)
   pl. ta·pir *or* ta·pirs
tap·room
tap·root
tar·an·tel·la
ta·ran·tu·la
   pl. ta·ran·tu·las *or* ta·ran·tu·lae
tar·dy
   tar·di·ness
tare *n*. (*counterweight; see tear*)
tar·get

tar·iff
tar·la·tan
tar·nish
ta·rot
tar·pau·lin
tar·pon
tar·ra·gon
tar·ry
tar·tan
tar·tar *n*. (*encrustation on teeth; see Tartar*)
   tar·tar·ic
Tar·tar *n*. (*Turk; see tartar*)
Tar·ta·rus
task force
task·mas·ter
tas·sel
taste·ful
taste·less
tast·y
   tast·i·ly
tat·ter·de·ma·lion
tat·ter·sall
tat·ting
tat·too
   pl. tat·toos
taught *v*. (*pt. of teach; see taut*)
taunt
taut *adj*. (*tight; see taught*)
tau·tol·o·gy
tav·ern
taw·dry
   taw·dri·ness
taw·ny
tax·a·ble
tax·a·tion
tax-ex·empt
tax·i
   tax·i·cab
   tax·i danc·er
   tax·ied
   tax·i·ing
   tax·i·man
   tax·i·me·ter

tax·i·der·my
  tax·i·der·mist
tax·pay·er
tax shel·ter
T-bone
tea *n.* (*beverage*; see *tee*)
  tea bag
  tea ball
  tea·cup
  tea dance
  tea gown
  tea·house
  tea·ket·tle
  tea·pot
  tea·room
  tea·spoon·ful
  pl. tea·spoon·fuls *or*
  tea·spoons·ful
  tea time
  tea·tray
  tea wag·on
teach·a·ble
teach·er
teak·wood
team *n., v.* (*group*; see *teem*)
  team·mate
  team·ster
  team·work
tear *v., n.* (*to rip*; see *tare* and *tier*)
  tear·drop
  tear·ful
  tear gas
  tear sheet
  tear·stain
tease
tech·ni·cal
  tech·ni·cal·i·ty
tech·ni·cian
Tech·ni·col·or (*trademark*)
tech·nique
tech·noc·ra·cy
tech·nol·o·gy
  tech·no·log·i·cal

te·di·ous
te·di·um
tee *n., v.* (*golf area*; see *tea*)
teem *v.* (*to abound*; see *team*)
teen·age
  teen·ag·er
teens
tee·ter
tee·to·tal·er *or* tee·to·tal·ler
Tel·Au·to·graph (*trademark*)
tel·e·cast
tel·e·gram
te·leg·ra·phy
  tel·e·graph
  te·leg·ra·pher
  tel·e·graph·ic
tel·e·me·ter
tel·e·ol·o·gy
te·lep·a·thy
  tel·e·path·ic
tel·e·phone
  tel·e·phon·ic
  te·leph·o·ny
tel·e·pho·to
tel·e·print·er
Tel·e·Promp·Ter (*trademark*)
tel·e·scope
  tel·e·scop·ic
Tel·e·type (*trademark*)
  Tel·e·type·set·ter
  Tel·e·type·writ·er
tel·e·vi·sion
Tel·ex (*trademark*)
tell·tale
tel·pher
tem·blor
te·mer·i·ty
tem·per
  tem·per·a·ment
  tem·per·ance
  tem·pered
tem·per·ate
tem·per·a·ture

tem·pest
  tem·pes·tu·ous
tem·plate
tem·ple
tem·po
  pl. tem·pi *or* tem·pos
tem·po·ral
tem·po·rar·y
  tem·po·rar·i·ly
tem·po·rize
tempt
  temp·ta·tion
  tempt·ress
ten·a·ble
te·nac·i·ty
  te·na·cious
ten·ant
  ten·an·cy
  ten·ant·a·ble
ten-cent store
tend·en·cy
  ten·den·tious
ten·der
  ten·der·foot
  ten·der·heart·ed
  ten·der·iz·er
  ten·der·loin
ten·don
ten·dril
ten·e·ment
ten·es·mus
ten·et
Ten·nes·see
ten·nis
ten·on
ten·or
ten·pin
ten·sion
  ten·sile
ten-strike
ten·ta·cle
ten·ta·tive
ten·ter·hook
tent·mak·er

te·nu·i·ty
ten·u·ous
ten·ure
te·pee
tep·id
te·qui·la
ter·cen·ten·a·ry
te·re·do
  pl. te·re·dos
ter·gi·ver·sate
ter·ma·gant
ter·mi·nal
ter·mi·nate
  ter·mi·na·tion
  ter·mi·ni·ble
ter·mi·nol·o·gy
ter·mi·nus
  pl. ter·mi·ni *or* ter·mi·nus·es
ter·mite
tern
terp·sich·o·re·an
ter·race
ter·ra-cot·ta
  pl. ter·ra-cot·tas
ter·ra fir·ma
ter·rain
ter·ra·pin
ter·rar·i·um
  pl. ter·rar·i·a *or* te·rar·i·ums
ter·raz·zo
ter·res·tri·al
ter·ri·ble
ter·ri·er
ter·rif·ic
ter·ri·fy
ter·ri·to·ry
  ter·ri·to·ri·al
  ter·ri·to·ri·al·i·ty
ter·ror
  ter·ror·ism
  ter·ror·ist
  ter·ror·ize
terse
ter·ti·ar·y

tes·sel·la·tion
tes·ta·ment
  tes·ta·men·ta·ry
  tes·ta·tor
tes·ti·fy
tes·ti·mo·ny
  tes·ti·mo·ni·al
tes·tos·ter·one
test tube *n.*
test-tube *adj.*
tet·a·nus
tête-à-tête
  pl. tête-à-têtes *or* têtes-à-têtes
teth·er·ball
tet·ra·cy·cline
tet·ra·he·dral
te·tral·o·gy
te·tram·e·ter
Teu·ton·ic
Tex·as
text·book
tex·tile
tex·tu·al
tex·ture
Thai·land
tha·lid·o·mide
thank·ful
thank·less
thanks·giv·ing
the·a·ter *or* the·a·tre
  the·at·ri·cal
their *adj.* (*belonging to them;*
  see *there* and *they're*)
the·ism
the·mat·ic
thence·forth
the·od·o·lite
the·ol·o·gy
  the·o·lo·gian
  the·o·log·i·cal
the·o·rem
the·o·ry
  the·o·ret·i·cal
  the·o·rize

the·os·o·phy
ther·a·peu·tics
ther·a·py
  ther·a·pist
there *adv., n.* (*that place;*
  see *their* and *they're*)
there·af·ter
there·by
there·for *adv.* (*in return for;*
  see *therefore*)
there·fore *adv.* (*consequently;*
  see *therefor*)
there·in·af·ter
there·in·to
there·of
there·on
there·to·fore
there·up·on
there·with
ther·mal
ther·mo·dy·nam·ics
ther·mo·e·lec·tric
ther·mom·e·ter
ther·mo·nu·cle·ar
ther·mo·plas·tic
ther·mo·stat
the·sau·rus
  pl. the·sau·ri *or* the·sau·rus·es
the·sis
they're (*they are;* see *their*
  and *there*)
thick·et
thick·set
thick-skinned
thief
  pl. thieves
  thiev·ish
thim·ble·ful
thin
  thin·ner
  thin-skinned
third class *n.*
third-class *adj., adv.*
third-rate *adj.*

thirst·y
  thirst·i·ly
this·tle·down
thith·er
tho·rax
  pl. tho·rax·es *or* tho·ra·ces
  tho·rac·ic
tho·ri·um
thorn·y
  thorn·i·ness
thor·ough
  thor·ough·bred
  thor·ough·fare
  thor·ough·go·ing
thought·ful
thou·sand
  pl. thou·sands *or* thou·sand
  thou·sand-leg·ger
thrall·dom *or* thral·dom
thread·bare
thread·worm
threat·en·ing·ly
three·fold
three-piece
three-ply
three·score
three·some
thren·o·dy
thresh·old
threw *v*. (*pt. of throw*; see
  through)
thrift·less
thrift·y
  thrift·i·ly
thrive
throat·y
  throat·i·ness
throe *n*. (*spasm*; see *throw*)
throm·bo·sis
  pl. throm·bo·ses
throne
throng
throt·tle·hold

through *or* thru *prep., adv.,
  adj*. (*finished; by way of;
  *see *threw*)
through·out
through·put
through·way
throw *v., n*. (*to toss*; see
  throe)
throw·a·way
throw back *v*.
throw·back *n*.
thrown
thrum
  thrummed
  thrum·ming
thumb·nail
thumb·print
thumb·screw
thumb·tack
thun·der·bolt
thun·der·clap
thun·der·cloud
thun·der·head
thun·der·ous
thun·der·show·er
thun·der·storm
thwart
thyme *n*. (*herb*; see *time*)
thy·mus
  pl. thy·mus·es *or* thy·mi
thy·roid
tib·i·a
  pl. tib·i·ae *or* tib·i·as
tic *n*. (*muscular spasm*; see
  tick)
tick *n., v*. (*bloodsucking
  insect*; see *tic*)
  tick·er
tick·et
tick·le
  tick·ler
tid·al *adj*. (*subject to tides*;
  see *title*)

tide
  tide·land
  tide·mark
  tide·wa·ter
ti·dy
  ti·di·ly
tie
  tied
  ty·ing
tie-in *n.*, *adj.*
tie in *v.*
tie·pin
tier *n.* (*a row*; see *tear*)
tie up *v.*
tie-up *n.*
ti·ger
  pl. ti·gers *or* ti·ger
tight·fist·ed
tight-lipped
tight-mouthed
tight·rope
tight·wad
tilt·yard
tim·bal *n.* (*kettledrum*; see *timbale*)
tim·bale *n.* (*food*; see *timbal*)
tim·ber *n.*, *adj.* (*wood*; see *timbre*)
  tim·ber·land
  tim·ber·line
  tim·ber·man
  tim·ber·work
tim·bre *n.* (*distinctive tone*; see *timber*)
time *n.*, *v.* (*measurable period*; see *thyme*)
  time clock
  time-con·sum·ing
  time draft
  time-hon·ored
  time·keep·er
  time·less
  time·li·ness
  time·ly

  time·piece
  time-sav·er *n.*
  time-sav·ing
  time shar·ing
  time·ta·ble
  time·worn
  time zone
tim·id
  ti·mid·i·ty
tim·o·rous
tim·o·thy
tim·pa·ni *pl.*
tinc·ture
tin·der·box
tin·foil
tin·gle
tin·ker
tin·plate *n.*
tin-plate *v.*
tin·sel
  tin·seled
tin·smith
tin·type
tin·ware
tin·work
ti·ny
tip
  tipped
  tip·ping
tip·ple
tip·staff
  pl. tip·staves *or* tip·staffs
tip·ster
tip·sy
tip·toe
tip-top
ti·rade
tire·some
tis·sue
Ti·tan
  ti·tan·ic
tithe
  tith·ing
tit·il·late

tit·i·vate
ti·tle *n.* (*inscription, heading;*
  see *tidal*)
  ti·tle·hold·er
tit·mouse
ti·trate
  ti·tra·tion
tit·u·lar
to *prep., adv.* (*toward;* see
  too and *two*)
toad·stool
toast·mas·ter
to·bac·co
  pl. to·bac·coes
  to·bac·co·nist
to·bog·gan
toc·ca·ta
toc·sin *n.* (*alarm bell;* see
  toxin)
to·day
tod·dy
toe *n., v.* (*appendage on foot;*
  see *tow*)
  toe cap
  toed
  toe dance *n.*
  toe-dance *v.*
  toe·hold
  toe·ing
  toe·nail
tof·fee *or* tof·fy
to·ga
  to·gaed
to·geth·er
tog·gle
toi·let *n.* (*bathroom fixture;*
  see *toilette*)
toi·lette *n.* (*fashionable attire;*
  see *toilet*)
toil·some
toil·worn
to·ken
tol·er·ant
  tol·er·ance

tol·er·ate
  tol·er·a·ble
  tol·er·a·tion
toll·booth
toll call
toll·gate
tom·a·hawk
to·ma·to
tom·boy
tomb·stone
tom·cat
tom·fool·er·y
to·mor·row
tom-tom
ton·al
  to·nal·i·ty
tone
  tone arm
  tone-deaf *adj.*
tongue
  tongue-lash *v.*
  tongue-lash·ing *n.*
  tongue-tied
ton·ic
to·night
ton·nage
ton·neau
to·nom·e·ter
ton·sil
  ton·sil·lec·to·my
  ton·sil·li·tis
ton·so·ri·al
ton·sure
ton·tine
too *adv.* (*also;* see *to* and *two*)
tool *n., v.* (*implement;* see
  tulle)
  tool·box
  tool·hold·er
  tool·house
  tool·mak·er
  tool·room
tooth·ache
tooth·brush

tooth·pick
tooth·some
to·paz
top·coat
top flight *n.*
top-flight *adj.*
top hat *n.*
top-hat *adj.*
top-heav·y *adj.*
to·pi·ar·y
top·ic
  top·i·cal
top·knot
top·mast
top·most
top·notch *n.*
top-notch *adj.*
to·pog·ra·phy
  to·pog·ra·pher
top·ping
top·sail
top·side
top·soil
top·sy-tur·vy
  top·sy-tur·vi·ness
toque
torch·light
to·re·a·dor
tor·ment
  tor·men·tor
tor·na·do
  pl. tor·na·does *or* tor·na·dos
tor·pe·do
tor·pid
tor·por
torque
tor·rent
  tor·ren·tial
tor·rid
tor·sion
tor·so
  pl. tor·sos *or* tor·si *or* tor·soes
tort *n.* (*wrongful act*; see
  torte)

tor·te *n.* (*kind of cake*; see
  tort)
  pl. tor·ten *or* tor·tes
tor·ti·lla
tor·toise
  pl. tor·tois·es *or* tor·toise
tor·toise·shell
tor·to·ni
tor·tu·ous *adv.* (*winding*; see
  torturous)
tor·ture
  tor·tur·ous *adj.* (*cruelly
  painful*; see *tortuous*)
toss·pot
toss-up *n.*
to·tal
  to·taled
  to·tal·ing
  to·tal·i·tar·i·an
  to·tal·i·ty
  to·tal·ize
  to·tal·ly
to·tem
touch down *v.*
touch·down *n.*
tou·ché
touch·i·ly
touch·i·ness
touch·stone
tough *adj.* (*strong*; see *tuff*)
  tough·en
  tough-mind·ed
tou·pee
tour de force
  pl. tours de force
tour·ism
  tour·ist
tour·ma·line
tour·na·ment
tour·ney
tour·ni·quet
tout
tow *v., n.* (*to pull*; see *toe*)
  tow·age

tow·boat
tow·head
tow·line
tow·path
tow·rope
to·ward *adj., prep.*
to·wards *prep.*
tow·el
  tow·el·ing
tow·er
towns·folk
town·ship
towns·man
towns·peo·ple
tox·e·mi·a
tox·ic
  tox·i·col·o·gy
tox·in *n. (poison; see tocsin)*
trace·a·ble
trac·er·y
tra·che·a
  pl. tra·che·ae *or* tra·che·as
tra·che·ot·o·my
tra·cho·ma
trac·ing
track *n., v. (path; see tract)*
  track·age
  track·less
  track·walk·er
tract *n. (pamphlet; see track)*
trac·ta·ble
trac·tion
trac·tor
trade-in *n.*
trade in *v.*
trade-last
trade·mark
trade name
trade school
trades·man
trade wind
tra·di·tion
tra·duce
traf·fic

trag·e·dy
  tra·ge·di·an
  tra·ge·di·enne *f.*
trag·ic
trail·blaz·er
trail·er
train·bear·er
train·load
train·man
train·sick
trait
trai·tor
  trai·tor·ous
  trai·tress *or* trai·tor·ess *f.*
tra·jec·to·ry
tram·car
tram·mel
tram·ple
tram·po·line
tram·way
tran·quil
  tran·quil·iz·er
  tran·quil·li·ty
trans·act
  trans·ac·tion
trans·at·lan·tic
tran·scend
  tran·scen·dent
  tran·scen·den·tal
trans·con·ti·nen·tal
tran·scribe
  tran·script
  tran·scrip·tion
trans·duc·er
tran·sept
trans·fer
  trans·fer·a·ble
  trans·fer·ence
trans·fig·ure
  trans·fig·u·ra·tion
trans·fix
trans·form
  trans·for·ma·tion
  trans·form·er

trans·fuse
trans·gress
  trans·gres·sion
  trans·gres·sor
tran·sient
tran·sis·tor
tran·sit
tran·si·tion
tran·si·tive
tran·si·to·ry
trans·late
  trans·la·tion
  trans·la·tor
trans·lit·er·ate
trans·load·ing
trans·lu·cent
trans·mi·grate
trans·mit
  trans·mis·si·ble
  trans·mis·sion
  trans·mit·tal
  trans·mit·ter
trans·mute
  trans·mu·ta·tion
tran·som
trans·par·ent
  trans·par·en·cy
tran·spire
trans·plant
trans·port
  trans·por·ta·tion
trans·pose
  trans·po·si·tion
trans·verse
trap·door
tra·peze
trap·nest
trap·per
trap·ping
Trap·pist
trash·y
trau·ma
  pl. trau·ma·ta *or* trau·mas
tra·vail *n.* (*toil;* see *travel*)

trav·el *v., n.* (*journey;* see
  travail)
  trav·eled
  trav·el·er
  trav·el·ing
tra·verse
trav·er·tine
trav·es·ty
treach·er·y
  treach·er·ous
trea·cle
trea·dle
tread·mill
trea·son
trea·sure
  trea·sur·er
  trea·sur·y
treat
  treat·ment
trea·tise
trea·ty
tre·ble
tree fern
tree·nail
tree·top
tre·foil
trel·lis
trem·ble
tre·men·dous
trem·o·lo
trem·or
trem·u·lous
trench
  tren·cher
tren·chant
  tren·chan·cy
tre·pan
tre·phine
trep·i·da·tion
tres·pass
  tres·pass·er
tres·tle
  tres·tle·work
tri·ad

tri·al
tri·an·gle
  tri·an·gu·lar
  tri·an·gu·la·tion
tribe
  trib·al
  tribes·man
trib·u·la·tion
tri·bune
  tri·bu·nal
trib·u·tar·y
trib·ute
trick·er·y
trick·i·ly
trick·i·ness
trick·le
trick·ster
tri·col·or
tri·cy·cle
tri·dent
tri·en·ni·al
tri·fle
tri·fo·cal
trig·ger
  trig·ger-hap·py
tri·glyc·er·ide
trig·o·nom·e·try
tril·lion
tril·li·um
tril·o·gy
Trin·i·dad
trin·i·ty
trin·ket
tri·o
tri·par·tite
trip-ham·mer
triph·thong
tri·ple
  tri·ple-space v.
  trip·let
  tri·plex
  trip·li·cate
  trip·li·ca·tion
tri·pod

trip·tych
tri·reme
tri·sect
trite
trit·u·rate
tri·umph
  tri·um·phal
  tri·um·phant
tri·um·vi·rate
triv·et
triv·i·a
  triv·i·al
  triv·i·al·i·ty
tro·che n. (lozenge; see
  trochee)
tro·chee n. (poetic meter; see
  troche)
trog·lo·dyte
trol·ley
trom·bone
troop n., v. (group, esp. of
  soldiers; see troupe)
  troop·ship
trope
tro·phy
trop·ic
  trop·i·cal
trot
  trot·ted
  trot·ting
trou·ba·dour
trou·ble·mak·er
trou·ble·shoot·er
trou·ble·some
trou·blous
troupe n. (group, esp. of
  performers; see troop)
trou·sers
trous·seau
  pl. trous·seaux or trous·seaus
tro·ver
trow·el
tru·ant
  tru·an·cy

truck·le
truck·load
truck·man
truc·u·lent
  truc·u·lence
true-blue *adj.*
true·born
true·heart·ed
true-life *adj.*
truf·fle
tru·ism
tru·ly
trum·per·y
trum·pet
  trum·pet·er
trun·cate
trun·cheon
trun·dle
trunk line
trun·nion
trust·bust·er
trust·ee *n.* (*guardian;* see
  trusty)
  trust·ee·ship
trust·ful
trust fund
trust·wor·thy
  trust·wor·thi·ness
trust·y *adj.* (*reliable;* see
  trustee)
truth·ful
try·out *n.*
try out *v.*
try square
tryst
tset·se
T-shirt
T-square
tsu·na·mi
tu·ba
tu·ber
tu·ber·cu·lo·sis
  tu·ber·cu·lar
  tu·ber·cu·lin
  tu·ber·cu·lous

tube·rose
tu·bu·lar
Tu·dor
Tues·day
tuff *n.* (*volcanic rock;* see
  tough)
tug·boat
tug-of-war
  pl. tugs-of-war
tu·i·tion
tu·la·re·mi·a
tu·lip
tu·lip·wood
tulle *n.* (*sheer material;* see
  tool)
tum·ble
  tum·bler
  tum·ble·weed
tum·brel *or* tum·bril
tu·mor
tu·mult
  tu·mul·tu·ous
tun·dra
tune·ful
tune·less
tune-up *n.*
tune up *v.*
tung·sten
tu·nic
Tun·i·sia
tun·nel
  tun·neled
  tun·nel·ing
tur·ban *n.* (*headdress;* see
  turbine)
tur·bid
tur·bine *n.* (*rotary engine;*
  see *turban*)
tur·bo·jet
tur·bot
  pl. tur·bot *or* tur·bots
tur·bu·lence
tur·gid
tur·key *n.* (*bird;* see *Turkey*)

Tur·key n. (country; see
   turkey)
tur·mer·ic
tur·moil
turn
  turn·a·bout
  turn·buck·le
  turn·coat
  turn down v.
  turn·down adj., n.
  turn·key
  turn·key op·er·a·tion
  turn off v.
  turn·off n.
  turn out v.
  turn·out n.
  turn o·ver v.
  turn·o·ver adj., n.
  turn·pike
  turn·spit
  turn·stile
  turn·ta·ble
tur·nip
tur·pen·tine
tur·pi·tude
tur·quoise
tur·ret
tur·tle·dove
tur·tle·neck
tus·sle
tus·sock
tu·te·lage
  tu·te·lar
  tu·te·lar·y
tu·tor
tut·ti-frut·ti
tweez·ers
twelfth
twelve
twen·ti·eth
twerp
twice-told
twi·light
twill

twine
twin·kle
twist
twitch
two n., adj., pron. (number;
  see to and too)
  two-ply
  two-sid·ed
  two·some
  two-step n.
  two-way
ty·coon
ty·ing
type·cast v. (cast performer;
  see type-cast)
type-cast v. (cast type; see
  typecast)
type·face
type·found·er
type·script
type·set·ter
type·write
  type·writ·er
  type·writ·ing
ty·phoid
ty·phoon
ty·phus
typ·i·cal
typ·i·fy
typ·ist
ty·pog·ra·phy
  ty·pog·ra·pher
  ty·po·graph·i·cal
tyr·an·ny
  ty·ran·ni·cal
  ty·ran·ni·cide
  tyr·an·nize
  ty·ran·nous
  ty·rant
ty·ro
tzar

U

u·biq·ui·tous
  u·biq·ui·ty
ud·der
U·gan·da
ug·ly
  ug·li·ness
u·ku·le·le
ul·cer
  ul·cer·a·tion
  ul·cer·a·tive
  ul·cer·o·gen·ic
  ul·cer·ous
Ul·ster
ul·te·ri·or
ul·ti·mate
ul·ti·ma·tum
  pl. ul·ti·ma·tums *or* ul·ti·ma·ta
ul·ti·mo
ul·tra·fash·ion·a·ble
ul·tra·ma·rine
ul·tra·mod·ern
ul·tra·vi·o·let
ul·u·la·tion
U·lys·ses
um·bil·i·cus
  um·bil·i·cal
um·brage
  um·bra·geous
um·brel·la
um·laut
um·pire
un·a·bashed
un·a·bat·ed
un·a·ble
un·ac·com·pa·nied
un·ac·count·a·ble
un·ac·cus·tomed
un·a·dorned
un·a·dul·ter·at·ed
un·af·fect·ed
un·a·ligned

un·al·loyed
un·al·ter·a·ble
un-A·mer·i·can
u·na·nim·i·ty
  u·nan·i·mous
un·as·sum·ing
un·a·void·a·ble
un·a·ware
un·bal·anced
un·be·com·ing
un·be·lief
  un·be·liev·er
un·bend
un·bi·ased
un·bid·den
un·bo·som
un·bound·ed
un·but·ton
un·called-for
un·cer·tain
un·char·i·ta·ble
un·civ·i·lized
un·cle
un·clean
un·com·fort·a·ble
un·com·mit·ted
un·com·mu·ni·ca·tive
un·com·pli·men·ta·ry
un·com·pro·mis·ing
un·con·cerned
un·con·di·tion·al
un·con·quer·a·ble
un·con·scion·a·ble
un·con·scious
un·couth
unc·tion
unc·tu·ous
un·de·ni·a·ble
un·der·age
un·der·arm
un·der·brush
un·der·class·man
un·der·clothes
un·der·cov·er

un·der·cur·rent
un·der·de·vel·oped
un·der·dog
un·der·es·ti·mate
un·der·ex·pose
un·der·feed
un·der·foot
un·der·glaze
un·der·go
un·der·grad·u·ate
un·der·ground
un·der·hand·ed
un·der·line
un·der·mine
un·der·neath
un·der·pants
un·der·pass
un·der·priv·i·leged
un·der·rate
un·der·score
un·der·sell
un·der·shirt
un·der·sized
un·der·slung
un·der·stand
   un·der·stood
un·der·stud·y
un·der·tak·er
un·der·tone
un·der·tow
un·der·val·ue
un·der·wa·ter
un·der·wear
un·der·weight
un·der·world
un·der·write
un·do *v.* (*to unfasten;* see *undue*)
un·doubt·ed·ly
un·due *adj.* (*undeserved;* see *undo*).
un·du·la·tion
un·du·ly
un·earned

un·earth·ly
un·eas·y
un·em·ployed
un·e·qual
un·e·quiv·o·cal
un·err·ing
un·eth·i·cal
un·e·vent·ful
un·ex·cep·tion·a·ble
un·ex·pect·ed
un·fail·ing
un·faith·ful
un·fa·mil·iar
un·fa·vor·a·ble
un·fet·tered
un·fin·ished
un·flap·pa·ble
un·fore·seen
un·for·get·ta·ble
un·for·tu·nate
un·furl
un·gain·ly
un·god·ly
un·gram·mat·i·cal
un·grate·ful
un·guent
un·health·y
u·ni·cam·er·al
u·ni·form
   u·ni·form·i·ty
u·ni·fy
   u·ni·fi·ca·tion
u·ni·lat·er·al
un·im·peach·a·ble
un·im·proved
un·in·hib·it·ed
un·in·tel·li·gent
un·in·tel·li·gi·ble
un·in·ter·est·ed
un·ion
   un·ion·ize
u·nique
u·ni·son
u·nit

u·nite
  u·ni·ty
u·ni·verse
  u·ni·ver·sal
  u·ni·ver·sal·i·ty
u·ni·ver·si·ty
un·just
un·kempt
un·know·ing
un·lace
un·law·ful
un·leash
un·less
un·let·tered
un·like·ly
un·lim·it·ed
un·list·ed
un·luck·y
un·man·ly
un·mer·ci·ful
un·mind·ful
un·mit·i·gat·ed
un·nat·u·ral
un·nec·es·sar·y
un·nerve
un·oc·cu·pied
un·of·fi·cial
un·or·gan·ized
un·or·tho·dox
un·par·al·leled
un·plea·sant
un·pop·u·lar
un·prec·e·dent·ed
un·pre·dict·a·ble
un·prej·u·diced
un·prin·ci·pled
un·print·a·ble
un·prof·it·a·ble
un·qual·i·fied
un·ques·tion·a·ble
un·quote
un·rav·el
un·re·al
un·rea·son·a·ble

un·re·con·struct·ed
un·re·gen·er·ate
un·re·li·a·ble
un·re·mit·ting
un·re·strained
un·righ·teous
un·ri·valed
un·rul·y
  un·rul·i·ness
un·sa·vor·y
un·scathed
un·schooled
un·scru·pu·lous
un·seem·ly
un·skill·ful
un·so·cia·ble
un·so·phis·ti·cat·ed
un·speak·a·ble
un·sprung
un·sub·stan·tial
un·suc·cess·ful
un·suit·a·ble
un·ten·a·ble
un·think·a·ble
un·ti·dy
un·tie
un·til
un·time·ly
  un·time·li·ness
un·told
un·touch·a·ble
un·to·ward
un·truth·ful
un·tu·tored
un·u·su·al
un·var·nished
un·want·ed
un·war·y
un·well
un·whole·some
un·wield·y
  un·wield·i·ness
un·wont·ed
un·world·ly

un·wor·thy
  un·wor·thi·ness
un·writ·ten
up·beat
up·braid
up·bring·ing
up-coun·try
up·date
up·draft
up·grade
up·heav·al
up·hill
up·hold
up·hol·ster
  up·hol·ster·er
  up·hol·ster·y
up·keep
up·land
up·lift
up·on
up·per
  up·per-class *adj.*
  up·per class *n.*
  up·per·class·man
  up·per·cut
  up·per·most
up·right
up·ris·ing
up·roar·i·ous
up·root
up·set
up·shot
up·side-down *adj.*
up·side down *adv.*
up·stage
up·stairs
up·start
up·state
up·stream
up·stroke
up·swept
up-to-date
up·town
up·turn

up·ward *n., adj., prep., adv.*
up·wards *adv.*
u·ra·ni·um
ur·ban *adj. (pertaining to a city; see urbane)*
ur·bane *adj. (polished; see urban)*
  ur·ban·i·ty
ur·chin
u·re·mi·a
u·re·ter
u·re·thra
ur·gent
  ur·gen·cy
u·ric
u·ri·nal
urn *n. (vase; see earn)*
ur·ti·car·i·a
U·ru·guay
us·a·ble
us·age
use·ful
  use·ful·ness
use·less
ush·er
u·su·al
u·su·fruct
u·surp
  u·surp·pa·tion
  u·surp·er
u·su·ry
  u·su·rer
  u·su·ri·ous
U·tah
u·ten·sil
u·ter·ine
u·til·i·ty
  u·til·i·tar·i·an
u·ti·lize
  u·ti·liz·a·ble
ut·most
u·to·pi·an·ism
ut·ter
  ut·ter·ance

u·vu·la
ux·o·ri·ous

V

va·cate
  va·can·cy
  va·cant
va·ca·tion
  va·ca·tion·ist
vac·ci·nate
  vac·ci·na·tion
  vac·cine
vac·il·late
  vac·il·la·tion
va·cu·i·ty
vac·u·ous
vac·u·um
  pl. vac·u·ums *or* vac·u·a
vag·a·bond
va·gar·y
vag·i·ni·tis
va·grant
  va·gran·cy
vague
vain *adj.* (*conceited;* see *vane* and *vein*)
  vain·glo·ri·ous
  vain·glo·ry
va·lance *n.* (*short decorative drapery;* see *valence*)
vale *n.* (*valley;* see *veil*)
val·e·dic·to·ry
  val·e·dic·to·ri·an
va·lence *n.* (*interactive chemical ability;* see *valance*)
val·en·tine
val·et
val·e·tu·di·nar·i·an
Val·hal·la
val·iant

val·id
  val·i·date
  val·i·da·tion
  va·lid·i·ty
va·lise
Va·li·um (*trademark*)
val·ley
val·or
  val·o·ri·za·tion
  val·or·ous
val·u·a·ble
val·ue
  val·u·a·tion
  val·ue·less
val·vu·lar
vam·pire
van·dal·ism
vane *n.* (*indicates wind direction;* see *vain* and *vein*)
van·guard
va·nil·la
van·ish
van·i·ty
van·quish
van·tage
va·pid
va·por
  va·por·i·za·tion
  va·por·ize
  va·por·iz·er
  va·por·ous
var·i·a·ble
var·i·ant
  var·i·ance
var·i·a·tion
var·i·col·ored
var·i·cose
var·i·e·gate
  var·i·e·ga·tion
va·ri·e·ty
var·i·o·rum
var·i·ous
var·nish

var·y v. (to change; see very)
 var·ied
vas·cu·lar
vas de·fe·rens
Vas·e·line (trademark)
vas·sal
Vat·i·can
vaude·ville
 vaude·vil·lian
vault
vec·tor scan
veg·e·ta·blc
veg·e·tar·i·an
 veg·e·tar·i·an·ism
veg·e·tate
 veg·e·ta·tion
 veg·e·ta·tive
ve·he·ment
 ve·he·mence
ve·hi·cle
 ve·hic·u·lar
veil n. (covering; see vale)
vein n., v. (blood vessel; see
 vain and vane)
vel·lum
vc·loc·i·pede
ve·loc·i·ty
ve·lour
vel·vet
vel·vet·ecn
ve·nal adj. (mercenary; see
 venial)
vend·ee
ven·det·ta
ven·dor
ve·neer
ven·er·a·ble
ven·er·ate
 ven·er·a·tion
Ve·ne·tian
Ven·e·zue·la
ven·geance
venge·ful

ve·ni·al adj. (pardonable; see
 venal)
ven·i·son
ven·om·ous
ve·nous
ven·ti·late
 ven·ti·la·tion
 ven·ti·la·tor
ven·tral
ven·tri·cle
ven·tril·o·quism
 ven·tril·o·quist
ven·ture·some
ven·tur·ous
ven·ue
ve·rac·i·ty
 vc·ra·cious adj. (truthful; see
 voracious)
ve·ran·da or ve·ran·dah
ver·bal
 ver·bal·ism
 ver·bal·i·za·tion
 ver·bal·ly
ver·ba·tim
ver·be·na
ver·bi·age
ver·bose
ver·dant
ver·dict
ver·di·gris
ver·dure
verg·er
ver·i·fy
 ver·i·fi·ca·tion
ver·i·ly
ver·i·si·mil·i·tude
ver·i·ta·ble
ver·i·ty
ver·meil
ver·mi·cel·li
ver·mi·cide
ver·mi·form
ver·mi·fuge
ver·mil·ion or ver·mil·lion

ver·min
  pl. ver·min
  ver·min·ous
Ver·mont
ver·mouth
ver·nac·u·lar
ver·nal
ver·ni·er
ver·sa·tile
  ver·sa·til·i·ty
ver·si·fy
  ver·si·fi·ca·tion
ver·sion
ver·sus
ver·te·bra
  pl. ver·te·brae *or* ver·te·bras
  ver·te·bral
  ver·te·brate
ver·tex
  pl. ver·ti·ces *or* ver·tex·es
ver·ti·cal
  ver·ti·cal·ly
ver·ti·go
  pl. ver·ti·goes *or* ver·tig·i·nes
  ver·tig·i·nous
ver·y *adj*., *adv*. (*exceedingly*;
  see *vary*)
ves·i·cle
ves·pers
ves·sel
ves·tal
ves·ti·bule
ves·tige
  ves·tig·i·al
vest·ment
vest-pock·et
ves·try
  ves·try·man
vet·er·an
vet·er·i·nar·y
ve·to
  pl. ve·toes
  ve·toed

vex·a·tion
  vex·a·tious
vi·a·ble
vi·a·duct
vi·al *n*. (*small container*; see
  vile and *viol*)
vi·and
vi·brant
vi·bra·phone
vi·brate
  vi·bra·tion
  vi·bra·to
  vi·bra·tor
  vi·bra·to·ry
vic·ar
  vic·ar·age
vi·car·i·ous
vice *n*., *prep*. (*wickedness*;
  see *vise*)
  vice ad·mi·ral
  vice-chair·man
  vice-chan·cel·lor
  vice-con·sul
  vice-ge·rent
  vice-pres·i·dent
  vice-re·gal
  vice·roy
  vice ver·sa
vi·chys·soise
vic·i·nage
vi·cin·i·ty
vi·cious *adj*. (*savage*; see
  viscose and *viscous*)
vi·cis·si·tude
vic·tim
  vic·tim·ize
vic·tor
  vic·to·ri·ous
  vic·to·ry
Vic·to·ri·an
vict·ual
vi·cu·ña *or* vi·cu·na
vid·e·o
Vi·et·nam

vig·il
  vig·i·lance
  vig·i·lant
  vig·i·lan·te
vi·gnette
vig·or·ous
vile *adj.* (*horrible;* see *vial*
  and *viol*)
vil·i·fy
vil·la
vil·lage
vil·lain
  vil·lain·ous
  vil·lain·y
vin·ai·grette
vin·cu·lum
  pl. vin·cu·lums *or* vin·cu·la
vin·di·cate
  vin·di·ca·tion
vin·dic·tive
vin·e·gar
  vin·e·gar·y
vine·yard
vin·tage
vint·ner
vi·nyl
vi·ol *n.* (*musical instrument;*
  see *vial* and *vile*)
vi·o·la
vi·o·late
vi·o·lent
  vi·o·lence
vi·o·let
vi·o·lin·ist
VIP
vi·per
vi·ra·go
  pl. vi·ra·goes *or* vi·ra·gos
vi·re·mi·a
vir·e·o
vir·gin
Vir·gin·ia
vir·ile
  vi·ril·i·ty

vir·tu·al
vir·tue
vir·tu·os·i·ty
  vir·tu·o·so
  pl. vir·tu·o·si
vir·tu·ous
vir·u·lent
  vir·u·lence
vi·rus
vis·age
vis·à·vis
vis·cer·al
vis·cid
vis·cose *n.* (*kind of rayon;*
  see *vicious* and *viscous*)
vis·count
vis·cous *adj.* (*thick;* see *vicious*
  and *viscose*)
  vis·cos·i·ty
vise *n.* (*tool for holding work;*
  see *vice*)
vis·i·ble
  vis·i·bil·i·ty
vi·sion
  vi·sion·ar·y
vis·it
  vis·i·ta·tion
  vis·i·tor
vi·sor
vis·ta
vi·su·al
  vi·su·al·ize
vi·ta
vi·tal
  vi·tal·i·ty
  vi·tal·ize
vi·ta·min
vi·ti·ate
vit·re·ous
vit·ri·fy
vit·ri·ol
vi·tu·per·a·tive
  vi·tu·per·a·tion

vi·vac·i·ty
 vi·va·cious
viv·id
vi·vip·a·rous
viv·i·sec·tion
vix·en
vi·zier
vo·cab·u·lar·y
vo·cal
 vo·cal·ist
 vo·cal·ize
vo·ca·tion
 vo·ca·tion·al
voc·a·tive
vo·cif·er·ous
vod·ka
vogue
voice·less
void·a·ble
vol·a·tile
 vol·a·til·i·ty
vol·ca·no
 pl. vol·ca·noes *or* vol·ca·nos
 vol·can·ic
vo·li·tion
vol·ley
 vol·ley·ball
volt·age
vol·u·ble
 vol·u·bil·i·ty
vol·ume
 vol·u·met·ric
 vo·lu·mi·nous
vol·un·tar·y
 vol·un·tar·i·ly
vol·un·teer
vo·lup·tu·ous
 vo·lup·tu·ar·y
vom·it
voo·doo
vo·ra·cious *adj*. (*ravenous*;
 see *veracious*)
 vo·rac·i·ty

vor·tex
 pl. vor·ti·ces *or* vor·tex·es
vo·ta·ry
vo·tive
vouch
 vouch·er
 vouch·safe
vow·el
voy·age
voy·eur
vul·can·ize
 vul·can·i·za·tion
vul·gar
 vul·gar·ism
 vul·gar·i·ty
 vul·gar·i·za·tion
vul·ner·a·ble
vul·ture
 vul·tur·ous
vy·ing

W

wad
 wad·ded
 wad·ding
wade
wa·fer
waf·fle
wa·ger
Wag·ne·ri·an
wag·on
wail *v., n.* (*to lament*; see
 wale and *whale*)
wain·scot
waist *n.* (*human midsection*;
 see *waste*)
 waist·band
 waist·coat
 waist·line
wait *v., n.* (*to stay in
 expectation of*; see *weight*)
 wait·ress

waive v. (*to forgo*; see *wave*)
waiv·er n. (*a document*; see
waver)
wale n. (*ridge*; see *wail* and
whale)
Wales
walk·a·way
walk·ie-talk·ie
walk in v.
walk-in *adj.*, n.
walk-on n.
walk on v.
walk out v.
walk·out n.
walk·o·ver n.
walk o·ver v.
walk-up n., *adj.*
walk up v.
wal·let
wall·eyed
wall·flow·er
wal·low
wall·pa·per
wal·nut
wal·rus
wam·pum
wan·der
wan·der·lust
want n., v. (*to desire*; see
wont)
wan·ton
war·bler
war chest
war cry
war dance
war·den
ward·robe
ward·room
ware n. (*manufactured
article*; see *wear* and
where)
ware·house·man
ware·room
war·fare

war·head
war·horse
war·i·ly
war·i·ness
war·like
war·lord
warm·blood·ed
warmed-o·ver
warm·heart·ed
war·mon·ger
warmth
warm up v.
warm-up n.
warp
war·path
war·plane
war·ran·ty
war·rant·a·ble
war·ran·tor
war·ren
war·rior
war·ship
wart·hog
war·time
war whoop
war·y
war zone
wash·a·ble
wash and wear *adj.*
wash·ba·sin
wash·board
wash·bowl
wash·cloth
washed-out *adj.*
washed-up *adj.*
wash·er
wash·house
Wash·ing·ton
wash out v.
wash·out n.
wash·room
wash·stand
wash·tub
wash up v.

wash·up *n.*
was·sail
waste *v., n., adj. (to use inefficiently;* see *waist)*
  wast·age
  waste·bas·ket
  waste·ful
  waste·land
  waste·pa·per
was·trel
watch·band
watch·case
watch·cry
watch·dog
watch fire
watch·ful
watch·mak·er
watch·man
watch out *v.*
watch·out *n.*
watch·tow·er
watch·word
wa·ter
  wa·ter·bed
  wa·ter·borne
  wa·ter·buf·fa·lo
  wa·ter·col·or
  wa·ter·course
  wa·ter·craft
  wa·ter·cress
  wa·ter·fall
  wa·ter·fowl
  wa·ter·front
  Wa·ter·gate
  wa·ter·line
  wa·ter·logged
  Wa·ter·loo
  wa·ter·man
  wa·ter·mark
  wa·ter·mel·on
  wa·ter pipe
  wa·ter po·lo
  wa·ter·pow·er
  wa·ter·proof

wa·ter·re·pel·lent *adj.*
wa·ter·re·sist·ant
wa·ter·shed
wa·ter·side
wa·ter·ski·er
wa·ter·spout
wa·ter ta·ble
wa·ter·tight
wa·ter tow·er
wa·ter·way
wa·ter·wheel
wa·ter·works
wa·ter·y
watt·age
wave *v., n. (to flutter;* see *waive)*
  wave band
  wave·length
wa·ver *n., v. (to vacillate;* see *waiver)*
wav·y
wax·en
wax·work
way *n. (path;* see *weigh* and *whey)*
  way·bill
  way·far·er
  way·lay
  way·side
  way·ward
weak *adj. (not strong;* see *week)*
  weak·fish
  weak·heart·ed
  weak-kneed
  weak·ling
  weak·ly *adj., adv.* (see *weekly)*
  weak-mind·ed
  weak·ness
weal *n. (prosperous state;* see *we'll, wheal,* and *wheel)*
wealth
  wealth·i·ness
  wealth·y

wean *v.* (*to withdraw from breast-feeding*; see *ween*)

weap·on

wear *v., n.* (*to put on*; see *ware* and *where*)
wear·a·ble
wear out *v.*
wear-out *n.*

wea·ry
wea·ri·less
wea·ri·ly
wea·ri·ness
wea·ri·some

wea·sand

wea·sel

weath·er *n., v.* (*climate*; see *whether*)
weath·er·proof

weave *v., n.* (*to loom*; see *we've*)
weav·er

web·foot *n.*
web-foot·ed *adj.*

wed
wed·ding
wed·lock

we'd

Wedg·wood (*trademark*)

Wednes·day

wee

week *n.* (*seven days*; see *weak*)
week·day
week·end
week·ly *adj., adv., n.* (see *weakly*)

ween *v.* (*to suppose*; see *wean*)

wee·vil

weigh *v.* (*to measure heaviness*; see *way* and *whey*)
weighed

weight *n., v.* (*heaviness*; see *wait*)
weight·i·ly
weight·i·ness
weight·less
weight·less·ness
weight·y

weir *n.* (*dam*; see *we're*)

weird

wel·come

wel·fare
wel·far·ism

wel·kin

well

we'll (*contraction of we will*; see *weal*, *wheal*, and *wheel*)

well-ad·vised

well-be·ing

well-be·loved

well·born

well-bred

well-con·di·tioned

well-dis·posed

well-done

well-fa·vored

well-fixed

well-found·ed

well-groomed

well-ground·ed

well-han·dled

well·head

well-heeled

well-knit

well-known

well-man·nered

well-mean·ing

well-nigh

well-off

well-or·dered

well-read

well-spo·ken

well·spring

well-thought-of

well-timed

well-to-do
well-turned
well-wish·er
well-worn
wel·ter
we're (*contraction of we are;*
  see *weir*)
weren't
were·wolf
west·er·ly
west·ern
West·ern·er
West In·dies
west·ward *n.*
wet *adj., v., n.* (*watery;* see
  whet)
  wet·back
  wet blan·ket *n.*
  wet-blan·ket *v.*
  wet·land
  wet nurse *n.*
  wet-nurse *v.*
  wet wash
we've (*contraction of we have;*
  see *weave*)
whale *n., v.* (*large sea
  mammal;* see *wail* and *wale*)
  whale·back
  whale·boat
  whale·bone
wham·my
wharf
  pl. wharves
  wharf·age
  wharf·in·ger
what·ev·er
what·not
what·so·ev·er
wheal *n.* (*swelling;* see *weal,
  we'll,* and *wheel*)
wheat germ
whee·dle
wheel *n., v.* (*circular object;*
  see *weal, we'll,* and *wheal*)
  wheel·bar·row

wheel·base
wheel·chair
wheel·horse
wheel·house
wheel·wright
whence
when·ev·er
when·so·ev·er
where *adj., conj., pron.* (*in
  what place;* see *ware* and
  wear*)
where·a·bouts
where·as
where·at
where·by
where·fore
where·in
where·of
where·so·ev·er
wher·ev·er
where·with
  where·with·al
wher·ry
whet *v.* (*to sharpen;* see *wet*)
  whet·stone
wheth·er *conj.* (*either;* see
  weather)
whey *n.* (*watery part of milk;*
  see *way* and *weigh*)
which *pron., adj.* (*what one;*
  see *witch*)
which·ev·er
which·so·ev·er
while *n., conj., v.* (*period of
  time;* see *wile*)
whi·lom
whim·per
whim·si·cal
whine *n., v.* (*distressed cry;*
  see *wine*)
whip·cord
whip hand
whip·lash
whip·per·snap·per
whip·pet

whip·ping
whip·poor·will
whip·stitch
whirl·i·gig
whirl·pool
whirl·wind
whisk broom
whisk·er
whis·key *or* whis·ky
whis·per
whist
whis·tle
  whis·tle-stop
whit *n.* (*smallest part*; see *wit*)
white·beard
white book
white·cap
white-col·lar
white·fish
white flag
white-head·ed
white-hot
white lead
white-liv·ered
whit·en
white·wash
white·wood
whith·er *adv., conj.* (*to what place*; see *wither*)
whit·tle
who·dun·it
who·ev·er
whole *adj., n.* (*complete*; see *hole*)
  whole·heart·ed
  whole·sale
  whole·some
  whole-souled
whol·ly *adv.* (*completely*; see *holey* and *holy*)
whoop
whore *n., v.* (*prostitute*; see *hoar*)

who's (*contraction of who is*; see *whose*)
whose *pron.* (*indicates possession*; see *who's*)
who·so·ev·er
wick·ed·ness
wick·er·work
wick·et
wide-an·gle *adj.*
wide-a·wake *adj.*
wide-eyed
wide·mouthed
wide·spread
wid·ow
  wid·ow·er
  wid·ow·hood
wid·ow's peak
wield
Wie·ner schnit·zel
wig·wag
wig·wam
wild·cat
  wild·cat·ter
wil·der·ness
wild-eyed
wild·fire
wild·fowl
wild-goose chase
wild·life
wild·wood
wile *n., v.* (*trick*; see *while*)
will·ful
will-o'-the-wisp
wil·low·ware
will·pow·er
wind·age
wind·bag
wind·blown
wind·break
wind·burn
wind chill
wind·fall
wind·jam·mer

wind·lass *n.* (*mechanism for hoisting*; see *windless*)
wind·less *adj.* (*without wind*; see *windlass*)
wind·mill
win·dow
  win·dow·pane
  win·dow-shop *v.*
  win·dow-shop·per *n.*
  win·dow·sill
wind·pipe
wind·proof
wind·shield
wind·sock
wind·storm
wind·swept
wind up *v.*
wind·up *adj., n.*
wind·ward
wine *n., v.* (*fermented grape beverage*; see *whine*)
  wine·glass
  wine·grow·er
  wine·press
  wine·shop
  wine·skin
wing chair
wing-foot·ed
wing nut
wing·span
wing·spread
wing tip
win·ner
win·now
win·some
win·ter
  win·ter·green
  win·ter·ize
  win·ter-kill *v.*
  win·ter-kill *n.*
wire·haired
wire·less
wire-pull·er *n.*
wire-pull·ing *n.*

wire·tap
  wire·tap·per
Wis·con·sin
wis·dom
wise·a·cre
wise·crack
wise·ly
wish·bone
wish·ful
wish·y-wash·y
wis·te·ri·a
wist·ful
wit *v., n.* (*mind*; see *whit*)
witch *n.* (*worker of magic*; see *which*)
  witch·craft
  witch·er·y
  witch-hunt
with·al
with·draw
  with·draw·al
with·er *v.* (*to shrivel*; see *whither*)
with·hold
with·in
with·out
with·stand
wit·ness
wit·ting·ly
wit·ty
  wit·ti·cism
  wit·ti·ly
wiz·ard
wiz·ened
wob·ble
woe·be·gone
wok
wolf·hound
wol·ver·ine
wom·an
  wom·an·hood
  wom·an·ish
  wom·an·kind
  wom·an·like

wom·an·li·ness
wom·an·ly
wom·en·folk
won v. (pt. of win; see one)
won·der·ful
won·der·land
won·der·ment
won·der·work
won·drous
wont adj., n. (accustomed to; see want)
won't
wood n., adj. (lumber; see would)
wood·bin
wood·bine
wood-bor·ing
wood-carv·er
wood carv·ing
wood·chop·per
wood·chuck
wood·craft
wood·cut
wood·cut·ter
wood·ed
wood·en
wood·en·head
wood·en·ware
wood·land
wood·lot
wood·man
wood·peck·er
wood·pile
wood pulp
wood·shed
woods·man
wood·turn·er
wood turn·ing
wood·wind
wood·work·ing
wood·yard
wool·en or **wool·len**
wool-gath·er
wool·gath·er·ing

wool·ly or **wool·y**
wool·li·ness
wool·sack
word·age
word·book
word for word adv.
word-for-word adj.
word·i·ly
word·i·ness
word·ing
word-of-mouth adj.
word pro·cess·ing
word pro·cess·or
word·smith
word square
work·a·ble
work·a·day
work·bag
work·bas·ket
work·bench
work·book
work·box
work camp
work·day
worked
work force
work·horse
work·house
work·ing
work·ing·man
work load
work·man
work·man·like
work·man·ship
work out v.
work·out n.
work·room
work·shop
work·ta·ble
work·week
world-beat·er
world·ly
world·li·ness
world·ly-mind·ed
world·ly-wise

world-shak·ing
world-wea·ri·ness
world·wide
worm-eat·en
worm gear
worm·hole
worm·wood
worn-out
wor·ri·ment
wor·ri·some
wor·ry·wart
wor·ship
  wor·ship·ful
worst *adj.*, *v.*, *n.* (*most bad*;
  see *wurst*)
wor·sted
worth·less
worth·while
  worth·while·ness
wor·thy
  wor·thi·ly
would *v.* (*strongly desire*; see
  wood)
wound
wrack *n.* (*to wreck*; see *rack*)
wraith
wran·gle
wrap·a·round
wrapped
wrap·per
wrap up *v.*
wrap-up *n.*
wrath·ful
wreak *n.*, *v.* (*to inflict*; see
  reek)
wreath *n.* (*garland*; see
  wreathe)
wreathe *v.* (*to interweave*;
  see *wreath*)
wreck *v.* (*to destroy*; see
  reck)
  wreck·age
  wreck·er
wren

wrench
wrest *v.* (*pull violently*; see
  rest)
wres·tle
  wres·tler
  wres·tling
wretch *n.* (*miserable person*;
  see *retch*)
wretch·ed
wrig·gle
  wrig·gly
wring *v.*, *n.* (*to twist*; see
  ring)
  wring·er
wrin·kle
  wrin·kling
wrist·band
wrist·let
wrist·lock
wrist pin
wrist·watch
writ
write *v.* (*inscribe symbols*;
  see *right* and *rite*)
  write down *v.*
  write-down *n.*
  write in *v.*
  write-in *n.*
  write off *v.*
  write-off *n.*
  write out *v.*
  writ·er
  write up *v.*
  write-up *n.*
  writ·ing
  writ·ten
writhe
wrong
  wrong·do·er
  wrong·do·ing
  wrong·ful
  wrong·head·ed
wrote *v.* (*pt. of write*; see
  rote)

wrought
wrung v. (pt. of wring; see rung)
wry adj. (twisted; see rye)
wurst n. (sausage; see worst)
Wy·o·ming

X

xe·non
xen·o·pho·bi·a
xe·rog·ra·phy
Xer·ox (trademark)
X ray n.
   X-ray v., adj.
   X-ray tube
xy·lo·phone

Y

yacht
   yachts·man
yak
yam
Yan·kee
yard·age
yard·arm
yard·bird
yard goods
yard·man
yard·mas·ter
yard·stick
yar·row
yawl
yawn
year·book
year·ling
year·ly
yearn
yeast
yel·low
yel·low·jack·et

Yem·en
yeo·man·ry
ye·shi·va
yes-man
yes·ter·day
yew n. (tree; see ewe and you)
Yid·dish
yield
yo·del
yo·ga
yo·gurt or yo·ghurt
yoke n., v. (wooden harness; see yolk)
yo·kel
yolk n. (yellow of egg; see yoke)
yon·der
yore
you pron. (person addressed; see ewe and yew)
you'll (contraction of you will; see yule)
young
   young·ster
your adj. (relating to you; see you're)
   your·self
   pl. your·selves
you're (contraction of you are; see your)
youth·ful
yt·ter·bi·um
yt·tri·um
yuc·ca
Yu·go·slav·i·a
yule n. (Christmas season; see you'll)
   yule·tide

Z

Za·ire
Zam·bi·a

za·min·dar
za·ny
zar·zue·la
zeal
  zeal·ot
  zeal·ot·ry
  zeal·ous
ze·bra
  pl. ze·bras *or* ze·bra
ze·bu
ze·na·na
ze·nith
zeph·yr
zep·pe·lin
ze·ro
  pl. ze·ros *or* ze·roes
zest
zig·gu·rat
zig·zag
  zig·zagged
  zig·zag·ging
Zim·bab·we
zinc
zin·fan·del
zin·ni·a
Zi·on·ism

zip
  zipped
  zip·per
  zip·ping
zir·con
  zir·co·ni·um
zith·er
zo·di·ac
  zo·di·a·cal
zom·bi *or* **zom·bie**
zon·al
zo·ol·o·gy
  zo·o·log·i·cal
zoot suit
Zou·ave
zoy·si·a
zuc·chet·to
zuc·chi·ni
  pl. zuc·chi·ni *or* zuc·chi·nis
Zu·lu
  pl. Zu·lu *or* Zu·lus
Zu·ñi
zwie·back
  pl. zwie·back *or* zwie·backs
zy·gote
zy·mase
zy·mot·ic

Appendices

I. Standard Rules of Spelling

Here are eleven rules that will help you with most difficult spelling situations. If you master these rules, you will be able to choose correct spellings in most cases without referring to a dictionary or word list.

Spelling Rule 1: Pronounce words carefully and correctly.

This rule is easy to follow, and will become your chief weapon in the battle against spelling mistakes. This recommendation is really much more than a rule: it should become a constant habit. If you form the habit of pronouncing words carefully and correctly, you will find you can correct many spelling problems automatically and, at the same time, add to your arsenal of new vocabulary. You can tackle all sorts of tough words, familiar and completely new, if you pronounce them accurately and listen closely to the pronunciation: simply sound out the word, syllable by syllable. Then write the word out, choosing a combination of letters to match the sounds.

The technique of sounding out words to gain control over them is no doubt familiar to you. You probably learned it first when you were taught to read many years ago. Perhaps you now use the technique unconsciously when you come across an unfamiliar word in your reading. Begin now to sound out words deliberately, especially those you frequently misspell. As you sound out your personal troublemakers, concentrate on the problem sounds and problem syllables in them.

There are six categories of spelling errors that stem from faulty pronunciation:

1. Confusing words that are very similar in sound
If you distinguish the pronunciations of these words carefully, you won't misspell or misuse them. These are the most common examples:

accept/except	elicit/illicit
access/excess	emigrate/immigrate
advice/advise	eminent/imminent
affect/effect	finally/finely
allude/elude	impostor/imposture
allusion/illusion	pastor/pasture
casualty/causality	persecute/prosecute
celery/salary	plaintiff/plaintive
cemetery/symmetry	tenet/tenant

(You'll find definitions and sample uses for many of these in Appendix II, Common Mix-ups.)

2. Adding an extra syllable

Because some words are hard to pronounce in combination, some words seem to cry out for an extra syllable. People pronounce them incorrectly so often that the bad habit spreads by imitation. If you pronounce these words correctly, you won't be tempted to add that offending extra syllable when you write the word out. Some very common examples:

athlete (not athelete)	laundry (not laundery)
barbarous (not barbarious)	mischievous (not mischievious)
disastrous (not disasterous)	monstrous (not monsterous)
drowned (not drownded)	nervous (not nerveous)
entrance (not enterance)	partner (not partener)
grievous (not grievious)	remembrance (not rememberance)
hindrance (not hinderance)	similar (not similiar)
hundred (not hundered)	umbrella (not umberella)

3. Dropping a syllable

Some words, on the other hand, lose necessary syllables easily, usually because their sounds run together and slur in pronunciation. If you are conscious of pronouncing these words accurately, you won't drop letters when you spell them. Some common problem words in this category:

accidentally (not acciden*tly*)

actually (not act*ully*)

auxiliary (not auxi*lary*)

chocolate (not cho*clate*)

conscientious(not conscien*tous*)

convenient (not conven*ent*)

familiar (not fami*lar*)

grammatically(not grammati*cly*)

incidentally (not inciden*tly*)

laboratory (not labor*tory*)

miniature (not mi*nature*)

poem (not po*me*)

probably (not pro*bly*)

temperature (not temper*ture*)

4. Dropping a letter

Another group of words tends to lose single letters instead of syllables, again due to hasty and slurred pronunciation. Perhaps the most slippery of these words is "sur*prise*," which people often misspell as "su*prise*." Other words in this category (with the tricky letter indicated):

ar*C*tic

can*D*idate

di*PH*theria

gover*N*ment

enviro*N*ment

Feb*R*uary

lib*R*ary

quan*T*ity

sacril*E*gious

su*R*prise

represen*T*ative

5. Reversing letters

Some words tend to get their letters reversed, usually because people pronounce them incorrectly and then write out the pronunciation without looking them up in a dictionary. Some examples:

cavalry (easily pronounced as "Calvary"—which is the name of the hill on which Christ was crucified)

height (not hei*ghth*)

irrelevant (not irr*evel*ant)

perspiration (not *pre*spiration)

perversely (not *pre*versely)

perform (not *pre*form)

tragedy (not tra*degy*)

6. Unstressed vowel sounds

Perhaps the trickiest words in the language are those that contain unstressed, or lightly stressed, vowel sounds. These

words account for a vast number of common spelling errors.
The problem is that many vowels, when appearing in unstressed syllables, naturally lose their unique character and
are correctly pronounced as a vague, indistinguishable "uh"
sound. (The technical name for this sound is "schwa.") Think,
for example, of the middle syllables of "separate" and "definite": one is spelled with an "a," and the other with an "i,"
yet both are pronounced "uh." How can you choose the
correct vowel when writing these troublesome words? First,
you can make yourself aware of the most commonly misspelled ones, and pronounce the unstressed vowel in an
exaggerated manner until you've formed the correct spelling
habit. Pronounce "definite" as "de-FI-nite," for example.
While your pronunciation may be overstated for a while,
you will soon recall the correct spelling automatically. Some
other commonly misspelled examples:

accident	dollar
benefit	existence
calendar	origin
category	privilege
definite	separate
despair	sponsor

Second, you can often determine the correct vowel in an
unstressed syllable by thinking of a closely related word in
which the vowel is stressed, and therefore clearly heard. The
list of these words is enormous, but here are a few to start:

Indistinct vowel in un-stressed syllable	*Same vowel in clearly heard (stressed) syllable*
arithmetic	arithmetical
celebrate	celebrity
competition	compete
frivolous	frivolity
hypocrisy	hypocritical
narrative	narrate
revolution	revolt
sedative	sedate

Spelling Rule 2: Distinguish between regular and irregular plurals.

A regular plural is simple to form—people seldom make mistakes here. But irregular plural forms cause trouble. ("Singular" and "plural" refer to the number of a noun: how many are being discussed. "Singular" means "one"; "plural" means "more than one.") If you distinguish between regular and irregular plural forms, and remember a few rules about spelling irregular plurals, you will eliminate spelling errors.

Regular plurals

Form the plural of most nouns by adding "s" to the singular:

arrow, arrows	pencil, pencils
boy, boys	sidewalk, sidewalks
cat, cats	tree, trees
desk, desks	truck, trucks

However, if a word ends in *ch*, *sh*, *s*, *x*, or *zz* (sibilant sounds), form the plural by adding "es":

bush, bushes	gas, gases
buzz, buzzes	hitch, hitches
church, churches	loss, losses
fizz, fizzes	squash, squashes
fox, foxes	tax, taxes

Irregular plurals

1) "y" endings

Be careful when pluralizing nouns that end in a "y" preceded by a consonant. These words form their purals by changing the "y" to "i" and adding "es":

activity, activities	cry, cries
baby, babies	library, libraries
blueberry, blueberries	pantry, pantries
country, countries	puppy, puppies

Note: words that end in "y" preceded by a vowel are regular plural forms. They do *not* change the "y" to "i" or add "es":

attorney, attorneys

boy, boys

guy, guys

honey, honeys

monkey, monkeys

ray, rays

2) "o" endings
If a word ends in "o," preceded by a vowel, always add "s" to form the plural:

cameo, cameos

patio, patios

radio, radios

studio, studios

Many musical terms ending in "o" form their plurals by adding "s," even when the "o" is preceded by a consonant:

alto, altos

banjo, banjos

concerto, concertos

contralto, contraltos

piano, pianos

soprano, sopranos

Words ending in "o," preceded by a consonant, usually add "es" to form the plural:

cargo, cargoes

hero, heroes

Negro, Negroes

potato, potatoes

tomato, tomatoes

volcano, volcanoes

3) "f" endings
"F" endings are so irregular as to be nearly random. When you want to pluralize one of these words, and have any doubts at all, you should consult a dictionary or the word list in this book. Generally, nouns ending in "fe" change "fe" to "ve" before adding "s"; nouns ending in "ff" simply add "s." But these rules have many exceptions. Here are some examples of nouns with "f" endings put into their plural forms:

belief, beliefs

chief, chiefs

half, halfs (or halves)

leaf, leaves

life, lives

roof, roofs

self, selves	tiff, tiffs
shelf, shelves	wife, wives
sheriff, sheriffs	wolf, wolves

4) Words of foreign origin

Many words have entered the English language from other languages (usually Latin) without any change in spelling, and these words form their plurals in a number of ways, governed by the rules of their language of origin. Some even have more than one correct plural form. Use your dictionary if you are in doubt when spelling these plurals. Some commonly used examples:

alumna, alumnae (female)	index, indexes, indices
alumnus, alumni (male)	memorandum, memorandums,
analysis, analyses	memoranda
axis, axes	parenthesis, parentheses
basis, bases	phenomenon, phenomena
crisis, crises	stimulus, stimuli
criterion, criteria	thesis, theses
hypothesis, hypotheses	

5) Total word shifts

A few nouns don't change endings to indicate a shift from the singular to the plural—they change form entirely. When you pluralize these nouns, change the word completely:

brother, brothers, brethren	man, men
child, children	mouse, mice
foot, feet	ox, oxen
goose, geese	tooth, teeth
louse, lice	woman, women

Spelling Rule 3: Handle the final "y" correctly whenever you add a suffix to a word ending in "y."

We have already discussed the plurals of nouns ending in "y." Added suffixes follow the same principle: whenever you add a suffix to a word ending in "y," preceded by a consonant, change the "y" to "i" *unless* the suffix begins with "i." Some common suffixes are *-ance, -ed, -er, -est, -ful, -ing, -ish, -ly, -ment,* and *-ness.*

accompany, accompaniment	hearty, heartily
ally, alliance	lazy, lazily
comply, complies, complied, *but* complying	merry, merriment
cry, cried, *but* crying	pity, pitiful
empty, emptier, emptiest	slovenly, slovenliness
	tiny, tinier, tiniest

When the final "y" is preceded by a vowel, keep the "y" and add the suffix.

annoy, annoying, annoyance	play, played, playing
boy, boyish	relay, relayed, relaying
convey, conveyed, conveyor	slay, slays, slaying
employ, employer	survey, surveying, surveyor

But remember these important exceptions:

baby, babyhood	lay, laid
day, daily	pay, paid
gay, gaily	say, said

Spelling Rule 4: When adding a suffix beginning with a vowel, decide whether or not the final consonant of the word should be doubled.

The following rule sounds complicated, but it's not as complex as it seems, and it will be useful to you in a great number of problem spelling situations. The rule has two parts: If a word ends in a single consonant, preceded by a single vowel, and if the last syllable of the word is accented, double the final consonant before adding any suffix beginning with a vowel. On the other hand, if a word ends in a single consonant, preceded by a single vowel, and the last syllable of the word is unaccented, do not double the final consonant before adding any suffix beginning with a vowel.

An accented syllable is an emphasized syllable. All words of more than one syllable fall into a natural rhythmic pattern of pronunciation, in which one syllable is said with more stress or force than the others. This emphasized syllable is said to be accented. Compare the pronunciations of *"hin-der"* and *"for-get."* If you listen to the pattern of emphasis as you say these words aloud, you will see that the first syllable of *"hinder"* is accented, while the last syllable of *"forget"* is accented. As a result, the final consonants are treated in the following manner when adding suffixes beginning with vowels:

hinder, hindered, hindering   forget, forgetting, forgettable

Here are longer lists of examples, drawn from the thousands of words to which this rule applies. As you can see, the rule is especially useful in forming the various tenses of verbs and the comparative and superlative degrees of adjectives. In the first list, suffixes beginning with vowels have been added to words ending in a single consonant, preceded by a single vowel, whose last syllable is accented. The final consonant, therefore, is doubled:

admit, admitted, admittance   occur, occurred, occurrence

begin, beginner, beginning   submit, submitted, submitting

control, controlling, controller transmit, transmitter,
                                  transmittal
equip, equipped, equipping

expel, expelled, expelling

In the next list, suffixes beginning with vowels have been added to words ending in a single consonant, preceded by a single vowel, whose last syllable is unaccented. The final consonant, therefore, is not doubled:

benefit, benefited, benefiting   label, labeled, labeling

edit, edited, editor   wonder, wondered, wondering

happen, happening, happened

The accent naturally falls on the single syllable of one-syllable words. Therefore, if words of one syllable end in a single consonant, preceded by a single vowel, the final consonant should be doubled before adding a suffix beginning with a vowel:

bat, batting, batted   ship, shipping, shipper

fat, fatter, fattest   sit, sitting, sitter

knot, knotting, knotted   strip, stripping, stripper

red, redder, reddest

Cautions:

1) The doubling rule does not apply to words ending in a double consonant:

bend, bending   short, shorter, shortest

dumb, dumber, dumbest   stack, stacked, stacking

2) Nor does it apply to words ending in a single consonant preceded by two vowels. If you add a suffix beginning with a vowel to one of these words, do not double the final consonant first:

appear, appearing, appearance   clean, cleaning, cleanest

book, booking, booked   neat, neater, neatest

3) The doubling rule does not apply to words ending in "x," since the English language avoids double "x's":

tax, taxed, taxing   wax, waxed, waxing

4) If the accent is shifted to an earlier syllable when the suffix is added, do not double the final consonant. This procedure is entirely consistent with the final accented syllable/doubled-consonant rule, but it takes note of the fact that emphasis in a word sometimes shifts when the form changes. This shift tends to occur especially with words ending in "fer":

confer, conferring *but* conference	prefer, preferred *but* preference
defer, deferred *but* deference	refer, referring *but* reference
infer, inferring *but* inference	

5) There are, of course, always exceptions. It is best simply to remember these, perhaps by using some of the techniques described in Appendix III. Here are some of the most commonly used and misspelled:

cancel, cancellation	handicap, handicapped
chagrin, chagrined	question, questionnaire
crystal, crystallize	tranquil, tranquillity
excel, excellent	zigzag, zigzagged
gas, gaseous	

Spelling Rule 5: *When adding suffixes to words ending in silent "e," decide whether the "e" should be dropped.*

Thousands of words in our language end in a silent "e," and many of them cause spelling headaches. This rule should help you out of numerous difficulties—the rule probably covers more words than any other one we'll discuss.

A silent "e" occurs at the close of words such as "hope" and "fine." It is not pronounced; its job is to indicate that the vowel it follows is pronounced as a long vowel rather than a short vowel. Without the silent "e," "hope" and "fine" would dissolve into "hop" and "fin." The same is true of "note" and "not," "tine" and "tin," and a huge number of other word pairs.

Whenever you want to add a suffix to a word ending in a silent "e," decide whether to drop or retain the "e" by following this rule: a final silent "e" is usually dropped before adding a suffix beginning with a vowel; it is generally retained before adding a suffix beginning with a consonant.

abate, abating, abatement	desire, desirable, desirous
bare, baring, bareness	grieve, grieved, grievance
console, consoling, consolation	hate, hating, hateful

incite, incited, incitement | rate, rating

move, moving, movement | use, usable, useless

There are a few specific and logical exceptions to the first half of this rule. If the word ends in a final silent "e," and you're adding a suffix beginning with a vowel, do *not* drop the "e" in the following instances:

1) To prevent confusion between words. Only a few words fall into this category.

dye, dyeing   to prevent confusion with   die, dying

singe, singeing   to prevent confusion with   sing, singing

tinge, tingeing   to prevent confusion with   ting, tinging

2) To avoid pronunciation difficulties

canoe, canoeing   shoe, shoeing

hoe, hoeing   toe, toeing

3) To preserve the soft sound in "ce" and "ge" endings (a "ce" sound is said to be soft when it sounds like "s" instead of "k"; a "ge" sound is soft when it sounds like "j" rather than like the "g" in "gable")

advantage, advantageous | manage, manageable

change, changeable | outrage, outrageous

courage, courageous | service, serviceable

The second half of the rule, sadly, isn't as reliable. If you want to add a suffix beginning with a consonant to a word ending in a silent "e," you *generally* retain the final "e." There are so many exceptions, however, that you should refer to your dictionary if you have any doubts. These are some of the most commonly used and misspelled exceptions:

acknowledge, acknowledgment | possible, possibly

argue, argument | probable, probably

incredible, incredibly | true, truly

judge, judgment | whole, wholly

Spelling Rule 6: Watch out for words with the letters "ie" and "ei."

Next to the jingle for remembering the number of days in every month, this rule is probably the most widely known piece of verse in the English language:

> Write "i" before "e"
> Except after "c"
> Or when sounded like "a"
> As in "neighbor" and "weigh"

Since you probably already know the verse—or at least the first two lines of it—you need only look closely at your "ie" and "ei" word, and then pronounce the word to yourself. Does the puzzling "ie" or "ei" combination sound like the long "a" of "neighbor" and "weigh"? If so, the correct spelling is "ei":

beige	reign
eight	rein
feint	sleigh
freight	surveillance
heir	veil
neighbor	vein

Does the troublesome "ie" or "ei" combination sound like the long "e" of "thief"? If so, the spelling will be *either* "ie" or "ei," depending upon whether the combination is preceded by a "c":

ceiling	perceive
conceited	receipt
deceit	receive

(Watch "receive" especially—it is one of the most widely misspelled words in the language.)

apiece	brief
believe	chief

fiend	relieve
grief	shield
piece	siege
pier	yield

As usual, there are exceptions even to this venerable old rule. Try to remember these common ones by using the techniques discussed in Appendix III.

either	neither
Fahrenheit	protein
fiery	seize
height	sheik
leisure	weird

Spelling Rule 7: When adding prefixes to words, recognize when initial letters should be doubled.

This rule is even more straightforward than the last one. A prefix is any syllable attached to the beginning of a word to change its meaning. Some common prefixes are *dis-*, *im-*, *in-*, *mis-*, *re-*, and *un.* If the prefix ends in a letter different from the first letter of the root word, do not double the initial letter of the word.

disappear	inspirit
disembodied	misadventure
impossible	recall
inappropriate	unrealistic

If, on the other hand, the prefix ends in the same letter that begins the root word, double the initial letter of the root word.

dissatisfied	misspell
disservice	reevaluate
dissimilar	reexamine
immobile	unnecessary
innumerable	unnerving

"Dis-" is probably the trickiest of these prefixes. It's worth remembering that there are only about thirty common words beginning with "diss-" in the language, and almost ten times that number beginning with "dis-."

Spelling Rule 8: Proceed carefully when spelling words that end in these suffixes: -able and -ible; -ally and -ly; -efy and -ify; -full and -ful; -sede, -cede, and -ceed; -ary and -ery.

Some of these suffixes cause complicated problems that stump even excellent spellers; others are relatively easy to handle. We'll take the simple ones first.

1) "-ary" and "-ery"
This spelling decision is very easy to make: use "-ary" most of the time. While there are hundreds of English words ending in "-ary," only six or seven common ones end in "-ery." If you remember the few "-ery" words you are likely to use, you can spell the rest with "-ary" and be confident of your accuracy. These are the commonly used "-ery" words:

cemetery (this is the most commonly misspelled)

confectionery	millinery
distillery	monastery
dysentery	stationery (writing paper)

Other common words all end in "-ary." Here are some that people misspell frequently; you can use this rule to erase your difficulties with them:

auxiliary	
boundary	military
dictionary	secretary
elementary	stationary (not moving)
imaginary	voluntary

2) The "-ful" ending
The "-ful" ending converts a noun into an adjective form. Though the suffix means "full of," generally drop one of the "l's" when you add the suffix to another word.

| cheer, cheerful | pity, pitiful |
| hate, hateful | spite, spiteful |

3) "-sede," "-cede," and "-ceed"

These suffixes cause a great deal of confusion, but they too are very easy to distinguish if you examine them closely. There are only about a dozen words in the English language ending in the "-seed" sound. Of these:

Only one word ends in "-sede": supersede

Three words end in "-ceed": exceed, proceed, succeed

All others end in "-cede": accede, concede, intercede, precede, recede, secede

Perhaps the most commonly misspelled of these is "precede" (to go before), which people often incorrectly spell "preceed." Note, too, that none of these words ends in "-seed," even though "-seed" is the most logical spelling of the sound of the suffix.

4) "-efy" and "-ify"

This spelling decision is very easy to make, too: use "-ify" most of the time. There are only four words you are likely to use that end in "-efy." Remember them and spell the rest with "-ify." These are the "-efy" words:

| liquefy (even though "liquid" is the root word) | rarefy |
| putrefy | stupefy |

Note, too, that other forms of these words retain the "e":

liquefy, liquefaction, liquefied
stupefy, stupefies, stupefaction

All other words are spelled with the "-ify" ending.

classify	purify
codify	qualify (one of the most misspelled)
fortify	
pacify	

The next two suffix rules are somewhat more complicated, but their logic is still clear.

5) "-ally" and "-ly"
These two endings are used to change adjective forms into adverbs, and "-ly" appears far more frequently. To spell adverbs correctly, write out the adjective form first. Then look at the final consonant of the adjective and add the correct suffix according to the following rules.

Add "-ly" to form the adverbs of adjectives ending in most consonants:

formerly	poorly
newly	slowly

Add "-ly" to form the adverbs of adjectives ending in silent "e." Do not drop the silent "e" first. This procedure follows the logic of Spelling Rule 5: Keep the final "e" of a word before adding any suffix beginning with a consonant.

absolute, absolutely	extreme, extremely
complete, completely	immediate, immediately
definite, definitely	late, lately
entire, entirely	rare, rarely

Add "-ly" to form the adverbs of adjectives ending in "y." But first change the "y" to "i" as outlined in Spelling Rule 3:

easy, easily	ready, readily
heavy, heavily	wary, warily
necessary, necessarily	

If an adjective ends in "-able" or "-ible," simply change the final "e" to "y":

able, ably	incredible, incredibly
capable, capably	probable, probably
considerable, considerably	possible, possibly

Add "-ly" to form the adverbs of adjectives ending in "-l" and "-al." This category causes the most difficulty. Adjectives that end in "-al" add the "-ly" ending to form their adverbs, so their full endings are always spelled "-ally." Some common problem words:

accidental, accidentally	occasional, occasionally
actual, actually	oral, orally
exceptional, exceptionally	physical, physically
fundamental, fundamentally	skillful, skillfully
incidental, incidentally	successful, successfully
logical, logically	usual, usually

The "-ally" ending is added to adjectives much less often than the "-ly" ending. Always add "-ally" to form the adverbs of adjectives ending in "-ic":

academic, academically	emphatic, emphatically
automatic, automatically	scholastic, scholastically
basic, basically	systematic, systematically

The only exception to this clear-cut rule is "public," whose adverb form is spelled "publicly."

6) "-able" and "-ible"
These two endings cause headaches even for excellent spellers. The rule for deciding between them has numerous exceptions, so consult your dictionary or the word lists in this book whenever possible. When you don't have the word lists handy, however, use these guiding principles:

"-able"

Use "-able" if the base word stands alone as a complete word. Many common adjectives are formed by adding "-able" to the root. Note that the full word remains if the ending is dropped from each of the following:

acceptable	changeable
avoidable	comfortable

considerable	noticeable
dependable	peaceable
fashionable	predictable
favorable	profitable

Use "-able" if the base word stands alone as a complete word, except for a final "e":

advisable	excusable
believable	lovable
comparable	receivable
desirable	usable

Use "-able" if the base ends in "i." Usually, these roots ended in a "y" that was changed to an "i" before adding a suffix. Using "-able" in these cases is logical: it avoids a double "i."

classifiable	pitiable
enviable	reliable
justifiable	

Use "-able" if the base ends in a hard "g" or hard "c." (The hard "g" sound is the "g" in "got"; the hard "c" sound is the "c" in "cane.")

applicable	implacable
despicable	indefatigable
explicable	irrevocable

Use "-able" if a related word form contains a long "a" sound:

duration	durable
estimate	estimable
inflammation	inflammable
irritate	irritable
penetrate	impenetrable
tolerate	tolerable

"-ible"

Use "-ible" if the base is *not* a full word:

audible	infallible
credible	intelligible
divisible	plausible
feasible	visible

Use "-ible" if the base word ends in a soft "c" or "g." (The soft "c" sound is the "c" in "ceiling"; the soft "g" sound is the "g" in "gesture.")

deducible	illegible
eligible	legible
forcible	tangible

Use "-ible" if "-ion" can be added to the base without intervening letters:

access	accession	accessible
collect	collection	collectible
corrupt	corruption	corruptible
deduct	deduction	deductible
digest	digestion	digestible

This rule is tricky. If intervening letters are needed to spell the "-ion" form, chances are good the adjective form will end in "-able": present, presentation, presentable.

There are numerous exceptions to these guidelines, so the initial warning is worth repeating: Consult the word lists in this book or a dictionary whenever possible. Concentrate, too, on the following common exceptions, many of which are often misspelled:

affable	inevitable
amenable	portable
capable	vulnerable
equitable	contemptible
formidable	flexible

7) One final word on adding suffixes. If you add a suffix whose first letter is the same as the last letter of the root word, be sure to double the consonant:

accidentally

brownness

cleanness

cruelly

drunkenness

occasionally

soulless

suddenness

Spelling Rule 9: Always place a "u" after the letter "q."

Don't worry about exceptions to this rule—the tiny number of exceptions never appear in ordinary discourse. (A "qintar," for example, is a unit of Albanian money; a "qasida" is an Arabic poetic form. But how often do you use either of these words?) Simply remember, always, to place a "u" after every "q," no matter where in the word the "q" appears.

quality

question

quickly

equality

equipment

iniquity

Spelling Rule 10: When you use an apostrophe, distinguish between plurals, possessives, and contractions.

Possessives

Apostrophes are used most often to indicate possession. The basic rule is this: Use an apostrophe and "s" to form the possessive of any noun not ending in the letter "s." Use an apostrophe alone to form the possessive of any noun already ending in the letter "s."

For words not ending in "s," add an apostrophe and "s":

the boy's hat

Fred's wife

the geese's pond

the rifle's trigger

the teacher's book

the children's room

For words already ending in the letter "s," add the apostrophe alone. Note that this group includes plurals formed with "s" where the addition of "s" would produce an awkward sound or visual effect.

both boys' hats (two boys)

all the cars' motors (several cars)

the ladies' gowns

Hugh and Millie Clements' car

James' suit

There are a few slightly more complicated possessive forms. If you want to form the possessive of a group of two or more, the last word receives the apostrophe and "s":

Send that letter to Gen and Joe Hill's house.

Was that brief prepared by Brunngraber and Riley's firm?

I'm tired of every Tom, Dick, and Harry's opinion.

When you form the possessive of a hyphenated word, add the apostrophe and "s" to the last word of the group:

my father-in-law's piano

her brother-in-law's cello

Note: Personal possessive pronouns are *not* spelled with an apostrophe.

Correct	*Incorrect*
ours	our's or ours'
yours	your's or yours'
his	his'
hers	her's or hers'
its	it's or its'
theirs	their's or theirs'
whose	who's

Plurals

Plurals are not generally formed with an apostrophe. As we discussed in Spelling Rule 1, regular plurals are formed by adding "s" or "es" to the end of the noun. The only plurals formed with apostrophes are plurals of numbers, letters, and words highlighted as words, as in these examples:

How many 3's does your phone number have?

Be sure to watch your *p*'s and *q*'s.

How many *s*'s does the word "Mississippi" have?

Her sentence had too many *and*'s.

Contractions

Finally, the apostrophe is used in contractions, to indicate that some letter has been left out. Be careful where you place the apostrophe: it should appear where the dropped letter or letters would normally be.

are not: aren't (not are'nt)

is not: isn't (not is'nt)

he is: he's

was not: wasn't (not was'nt)

were not: weren't (not were'nt)

they are: they're

it is: it's (not its')

"Its" and "it's" deserve some special attention since they are two of the most commonly confused words in the language. "It's" is a contraction meaning "it is." "Its" is a personal pronoun indicating possession. Confusion arises so often between these two words because people are generally accustomed, and correctly so, to forming possessives by adding an apostrophe and "s" to the end of nouns. Therefore, when someone wants to write about a dog wagging a tail, the first impulse is to choose "it's," since the apostrophe and "s" is associated with possession: "The dog wagged it's tail." Though this form seems natural, it is incorrect. The usual logic of the apostrophe and "s" indicating possession doesn't work with "it's" and "its." The first is a contraction and the second indicates possession. To correct your spelling of these two forms, use these methods. Remember, first of all, that the personal possessive pronouns are never formed with an apostrophe and "s" (see above). Further, if you remember that "it's" means "it is," you can always test the spelling in your problem sentence by substituting "it is" to see if the sentence makes sense. Does it make sense, for example, to say "the dog wagged it is tail"? Since it doesn't, you know the correct spelling has to be "the dog wagged *its* tail."

Spelling Rule 11: When splitting a word to place it on two lines, always break the word accurately at the syllable divisions.

If you're typing and run out of room on a line in the middle of a word, you must be very careful about where you split your word to place part of it on the next line of type. You may only split a word between its syllables; you may not break up individual syllables. Though you should usually check syllabication (dividing into correct syllables) either in this book or with your dictionary, there are three rules that govern many syllabication decisions.

1) Words containing a double consonant usually divide into syllables between the consonants.

bit-ter	flat-ter
book-keeper	les-son
dap-per	sil-ly

2) If a word contains a single consonant between two vowels, the syllable division usually occurs after the consonant if the first vowel is short.

cab-in	pat-io
Lat-in	ref-ugee
med-al	

3) But if a word contains a single consonant between two vowels, and the first vowel is long, the syllable division usually occurs before the consonant.

mu-sic	scu-ba
ra-dio	tri-bal
sce-nic	va-por

Never leave any letter, vowel or consonant on a line of type by itself. For example, even though the syllable division is accurate, do not type "above" with the "a" on one line and "bove" on the next.

II. Common Mix-ups

This is an alphabetical list of seventy-five of the most commonly confused and misspelled words in the English language. Generally, confusion occurs because the misused word looks or sounds very much like another word. You can often eliminate the confusion for yourself by adhering to Spelling Rule 1: Concentrate on pronouncing the words carefully and correctly. This technique will help to distinguish, for example, between words such as "accept" and "except," or "advise" and "advice." In other cases, however, the troublesome related words have identical correct pronunciations. Such words are called homonyms, and they cannot be correctly identified by pronunciation alone. You may need to fix the correct spelling and definition in your mind by using one of the memory games described in the next appendix.

Use this list as a reference tool and as a self-instruction device. Read over the list quickly to acquaint yourself with the common mix-ups. Alert yourself to the ones that tend to trap you. Then keep this book on your desk and flip to the list whenever you are in doubt.

Ten Habitual Offenders

1) **a lot (not alot)** A large number. This expression is spelled as two words, not as one. Never, under any circumstances, spell this expression as a single word. Example: Fred made *a lot* of money on the stock market.

2) **category (not catagory)** A group or class. Example: Into what *category* would you place that type of food?

3) **definite (not definate or defanite)** Clear and unmistakable. "Definite" has no "a's" in it; both its middle vowels are "i's." Example: My vacation plans are *definite*: I leave tomorrow.

4) **develop (not develope)** To promote the growth or evolution of something. There is no silent "e" at the end of this word.

Likewise, the noun form is spelled "development." Example: How many years will it take for a new forest to *develop*?

5) **existence (not existance)** The state of living or being. The last syllable of "existence" is always spelled with an "e"—never an "a." Example: The student led a carefree *existence*.

6) **occasion (not occassion)** A time at which something happens. While "occasion" is spelled with two "c's," it has only one "s." Example: A birthday is an *occasion* for gifts.

7) **occurrence (not ocurrence or ocurence)** An event or happening. "Occurrence" contains two "c's" and two "r's." This spelling follows the logic of Spelling Rule 4. Example: Snowstorms are a common *occurrence* in the Northeast.

8) **privilege (not privalege or priviledge)** An advantage or favor. There is no "d" in "privilege"; the second vowel sound is "i." Example: Her invitation to the coronation was a rare *privilege*.

9) **receive (not recieve)** To get; to come into the possession of. This follows Spelling Rule 6: "i" before "e" except after "c." Example: She will *receive* her college diploma this June.

10) **separate (not seperate)** To keep distinct or apart. The second vowel sound is "a," never "e." Example: John and Mary have decided to keep *separate* bank accounts.

Sixty-five Perplexing Word Groups

1) **accept**	To receive. Will Ann *accept* Val's gift?
except	With the exclusion of. The building is open every day *except* Sunday.
2) **advice**	A recommendation or piece of information. Noun. Please pay attention to Paul's good *advice*.
advise	To give a recommendation or helpful information. Verb. Note that "advise" is the verb form of the noun "advice." Paul *advises* you to sell the stocks now.
3) **affect**	To influence. Most often used as a verb. How will the tax reduction *affect* your salary?

effect	A result or outcome. Most often used as a noun. The tax reduction will have a lovely *effect* on my salary.
4) **air**	The substance we breathe. The mountains have clean *air*.
heir	A person entitled to inherit something. John is the *heir* to his father's fortune.
5) **altar**	A place of worship. Noun. The minister stepped up to the *altar*.
alter	To change. Verb. Don't *alter* a word of your letter.
6) **angel**	A spiritual being. *Angels* are often pictured with wings.
angle	A corner formed when two lines meet. The *angle* of the turn was sharp.
7) **baring**	To uncover or unclothe. The thief was *baring* his conscience for the judge.
bearing	To hold up or support. How are you *bearing* up under the stress?
8) **breadth**	Width. Noun. The package was thirty-six inches in *breadth*.
breath	Exhalation. Noun. After running a mile, he lost his *breath*.
breathe	To inhale or exhale. Verb. Can you *breathe* easily after running two miles?
9) **canvas**	A strong linen fabric. Noun. The best sails are made of *canvas*.
canvass	To solicit or poll. Verb. Danny will *canvass* his neighborhood for votes.
10) **capital**	Chief in importance; also often relates to punishment by execution. Use for all meanings except "building." Should *capital* punishment be permitted?
capitol	Building where a legislature meets. We visited the *Capitol* when we toured Washington.

11) **casual**   Incidental; occurring by chance. Kate and Barry are only *casual* acquaintances.

    causal   Relating to cause and effect. Was the economy a *causal* agent in the firm's bankruptcy?

12) **cite**   To acknowledge or call attention to. Verb. He *cited* five authorities in his research.

    sight   Vision. Jules' new glasses makes his *sight* perfect.

    site   A place. The new museum will be built on the *site* of the old.

13) **clothes**   Garments. Deborah buys new *clothes* every fall.

    cloths   Pieces of fabric. These *cloths* may be used for cleaning the floor.

14) **complement**   Something that completes or goes with. That paint will *complement* the new wallpaper nicely.

    compliment   A flattering remark. Tony *complimented* Polly on her new dress.

15) **conscience**   Sense of right and wrong. The thief displayed no guilty *conscience*.

    conscious   Aware. The patient remained *conscious* throughout the operation.

16) **council**   A group or assembly. The local business *council* supported his plan.

    counsel   Advice. His lawyer gave him excellent *counsel*.

17) **desert**   (de-sert') To leave behind. Verb. Hal would never *desert* his wife.

    desert   (des'-ert) Wilderness without water. Noun. He wandered for days in the Sahara *Desert*.

    dessert   Last course in a meal. They served strawberry shortcake for *dessert*.

18) **discreet**   Prudently silent. She can be trusted to be *discreet* with your confidences.

discrete — Separate; distinct. The District of Columbia is a *discrete* governmental entity; it is supervised by no state.

19) **eminent** — Important; well-respected. Albert Einstein was an *eminent* scientist.

imminent — Immediate; near at hand. An outbreak of flu was *imminent*.

20) **foreword** — Introduction to a book. The author wrote an explanatory *foreword*.

forward — Movement toward the front. Several recruits stepped *forward* to volunteer for the dangerous mission.

21) **forth** — Onward. The soldiers marched *forth* to battle.

fourth — One more than three. This is the *fourth* time I've warned you!

22) **genius** — Brilliance. Jack has a *genius* for making money.

genus — Class; kind. Do you know the *genus* of this plant?

23) **groan** — Sound of dismay. Jerry gave a *groan* of pain.

grown — Increased in age or size. Joshua has *grown* four inches in a single year.

24) **hear** — To note sounds. Can you *hear* everything I say?

here — In this place. Please place your coats *here*.

25) **holy** — Sacred. The Greeks believed Delphi was a *holy* spot.

wholly — Completely. I am *wholly* convinced by your argument.

26) **human** — Relating to man. The wind sounded like a *human* voice.

humane — Relating to sympathy. The trial judge seemed *humane* when he gave her a suspended sentence.

27) **idle** Inactive. The strike kept the factory *idle*.
    idol Object of worship. She made Elvis Presley her *idol*.

28) **its** Possessive pronoun. The dog wagged *its* tail.
    it's Contraction for "it is." *It's* always wonderful to visit you.

29) **lessen** To diminish. The noise will *lessen* as we leave the city.
    lesson Something to be learned. He learned his *lesson* that time!

30) **loose** Not tightly fastened. She wore comfortable, *loose* clothing.
    lose To be parted from. Verb. Kathy is sure to *lose* her keys.
    loss A defeat. Noun. That politician may not recover from the *loss* of the last election.

31) **miner** Someone who works in a mine. The coal *miner* worked expertly with dynamite.
    minor Below the legal age. Do not serve an alcoholic beverage to a *minor*.

32) **moral** Virtuous; good. He was an utterly *moral* man.
    morale Spirit; enthusiasm. Always a noun. The doctor recommended a vacation to lift his patient's *morale*.

33) **morning** First part of the day. Fred rose at the crack of dawn every *morning*.
    mourning Grieving. The *mourning* family held a private funeral.

34) **oral** Spoken. The professor assigned an *oral* rather than a written report.
    aural Pertaining to the ear. A hearing aid will improve his *aural* capacity.

35) **pair** Two. Try on this *pair* of shoes.
    pare To peel. Must I *pare* all these apples before putting them into the pie?

36) **passed** — Moved by. Verb. We *passed* the oxcart in our car.

past — Just gone by. Adjective or noun. The *past* month has been very tiring for me.

37) **persecute** — To harass; to oppress. Small religious sects have often been *persecuted* for their beliefs.

prosecute — To bring to trial for a crime. The attorney *prosecuted* the case against Mr. Jones vigorously.

38) **personal** — Private; confidential. Adjective. Sally took the day off work to handle some *personal* business.

personnel — Employees; staff. Noun. The factory *personnel* demanded better fringe benefits.

39) **plain** — Simple; ordinary. Mary has a *plain* face.

plane — An airplane; also, a carpenter's tool. Shall we travel by *plane* or train? The carpenter smoothed the board with his *plane*.

40) **pray** — To address God; to beseech. Ministers try to *pray* daily.

prey — The victim of a hunt. The rabbit was the hawk's *prey*.

41) **precede** — To go before. The attendants *preceded* the bride down the aisle.

proceed — To advance. After completing one task, *proceed* quickly to the next.

42) **principal** — The supervisor of a school. The *principal* maintained strict discipline in his school. Central; foremost. When Joe took the new job, his *principal* concern was salary.

principle — A law or rule. Nancy adheres scrupulously to the *principle* that honesty is the best policy.

43) **prophecy** — A forecast; prediction. Noun. Jody didn't believe the gypsy's *prophecy* about her future.

prophesy   To predict the future. Verb. The psychic insisted she could *prophesy* the winner of the race.

44) **propose**   To suggest. He *proposed* marriage.

    purpose   A goal or intention. The treaty's *purpose* was to assure peace.

45) **quiet**   Silent; not loud. The room was *quiet* as a church.

    quite   Thoroughly; entirely. I am *quite* pleased with the result.

    quit   To stop or leave. Rich decided to *quit* school.

46) **rain**   Precipitation. Missouri had twelve inches of *rain* last week.

    reign   To rule over. The queen *reigns* over her loyal subjects.

    rein   To control or restrain. Can Darcy *rein* in the horse?

47) **raise**   To lift up. Will you *raise* the lid of this storage chest for me?

    raze   To tear down. The Planning Commission finally voted to *raze* the old building.

    rise   To get up. Please *rise* for the national anthem.

48) **right**   Correct, or direction. Emily is *right* to quit her job.
Turn *right* at the third traffic light.

    rite   Ceremony. The marriage *rite* is a joyous ceremony.

49) **stationary**   Immobile. The rabbit remained *stationary* while the hawk circled around it.

    stationery   Writing paper. Gen used her new *stationery* for her next letter.

50) **straight**   Without curves. Tony used a ruler to draw a perfectly *straight* line.

    strait   A narrow passage of water. The Bering *Strait* lies between Alaska and the Soviet Union.

51) **suit** Clothing. He bought a new three-piece *suit* for the interview.

   suite A group of rooms. Try to reserve a *suite* at the hotel.

52) **tale** A story. He told a horrifying *tale* of fraud and deceit.

   tail An appendage at the rear of an animal. The dog wagged its *tail*.

53) **than** Indicates comparison. My father is older *than* I.

   then Indicates time. It was *then* that Joe left for work.

54) **their** Personal pronoun indicating possession. *Their* coats were all new.

   there In that place. Please put the pitcher *there*.

   they're Contraction for "they are." *They're* not coming to our party.

55) **threw** Tossed. The quarterback *threw* the ball for a winning touchdown.

   through Preposition meaning from one end to the other. The trucks drove *through* the tunnel.

   thorough Complete. His doctor gave him a *thorough* examination.

   though Although. The room stayed warm even *though* the furnace was broken.

56) **to** Preposition with numerous meanings. He came *to* school yesterday.

   too Also; excessive. Let's include Susan *too*. She's *too* good to be left out.

   two The number after one. I'll have *two* hamburgers, please.

57) **vain** Conceited; also, worthless or failed. Barbara was a *vain* and cold woman. The police made a *vain* attempt to capture the escaped convict.

   vane Device that measures wind direction. The weather *vane* says the wind is out of the northwest.

vein	Blood vessel. The nurse drew blood for the test from the *vein* in his right arm.
58) **vice**	Immoral habit. The detectives were assigned to the *vice* squad.
vise	A tool that holds things still. Place the hinge in the *vise* until the glue dries.
59) **waist**	A person's midsection. She did daily exercises to firm her *waist*.
waste	To squander. Turn lights off when you're away; don't *waste* energy.
60) **waive**	To relinquish or put aside. The dean won't *waive* the language requirement for graduation.
wave	A swell of water. The boat was overturned by a thirty-foot *wave*.
61) **weather**	Atmospheric conditions. Listen to the radio for today's *weather* report.
whether	Implies alternatives. Sarah didn't know *whether* she would take a January vacation.
62) **where**	Indicates place. *Where* are you going on vacation?
were	Form of "to be." *Were* you both at home last night? We *were* in the area.
we're	Contraction for "we are." *We're* renting a car for the trip.
63) **who's**	Contraction for "who is." *Who's* coming with me to the theater?
whose	Pronoun indicating possession. *Whose* gloves are these?
64) **wring**	To twist or squeeze. Don't forget to *wring* out the mop.
ring	To sound, as a bell. At noon, all the chimes will *ring*.
65) **you're**	Contraction for "you are." *You're* too late to catch the train.
your	Pronoun indicating possession. *Your* plane just left without you.

III. Memory Games

Though improving your spelling may feel like a chore much of the time, your rewards will be enormous, and there are several techniques you can follow to make your work enjoyable. It's even possible to make correct spelling into an entertaining pastime. Some people take up crossword puzzles and acrostics. Others take up Scrabble.

Games such as these tend to improve your visual memory for words; if you see a word often enough, and concentrate on its correct spelling by "picturing" it to yourself, you'll soon find you won't misspell it anymore. Two other kinds of "memory" can be important for spelling skills too: your auditory memory and your motor memory.

Auditory memory is probably self-explanatory. It refers to anything you remember, or retain, by virtue of hearing. If you have an accurate auditory memory, you can use it to sound out difficult words, as we discussed in Spelling Rule 1. "Motor" memory refers to the memory that muscles possess. Think, for example, of tying a necktie or lacing a shoe. These tasks are probably firmly imbedded in your motor memory: your hands know how to do them automatically, without thought or reflection. Your muscular reactions are so automatic, in fact, that thinking about how to do the task would probably slow you down and make you stumble over it for a moment. Schoolteachers call upon motor memory when they instruct students to write out difficult words ten or twenty times. After a while, the movement of the hand in the correct spelling becomes automatic.

People possess accurate visual, auditory, and motor memories to different degrees. If you have an excellent visual memory, your auditory memory may be weak, or vice versa. We all, however, possess the three faculties to some degree, and we probably remember things most thoroughly when we use the three faculties in unison. You should apply the various memories to the task of improving your spelling. Decide, first of all, whether your visual, auditory, or motor memory is strongest. Once you've decided this, you can improve your spelling by emphasizing memory techniques that make use of your best faculty. Don't leave the other faculties out, however. Use your senses in concert. If you have a strong visual memory and you learn to picture the correct spellings of words that trap you, you'll remember those words even better if you reinforce your visual memory with auditory and motor devices.

But how should you put all this complicated advice about visual, auditory, and motor memories into practice? It's much simpler than it sounds. Imagine, for example, that the word "separate" is one of your personal troublemakers. Take a blank sheet of paper and write "separate" on it in large letters. Use your visual memory first of all: stare at the word on the page, isolate the letters that tend to give you difficulty, and fix the correct spelling in your mind. Picture it to yourself. Then look up, stare at a blank wall, and try to picture the letters there, as if projected onto a screen. Practice this exercise a few times until you can call up a mental picture of "separate"—spelled accurately—without straining.

Now reinforce your visual memory with an auditory image: say "separate" aloud, clearly and slowly. Listen to yourself as you speak. Exaggerate the pronunciation to highlight the tricky part of the word: say "separate" with a long "a" sound as its middle syllable. Repeat several times, concentrating on hearing yourself as you speak.

Next, reinforce both visual and auditory images with a motor device. Write "separate" on your sheet of paper several more times, concentrating on the feel of the "a" in the middle syllable. At first write the word in larger letters than you normally would—the exaggerated size tends to isolate the trouble spot for you in yet one more way. Then write "separate" in your normal handwriting, still focusing your mind on that tricky "a" in the middle syllable. By this time, you will have taught yourself the correct spelling of "separate." More practice after a few hours or days will imbed the correct spelling even deeper in your visual, auditory, and motor memories.

But there will always be devilish words that refuse to stick in your mind. For whatever reason, some words will not submit and remain in your memory, even after you've assaulted them with the techniques above. These stubborn words require a different approach. Try a different sort of memory game on them: *mnemonic devices*.

A mnemonic device is any sentence or statement that assists your memory. The imposing word "mnemonic" comes from the name of the Greek goddess of memory: Mnemosyne. Mnemonic devices work by association and the best ones are those you make up for yourself, using your personal connections and associations.

You've probably heard of people who use mnemonic devices to remember phone numbers. For example, someone might have a friend whose number is 555-1916. After scrambling the last four digits repeatedly, he may decide to invent a mnemonic device to help him keep the order straight. He looks at the phone number carefully, and sees that it ends in the four digits "1916"—the year of the Russian Revolution. He then remembers his friend has a Russian grandmother, and the connection is complete: if he associates the last four digits with his friend's heritage and the Russian Revolution, he won't forget the proper number is 555-1916.

You can use this same sort of mnemonic device to remind yourself of the correct spelling of those words that continue to trouble you. First of all, isolate the part of the word you tend to forget or misspell. Then make up some association to jog your memory. You can turn the procedure into a word game, and you'll end up with a series of jingles that keep your spelling accurate. A mnemonic device like this, for example, will help you decide when to use "principal" and "principle."

A princi*PAL* should be a *PAL*.

A princip*LE* can be *LE*gal.

Memory devices work best, though, if you invent them yourself. The very exercise of creating an association will fix a correct spelling firmly in your mind. So list your problem words; then compose jingles for them to remind yourself of the way they're spelled. Here are some examples to get you started:

If it's de*FIN*ite, it's *FIN*al.

LOP the "e" from the end of deve*LOP*.

Exis*TEN*ce is sometimes *TEN*se.

A pri*VILE*ge is hardly *VILE*.

When you *PAR*e an apple, you se*PAR*ate the skin from the fruit.

Accept: Please AC*cept* this pAC*kage*.

Except: To EX*cept* is to EX*clude*.

Capital: TALent is the best capiTAL for success.

Capitol: Senators TOil in the CapiTOl.

Emigrate: To Emigrate is to flEE.

Immigrate: To Immigrate is to come In.

Stationery: StationERy is for lettERs.

Stationary: StatioNARY means "NARY a movement."

Weather: WEAlthy people avoid bad WEAther: they fly to the Bahamas.

Whether: He'll tETHER you whETHER you like it or not.

Glossary

Accent: The emphasis or stress given to one syllable of a word when spoken.

Adjective: A word that modifies—that is, describes or limits—a noun or pronoun.

Adverb: A word that modifies—that is, describes or limits—a verb, adjective, or other adverb.

Consonant: One of these letters of the alphabet: b, c, d, f, g, h, j, k, l, m, n, p, q, r, s, t, v, w, x, y, z.

Noun: A word that names a person, place, thing, idea, or quality.

Plural: A designation for a noun or pronoun, denoting more than one.

Prefix: A letter or combination of letters added to the front of a word to change its meaning.

Pronoun: A word that takes the place of a noun. Used primarily to avoid repetition.

Singular: A designation for a noun or pronoun, denoting one.

Suffix: A letter or combination of letters added to the end of a word to change its meaning.

Syllable: A part of a word pronounced as a single unit.

Tense: The time sense of a verb, denoting when the action occurred.

Verb: A word that names an action.

Vowel: One of these letters of the alphabet: a, e, i, o, u, and sometimes y.

Bantam's
Reference Library